Experiments
in
College Physics

Experiments in College Physics

FIFTH EDITION

Bernard Cioffari

College of New Rochelle

D. C. HEATH AND COMPANY
Lexington, Massachusetts Toronto London

PUBLISHER'S PREFACE

D. C. Heath and Company is pleased to present the fifth edition of Bernard Cioffari's *Experiments in College Physics*.

The fourth edition has won widespread acceptance by teachers throughout the country. Therefore, all the experiments in that edition have been retained and two new ones added. The contents now include nine experiments on atomic physics as well as the fifty experiments in classical physics that were selected by an extensive study of experiments most used by colleges in the United States.

The manual was planned for the convenience of the instructor and the student. It is written in a remarkably clear style. Each experiment contains a brief review of related physics principles to orient the student. Directions for procedures are logical, easy to understand, and definite. Adequate space has been allowed for data, calculations, and answers to questions. The illustrations are uniformly clear and exact.

It is hoped that the fifth edition will please its users to the same extent as the earlier editions. Criticism and suggestions from persons using the manual will be gratefully received.

CONTENTS

Contents

INTRODUCTION

The purpose of the physics laboratory is to supply the practical knowledge necessary for a complete understanding of the subject of physics. A further aim is to develop familiarity with the experimental method, upon which science depends, and to help the student to develop a technique for meeting and solving the difficulties which arise in all problems of scientific measurement.

INSTRUCTIONS

The instructions for each experiment should be read before the regular laboratory period. The student should know well in advance which experiment is to be performed on a given date.

The student should work at his own assigned place. He should not borrow apparatus without permission from the instructor. Whenever he needs additional information, he should consult only the instructor.

All observations and data should be neatly recorded in a suitable tabular form previously arranged for the particular experiment. The columns should be labeled clearly, and the units in which the quantities are measured should be denoted. Instruments should be read to the limit of their possibilities by estimating the last figure of the reading, i.e. the fraction of the smallest scale division. Each measurement should be recorded directly on the data sheet and exactly in the form in which it is made, without any mental calculation. The observations should be labeled in such a way that it will be easy to know what they mean.

The calculations are to be made in the space provided in the manual, whenever it is feasible. When the required computations are too lengthy, they should be completed on a separate sheet of paper, which is to be included as part of the report. In making the calculations, it is well to include the mathematical equations used, to indicate the operations performed, and to show clearly how the results have been obtained. Students are urged to use a slide rule, or tables of logarithms, as much as possible, to save time.

The questions at the end of each experiment are to be answered in the space provided after each question. Complete sentences should be used. As far as time permits, the computations should be carried out during the regular laboratory period. The report itself should be completed during the period whenever it is possible.

CARE OF APPARATUS

It is expected that every student exercise the greatest care in the use of laboratory apparatus. Each one will be held personally responsible for the apparatus entrusted to his care.

The instructions for each experiment contain a list of the apparatus required. At the beginning of each laboratory period, the student should check over the apparatus and make sure that he has all the items listed, and that the apparatus is in good condition. If anything is missing or broken, he should report it to the instructor. At the end of the period, the student should again check the apparatus and leave it neatly arranged.

In connecting apparatus in electrical circuits, very special care must be exercised to avoid making wrong connections. If this is not done, the apparatus may be seriously damaged. The source of power (dry cells, storage batteries, or power line) should always be connected last; but before this final connection is made, the circuit must be checked and approved by the instructor. In disconnecting any circuit, the source of power should always be disconnected first.

THE REPORT

A report of the work done in each experiment must be prepared by the student and must be submitted at the beginning of the next laboratory period, or at some other time appointed by the instructor. The report will be graded by the instructor and returned as soon as possible. The student may then keep the reports in a loose-leaf notebook for future reference. The report should include the following:

Introduction

1. The title. This includes the name of the student, the date, the name and number of the experiment.

2. The instruction sheets. These include the object of the experiment, the theory, the apparatus, and the procedure. The student tears out the perforated pages and hands them in as part of the report.

3. All original data and observations. These should be arranged in tabular form and properly labeled. For convenience, the tables for the data are laid out in the manual. The student fills in the results of his observations.

4. All the required computations. These are to be made in the space provided, wherever it is feasible.

5. Graphs and diagrams, whenever these are required.

6. A summary of the results. This is included in tabular form under the data. This summary may also include a comparison of the computed results with the accepted values, and the percentage errors involved.

7. Answers to the questions at the end of the experiment. The answers are placed in the space provided after each question. Complete sentences should be used.

PLOTTING OF CURVES

All curves must be drawn on the graph paper provided in the manual. Scales for the coordinate axes should be so chosen that the curve extends over almost all of a full-sized sheet of paper, and that the decimal parts of units can be easily located. This can be done if each small division is made equal to one, two, five, or ten units. The same scale need not be used on both axes. The independent variable should be plotted along the x axis and the dependent variable along the y axis. Each axis should be labeled with the name of the quantity being plotted and the scale divisions used. The numbers should increase from left to right and from bottom to top. The graph should be labeled to indicate what the curve intends to show.

Each plotted point should be a small dot surrounded by a small circle, so that the point will be clearly visible on the graph. Finally, a smooth curve should be drawn through the plotted points. The curve need not pass through all the points, but should be drawn in such a way as to fit the points as closely as possible; in general, as many points will be on one side of the curve as on the other. The extent to which the plotted points coincide with the curve is a measure of the accuracy of the results.

SIGNIFICANT FIGURES

In carrying out computations, only significant figures should be retained. Significant figures are those figures which are known to be reasonably trustworthy; they are figures actually obtained from the measuring instruments, including zeros and estimated figures. The position of the decimal point does not affect the number of significant figures; if a zero is used merely to locate the decimal point, it is not significant, but if it actually represents a value read on the instrument, or estimated, then it is significant.

For example, suppose that a distance is measured with an ordinary centimeter ruler and found to be 52.3 millimeters, where the 3 is estimated, then all three figures are significant. If this number is recorded as 0.0523 meters, then the two zeros are not significant, because they are used merely to locate the decimal point; the number still contains three significant figures. However, if the estimated figure had been a zero, then the distance should be recorded as 52.0 millimeters, and not 52 millimeters, since the zero would then be a significant figure.

In computations, figures which are not significant should be dropped out continually. This not only saves labor, but avoids drawing false conclusions, because the retaining of too many figures implies an accuracy greater than the figures actually represent. The following rules may be used for the retention of significant figures in a computation:

1. In addition and subtraction, do not carry the result beyond the first column that contains a doubtful figure. This means that all figures lying to the right of the last column in which all figures are significant should be dropped.

2. In multiplication and division, retain in the result only as many significant figures as the least precise quantity in the data contains.

3. In dropping figures which are not significant, the last figure retained should be unchanged if the first figure dropped is less than 5. It should be increased by 1 if the first figure dropped is 5 or greater.

These rules give the number of significant figures which should appear in the final result. But in computing, in all the intermediate steps, it is better to carry one more significant figure than is needed in the final result.

The following examples illustrate the principles just mentioned:

In obtaining the sum of these numbers

806.5		806.5
32.03		32.0
0.0652	they should be written as	0.1
125.0		125.0
		963.6

Then the sum is expressed to the correct number of significant figures.

Again, suppose that a length is measured as 7.62 cm., and a width as 3.81 cm. In these numbers the third figure has been estimated, and therefore it is a doubtful figure. In computing the area by direct long-hand multiplication, one obtains the result 29.0322 square centimeters. This number has six significant figures, but neither one of the original quantities is known to this number of figures. There are only three significant figures in each one of the factors. Therefore, only three significant figures should be retained in the result, which should be written as 29.0 square centimeters.

THEORY OF ERRORS

All measurements are affected by errors; this means that measurements are always subject to some uncertainty. There are many different types of errors, such as personal, systematic, instrumental, and accidental errors. Personal errors include blunders, such as mistakes in arithmetic, in recording an observation, or in reading scale divisions. Another important kind of personal error is known as personal bias, such as trying to fit the measurements to some preconceived idea, or being prejudiced in favor of the first observation. Systematic errors are characterized by their tendency to be in one direction only, either positive or negative. For example, if a meter stick is slightly worn at one end, and measurements are taken from this end, then a constant error will occur in all these measurements. Instrumental errors are those introduced by slight imperfections in the manufacture or calibration of the instrument. Accidental errors are deviations which are beyond the control of the observer. These errors are due to jarring, noise, fluctuations in temperature, variations in atmospheric pressure, and the like.

The accuracy of a measurement, then, depends upon a number of factors, many of which cannot be easily determined. It will be assumed that in these experiments the apparatus is sufficiently accurate so that instrumental errors are negligible, and that systematic errors, personal errors, and personal bias are eliminated. Under these conditions, all variations in the readings are due to accidental errors. In this case, experience tells us that the arithmetic mean of a number of observations will give the most probable result. The arithmetic mean, or average, is found by adding all the observed values and dividing by the number of observations made. But this is still not the true value of the quantity that is being measured, since the true value is seldom known. Hence it is important to know how reliable the result is, that is, to set limits within which it is probable that the true value lies. It is known from the theory of probability that an arithmetic mean computed from n equally reliable observations is more accurate than any one observation in the ratio of $\sqrt{n}$ to 1. It can also be shown that the arithmetic mean will approach the true value as the number of observations increases. Thus, one way of increasing the accuracy of a measurement is to take a large number of observations.

It is very desirable in experimental work to have an estimate of the reliability of the mean of a number of observations. Since the true value of a quantity is not known, the best that can be done is to set limits within which it is highly probable that the true value lies. The closer these limits are, the more reliable is the value of the mean obtained.

There are several ways of expressing the measure of reliability of the arithmetic mean. These are: the average deviation from the mean, the average deviation of the mean, and the per cent deviation of the mean.

When the mean of a number of observations is taken, the departures of the individual values from the mean are called deviations. The average deviation from the mean (the a.d.) is the average of the differences between each observed value and the arithmetic mean, without regard to sign. It is a measure of the scatter of the observed values from their average value; it represents the average deviation, or error, of a single observation. Its value is found by subtracting the mean from each reading, adding these differences without taking into account the algebraic signs, and dividing by the number of readings.

For example, suppose that six measurements of the length of a body have been made. Then the average deviation is found as follows:

READINGS	DEVIATIONS
7.85 cm.	+0.02 cm.
7.81	−0.02
7.84	+0.01
7.82	−0.01
7.85	+0.02
7.80	−0.03
6)46.97	6)0.11
Mean 7.83 cm.	a.d. 0.02 cm.

The average deviation thus found is sometimes called the average error and, for the purposes of the elementary laboratory, it may be taken as the possible error in the mean value.

The average deviation of the mean (the A.D.) is equal to the a.d. divided by the square root of the number of observations. Thus $A.D. = \dfrac{a.d.}{\sqrt{n}}$.

This quantity is a measure of the deviation of the arithmetic mean from the true value; it is the quantity that is generally known as the probable error. The significance of the A.D., from probability theory, is that the chances that the true value M_t will lie within the range $M \pm A.D.$, or outside of that range, are one to one; M is the observed arithmetic mean.

Thus, in the example given above, the mean of the readings is 7.83 cm. The average deviation from the mean (the a.d.) is 0.02 cm. The significance of the a.d. is that on the average, the readings differ from the mean (7.83 cm.) by ± 0.02 cm. The average deviation of the mean (the A.D.) is $\dfrac{0.02}{\sqrt{6}} = 0.008$ cm.

The significance of the A.D. is that the chances that the true value of the length will lie within the range 7.83 ± 0.008 cm. are 50%, while the chances that it will lie outside of that range are also 50%.

The per cent deviation of the mean, or the per cent A.D., is equal to the A.D. divided by the mean, times 100.

$$\% \ A.D. = \frac{A.D.}{M} \times 100\%$$

Sometimes it is important to know the ratio of the average deviation of the mean to the value of the quantity measured. Expressed in per cent, this is the per cent A.D., which is the quantity usually considered in judging the accuracy of a series of measurements.

Thus, in the example given above, the per cent deviation of the mean is $\dfrac{0.008}{7.83} \times 100\% = 0.1\%$.

PER CENT ERROR

If the true value of a quantity is known, then the error can be calculated. The error is the difference between the result actually observed (M) and the true value (M_t). The relative error is the ratio of the error to the true value. The per cent error is equal to the error divided by the true value and multiplied by 100.

$$\% \ error = \frac{M - M_t}{M_t} \times 100\%$$

where M is the observed value, or the arithmetic mean of the observations, and M_t is the true value.

For example, suppose that a student measures the velocity of sound in dry air at 0°C. and finds it to be

333.1 meters per second, while the accepted value is 331.4 meters per second. The error is 1.7 meters per second. The relative error is $\dfrac{1.7}{331.4}$ or 0.005. The per cent error is $\dfrac{1.7}{331.4} \times 100\% = 0.5\%$.

There is no definite value for the allowable per cent error to be expected in the following experiments. In many cases it is reasonable to expect results within 1%, while in some cases the error may be 5% or more, depending on the apparatus used. However, all measurements should be made with the greatest care, so as to reduce the error as much as possible.

1

MEASUREMENT OF LENGTH

Physics is an exact experimental science, and as such it is largely a science of measurement. Many measuring instruments of great accuracy and sensitivity have been developed to meet the requirements of the physics laboratory. The measurement of length is of fundamental importance in scientific work, hence it is fitting to begin experimental work with this type of measurement. The purpose of this experiment is to measure the length of an object by means of a meter ruler, vernier caliper, and micrometer caliper; to determine the probable error; and to compare the English and metric units of length.

THEORY

The simplest way of measuring length is with the aid of an ordinary meter scale, or an English ruler. For ordinary measurements a length is determined by a rough comparison with the scale, and the result is given at a glance and in round numbers. For a more precise determination the scale has to be very accurately made, and it has to be read to a fraction of its smallest scale division.

It is found that when an instrument is used to the limit of its precision, certain errors occur which cannot be eliminated; these are called accidental errors. Thus, in taking a series of measurements of a physical quantity, it is found that these usually differ among themselves, because of the accidental errors involved. The best value of the quantity measured, i.e. the most probable value, is the arithmetic mean, or the average of the values obtained.

The precision of measurement can usually be increased by using more complex and more accurate equipment and by taking precautions to eliminate errors as much as possible. However, the student should always aim to make his measurements with the greatest accuracy attainable with the given apparatus.

The Vernier Caliper

When a measurement is made with an ordinary meter stick, it is necessary to estimate the tenths of a millimeter, the smallest division on the scale. A vernier is a device which helps in reading accurately the fractional part of a scale division. It consists of a small auxiliary scale, called a vernier, which slides along the main scale; the graduations of the vernier are different from those of the main scale, but they bear a simple relation to them.

The vernier caliper, which is illustrated in Fig. 1, consists of a fixed part and a movable jaw. The fixed part includes a stem, on which is engraved the main scale, and a fixed jaw which is attached to the stem. The

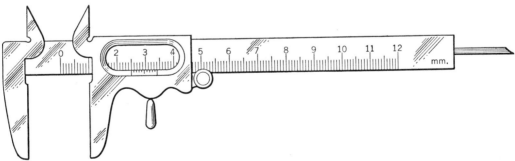

Fig. 1. The Vernier Caliper

movable jaw is free to slide on the fixed stem and has a vernier scale engraved on it. The fixed scale is divided into centimeters and millimeters. The vernier is divided so that 10 divisions on it cover the same interval as 9 divisions on the main scale. Hence the length of each vernier division is $\frac{9}{10}$ the length of a main scale division. When the jaws are closed, the first line at the left end of the vernier, called the zero line or the index, coincides with the zero line on the main scale. However, the first vernier division is 0.1 mm. away from the next main scale division, the second vernier division is 0.2 mm. away from the next main scale division, and so on. If the jaws are slightly opened, it is easy to tell the fraction of a main scale division which the vernier index has moved, by noting which vernier division coincides with a main scale division.

A measurement is made with the vernier caliper by closing the jaws on the object to be measured and then reading the position where the zero line of the vernier falls on the main scale. This setting of the zero line of the vernier on the main scale is the required measurement, except that no attempt is made to estimate to a fraction of a main scale division. The fractional part of a main scale division is obtained by noting which line on the vernier coincides with a line on the main scale. Several possible vernier readings are illustrated in Fig. 2.

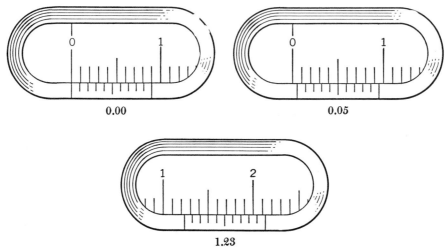

0.00   0.05

1.23

Fig. 2. Vernier Readings

Frequently a vernier does not read zero when the jaws are completely closed. In such cases a zero correction has to be applied to every reading; this correction may be either positive or negative. If the errors in the direction of increasing main scale readings are called positive, then the zero correction is always made by subtracting the zero reading from the final reading.

Vernier scales are attached to many different kinds of instruments, and not all of them divide a main scale division into ten equal parts. In actual practice the number of vernier divisions equal in length to a certain smaller number of scale divisions has to be observed for the vernier being used.

The Micrometer Caliper

The micrometer caliper (see Fig. 3) is an instrument used for the accurate measurement of short lengths. It consists essentially of a carefully machined screw mounted in a strong frame. The object to be measured

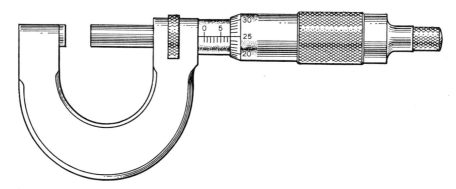

Fig. 3. The Micrometer Caliper

is placed between the end of the screw and the projecting end of the frame, called the anvil. The screw is then advanced until the object is gripped gently between the two jaws of the instrument. Most micrometers are provided with a ratchet which is arranged to slip on the screw as soon as a light and constant force is exerted on the object. By using the ratchet it is possible to tighten up the screw by the same amount each time,

2

and thus avoid using too great a force. If this arrangement is absent, great care should be taken not to force the screw, for the instrument may be easily damaged.

The micrometer caliper used in this experiment consists of a screw with a pitch of 0.5 mm., a longitudinal scale engraved along a barrel containing the screw, and a circular scale engraved around a thimble which rotates with the screw and moves along the scale on the barrel. The longitudinal scale is divided into millimeters. The circular scale has 50 divisions. Since the pitch of the screw is 0.5 mm., which is the distance advanced by the screw on turning through one revolution, it is clear that rotating the thimble through one scale division will cause the screw to move a distance of $\frac{1}{50}$ of 0.5 mm., or 0.01 mm. Hence readings may be taken directly to one hundredth of a millimeter, and by estimating tenths of a thimble scale division, they may be taken to one thousandth of a millimeter.

The reading of the micrometer is taken by noting the position of the edge of the thimble on the longitudinal scale and the position of the axial line of the barrel on the circular scale, and adding the two readings. The reading of the main scale gives the measurement to the nearest whole main scale division; the fractional part of a main scale division is read on the circular scale. Since it requires two revolutions of the screw to make it advance a distance of one millimeter, it is necessary always to be careful to note whether the reading on the circular scale refers to the first half or the second half of a millimeter. (In Fig. 3 the reading is 7.75 mm.)

The micrometer should be checked for a zero error, for it may not read zero when the jaws are completely closed. In such cases a zero correction has to be applied to every reading; this correction may be either positive or negative. The value of the zero reading is obtained by rotating the screw until it comes in contact with the anvil, and then noting the reading on the circular scale.

APPARATUS

1. English ruler.
2. Metric ruler.
3. Vernier caliper.
4. Micrometer caliper.

5. Unknown length.
6. Brass plate.
7. Metal cylinder.

PROCEDURE

1. Measure the unknown length with the metric ruler. Read the position of both ends of the unknown length, estimating to the nearest tenth of a millimeter. Record both readings in cm., and read to 0.01 cm. Make four independent measurements, i.e. use a different part of the ruler for each measurement, and record all the readings.

2. Measure the unknown length with the English ruler. Read the position of both ends of the unknown length, estimating to the nearest tenth of the smallest scale division. Record both readings, expressed in inches, to the nearest 0.01 inch. Make four independent measurements, i.e. use a different part of the ruler for each measurement, and record all the readings.

3. Determine the zero reading of the vernier caliper, i.e. the reading when the jaws of the instrument are in contact with each other. Record the value of this reading to 0.01 cm. Make four independent determinations of the zero reading, i.e. open and close the jaws before each setting, and record the readings.

4. Measure the length of the brass plate with the vernier caliper. The measurement is made by closing the jaws of the caliper on the brass plate and reading the position where the zero line of the vernier falls on the main scale. The fractional part of a main scale division is obtained by noting which line on the vernier coincides with a line on the main scale. Record the reading in cm., and read to 0.01 cm. Make four independent measurements, i.e. open and close the jaws before each setting, and record the readings.

5. Determine the zero reading of the micrometer caliper, i.e. the reading when the jaws of the instrument are in contact with each other. The movable jaw may be brought almost into contact with the fixed jaw by turning the spindle directly, but actual contact must always be made by turning the ratchet slowly until it clicks several times. If the ratchet is absent, great care must be taken not to force the screw; merely let the movable jaw approach the fixed jaw very slowly and stop turning the screw as soon as the two jaws touch. Record the value of this reading in cm., and read to 0.0001 cm., estimating to one tenth of the smallest scale division. Make four independent determinations of the zero reading, i.e. open and close the jaws before each setting, and record the readings.

6. Measure the diameter of the metal cylinder with the micrometer caliper. The measurement is made by placing the cylinder between the jaws of the caliper and advancing the screw until the cylinder is gripped gently between the two jaws of the instrument. Again, care should be taken not to force the screw. Record the value of this reading in cm., and read to 0.0001 cm., estimating to one tenth of the smallest scale division. Make four independent measurements of the diameter of the cylinder, i.e. open and close the jaws before each setting, and record the readings.

DATA

MEASUREMENT OF UNKNOWN LENGTH USING A METRIC RULER

RULER READINGS		LENGTHS	DEVIATIONS
LEFT END	RIGHT END		
AVERAGE VALUE OF THE UNKNOWN LENGTH			

MEASUREMENT OF UNKNOWN LENGTH USING AN ENGLISH RULER

RULER READINGS		LENGTHS	DEVIATIONS
LEFT END	RIGHT END		
AVERAGE VALUE OF THE UNKNOWN LENGTH			

Number of centimeters in one inch, calculated value.....................................

Number of centimeters in one inch, accepted value.....................................

Per cent error.....................................

LENGTH OF BRASS PLATE USING A VERNIER CALIPER

	VERNIER CALIPER READINGS				
	1	2	3	4	AVERAGE
ZERO READING					
READING WITH BRASS PLATE					
LENGTH OF BRASS PLATE					

DIAMETER OF METAL CYLINDER USING A MICROMETER CALIPER

	MICROMETER READINGS				
	1	2	3	4	AVERAGE
ZERO READING					
READING WITH METAL CYLINDER					
DIAMETER OF METAL CYLINDER					

Measurement of Length

NAME_____ SECTION_____ DATE_____ EXPERIMENT ONE

CALCULATIONS

1. From the data of procedure (1), compute the length of the object measured for each set of measurements. Calculate the average value of the length by finding the arithmetic mean of the lengths obtained, to the proper number of significant figures.

2. From the data of procedure (2), compute the length of the object measured for each set of measurements. Calculate the average value of the length by finding the arithmetic mean of the lengths obtained, to the proper number of significant figures.

3. Compute the number of centimeters in one inch from your measurements in procedures (1–2). Use the calculated average values of the unknown length in making the computations. Compare your result with the accepted value by finding the per cent error.

4. From the data of procedure (3), compute the average value of the zero reading of the vernier caliper. From the data of procedure (4), compute the average value of the setting of the vernier caliper for the length of the brass plate. Calculate the length of the brass plate, making sure to properly include the algebraic sign of the zero correction.

5. From the data of procedure (5), compute the average value of the zero reading of the micrometer caliper. From the data of procedure (6), compute the average value of the setting of the micrometer caliper for the diameter of the metal cylinder. Calculate the diameter of the metal cylinder, making sure to properly include the algebraic sign of the zero correction.

6. From the data of procedures (1–2), calculate the deviations of the lengths obtained from the average value of the length. Compute the average deviation from the mean (the a.d.), the average deviation of the mean (the A.D.), and the per cent deviation of the mean (the per cent A.D.) for both sets of measurements. (See the Introduction on the Theory of Errors.)

QUESTIONS

1. Why are several observations taken for each measurement?

2. (a) What is the smallest part of a centimeter that can be read or estimated with a meter stick? (b) What is the smallest part of a centimeter that can be read or estimated with your vernier caliper? (c) Which readings are more reliable? Why?

3. What is the smallest part of a centimeter that can be read or estimated with your micrometer caliper? This represents the sensitivity of the micrometer, for the sensitivity of a measuring instrument is the value of the smallest quantity that can be read or estimated with it.

4. State the number of significant figures in the data of procedures (1), (4), and (6).

5. (a) What is the significance of the average deviation from the mean (the a.d.)? (b) What is the significance of the average deviation of the mean (the A.D.)?

2

MASS, VOLUME, AND DENSITY

Density is one of the important characteristics of materials. The engineer uses tables of densities in calculating the weights of bridges and other structures which it would be impossible to weigh; from the dimensions he can compute the volume and then from tables of densities he can calculate the total weight. It is the object of this experiment to determine the masses, volumes, and densities of several substances.

THEORY

In measuring various physical quantities it is important to be able to use the proper instruments. In this experiment the mass of an object is measured by weighing it on a balance, the volume is computed from the measurements of its dimensions, and the density is then calculated. Density is defined as the mass per unit volume, or

$$D = \frac{M}{V}$$

where M is the mass in grams, V is the volume in cubic centimeters, and D is the density in grams per cubic centimeter.

The volume of a cylinder is given by

$$V = \frac{\pi d^2 L}{4}$$

where d is the diameter and L is the length of the cylinder.

APPARATUS

1. Equal arm balance.
2. Set of weights.
3. Triple beam balance.
4. Metric ruler.
5. Vernier caliper.
6. Micrometer caliper.
7. Three cylinders of different metals:
   a. Aluminum.
   b. Brass.
   c. Iron.

8. Two pieces of wire of different metals:
   a. Aluminum.
   b. Copper.
9. An irregular solid.
10. A 250 c.c. graduated cylinder.

PROCEDURE

1. Determine the mass of each cylinder, using the equal arm balance.

2. Determine the mass of each wire, using the triple beam balance.

3. Measure the diameter of each cylinder and of each wire with the micrometer caliper. Take four readings at different places for each set of measurements, estimating to one tenth of the smallest scale division. The readings should be to 0.0001 centimeter. Record the zero reading of the instrument.

4. Measure the length of each cylinder with the vernier caliper.

5. Measure the length of each wire with the metric ruler.

6. Weigh the irregular solid, using the equal arm balance.

7. Determine the volume of the irregular solid by the displacement method. Suspend the solid by means of a string and lower it into the graduated cylinder, which has been partly filled with water. Read the level of the water before and after immersing the irregular solid. Subtract the first reading from the second to obtain the volume in cubic centimeters.

DATA

OBJECT USED	MASS IN GM.	LENGTH IN CM.	VOLUME IN C.C.	DENSITY COMPUTED	DENSITY FROM TABLE III, APPENDIX	PER CENT ERROR
ALUMINUM CYLINDER						
BRASS CYLINDER						
IRON CYLINDER						
ALUMINUM WIRE						
COPPER WIRE						
IRREGULAR SOLID						

| OBJECT USED | MICROMETER READINGS | | | | | DIAMETER IN CM. |
	1	2	3	4	AVERAGE	
ALUMINUM CYLINDER						
BRASS CYLINDER						
IRON CYLINDER						
ALUMINUM WIRE						
COPPER WIRE						
ZERO READING						

CALCULATIONS

1. Compute the average of the readings for each diameter measured. Calculate and record each diameter, properly corrected for the zero reading of the micrometer.

2. Compute the volume of each object measured.

3. Calculate the density of each substance used.

4. Compare your results with those given in Table III, Appendix, and find the per cent error.

QUESTIONS

1. In measuring the length and diameter of a cylinder, which dimension should be measured more carefully?
Why?

2. Why was the triple beam balance used in determining the masses of the wires?

3. (a) What is the volume in cubic millimeters of the largest cylinder you measured? (b) What is the volume in liters? (c) What is the mass in kilograms?

4. A thin circular sheet of copper has a diameter of 30.0 centimeters and a thickness of 1 millimeter. Find the weight of the sheet in grams.

3

ADDITION OF VECTORS. EQUILIBRIUM OF A PARTICLE

When a system of forces, all of which pass through the same point, acts on a body, they may be replaced by a single force called the resultant. The purpose of this experiment is to show that the magnitude and direction of the resultant of several forces acting on a particle may be determined by drawing the proper vector diagram, and that the particle is in equilibrium when the resultant force is zero.

THEORY

A scalar is a physical quantity that possesses magnitude only; examples of scalar quantities are length, mass, and density. A vector is a quantity that possesses both magnitude and direction; examples of vector quantities are velocity, acceleration, and force. A vector may be represented by drawing a straight line in the direction of the vector, the length of the line being made proportional to the magnitude of the vector; the sense of the vector, for example, whether it is pointing toward the right or toward the left, is indicated by an arrowhead placed at the end of the line.

Vectors may be added graphically. For example, if two or more forces act at a point, a single force may act as the equivalent of the combination of forces. The resultant is a single force which produces the same effect as the sum of several forces, when these pass through a common point (see Fig. 4). The equilibrant is a force

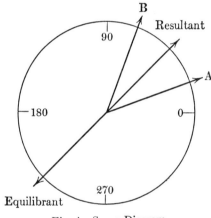

Fig. 4. Space Diagram

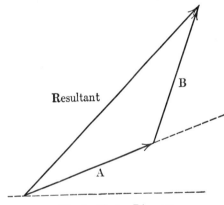

Fig. 5. Vector Diagram

equal and opposite to the resultant. A vector may also be broken up into components. The components of a vector are two vectors in different directions, usually at right angles, which will give the original vector, when added together (see Fig. 7).

The operation of adding vectors graphically consists in constructing a figure in which a straight line is drawn from some point as origin to represent the first vector, the length of the line being proportional to the magnitude of the vector and the direction of the line being the same as the direction of the vector. From the arrowhead end of this line and at the proper angle with respect to the first vector, another line is drawn to represent the second vector, and so on with the remaining ones. The resultant is the vector drawn from the origin of the first vector to the arrowhead of the last (see Fig. 5). If a closed polygon is formed, that is, if the arrowhead of the last vector falls upon the origin of the first, then the resultant is zero. If the vectors represent forces, they are in equilibrium.

Vectors may also be added analytically by calculating the x and y components of each vector (see Fig. 7), getting the algebraic sum of all the x components and the algebraic sum of all the y components, and then adding these sums by the parallelogram method.

To find the resultant of two vectors by the parallelogram method, the two vectors A and B to be added are laid off graphically to scale and in the proper directions from a common origin, so as to form two adjacent sides of a parallelogram (see Fig. 6). The parallelogram is then completed by drawing the other two sides parallel respectively to the first two. The diagonal R of the parallelogram drawn from the same origin gives the

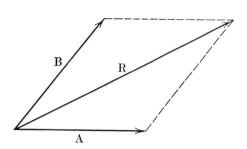

Fig. 6. Parallelogram Method of
Adding Vectors

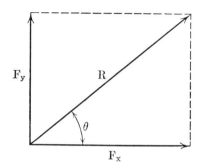

Fig. 7. Resolution of a Vector
into Components

resultant, both in magnitude and direction. This method may be used for the addition of any number of vectors, by first finding the resultant of two vectors, then adding the third one to this resultant in the same way, and continuing the process with the other vectors.

The apparatus used in this experiment (see Fig. 8) consists of a horizontal force table graduated in degrees and provided with pulleys which may be set at any desired angles. A string passing over each pulley supports a weight holder upon which weights may be placed. A pin holds a small ring to which the strings are attached and which acts as the particle. When a test for equilibrium is to be made, the pin is removed; if the forces are in equilibrium, the particle will not be displaced.

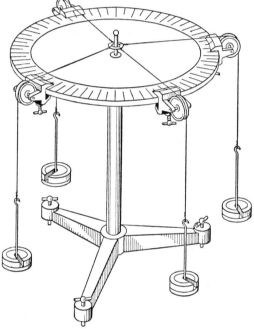

Fig. 8. Force Table

APPARATUS

1. Force table.
2. Four pulleys.
3. Four weight hangers.
4. Set of slotted weights, including:
      four 100-gm. weights
      four 50-gm. weights
      two 20-gm. weights
      two 10-gm. weights.
5. Set of small weights (5, 2, 2, 1 gram).
6. Protractor.
7. Metric ruler.

PROCEDURE

1. Mount a pulley on the 20° mark on the force table and suspend a total of 100 grams over it. Mount a second pulley on the 120° mark and suspend a total of 200 grams over it. Draw a vector diagram to scale, using a scale of 20 grams per centimeter, and determine graphically the direction and magnitude of the resultant, by using the parallelogram method.

2. Check the result of procedure (1) by setting up the equilibrant on the force table. This will be a force equal in magnitude to the resultant, but pulling in the opposite direction. Set up a third pulley 180° from the calculated direction of the resultant and suspend weights over it equal to the magnitude of the resultant. Cautiously remove the center pin to see if the ring remains in equilibrium. Before removing the pin, make sure that all the strings are pointing exactly at the center of the pin, otherwise the angles will not be correct.

3. Mount the first two pulleys as in procedure (1), with the same weights as before. Mount a third pulley on the 220° mark and suspend a total of 150 grams over it. Draw a vector diagram to scale and determine graphically the direction and magnitude of the resultant. This may be done by adding the third vector to the sum of the first two, which was obtained in procedure (1). Now set up the equilibrant on the force table and test it as in procedure (2).

4. Clamp a pulley on the 30° mark on the force table and suspend a total of 200 grams over it. By means

of a vector diagram drawn to scale, find the magnitude of the components along the 0° and the 90° directions. Set up these forces on the force table as they have been determined. These two forces are equivalent to the original force. Now replace the initial force by an equal force pulling in a direction 180° away from the original direction. Test the system for equilibrium.

CALCULATIONS

1. Calculate the resultant in procedure (1) by solving for the third side of a triangle algebraically. The magnitude of the vector may be obtained by using the law of cosines, and the direction may be obtained by using the law of sines.

2. Calculate the resultant in procedure (1) by using the analytical method of adding vectors.

QUESTIONS

1. State how this experiment has demonstrated the vector addition of forces.

2. In procedure (3) could all four pulleys be placed in the same quadrant or in two adjacent quadrants and still be in equilibrium? Explain.

3. State the condition for the equilibrium of a particle.

4
EQUILIBRIUM OF A RIGID BODY

When a rigid body is acted upon by a system of forces which do not all pass through the same point, a change may be produced in the linear velocity or in the angular velocity of the body. Under certain conditions the body will be in equilibrium. This experiment presents a study of the conditions for the equilibrium of a rigid body under the action of several forces.

THEORY

The torque, or the moment of a force, is a measure of the force's tendency to produce rotation. It is equal to the product of the force and the perpendicular distance from the axis of rotation to the line of action of the force. In computing moments the rules of coordinate geometry are used, hence clockwise moments, that is those which tend to produce clockwise rotation, are regarded as negative, and counterclockwise moments are regarded as positive.

A rigid body is a body whose particles do not change their distances from one another. If a system of forces is acting on a rigid body and the forces considered collectively have no tendency to produce any motion of translation or rotation, then the body is in equilibrium. That is, a rigid body is in equilibrium when it has no linear or angular acceleration. The two conditions for the equilibrium of a rigid body are: (1) the vector sum of all the forces acting on the body must be zero; (2) the algebraic sum of all the torques (or moments of force) about any axis must be zero. The first condition means that the sum of the forces in any direction must be equal to the sum of the forces in the opposite direction. The second condition means that the sum of the clockwise moments around any point must be equal to the sum of the counterclockwise moments around the same point.

Suppose one takes for illustration a horizontal bar having its axis of rotation near the center and having various forces acting upward and downward on it (see Fig. 9). The moment of each force is calculated, and

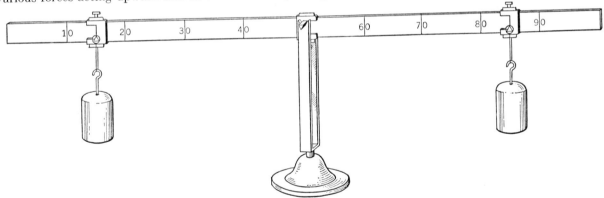

Fig. 9. Equilibrium of a Rigid Body

by making use of the two conditions for the equilibrium of a rigid body, the unknown force or distance may be computed. The weight of the bar itself has to be considered. The weight of a body is the gravitational force with which the earth pulls on the body; it is made up of the sum of the weights of its particles and acts throughout the body. This constitutes a system of parallel forces. The resultant of this system of forces passes through a point called the center of parallel forces, which is the center of gravity of the body. The resultant of the parallel forces is the weight of the body. Thus in computing moments it is convenient to use the concept of center of gravity. This, then, is the point in a body where the entire weight may be regarded as concentrated, in so far as the force action due to the weight is concerned. Thus the moment of force exerted by the weight of the bar is the same as if all its weight were concentrated at the center of gravity and is calculated accordingly.

APPARATUS

1. Meter stick.
2. Three meter stick knife-edge clamps.
3. Stand for supporting the meter stick with a clamp.

4. Set of hooked weights.
5. Equal arm balance and weights.
6. Body of unknown weight (about 100 grams).

15

PROCEDURE

1. Weigh the meter stick and record the weight.

2. Weigh the three meter stick clamps together and compute their average weight.

3. Find the center of gravity of the meter stick to the nearest 0.5 millimeter by balancing it in one of the clamps.

4. Put another clamp near one end of the stick and hang a 100-gram weight from it. Slide the stick through the supporting clamp until the position of balance is found. Record the position of the axis of rotation, that is the point of support, and the position of the weight.

5. Put another clamp near the other end of the stick and suspend a 200-gram weight from it. Leaving the other weight in place, find the new point of balance by again sliding the meter stick through the supporting clamp. Record the position of the 200-gram weight and of the new point of balance.

6. Remove the weights and clamps. Clamp the meter stick in the support clamp at its center of gravity. Put another clamp near one end of the stick and suspend the body of unknown weight from it. Slide another clamp, with a 200-gram weight attached, along the other end of the stick until the position of equilibrium is found. Record the positions of both weights.

7. Weigh the body of unknown weight used.

DATA

Weight of the meter stick...

Weight of the three meter stick clamps...

Average weight of the meter stick clamps..

Center of gravity of the meter stick...

Position of the 100-gram weight..

Position of the axis of rotation...

Position of the 200-gram weight..

New point of balance...

Position of the unknown weight...

New position of the 200-gram weight..

Actual weight of the unknown mass..

Weight of the meter stick computed by the method of moments.......................

Weight of the unknown mass computed by the method of moments...................

CALCULATIONS

1. Compute the weight of the meter stick from the data of procedure (4) by the method of moments. Compare the result with the known weight of the stick.

2. Using the point of support as the axis in procedure (5), compute the moment of force of each of the weights. Add all the positive moments together and all the negative moments together, then find their algebraic sum. Calculate what percentage of the total positive moment this sum represents.

3. Compute the weight of the body used in procedure (6) by the method of moments. Compare the actual mass of the body of unknown weight with the computed weight.

QUESTIONS

1. State the two conditions for the equilibrium of a rigid body.

2. How do your results from calculation (2) compare with the equilibrium condition for moments?

3. Why was the meter stick clamped at its center of gravity in procedure (6)? Was there any advantage in doing this?

4. Using the data of procedure (5), assume the axis of rotation to be at one end of the stick and compute the moments of all the forces about this axis. The total upward force at the point of support is equal to the sum of all the downward forces. Add all the positive moments together and all the negative moments together, then find their algebraic sum. What conclusion do you draw from the result?

5
THE SIMPLE PENDULUM

The acceleration of a freely falling body is called the acceleration of gravity. It may be measured by observing the time required for a body to fall freely through a known distance. But this method is not capable of yielding very accurate results. The simple pendulum offers a method of measuring this constant very precisely. The object of this experiment is to study the law of the simple pendulum and to measure the acceleration of gravity g.

THEORY

The simple pendulum consists of a concentrated mass suspended at the end of a cord of negligible weight. A close approximation to this is a small metal sphere on a long, thin thread. The period of such a pendulum is given by the expression

$$T = 2\pi\sqrt{\frac{L}{g}}$$

where L is the length of the pendulum measured to the center of the sphere and g is the acceleration of gravity at the place where the pendulum is located. The period T is the time for one vibration, or the time it takes the pendulum to swing from its maximum displacement on one side, to the other side, and back again. The length of the pendulum is expressed in centimeters, the period is in seconds, and the acceleration of gravity is in centimeters per second per second.

APPARATUS

1. Metal sphere on a long string (the simple pendulum).
2. Supporting rod and pendulum clamp.
3. Two-meter stick with caliper jaws.

4. Vernier caliper.
5. Stop watch or stop clock,

PROCEDURE

1. Measure the diameter of the metal sphere with the vernier caliper.

2. Clamp the string so that the center of the sphere is about 20 cm. below the point of support. Carefully measure the distance from the lower edge of the support to the upper surface of the sphere. Record this distance as the length of string used. The length of the pendulum will be this distance plus the radius of the metal sphere.

3. Displace the sphere to one side, through an angle of not more than about five degrees, and let the pendulum oscillate. Record the time it takes the pendulum to make 50 vibrations. In counting vibrations be sure to start the stop watch on the count of zero and not on the count of one.

4. Make the length of the pendulum about 40 cm., and measure the distance from the lower edge of the support to the upper surface of the sphere. Record this distance as the length of string used. The length of the pendulum will be this distance plus the radius of the metal sphere. Again record the time for 50 vibrations.

5. Repeat procedure (4), making the length of the pendulum successively about 60, 80, 100, 120, 140, and 160 cm. In the last three cases record the time for 25 vibrations instead of 50.

6. Using a length of about 50 cm., determine the time for 50 vibrations when the sphere is displaced about 5 degrees, 30 degrees, and 45 degrees from the equilibrium position. Record the length of the pendulum and the time.

DATA

Diameter of sphere. . . . . : . . . .

Radius of sphere. . . . .

LENGTH OF STRING USED	LENGTH OF PENDULUM	NUMBER OF VIBRATIONS	TIME	PERIOD	SQUARE OF PERIOD	VALUE OF g

CALCULATIONS

1. Calculate the period for each observation.

2. Calculate the square of the period for each observation. Use only three significant figures in recording the square of the period, rounding off the third figure.

3. Compute the value of g from each measurement in procedure (5).

4. Calculate the average value of g, and compare it with the known value, $g = 980$ cm./sec.^{2}, by finding the per cent error. The acceleration of gravity varies slightly with latitude and elevation. The value given is approximately correct for sea level and 45° latitude.

5. Plot a curve using the values of the square of the period as ordinates and the lengths of the pendulum as abscissas. Use the entire sheet of graph paper. Read the instructions on plotting graphs in the introduction.

6. Plot a second curve using the values of the period as ordinates and the lengths of the pendulum as abscissas. Use the entire sheet of graph paper.

QUESTIONS

1. State what this experiment has shown.

2. Why must the angle through which the pendulum swings be no more than about 10 degrees?

3. Did you actually measure the period of the pendulum in this experiment? Explain.

4. What do the results of procedure (6) show?

5. What kind of curves should you obtain if your experimental results verify the formula for the simple pendulum?

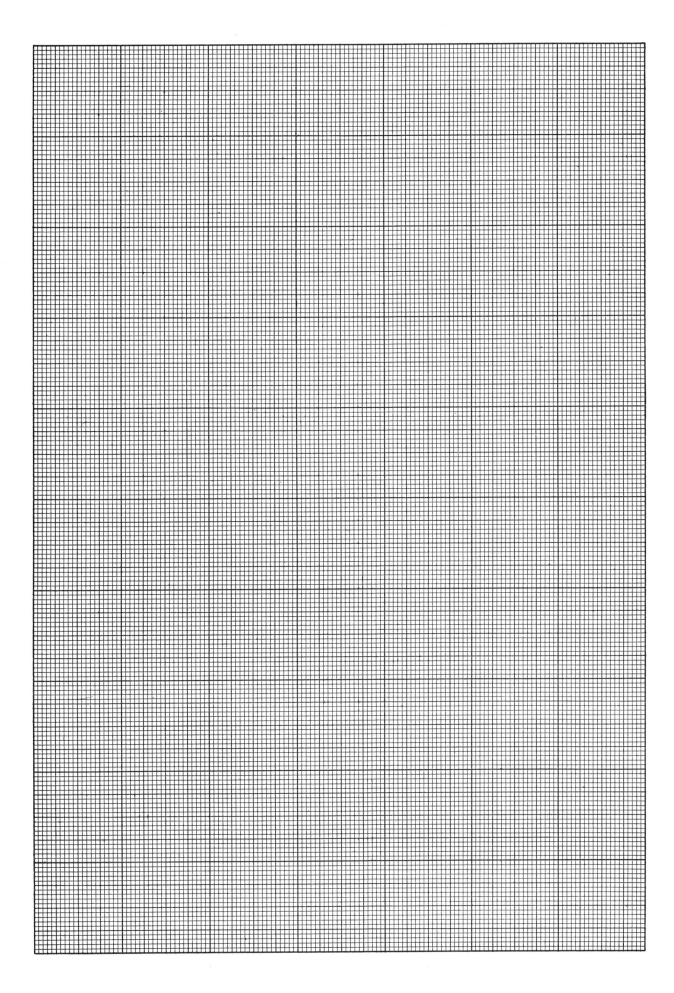

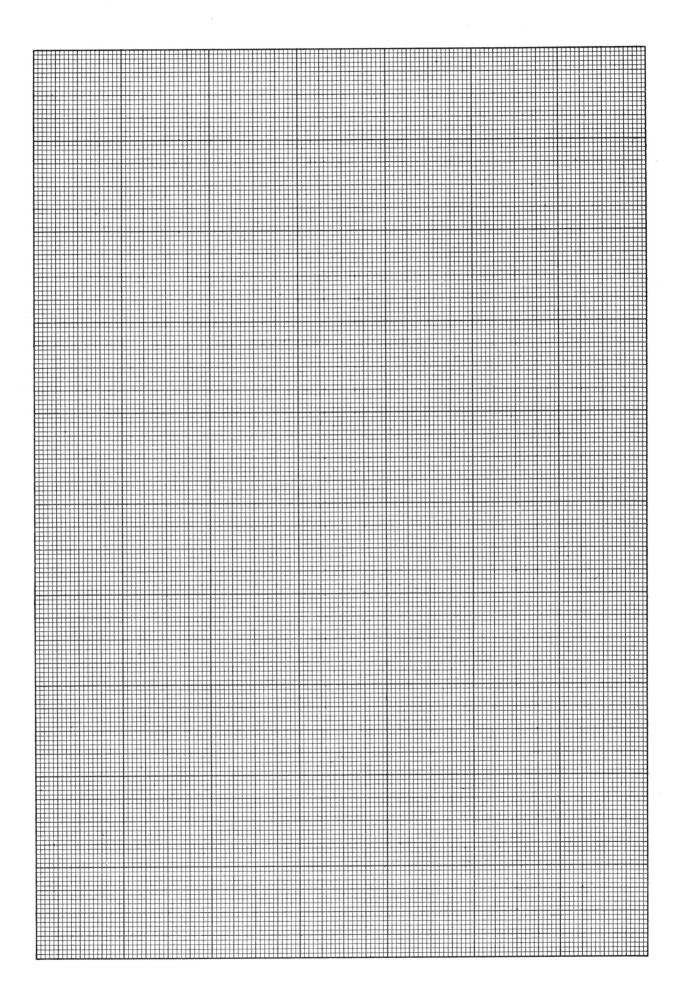

6

UNIFORMLY ACCELERATED MOTION. THE ATWOOD MACHINE

In accordance with Newton's first law of motion, when the resultant of all the forces acting on a body is zero, if the body is at rest, it will remain at rest, and if it is in motion, it will continue to move with uniform speed in a straight line. Newton's second law of motion describes what happens if the resultant is different from zero. The law states that if an unbalanced force is acting on a body, it will produce an acceleration in the direction of the force, the acceleration being directly proportional to the force and inversely proportional to the mass of the body. If the acceleration is constant, the body is said to be moving with uniformly accelerated motion. The purpose of this experiment is to measure the acceleration of a given mass produced by a given force and to compare it with that calculated from Newton's second law of motion.

THEORY

The Atwood machine consists of two weights connected by a light, flexible string which passes over a light pulley; the pulley should be as nearly frictionless as possible. The machine is used in measuring the acceleration produced by an arbitrarily chosen force acting upon a given mass. Once the mass and the force have been chosen, the acceleration produced is determined by Newton's second law of motion

$$F = ma$$

where F is the net force in dynes acting on a body, m is the mass of the body in grams, and a is the acceleration in centimeters per second per second.

In the Atwood machine the total mass that is being accelerated is the sum of the two masses. The driving force, which is expressed in dynes, is the difference in the weights on the two ends of the string. The immediate object in performing this experiment is to bring out the dependence of acceleration on force when the mass is kept constant. The only way in which the force can be varied without varying the total mass is to transfer masses from one side of the moving system to the other. First of all, the force of friction must be overcome, and that is done by transferring masses from the ascending side to the descending side, until the mass on the descending side moves downward with uniform velocity when it is given a very slight push. In this manner friction is compensated for. The value of the force of friction should be recorded.

For convenience the distance should be the same in all of the observations. The starting point is taken as the position of the moving system in which one of the masses rests on the floor. As this mass ascends, the other will descend an equal distance, and the stopping point is taken as the instant at which this mass strikes the floor. The distance traversed should be about one and a half meters. The time required for the mass to move through this distance is measured with a stop watch.

In uniformly accelerated motion the velocity is increased by the same amount in each succeeding second. The distance traveled is equal to the average velocity multiplied by the time. Since the system starts from rest and experiences a uniform acceleration, the final velocity will be twice the average velocity. From the time taken to acquire this final velocity, the corresponding acceleration can be computed. The equations of motion involved in uniformly accelerated motion are discussed below. The distance is given by

$$s = \bar{v}t$$

where s is the distance in centimeters, $\bar{v}$ is the average velocity in centimeters per second, and t is the time in seconds. The average velocity is given by

$$\bar{v} = \frac{v_1 + v_2}{2}$$

where $\bar{v}$ is the average velocity; v_1 is the initial velocity, which is zero in this case; and v_2 is the final velocity. The final velocity is given by

$$v_2 = v_1 + at$$

where v_2 is the final velocity; v_1 is the initial velocity, which is zero in this case; a is the acceleration in centimeters per second per second; and t is the time in seconds.

APPARATUS

1. Pulley clamped to a vertical rod.
2. Two weight holders.
3. Set of slotted weights.
4. Set of small weights, including:
   one 10-gm. weight
   one 5-gm. weight
   five 2-gm. weights
   one 1-gm. weight.
5. String (strong fishing line).
6. Stop watch or stop clock.
7. Two-meter stick.

PROCEDURE

1. Using a total mass of about 2000 grams, determine the force of friction in the machine by transferring masses from the ascending side to the descending side until the mass on the descending side moves downward with uniform velocity when given a very slight push. Record the mass on the descending side, the mass on the ascending side, and the force of friction. Be sure to include the mass of each weight hanger. Arrange the weights so as to have five two-gram weights on the ascending side when the machine is in the balanced condition. CAUTION: Always stand clear of the suspended weights, for the string may break.

2. Transfer two more grams from the ascending side to the descending side, and thus determine the acceleration produced by a net force of four grams. Begin the observation when the ascending mass is on the floor, starting the stop watch at the instant when you let the weights go, and stopping it at the instant when the other mass strikes the floor. Make and record four independent observations.

3. Measure the distance traversed.

4. Repeat procedure (2), using accelerating forces of 8, 12, 16, and 20 grams, by transferring two additional grams each time. Make four independent observations for each accelerating force.

DATA

Distance traversed. . . . .

Descending mass, for uniform velocity. . . . .

Ascending mass, for uniform velocity. . . . .

Force of friction. . . . .

DESCENDING MASS	ASCENDING MASS	NET FORCE	TIME 1	2	3	4	AVERAGE

NET FORCE	AVERAGE VELOCITY	FINAL VELOCITY	ACCELERATION EXPERIMENTAL VALUE	ACCELERATION FROM $F = ma$	PER CENT ERROR

CALCULATIONS

1. Compute the average time taken with each accelerating force. From the known distance and the time taken in each case, compute the average velocity corresponding to each accelerating force.

2. Calculate the final velocity for each set of observations.

3. Calculate the acceleration produced by each accelerating force, from the values of the final velocity and the time.

4. Compute the theoretical value for the acceleration from Newton's second law of motion. Assuming this to be the correct value, compute the per cent error of the observed value for each case.

QUESTIONS

1. (a) State what this experiment tested. (b) State the relation between force and acceleration observed in this experiment.

2. What is the difference between uniform motion and uniformly accelerated motion?

3. If you gave the system an initial velocity different from zero, how would this affect your results?

4. What is the advantage of transferring masses from one side to the other, instead of adding masses to one side?

7

THE BALLISTIC PENDULUM. PROJECTILE MOTION

The principle of conservation of momentum follows directly from Newton's laws of motion. According to this principle, if there are no external forces acting on a system containing several bodies, then the momentum of the system remains constant. In this experiment the principle is applied to the case of a collision, using a ballistic pendulum. A ball is fired by a gun into the bob of a ballistic pendulum. The initial velocity of the ball is determined in terms of the masses of the ball and pendulum bob and the height which the bob rises after impact. This velocity can also be obtained by firing the ball horizontally and allowing it to fall freely toward the earth. The velocity is then determined in terms of the range and the vertical distance of fall. It is the object of this experiment to study the law of conservation of momentum and the elements of projectile motion; more precisely, the purpose is to determine the initial velocity of a projectile (1) by measurements of its range and vertical distance of fall and (2) by means of a ballistic pendulum.

THEORY

The momentum of a body is defined as the product of the mass of the body and its velocity. Newton's second law of motion states that the net force acting on a body is proportional to the time rate of change of momentum. Hence if the sum of the external forces acting on a body is zero, the linear momentum of the body is constant. This is essentially a statement of the principle of conservation of momentum. Applied to a system of bodies, the principle states that if no external forces act on a system containing two or more bodies, then the momentum of the system does not change.

In a collision between two bodies, each one exerts a force on the other. These forces are equal and opposite, and if no other forces are brought into play, the total momentum of the two bodies is not changed by the impact. Hence the total momentum of the system after collision is equal to the total momentum of the system before collision. During the collision the bodies become deformed and a certain amount of energy is used to change their shape. If the bodies are perfectly elastic, they will recover completely from the distortion and will return all of the energy that was expended in distorting them. In this case, the total kinetic energy of the system remains constant. If the bodies are not perfectly elastic, they will remain permanently distorted, and the energy used up in producing the distortion is not recovered.

Inelastic impact can be illustrated by a device known as the ballistic pendulum, which is sometimes employed in determining the speed of a bullet. If a bullet is fired into a pendulum bob and remains imbedded in it, the momentum of the bob and bullet just after the collision is equal to the momentum of the bullet just before the collision. This follows from the law of conservation of momentum. The velocity of the pendulum before collision is zero, while after the collision, the pendulum and the bullet move with the same velocity. Hence the momentum equation gives

$$mv = (M + m)V$$

where m is the mass of the bullet in grams, v is the velocity in centimeters per second of the bullet just before the collision, M is the mass of the pendulum bob, and V is the common velocity of the pendulum bob and bullet just after the collision.

As a result of the collision, the pendulum with the imbedded bullet swings about its point of support, and the center of gravity of the system rises through a vertical distance h. From a measurement of this distance it is possible to calculate the velocity V. The kinetic energy of the system just after the collision must be equal to the increase in potential energy of the system as the pendulum reaches its highest point. This follows from the law of conservation of energy; here we assume that the loss of energy due to friction at the point of support is negligible. The energy equation gives

$$\tfrac{1}{2}(M + m)V^2 = (M + m)gh$$

where M is the mass in grams of the pendulum bob, m is the mass of the bullet, V is the common velocity in centimeters per second of the pendulum bob and bullet just after the collision, g is the known value of the acceleration of gravity, and h is the vertical distance in centimeters through which the center of gravity of the system rises. The left hand side of the equation represents the kinetic energy of the system just after the impact; the right hand side represents the change in the potential energy of the system. Solving the above equation for V, one obtains:

$$V = \sqrt{2gh}$$

By substituting this value of V and the values of the masses M and m in the momentum equation, it is possible to calculate the velocity of the bullet before the collision.

The velocity of the bullet can also be determined from measurements of the range and vertical distance of fall when the bullet is fired horizontally and allowed to fall to the floor without striking the pendulum bob.

The motion of a projectile is a special case of a freely falling body in which the initial velocity may be in any direction with respect to the vertical. The path of the projectile is a curved path produced by a combination of the uniform velocity of projection and the velocity due to the acceleration of gravity. This type of motion may be studied very effectively by considering it as made up of two independent motions, one of constant speed in the horizontal direction, and the other of constant acceleration in the vertical direction. Here the problem is simplified by neglecting the effect of air friction.

For the special case where the projectile is fired horizontally with an initial velocity v, the path is determined by the two equations of motion to be discussed presently, one for the horizontal direction, and the other for the vertical direction.

Since the horizontal component of the velocity remains constant, the distance in the horizontal direction is given by

$$x = vt$$

where x is the distance in centimeters that the projectile travels in the horizontal direction, v is the initial velocity in centimeters per second, and t is the time in seconds.

The initial velocity in the y direction is zero. Hence the motion in this direction is the same as that of a freely falling body with zero initial velocity. Therefore the distance traveled in the y direction is given by

$$y = \tfrac{1}{2}gt^2$$

where y is the distance in centimeters that the projectile travels in the vertical direction, g is the known value of the acceleration of gravity, and t is the time in seconds.

The apparatus used in this experiment (see Fig. 10) is a combination of a ballistic pendulum and a spring gun. The pendulum consists of a massive cylindrical bob, hollowed out to receive the projectile, and suspended

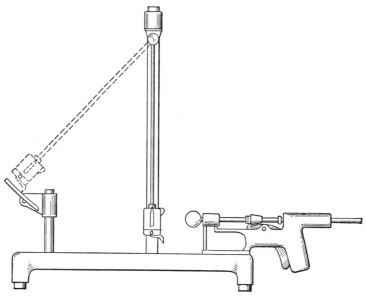

Fig. 10. The Blackwood Ballistic Pendulum

by a strong light rod, pivoted at its upper end. The projectile is a brass ball which is fired into the pendulum bob and is held there by a spring in such a position that its center of gravity lies in the axis of the suspension rod. A brass index is attached to the pendulum bob to indicate the height of the center of gravity of the loaded pendulum. When the projectile is fired into the bob, the pendulum swings upward and is caught at its highest point by a pawl which engages a tooth in the curved rack.

APPARATUS

1. Blackwood ballistic pendulum.
2. Equal arm balance and set of weights.
3. Metric steel scale.

4. Meter stick.
5. Plumb bob.
6. Carbon paper.

PROCEDURE

1. In the first part of the experiment, the initial velocity of the projectile is obtained from measurements of the range and fall. The apparatus should be set near one edge of a level table. In this part the pendulum is not used and should be swung up onto the rack so that it will not interfere with the free flight of the ball.

2. Get the gun ready for firing by placing the ball on the end of the firing rod and pushing it back, compressing the spring until the trigger is engaged. The ball is fired horizontally so that it strikes a target placed on the floor. Fire the ball and determine approximately where it strikes the floor. Place a sheet of white paper on the floor so that the ball will hit it near its center and cover it with carbon paper; place some weights at the corners of the paper to keep it from moving around. In this way a record can be obtained of the exact spot where the ball strikes the floor. Fire the ball five more times.

3. Measure the range for each shot; this is the horizontal distance from the point of projection to the point of contact with the floor. Use a plumb bob to locate the point on the floor directly below the ball as it leaves the gun.

4. Measure the vertical fall of the ball, that is, the vertical distance of the point of projection above the floor.

5. Get the gun ready for firing. Release the pendulum from the rack and allow it to hang freely. When the pendulum is at rest, pull the trigger, thereby firing the ball into the pendulum bob. This will cause the pendulum with the ball inside it to swing up along the rack where it will be caught at its highest point. Record the notch on the curved scale reached by the pawl when it catches the pendulum. To remove the ball from the pendulum, push it out with the finger or a rubber-tipped pencil, meanwhile holding up the spring catch.

6. Repeat procedure (5) four more times, recording the position of the pendulum on the rack each time.

7. From the data of procedures (5) and (6), compute the average value of the position of the pendulum on the rack. Set the pendulum with the pawl engaged in the notch which corresponds most closely with the average reading. Measure the vertical distance h_1 from the base of the apparatus to the index point attached to the pendulum. This index point indicates the height of the center of gravity of the pendulum and ball. Use the metric steel scale and read the measurement to 0.1 millimeter.

8. With the pendulum hanging in its lowest position, measure the vertical distance h_2 from the base of the apparatus to the index point.

9. Loosen the thumbscrew holding the axis of rotation of the pendulum and carefully remove the pendulum from its support. Weigh the pendulum and the ball separately and record the values obtained.

DATA

		Trials			
Range of the projectile	1.	2.	3.	4.	5.

Average range...

Vertical distance of fall..

Time of flight...

Velocity of projection from measurements of range and fall......................................

Highest position of ballistic pendulum:

		Trials			
Reading of curved scale	1.	2.	3.	4.	5.

Average reading..

Vertical distance h_1 or the average height of the center of gravity of the pendulum in its highest

    position...

Vertical distance h_2 or the height of the center of gravity of the pendulum in its lowest position

. . . .

Vertical distance h through which the center of gravity of the pendulum was raised. . . . .

Mass of the pendulum bob. . . . .

Mass of the ball. . . . .

Velocity of the pendulum and ball just after the collision. . . . .

Velocity of the ball before the collision. . . . .

CALCULATIONS

1. From the data of procedure (3), compute the average range of the projectile.

2. From the measured vertical distance that the ball falls and the known value of g, calculate the time of flight of the ball, by using the equation:

$$y = \tfrac{1}{2}gt^2$$

3. Compute the velocity of projection from the time of flight obtained in calculation (2) and the range obtained in calculation (1).

4. From the data of procedures (7) and (8), calculate the vertical distance h through which the center of gravity of the loaded ballistic pendulum was raised as a result of the collision.

5. Compute the value of V, the common velocity of the pendulum bob and ball just after the collision, by using the relation:

$$V = \sqrt{2gh}$$

6. Calculate the velocity of the ball before the collision by substituting the value of V found in calculation (5) and the measured values of the masses of the pendulum bob and of the ball in the momentum equation.

QUESTIONS

1. Using the data of your experiment, calculate the kinetic energy of the ball just before impact from the value of the velocity of the ball obtained with the ballistic pendulum and the mass of the ball.

2. Calculate the kinetic energy of the pendulum bob and ball just after impact from the value of their common velocity and of their masses.

3. (a) Using the results of questions (1) and (2), calculate the fractional loss of energy during this inelastic impact. Express it in per cent. (b) What became of the energy lost?

4. (a) Compute the ratio of the mass of the pendulum bob to the total mass of the bob and the ball. Express it in per cent. (b) How does this ratio compare with the fraction of energy lost during the impact?

5. A bullet weighing 10 grams is fired horizontally into a block of wood weighing 2000 grams and suspended like a ballistic pendulum.   The bullet sticks in the block and the impact causes the block to swing so that its center of gravity rises 10 centimeters.   Find the velocity of the bullet just before the impact.

6. Compare the momentum and the kinetic energy of an automobile weighing 2000 pounds and moving with a velocity of 60 miles per hour with the momentum and the kinetic energy of a projectile weighing 70 pounds and moving with a velocity of 2500 feet per second.

8

UNIFORM CIRCULAR MOTION

Whenever a body is moving in a circular path, a force directed toward the center of the circle must act on the body to keep it moving in this path. This force is called centripetal force. The reaction, which is equal and opposite, is the pull of the body on the restraining medium and is called centrifugal force. The purpose of this experiment is to study uniform circular motion and to compare the observed value of the centripetal force with the calculated value.

THEORY

If a body is moving with uniform speed in a circle, it is said to be moving with uniform circular motion. Even though the speed is constant, the velocity is continually changing, since the direction of the motion is constantly changing. Thus such a body has an acceleration. It can be shown that the direction of the acceleration is always toward the center of the circle and the magnitude of the acceleration is given by

$$a = \frac{v^2}{r}$$

where v is the speed of the body in centimeters per second and r is the radius of the path in centimeters.

A force is necessary to produce this acceleration, and this force is called centripetal force because it is always directed toward the center of rotation. By Newton's second law of motion, the magnitude of this force is given by the relation $F = ma$, or

$$F = m\frac{v^2}{r}$$

where F is the force in dynes and m is the mass in grams; v and r are the same as before. But by Newton's third law of motion, an equal and opposite force is exerted by the body on the restraining medium because of the inertia of the body. This reaction is called centrifugal force.

The centripetal force can also be expressed in terms of the angular speed, since

$$v = r\omega \quad \text{and} \quad \omega = 2\pi n$$

where v is the linear speed in centimeters per second, r is the radius of the path in centimeters, and ω is the angular speed in radians per second; n is the number of revolutions per second. Thus

$$F = mr\omega^2 \quad \text{or} \quad F = 4\pi^2 n^2 rm$$

where F is the centripetal force in dynes.

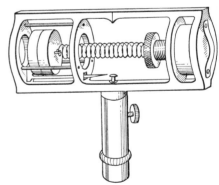

In the apparatus used for this experiment (see Fig. 11), the centripetal force of a stretched spring balances the centrifugal force due to the rotating mass. When the critical speed is reached, the sensitive indicator will stand opposite the index. This speed is kept constant and is measured by means of a revolution counter and a stop watch. The force required to stretch the spring the same amount is subsequently measured by applying weights.

Fig. 11. Centripetal Force Apparatus

APPARATUS

1. Centripetal force apparatus.
2. Rotator with counter.
3. Stop watch or stop clock.

4. Supporting stand.
5. Weight hanger and weights.
6. Vernier caliper.

PROCEDURE

1. Adjust the speed of the rotator and keep it constant at the critical speed for which the sensitive indicator of the centripetal force apparatus stands exactly opposite the index. Do not let this speed be exceeded. Begin by adjusting the variable speed rotator to a low speed and gradually increase the speed until the pointer of the

indicator is exactly opposite the index. Keep on adjusting the speed very gradually during the experiment so that the pointer is kept opposite the index, vibrating about this position as little as possible. CAUTION: It is dangerous to let the apparatus rotate at excessive speeds.

2. Measure the speed of rotation with the revolution counter and a stop watch. First record the reading of the counter. At the proper instant engage the counter and set the stop watch going. To perform the experiment more conveniently, it is a good plan to let one observer pay strict attention to the proper adjustment of the speed. The other observer can obtain the value of the speed by manipulating the stop watch and the revolution counter. At the end of exactly one minute, disengage the counter and record the reading.

3. Repeat procedure (2) and take three more readings of the speed.

4. Remove the apparatus, suspend it on a supporting stand, and determine the weight necessary to make the index and pointer coincide. Include the weight of the rotating mass and of the weight hanger in computing the total force needed to stretch the spring.

5. Measure the radius of rotation of the mass, using the vernier caliper, by measuring the distance from the axis of rotation to the center of the mass. Do this before removing the weight.

DATA

Weight of the rotating mass...

Weight applied to the spring...

Total weight necessary to stretch the spring..

Radius of rotation...

Average speed of rotation..

Centripetal force calculated from the theory..

Measured value of the centripetal force...

Per cent discrepancy...

TIME INTERVAL	READINGS OF THE REVOLUTION COUNTER		SPEED OF ROTATION
	AT THE BEGINNING	AT THE END	

CALCULATIONS

1. From the data of procedures (2) and (3) calculate the speed of rotation for each set of readings. Compute the average speed of rotation.

2. Calculate the centripetal force from the theory, using the average speed of rotation obtained in calculation (1).

3. Compare the calculated value of the centripetal force with the value measured directly, computing the per cent discrepancy.

QUESTIONS

1. State what the experiment checks.

2. (a) How does the centripetal force vary with the speed of rotation for a constant radius of the path? (b) How does it vary with the radius of the path for a constant speed of rotation?

3. Distinguish between centripetal force and centrifugal force. Explain in what direction each force is acting and on what it is acting.

4. Calculate at what speed the earth would have to rotate in order that objects at the equator would have no weight. Assume the radius of the earth to be 6400 kilometers. What would be the linear speed of a point on the equator?

FRICTION

Whenever a body slides along another body, a resisting force is called into play which is known as the force of friction. This is a very important force and serves many useful purposes, for a person could not walk without it, or a car could not propel itself along the road without the friction between the tires and the road. On the other hand, friction is very wasteful because it reduces the efficiency of machines, since work must be done to overcome it, and this energy is wasted as heat. The purpose of this experiment is to study the laws of sliding friction and to determine the coefficient of friction between two surfaces.

THEORY

Friction is the resisting force encountered when one tries to slide one surface over another; this force acts along the tangent to the surfaces in contact. The force necessary to overcome friction depends on the nature of the materials in contact, their roughness or smoothness, and on the normal force, but not on the area of contact, within wide limits. It is found experimentally that the force of friction is directly proportional to the normal force. The constant of proportionality is called the coefficient of friction.

The coefficient of friction is equal to the force of friction divided by the total normal force pressing the surfaces together. Thus

$$k = \frac{f}{N} \quad \text{or} \quad f = kN$$

where f is the force of friction to be overcome, N is the total normal force, or the perpendicular component of the force holding the two surfaces together, and k is the coefficient of friction.

A method of determining the above relation is to have one of the substances in the form of a plane placed horizontally, with a pulley fastened at one end. The other substance is made in the form of a block to which is attached a cord passing over the pulley and carrying weights; these may be varied until the block moves uniformly when given a very slight push. The normal force between the two surfaces can be changed by placing weights on top of the block, and the relation between the coefficient of friction, the force of friction, and the normal force can thus be tested.

The limiting angle of repose is the angle at which a body will just begin to slide down an inclined plane. The coefficient of friction is equal to the tangent of the angle of repose. It is found that the frictional force acting when actual sliding is taking place is slightly lower than the maximum frictional force that can act just before the body begins to slide. Thus the kinetic coefficient of friction is somewhat lower than the static coefficient of friction.

APPARATUS

1. Board with pulley at one end.
2. Supporting rod and clamp for adjusting the angle of the inclined plane.
3. Wood block with a cord attached to it.
4. Glass block.
5. Set of known weights.
6. Pan to support the known weights.
7. Equal arm balance and weights.
8. Protractor.

PROCEDURE

1. Weigh the wood block and record the weight.

2. Place the board in a horizontal position on the laboratory table with its pulley projecting beyond the edge of the table. Place the cord which is attached to the block over the pulley and attach it to the pan. Set the block on the plane with its largest surface in contact with the plane. Place some weights in the pan and slowly increase the load until it is just sufficient to keep the block sliding slowly with constant speed after it has been started with a very small push. Record the load needed.

3. Repeat procedure (2) placing weights of 200, 400, 600, 800, and 1000 grams successively on top of the wood block. Record the load needed in each case.

4. Turn the wood block on its side and repeat procedure (2) with a mass of 400 grams on top of the block. Record the load needed.

5. Again turn the wood block with the largest surface in contact with the plane and place 400 grams on top of the block. Gradually increase the load on the pan until the block just starts to move, without any initial push. Be careful to place the weights on the pan gently so as not to jerk the cord. Notice whether this time the block moves with uniform speed or whether it is being accelerated. Record the load needed under these conditions.

6. Adjust the board as an inclined plane. Place the wood block on the plane and find the smallest angle of the plane with the horizontal for which the block will slide down the plane with constant speed after it has been given a very small push. Measure this angle of the plane with the horizontal by means of a protractor and record the value. This angle is called the angle of repose.

7. Repeat procedure (6) using the glass block. Record the value of the angle of repose.

DATA

Weight of wood block. . . . .
Angle of repose for wood block. . . . .
Tangent of angle of repose for wood block. . . . .
Angle of repose for glass block. . . . .
Tangent of angle of repose for glass block. . . . .

POSITION OF BLOCK	WEIGHT PLACED ON THE BLOCK	TOTAL NORMAL FORCE	FORCE TO KEEP BLOCK MOVING UNIFORMLY	COEFFICIENT OF KINETIC FRICTION
FLAT	0 gm.			
FLAT	200 gm.			
FLAT	400 gm.			
FLAT	600 gm.			
FLAT	800 gm.			
FLAT	1000 gm.			
ON SIDE	400 gm.			

POSITION OF BLOCK	WEIGHT PLACED ON THE BLOCK	TOTAL NORMAL FORCE	FORCE TO START BLOCK MOVING	COEFFICIENT OF STATIC FRICTION
FLAT	400 gm.			

CALCULATIONS

1. From the data of procedures (1–4) calculate the coefficient of kinetic friction for wood on wood for all of the observations taken. The pull of the cord on the block is equal and opposite to the force of friction between the block and the plane. The normal force between the two surfaces, in this case, is equal to the weight of the block plus the weight placed on top of the block.

2. From the data of procedure (5) compute the coefficient of static friction for wood on wood.

3. From the data of procedure (6) calculate the coefficient of kinetic friction for wood on wood.

4. From the data of procedure (7) calculate the coefficient of kinetic friction for glass on wood.

5. From the data of procedures (2–3) plot a curve using the values of the total normal force as abscissas and the values of the force of friction as ordinates.

QUESTIONS

1. In this experiment why is it necessary that the body move with uniform velocity?

2. (a) How does the coefficient of friction depend upon the normal force between the surfaces in contact? (b) How does it depend upon the area of the surfaces in contact?

3. How does the coefficient of static friction compare with the coefficient of kinetic friction for the same surfaces, areas, and normal forces? In this connection explain what happened in procedure (5).

4. Deduce the relation that exists between the coefficient of friction and the limiting angle of repose of an object on an inclined plane.

5. Calculate the force needed to pull a mass of 20 kilograms at a uniform slow speed up a plane inclined at an angle of 30° with the horizontal, if the coefficient of kinetic friction is 0.20.

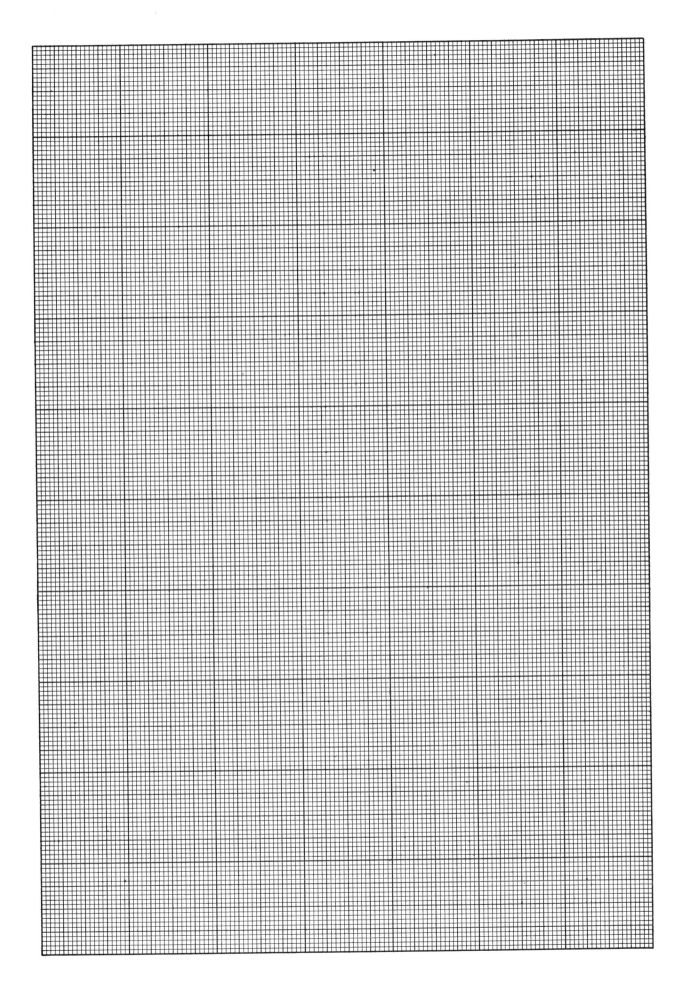

10

THE INCLINED PLANE. FRICTION. PRINCIPLE OF WORK

Machines are used to make work easier. All of the complicated machines of the modern age are made up of a few simple machines, one of which is the inclined plane. The purpose of this experiment is to study the inclined plane as a machine, to measure its mechanical advantage and efficiency, and to study frictional forces and the resolution of forces.

THEORY

When a weight W rests on an inclined plane (see Fig. 12), the force due to gravity, which acts vertically downward, may be resolved into two components, one perpendicular to the plane, and one parallel to it.

The component of the weight perpendicular to the plane is $W \cos \theta$, the component parallel to the plane is $W \sin \theta$, where θ is the angle made by the plane with the horizontal. The plane also exerts a force on the weight. If it is a frictionless plane, this force (designated by N in Fig. 12) is perpendicular to the plane and is equal to the component of the weight perpendicular to the plane. If there is no friction between the weight and the plane, then a force equal to $W \sin \theta$ directed up the plane will be sufficient to keep the weight in equilibrium, i.e. either at rest or moving up or down the plane with uniform velocity. If there is friction between the weight and the plane, then the force of friction will be directed up the plane when the weight is moving

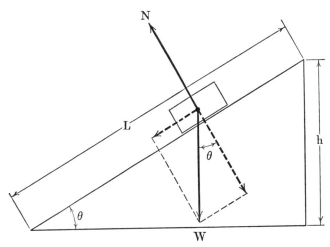

Fig. 12. The Inclined Plane

downward, and it will be directed down the plane when the weight is moving upward. Hence the force needed to make the weight move either up or down the plane will be different from $W \sin \theta$ and its value will depend on the direction of the motion.

The apparatus for this experiment consists of an inclined plane on which a car is made to roll either up or down, the motion being controlled by the pull on a string attached to the car. The plane is set at some convenient angle. The car is set on the plane and is attached to a weight holder by means of a string, which passes over a pulley. A few small weights are placed in the weight holder, and this constitutes the force which pulls the car up the plane. This force should be kept parallel to the plane; this is done by properly adjusting the pulley. A load is placed on the car and a condition of balance is found by varying the weights on the weight holder. It will be found that a condition of balance exists for a variety of weights placed on the weight holder. Thus any load between a certain small force F_1 and a certain large force F_2 will produce balance. This range of values for the balancing force is produced by the presence of friction. F_2 is the force pulling up the plane that will just make the car move up the plane with a small uniform velocity. F_1 is the force pulling up the plane that will just make the car move down the plane with a small uniform velocity. A force larger than F_2 will make the car accelerate up the plane. A force smaller than F_1 will make the car accelerate down the plane. If F is the force that would be needed to pull the car up the plane if there were no friction, and f is the force of friction, then

$$F_2 = F + f$$
$$F_1 = F - f$$

and

for in both cases the direction of the force of friction is opposite to the direction of the motion. From these equations the value of F is found to be

$$F = \tfrac{1}{2} (F_1 + F_2)$$

41

The value of F_2 is obtained by noticing what load placed on the weight holder will make the car move upward with uniform velocity when given a very slight push. If the load is different from F_2, the car will either slow down or speed up. The value of F_1 is determined in the same way, but with the car moving downward.

When one body is sliding over another, a frictional force is always acting in such a direction as to oppose the motion. The force of friction is the force exerted between two bodies opposing any tendency for their surfaces to slide relative to each other. It is found that the force of friction is proportional to the force with which one surface presses against the other. The coefficient of friction is the ratio of the maximum force of friction between two bodies to the normal force pressing the surfaces together (i.e. the component of the force perpendicular to the surface).

The work done by a force in moving a body is given by the product of the component of the force in the direction of the motion and the distance that the body moves. A machine is a device that makes work easier. The mechanical advantage of a machine is the ratio of the force overcome by the machine to the force applied to the machine. The ideal mechanical advantage is the ratio of the distance through which the force applied to the machine moves to the distance through which the force overcome by the machine moves. In calculating the ideal mechanical advantage, it is assumed that there is no friction in the machine. The actual mechanical advantage is smaller than the ideal one because some of the energy input is wasted in overcoming forces due to friction. The efficiency of a machine is the ratio of the output to the input, or the ratio of the useful work done by the machine to the total work done on the machine.

In considering the inclined plane as a machine, it should be noticed that the plane is used as a device to raise a weight vertically against the force of gravity. Thus the output is the work done against the force of gravity, where the height of the plane (designated by h in Fig. 12) is the distance that the body has been lifted. The input is the work done by the applied force, F_2, which moves over a distance (designated by L in Fig. 12) equal to the length of the plane.

APPARATUS

1. Inclined plane with attached pulley.
2. Small car.
3. Weight holder.
4. Set of slotted weights.

5. String.
6. Equal arm balance.
7. Set of weights.
8. Meter stick.

PROCEDURE

1. Weigh the empty car. Place a load of 500 grams in the car. Set the plane at an angle of 10 degrees. Put the car on the plane and pass the string attached to the car over the pulley at the top of the plane. Attach the weight holder to the string and adjust the load on it so that the car will move upward with uniform velocity when given a very slight push. This will be F_2. Then adjust the load so that the car will move downward with uniform velocity when given a very slight push. This will be F_1.

2. With the same load in the car, repeat procedure (1) using an angle of 20°.

3. With the same load in the car, repeat procedure (1) using an angle of 30°. Measure the length and the height of the plane.

4. Remove the load from the car, detach the car, and set it on the plane. Vary the inclination of the plane until the car rolls down with uniform velocity when given a very slight push. Record the angular setting of the plane.

5. Turn the car upside down and set it on the plane. Vary the inclination of the plane until the car slides down with uniform velocity when given a very slight push. Record the angular setting of the plane.

DATA

Weight of the empty car..

Load placed in the car...

Total weight lifted..

Length of the plane..

Height of the plane when it is set at 30 degrees...........................

Angular setting of the plane (angle of repose) for rolling friction. . . . .

Coefficient of rolling friction. . . . .

Angular setting of the plane (angle of repose) for sliding friction. . . . .

Coefficient of sliding friction. . . . .

ANGULAR SETTING OF THE PLANE	F_2	F_1	F	f	ACTUAL MECHANICAL ADVANTAGE
10°					
20°					
30°					

CALCULATIONS

1. From the data of procedures (1), (2), and (3) calculate the values of F and f for each set of observations.

2. From the angle of the plane in procedure (4) compute the coefficient of rolling friction.

3. From the angle of the plane in procedure (5) compute the coefficient of sliding friction between the two surfaces used.

4. Predict the value of F for the plane set at an angle of 30 degrees from a resolution of the forces acting. Draw a diagram illustrating this resolution of forces.

5. Consider the plane as a simple machine, when a force F_2 is lifting a load W. Calculate the actual mechanical advantage, W/F_2, for each case.

6. Calculate the efficiency of the machine for the plane set at an angle of 30 degrees. The input is the force F_2 times the length of the plane. The output is the weight W times the height of the plane.

QUESTIONS

1. State how the coefficient of sliding friction and the coefficient of rolling friction compare.

2. (a) What is the difference between the coefficient of starting friction and the coefficient of kinetic friction? (b) Which is larger?

3. State how the mechanical advantage of the inclined plane varies with the inclination of the plane. Neglect the effect of friction.

4. Calculate the amount of work done in drawing a mass of 20 kilograms at a uniform slow speed up a plane 2 meters long, making an angle of 30 degrees with the horizontal, if the coefficient of kinetic friction is 0.20.

SIMPLE MACHINES

A machine is a device by which a force applied at one point is changed into another force applied at a different point, for some useful advantage. The pulley system, the jackscrew, the lever, and the inclined plane are well-known examples of machines. The pulley is commonly used to lift heavy loads through great distances, while the jackscrew and the lever are employed to lift massive objects through short distances. The purpose of this experiment is to study an inclined plane, a wheel and axle, and a pulley system as examples of simple machines and to determine the mechanical advantage and efficiency of these machines.

THEORY

A simple machine is a device by means of which a force applied at one point gives rise to another force acting at some other point; the new force is usually greater in magnitude and different in direction from the applied force. Thus a machine is a device which makes work easier. In some cases the machine merely changes the direction of the force, in other cases it may actually give rise to a force smaller than the one that is being applied.

The actual mechanical advantage of a machine is the ratio of the force overcome by the machine to the force applied to the machine. Thus

$$\text{A.M.A.} = \frac{W}{F}$$

where W is the output force exerted by the machine, such as the weight lifted; F is the applied force.

The ideal mechanical advantage is the ratio of the distance that the force applied to the machine moves to the distance that the force exerted by the machine moves. It is the mechanical advantage obtained, on the assumption that there is no loss due to friction or other causes. Thus

$$\text{I.M.A.} = \frac{s}{h}$$

where s is the distance through which the force F moves and h is the distance through which the force W moves.

The efficiency of a machine is the ratio of the useful work done by the machine (the output) to the total work done on the machine (the input). Thus

$$\text{Efficiency} = \frac{\text{Output}}{\text{Input}}$$

The efficiency is usually expressed in per cent, in which case the above ratio is multiplied by 100. In any machine the efficiency is always less than 100% because some of the energy input is wasted in overcoming forces due to friction.

In this experiment an inclined plane, a wheel and axle, and a pulley system will be studied. In all of these cases a known load is raised against the gravitational force, and the applied force is measured. The ideal mechanical advantage of the inclined plane is given by the ratio of its length to its height; that of the wheel and axle is equal to the ratio of the radius of the wheel to the radius of the axle. A combination of fixed and moving pulleys, in which all the moving pulleys move at the same speed, has an ideal mechanical advantage equal to the number of sections of the cord supporting the moving block, if only a single cord is used.

APPARATUS

1. Board with pulley at one end.
2. Supporting rod and clamp for adjusting the angle of the inclined plane.
3. Wooden box with a cord attached to it.
4. Set of known weights.
5. Pan to support the known weights.
6. Equal arm balance and weights.
7. Meter stick.
8. Protractor.
9. Wheel and axle.
10. Pulley system.
11. Spring balance.

PROCEDURE

Inclined Plane

1. Weigh the wooden box and record the weight.

2. Adjust the board as an inclined plane and set the plane at an angle of 10 degrees with the horizontal.

3. Place the box on the plane, pass the attached cord over the pulley, and suspend the pan from it.

4. Place some weights in the pan and slowly increase this load until it is just sufficient to keep the box sliding slowly up the plane with constant speed, after it has been started with a very small push. Record the load.

5. Measure the length and the height of the inclined plane and record the values.

6. Set the plane at an angle of 20 degrees and repeat procedures (4–5).

7. Set the plane at an angle of 30 degrees and repeat procedures (4–5).

Wheel and Axle

8. Wind one string several times around the axle, and wind the other string several times around the wheel in the reverse direction. Hang a 500-gram mass on the string coming from the axle. This is the load to be lifted. Attach the pan to the string coming from the wheel and place masses in the pan until the load moves upward at a small constant speed. Record the value of the masses needed.

9. Measure the diameter of the wheel up to the surface on which the string is wound. Similarly, measure the diameter of the axle. Record the values.

Pulley System

10. Measure with a spring balance the force necessary to lift a mass of one kilogram with the pulley system set up in the laboratory. Observe the force while the mass is being lifted at a slow uniform speed and record the value of this force.

11. Count the number of supporting cords in the pulley system and record it.

DATA

INCLINED PLANE

	ANGLE OF THE INCLINED PLANE		
	10°	20°	30°
FORCE NEEDED TO PULL THE BOX UP THE PLANE			
LENGTH OF THE INCLINED PLANE			
HEIGHT OF THE INCLINED PLANE			

Weight of the wooden box...

WHEEL AND AXLE

Load used in the wheel and axle...
Force needed to lift this load...
Diameter of the wheel...
Diameter of the axle..

PULLEY SYSTEM

Load used in the pulley system...
Force needed to lift this load..
Number of supporting cords..

NAME_____ SECTION_____ DATE_____ EXPERIMENT ELEVEN

MECHANICAL ADVANTAGE AND EFFICIENCY

MACHINE	ACTUAL MECHANICAL ADVANTAGE	IDEAL MECHANICAL ADVANTAGE	EFFICIENCY
INCLINED PLANE AT 10°			
INCLINED PLANE AT 20°			
INCLINED PLANE AT 30°			
WHEEL AND AXLE			
PULLEY SYSTEM			

CALCULATIONS

1. From the data of procedures (4–5) calculate the actual mechanical advantage, the ideal mechanical advantage, and the efficiency of the inclined plane set at an angle of 10 degrees.

2. From the data of procedure (6) calculate the actual mechanical advantage, the ideal mechanical advantage, and the efficiency of the inclined plane set at an angle of 20 degrees.

3. From the data of procedure (7) calculate the actual mechanical advantage, the ideal mechanical advantage, and the efficiency of the inclined plane set at an angle of 30 degrees.

4. From the data of procedures (8–9) determine the actual mechanical advantage, the ideal mechanical advantage, and the efficiency of the wheel and axle used.

5. From the data of procedures (10–11) determine the actual mechanical advantage, the ideal mechanical advantage, and the efficiency of the pulley system used.

QUESTIONS

1. (a) State how the mechanical advantage of the inclined plane varies with the inclination of the plane. (b) Does this apply to both the ideal and the actual mechanical advantage?

2. (a) How does the efficiency of the inclined plane vary with the inclination of the plane? (b) Explain the reason for this.

3. A body weighing 400 pounds is pulled up an inclined plane 15 feet long and 5 feet high. The force required to pull the body up the plane at a slow uniform speed is 200 pounds. Compute the ideal mechanical advantage, the actual mechanical advantage, and the efficiency of the plane under these conditions.

4. A block and tackle consisting of two fixed pulleys and one movable pulley (see Fig. 13) is used to lift a stone weighing 300 pounds. The force required is 125 pounds. Compute the efficiency of the block and tackle, the actual mechanical advantage, and the ideal mechanical advantage.

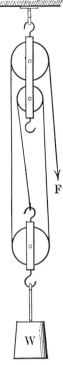

Fig. 13. Pulley System

12
YOUNG'S MODULUS

All bodies are deformed in some way by the application of a force. An elastic body is a body that changes in size or shape upon the application of a distorting force, but returns to its original condition when that force is removed. But there is a limit to the magnitude of the force which may be applied, if the body is to return to its original condition. This is called the elastic limit. A greater force will cause a permanent distortion or even a break. In this experiment a steel wire is stretched by the application of a force, and measurements are made of the changes in length produced. From these measurements, Young's modulus for a steel wire is calculated.

THEORY

When a wire is stretched by a mass hanging from it, the wire is said to experience a tensile strain, which is defined as the elongation per unit length. The force acting on the wire is a measure of the tensile stress, which is defined as the force per unit area over which it is acting.

Hooke's law states that as long as a body is not strained beyond its elastic limit, the stress is proportional to the strain. Thus the ratio of stress to strain is a constant and is called a modulus of elasticity. For the case of a wire stretched by a force, this constant is called Young's modulus. Thus

$$Y = \frac{\text{force per unit area}}{\text{elongation per unit length}} = \frac{F/A}{e/L} = \frac{FL}{eA}$$

where Y is Young's modulus in dynes per square centimeter, F is the force in dynes, L is the length of the wire in centimeters, e is the elongation in centimeters, and A is the area of cross section of the wire in square centimeters.

The arrangement of the apparatus used in this experiment is shown in Fig. 14. The elongations produced in this experiment are very minute, hence a method of magnifying them is used, i.e. the optical lever. This consists of a vertical mirror mounted on a horizontal T-shaped base having pointed legs at the three extremities. The wire whose elongation is to be measured is clamped at its upper end, and has a small cylinder attached to it near the lower end. This cylinder is free to move up and down through a hole in a shelf supporting the mirror and its base. The two front feet of the base form an axis of rotation for the mirror, the rear foot rests on the small cylinder attached to the wire and moves up and down, due to the elongation of the wire. At a distance of about one meter and a half from the mirror, there is placed a reading telescope to which is attached a vertical scale. The image of the illuminated scale as seen in the mirror is viewed through the

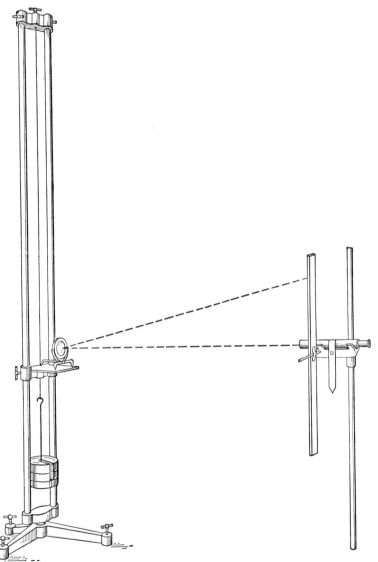

Fig. 14. Young's Modulus Apparatus

telescope. The position of the cross hairs upon the image of the scale, for the unstretched wire, is the zero reading. As the wire is stretched by applying a load, the angular movement of the mirror causes a different portion of the scale to appear on the cross hairs of the telescope. The elongation can be readily computed from geometrical considerations by using the relation

$$e = \frac{Sd}{2D}$$

where e is the elongation in centimeters, D is the distance in centimeters from the mirror to the scale, d is the perpendicular distance from the moving foot of the optical lever to the line joining the other two feet, and S is the difference in the scale readings before and after the application of the load. This relation is derived by using the principle of optics that the reflection of a beam of light falling on a plane mirror is turned through an angle twice as large as the angle through which the mirror is rotated, the incident beam remaining fixed.

APPARATUS

1. Young's modulus apparatus.
2. Telescope and scale, with support stand.
3. Mirror mounted on T-base (optical lever).
4. Desk lamp.

5. Slotted weights (ten 1-kg. weights).
6. Micrometer caliper.
7. Vernier caliper.
8. Two-meter stick.

PROCEDURE

1. Measure the length of the steel wire used, that is, the distance from the lower end of the upper chuck to the top of the cylinder at the lower end of the wire.

2. Measure the diameter of the wire in five places, using the micrometer caliper.

3. Measure the distance of the moving foot of the optical lever from the axis of rotation. This may be done by pressing the pointed legs on a piece of white paper and constructing the required distance. Use the vernier caliper for this measurement.

4. Carefully place the optical lever with its two front feet on the rigid support and its rear foot on the chuck which is clamped to the wire.

5. Carefully measure the distance from the mirror to the scale, using the two-meter stick.

6. Apply a load of one kilogram to the wire to take up any slack, using great care not to jar the apparatus. Adjust the apparatus so that the image of the scale illuminated with the desk lamp, as seen in the mirror, is viewed through the telescope. Record the reading of the scale to the nearest tenth of a millimeter. This will be the zero reading.

7. Add another kilogram to the load on the wire and again record the scale reading.

8. Add one kilogram at a time up to a total of 10 kilograms, reading the scale after each added load. Record the total load for each reading.

9. Remove the load, one kilogram at a time, recording the scale reading for each load. NOTE: The values of the load to be used apply only to a steel wire. If a different kind of wire is used, the proper values of the load will be suggested by the instructor.

DATA

Length of wire used..

Diameter of wire..

Micrometer readings:			Trials		
	1.	2.	3.	4.	5.

Average reading...

Zero reading..

Cross-sectional area of the wire...

Distance from front legs to the rear leg of the optical lever............

Distance from mirror to scale...

Young's modulus (computed value)..

Young's modulus (from Table IV, Appendix)...............................

Per cent error..

Young's Modulus

NAME_____ SECTION_____ DATE_____ EXPERIMENT TWELVE

LOAD IN KILOGRAMS	SCALE READING (INCREASING LOAD)	SCALE READING (DECREASING LOAD)	AVERAGE SCALE READING	ELONGATION
1				
2				
3				
4				
5				
6				
7				
8				
9				
10				

CALCULATIONS

1. Compute the average of the readings for the diameter of the wire. This will be the value of the diameter, when properly corrected for the zero reading of the micrometer.

2. Calculate the cross-sectional area of the wire in square centimeters.

3. Compute the total elongation for each total load, using the average of the scale readings obtained. Note that the value of the scale reading obtained when the load is one kilogram is taken as the zero reading. Hence the elongation produced by a load of one kilogram will be obtained by using the difference in the scale readings when the load is changed from 1 to 2 kilograms. A similar consideration is to be used for the other loads.

4. Compute Young's modulus for the wire using the data for the 9-kilogram load. Compare your result with the value given in Table IV, Appendix, and find the per cent error.

5. Plot a curve on the graph paper using total loads in kilograms as abscissas and total elongations in centimeters as ordinates.

QUESTIONS

1. State what the curve shows and hence what the experiment checked.

2. Why was not the whole length of the wire measured?

3. Define elasticity, elastic limit, stress, and strain.

4. (a) State Hooke's law. (b) Does your curve agree with it? (c) How would the curve look if the elastic limit were exceeded?

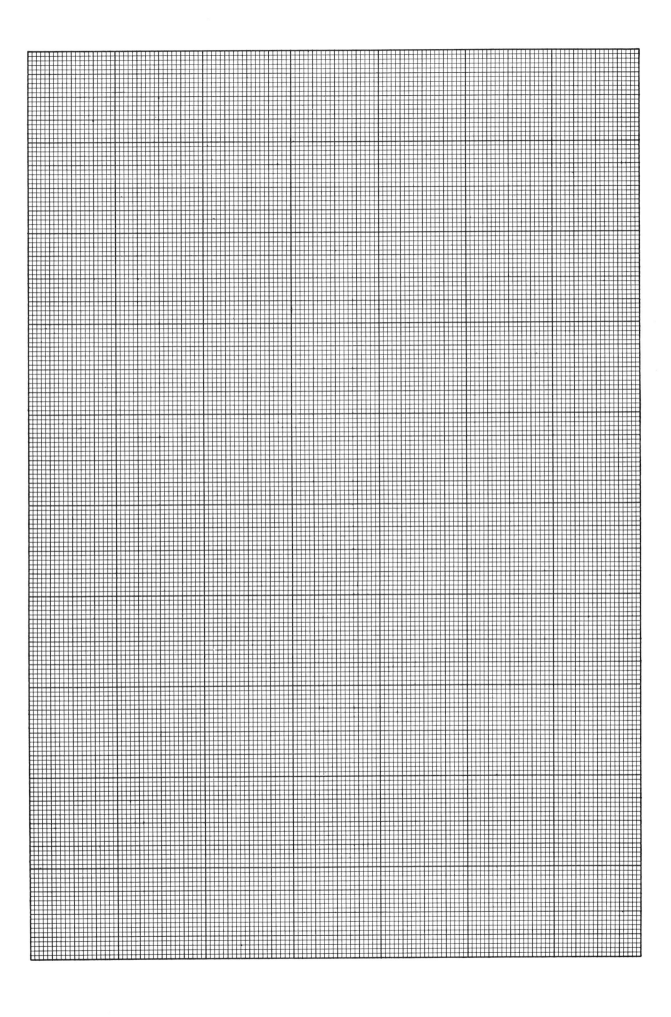

13
THE TORSION PENDULUM

The moment of inertia of a body may be measured by suspending it at the end of a wire of known torsion constant and observing the period of the rotational oscillations. From the value of the torsion constant and the period of the oscillations, the moment of inertia can be calculated. This is an experimental method of finding the moment of inertia of a body. But the method is applicable no matter what the shape of the body is. In order to check the experimental determination, the body is given such a regular form that it is also possible to compute its moment of inertia by the method of calculus. It is the object of this experiment to determine the moment of inertia of a disk and a ring by means of a torsion pendulum.

THEORY

A body executes linear simple harmonic motion when the resultant force acting on it is proportional to the displacement of the body from its equilibrium position and in the opposite direction to this displacement.

Similarly, a body executes angular simple harmonic motion when the resultant torque L acting on the body is proportional to the angular displacement θ of the body from its equilibrium position, and in the opposite direction to this displacement. The relation between the torque and the angular displacement is:

$$L = -k\theta$$

The factor of proportionality k is known as the torsion constant of the suspension; this is the torque expressed in centimeter-dynes which will produce an angular displacement of one radian. The torsion constant of the suspension depends on the dimensions of the wire and the modulus of rigidity of its material.

The period of oscillation is given by

$$T = 2\pi\sqrt{\frac{I}{k}}$$

where T is the period in seconds, k is the torsion constant of the suspension, and I is the moment of inertia of the body about the axis of rotation. The period is the time for one complete vibration, or the time it takes the body to swing from its maximum displacement on one side to the other side, and back again.

The torsion pendulum (see Fig. 15) consists of a solid disk suspended by a steel wire attached to the center of the disk; the upper end of the wire is attached to a fixed support. If the disk is turned about the axis of the suspending wire and then released, the elastic restoring torque set up in the wire by the twist will cause the disk to oscillate. If the angle of twist is not too great, the elastic restoring torque will be proportional to the angle and opposite in sense to the angular displacement. Therefore the disk will execute angular simple harmonic motion.

It may be shown by the methods of calculus that the moment of inertia of a disk about an axis through its center and perpendicular to the plane of the disk is

$$I = \tfrac{1}{2}MR^2$$

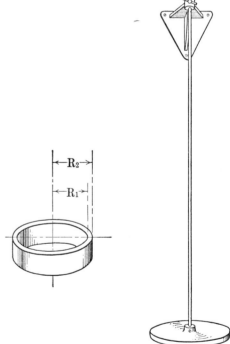

Fig. 15. The Torsion Pendulum

where M is the mass of the disk in grams, R is the radius in centimeters, and I is the moment of inertia in gm.-cm.^{2}

If the moment of inertia of the disk of a torsion pendulum is calculated by using the above relation, and if the period of oscillation is measured, then the torsion constant k can be calculated from the expression for the period of oscillation.

If the moment of inertia of another body about a particular axis is required, this body may be attached to the disk of the torsion pendulum so that the required axis and the wire coincide. Then the new period of oscillation will be given by

$$T = 2\pi\sqrt{\frac{I_1 + I_2}{k}}$$

where I_1 is the moment of inertia of the disk and I_2 is the moment of inertia of the other body.

In this experiment a ring is used as the other body. From the measured value of the new period of oscillation, the moment of inertia of the ring may be calculated. It will be noticed that the moment of inertia of the ring and disk taken together is the sum of their separate moments of inertia. The moment of inertia of a ring is also given by

$$I = \tfrac{1}{2}M(R_1^2 + R_2^2)$$

where M is the mass of the ring in grams, R_1 is the inner radius, and R_2 is the outer radius of the ring in centimeters.

APPARATUS

1. Torsion pendulum with disk and ring.
2. Stop watch or stop clock.
3. Vernier calipers.

4. Equal arm balance.
5. Set of weights.

PROCEDURE

1. Set the torsion pendulum into oscillation with an amplitude of about 10 degrees. Record the time for 20 complete vibrations. In counting vibrations, be sure to start the stop watch on the count of zero and not on the count of one.

2. Repeat procedure (1) two more times and record the results.

3. Detach the disk from the suspending wire. Weigh the disk, measure its diameter with the vernier calipers, and record the results.

4. Measure the inside and outside diameters of the ring with the vernier calipers, and record the measurements. Also weigh the ring.

5. Place the ring on the disk, centering it carefully, and attach the suspension wire to the disk.

6. Set the system into oscillation with an amplitude of about 10 degrees. Record the time for 20 complete vibrations of the torsion pendulum with the ring added to the disk.

7. Repeat procedure (6) two more times and record the results.

DATA

PERIOD OF THE DISK

	NUMBER OF VIBRATIONS	TIME
1.		
2.		
3.		
AVERAGE		
PERIOD		

PERIOD OF THE DISK AND RING

	NUMBER OF VIBRATIONS	TIME
1.		
2.		
3.		
AVERAGE		
PERIOD		

Mass of the disk...

Diameter of the disk...

Radius of the disk...

Moment of inertia of the disk...

Moment of torsion for the suspension wire......................................

Mass of the ring . . . .

Inside diameter of the ring . . . .

Outside diameter of the ring . . . .

Inside radius of the ring . . . .

Outside radius of the ring . . . .

Moment of inertia of the disk and ring . . . .

Moment of inertia of the ring . . . .

Moment of inertia of the ring computed from the formula . . . .

Per cent deviation . . . .

CALCULATIONS

1. Calculate the moment of inertia of the disk of the torsion pendulum, using the formula

$$I = \tfrac{1}{2}MR^2$$

where M is the mass of the disk in grams, R is the radius of the disk in centimeters, and I is the moment of inertia in gm.-cm.^{2}

2. From the data of procedures (1) and (2), calculate the average time for 20 vibrations. From the value of the average time, compute the period of the pendulum.

3. Using the value of the moment of inertia found in calculation (1) and the value of the period found in calculation (2), calculate the moment of torsion, or the torsion constant, of the suspension wire.

4. From the data of procedures (6) and (7), calculate the average time for 20 vibrations. From the value of the average time, compute the period of the pendulum with the ring added to the disk.

5. Using the value of the period found in calculation (4) and the value of the moment of torsion found in calculation (3), calculate the combined moment of inertia of the disk and ring. From this result and the moment of inertia of the disk computed in calculation (1), find the moment of inertia of the ring.

6. Compute the moment of inertia of the ring, using the formula

$$I = \tfrac{1}{2}M(R_1^2 + R_2^2)$$

where M is the mass of the ring in grams, R_1 is the inside radius and R_2 is the outside radius of the ring in centimeters, and I is the moment of inertia in gm.-cm.²

7. Calculate the per cent deviation between the computed value of the moment of inertia found in calculation (6) and the experimental value found in calculation (5).

QUESTIONS

1. Would the moment of inertia of the disk be the same if it was made thinner but with a larger radius, so that the mass remained the same? Explain.

2. Assuming that the same wire was used, what would happen to the period of the torsion pendulum if the length of the suspension wire were increased? Explain.

3. A solid uniform disk which weighs 2 kilograms and is 20 centimeters in diameter is suspended by a wire 100 centimeters long and 1 millimeter in diameter. In order to twist the disk through an angle of 180 degrees, two forces, each of 200 grams, must be applied tangentially to the disk at opposite ends of a diameter. What is the period of oscillation of this torsional pendulum?

4. Develop the equation for the moment of inertia of a ring

$$I = \tfrac{1}{2}M(R_1^2 + R_2^2)$$

by using the fact that the moment of inertia of a uniform solid cylinder about the axis of the cylinder (which is the same as the axis of the ring) is

$$I = \tfrac{1}{2}MR^2$$

14

ROTATIONAL MOTION

The motion of a flywheel of a steam engine, that of a propeller of an airplane engine, and that of any rotating wheel are examples of a very important type of motion called rotational motion. If a rigid body is acted upon by a system of torques, the body will be in equilibrium, as far as rotational motion is concerned, if the sum of the torques about any axis is zero. This means that if the body is at rest, it will remain at rest; if it is rotating about a fixed axis, it will continue to rotate about the same axis with uniform angular speed. If an unbalanced torque is acting on the body, it will produce an angular acceleration in the direction of the torque, the acceleration being proportional to the torque and inversely proportional to the moment of inertia of the body about its axis of rotation. The purpose of this experiment is to study rotational motion, to observe the effect of a constant torque upon a disk free to rotate, and to determine the resulting angular acceleration and the moment of inertia of the disk.

THEORY

Rotation refers to motion about some axis in space. In describing motion of rotation, it is necessary to give the angular displacement, the angular velocity, and the angular acceleration. The unit of angular measurement usually used is the radian. This is the angle subtended at the center of a circle by an arc equal in length to the radius. The angular velocity is the time rate of change of angular displacement. It is equal to the angle through which the body rotates divided by the time. The angular acceleration is the time rate of change of angular velocity.

The equations of motion involved in uniformly accelerated angular motion are discussed below. The angular displacement is given by

$$\theta = \bar{\omega}t$$

where θ is the angular distance in radians, $\bar{\omega}$ is the average angular velocity in radians per second, and t is the time in seconds. The average angular velocity is given by

$$\bar{\omega} = \frac{\omega_1 + \omega_2}{2}$$

where $\bar{\omega}$ is the average angular velocity, ω_1 is the initial angular velocity, and ω_2 is the final angular velocity. The final angular velocity is given by

$$\omega_2 = \omega_1 + \alpha t$$

where ω_2 is the final angular velocity, ω_1 is the initial angular velocity, α is the angular acceleration in radians per second per second, and t is the time in seconds.

The corresponding equations of motion involved in uniformly accelerated linear motion are

$$s = \bar{v}t$$
$$\bar{v} = \frac{v_1 + v_2}{2}$$
and
$$v_2 = v_1 + at$$

where s is the distance, $\bar{v}$ is the average velocity, v_1 is the initial velocity, v_2 is the final velocity, a is the acceleration, and t is the time.

There are some very simple relations between the linear quantities and the angular quantities, as a result of using the radian as the unit of angular measurement. Suppose that s represents the distance a particle moves around the circumference of a circle of radius r; let v be the linear velocity, or more accurately, the linear speed; and let a be the linear acceleration, or the tangential acceleration of the particle. Then the angular distance θ, the angular velocity ω, and the angular acceleration α are given by the relations

$$s = r\theta$$
$$v = r\omega$$
$$a = r\alpha$$

When a torque is applied to a body free to rotate about a fixed axis, then the body will acquire an angular acceleration given by the relation

$$L = I\alpha$$

where L is the sum in centimeter-dynes of all the torques about the fixed axis of rotation, I is the moment of inertia in gm.-cm.^{2} of the body about the same axis, and α is the angular acceleration in radians per second per second.

The moment of inertia is the inertia of a body as regards rotation about an axis. The moment of inertia of a body with respect to an axis is the sum of the products obtained by multiplying the mass of every particle of the body by the square of its distance from the axis. For a simple geometrical solid it can be readily determined by the use of integral calculus. For example, the moment of inertia of a uniform cylinder, or disk, with respect to its longitudinal axis is given by

$$I = \tfrac{1}{2}MR^2$$

where M is the mass in grams of the cylinder, or disk; R is the radius in centimeters; and I is the moment of inertia in gm.-cm.^{2}

The apparatus used in this experiment (see Fig. 16) consists of a massive disk mounted on an axle that can rotate freely in pivot bearings. The disk is set in motion by means of a weight attached to a string which is wound around the axle. As the weight descends, it will move with a constant linear acceleration, while the wheel and axle will rotate with a constant angular acceleration.

The angular acceleration of the wheel and axle depends on the applied torque, the frictional torque, and the moment of inertia. Assuming the last two to remain constant during the experiment, then the angular acceleration can be varied by changing the applied torque. This can be done by using different values of the suspended weight, or of the axle radius. The disk used in this experiment has two different axle radii. By varying the applied torque and thereby getting different values of the angular acceleration, it is possible to compute the moment of inertia and the frictional torque from the observations taken.

The value of the moment of inertia obtained can be checked by measurements of the dimensions of the wheel and the axles. From the total mass and the dimensions of the various parts, the separate masses of the disk and the axles may be calculated. Then, from their dimensions and masses, the moment of inertia of each shaft and of the disk can be calculated separately. The sum is the total moment of inertia.

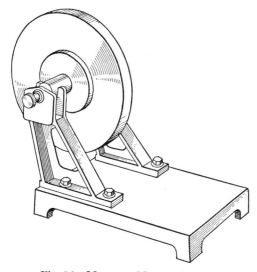

Fig. 16. Moment of Inertia Apparatus

APPARATUS

1. Moment of inertia apparatus, consisting of an aluminum wheel mounted on a fixed axle.
2. Two hooked weights (50 and 100 grams).
3. Stop watch or stop clock.
4. Meter stick.
5. Vernier calipers.
6. Large calipers.
7. String.

PROCEDURE

1. Wind the string on the smaller axle in a single layer. Choose a length of string so that the weight will be disconnected when it strikes the floor. This is accomplished by placing a loop in the string supporting the weight over a little pin set in the axle, adjusting the length of the string to make a small portion of it still touch the rim when the weight reaches the floor.

2. For the first set of measurements use a 50-gram weight. Measure the distance that the weight has to fall.

3. Find the time required for the 50-gram weight to reach the floor. With the string wound around the smaller axle and the weight at the top of its path, release the wheel and start the stop watch at the same

instant; make sure that no impulse is given to the wheel when it starts rotating. Stop the watch at the instant when the weight strikes the floor.

4. Repeat procedure (3), making two more observations of the time.

5. Repeat procedures (2) and (3), using a 100-gram weight with the string wound on the smaller axle. Make three observations of the time of descent.

6. Repeat procedures (1), (2), and (3), using a 50-gram weight with the string wound on the larger axle. Make three observations of the time of descent.

7. Repeat procedures (1), (2), and (3), using a 100-gram weight with the string wound on the larger axle. Make three observations of the time of descent.

8. Measure the diameter of each axle with the vernier calipers.

9. Measure the diameter of the wheel with the large calipers.

10. Record the total mass of the wheel and axle. This is stamped on the wheel.

DATA

Diameter of the smaller axle...
Radius of the smaller axle...
Diameter of the larger axle..
Radius of the larger axle..
Diameter of the wheel...
Radius of the wheel...
Total mass of the wheel and axle..
Moment of inertia of the wheel and axle from the slope of the line on the graph.............
Frictional torque from the *y* intercept on the graph..
Radius of gyration of the wheel and axle..

	USING SMALLER AXLE		USING LARGER AXLE	
	50-GM. MASS	100-GM. MASS	50-GM. MASS	100-GM. MASS
DISTANCE THAT THE MASS FALLS				
TIME OF FALL: 1.				
2.				
3.				
AVERAGE				
AVERAGE VELOCITY OF FALLING MASS				
FINAL VELOCITY OF FALLING MASS				
ACCELERATION OF FALLING MASS				
FINAL ANGULAR VELOCITY				
ANGULAR ACCELERATION				
TENSION IN THE STRING				
TORQUE ACTING ON WHEEL AND AXLE				

CALCULATIONS

1. From the data of procedures (3) and (4), calculate the average time of descent.

2. Similarly, calculate the average time of descent for each set of data in procedures (5), (6), and (7).

3. From the data of procedures (8) and (9), compute the radius of each axle and the radius of the wheel.

4. Using the average time of fall, compute the average velocity of the falling mass for each set of observations.

5. From the value of the average velocity, calculate the final velocity of the mass as it strikes the floor, for each set of observations. Notice that since the system starts from rest and experiences a uniform acceleration, the final velocity will be twice the average velocity.

6. The value of the final velocity found in calculation (5) is also the final tangential velocity of a point on the circumference of the axle. Using the expression

$$v = r\omega$$

find the final angular velocity ω for each set of observations.

7. From the average time of fall and the final velocity, calculate the acceleration of the falling mass for each set of observations.

8. The value of the acceleration found in calculation (7) is also the tangential acceleration of a point on the circumference of the axle. Using the expression

$$a = r\alpha$$

find the angular acceleration α for each set of observations.

9. There are two forces acting on the falling mass, the downward force of gravity, which is the weight, and the upward pull of the tension in the string.
Hence the resultant force acting on the falling mass is

$$F = mg - T$$

where F is the net force in dynes, m is the mass in grams, g is the acceleration of gravity, and T is the tension in the string in dynes. (See Fig. 17.) But by Newton's second law of motion, $F = ma$. Therefore

$$mg - T = ma$$

where m is again the mass in grams and a is the acceleration of the falling mass in centimeters per second per second.

From the value of the acceleration found in calculation (7), calculate the tension in the string for each set of observations.

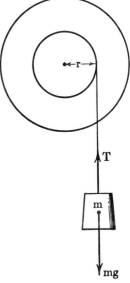

Fig. 17. Forces Acting on a Falling Mass

10. The torque acting on the wheel and axle is given by

$$L = Tr$$

where L is the applied torque in centimeter-dynes, T is the tension in the string in dynes, and r is the radius of the axle in centimeters.

Calculate the applied torque for each set of observations.

11. There are two torques acting on the rotating wheel and axle, the applied torque, calculated in (10), and the frictional torque. Hence the resultant torque is the difference between these two, since the frictional torque is acting in a direction opposite to the direction of rotation. But, from the laws of angular motion

$$\text{Resultant Torque} = I\alpha$$

we get the relation

$$L - L_f = I\alpha$$

where L is the applied torque in centimeter-dynes, L_f is the frictional torque, I is the moment of inertia in gm.-cm.^{2} of the wheel and axle, and α is the angular acceleration in radians per second per second.

The above equation may be written

$$L = I\alpha + L_f$$

In this equation, the quantities I and L_f are constant in the sets of observations taken, while L and α are variable. This is the equation of a straight line, since it is of the form

$$y = mx + b$$

Hence I is the slope of the line, and L_f is the y intercept.

Plot the values of the angular acceleration α along the x axis and the corresponding values of the applied torque L along the y axis. Draw the best straight line through the four points.

12. Determine the value of the moment of inertia I of the wheel and axle by computing the slope of the straight line drawn in (11).

13. Determine the value of the frictional torque L_f by reading the value of the y intercept of the straight line drawn in (11).

14. The radius of gyration of a rotating body is the distance from the axis of rotation to the point at which the entire mass of the body may be considered concentrated without altering the moment of inertia. It is defined by the expression

$$I = MK^2$$

where I is the moment of inertia in gm.-cm.^{2} of the body, M is the total mass of the body in grams, and K is the radius of gyration in centimeters.

Using the value of the moment of inertia computed in calculation (12) and the value of the total mass of the wheel and axle stamped on the wheel, calculate the radius of gyration of the wheel and axle.

QUESTIONS

1. By referring to your graph, determine if it is possible for the y intercept to be negative. What would this mean physically?

2. How does your calculated value of the radius of gyration compare with the radius of the wheel?

3. Could the radius of gyration be greater than the radius of the wheel? Explain.

4. A uniform disk 30 centimeters in diameter and having a mass of 2000 grams is free to rotate about its horizontal axle. An object with a mass of 50 grams is attached to a string wound around the rim of the disk. The object is released from rest and descends with constant linear acceleration. Calculate: (a) the moment of inertia of the disk; (b) the linear acceleration of the descending object; (c) the angular acceleration of the disk; and (d) the tension in the string. Neglect the moment of inertia of the axle and the friction at the axle.

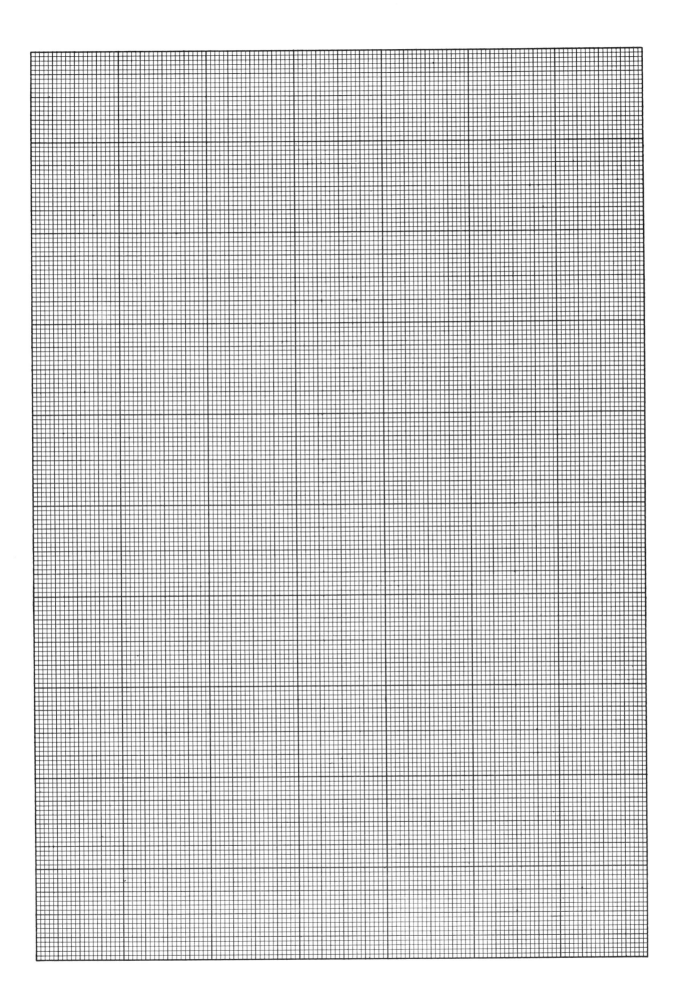

15

ARCHIMEDES' PRINCIPLE

Buoyancy is the ability of a fluid to sustain a body floating in it, or to diminish the apparent weight of a body immersed in it by an amount equal to the weight of the fluid displaced. It is the purpose of this experiment to study Archimedes' principle and its application to the determination of density and specific gravity; in particular, to find the specific gravity of a solid heavier than water, of a solid lighter than water, and of a liquid other than water.

THEORY

The density of a body is defined as the mass per unit volume. It is usually expressed in grams per cubic centimeter or in pounds per cubic foot. The specific gravity of a body is the ratio of its density to the density of water at the same temperature. Since for a given location the weight of a body is taken as a measure of its mass, the specific gravity may be taken as the ratio of the weight of a given volume of a substance to the weight of an equal volume of water.

Archimedes' principle states that the apparent loss of weight of a body immersed in a fluid is equal to the weight of the fluid displaced. The specific gravity of a solid heavier than water may be easily determined by the application of this principle. The body is weighed in air; then it is weighed in water, that is, suspended by a thread from the arm of a balance so as to be completely submerged (see Fig. 18). The loss of weight in water is $W - W_1$, where W is the weight in air and W_1 is the weight in water. But the loss of weight in water is equal to the weight of the water displaced, or the weight of an equal volume of water. Thus the specific gravity S will be

$$S = \frac{W}{W - W_1}$$

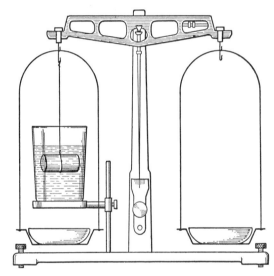

Fig. 18. Arrangement for Weighing a Body in Water

The specific gravity of a liquid may be found by measuring the loss of weight of a convenient solid body when immersed in that liquid and the loss of weight when immersed in water. The procedure is the following: A heavy body is weighed in air; this weight is called W. Then it is weighed in a liquid whose specific gravity is to be determined; this weight is called W_1. Finally it is weighed in water; this weight is called W_2. The specific gravity of the liquid will be

$$S = \frac{W - W_1}{W - W_2}$$

since this expression represents the weight of a certain volume of the liquid divided by the weight of an equal volume of water. Here $W - W_1$ is the loss of weight in the given liquid, and $W - W_2$ is the loss of weight in water.

In order to find the specific gravity of a solid lighter than water, it is necessary to employ an auxiliary body, or sinker, of sufficient weight and density to hold the other body completely submerged. The specific gravity of a solid lighter than water, as obtained by the sinker method, is given by

$$S = \frac{W}{W_1 - W_2}$$

where W is the weight of the solid in air; W_1 is the weight of the solid and the sinker, with the sinker alone immersed; and W_2 is the weight when both solids are immersed in water.

The hydrometer is an instrument designed to indicate the specific gravity of a liquid by the depth to which it sinks in the liquid. To measure the specific gravity of a liquid by means of a hydrometer, it is only necessary to let the hydrometer float in the liquid and to read the specific gravity directly on the calibrated scale.

71

The reading is taken, if possible, by placing the eye below the liquid surface and seeing where this surface cuts the hydrometer scale.

APPARATUS

1. Beam balance with platform.
2. Metal cylinder.
3. Wooden cylinder.
4. Lead sinker.
5. Distilled water.

6. Alcohol.
7. Hydrometer.
8. Hydrometer jar.
9. Two 400 c.c. beakers.
10. Fine thread.

PROCEDURE

1. Weigh the metal cylinder in air.

2. Weigh the metal cylinder in alcohol. Suspend the cylinder by a fine thread from the lower hook over the scale pan, without removing the pan. Place a beaker of alcohol on the adjustable circular platform over the scale pan and immerse the cylinder completely. Weigh the cylinder while it is immersed but not touching the beaker. Remove the beaker and dry the metal cylinder.

3. Repeat procedure (2) using a beaker of distilled water.

4. Weigh the wooden cylinder in air.

5. Attach the sinker to the wooden cylinder and weigh the combination with the sinker alone immersed in water.

6. Now weigh the two solids when they are both immersed in water.

7. Measure the specific gravity of the alcohol with the hydrometer. Pour some alcohol in a hydrometer jar and let the hydrometer float in the alcohol. Read the specific gravity directly.

DATA

Weight of metal cylinder in air. . . . .

Weight of metal cylinder in alcohol. . . . .

Weight of metal cylinder in water. . . . .

Specific gravity of metal cylinder. . . . .

Specific gravity of metal cylinder from Table III, Appendix. . . . .

Per cent error. . . . .

Specific gravity of alcohol. . . . .

Specific gravity of alcohol from Table III, Appendix. . . . .

Per cent error. . . . .

Weight of wooden cylinder in air. . . . .

Weight of cylinder in air and sinker immersed in water. . . . .

Weight of cylinder and sinker, both immersed in water. . . . .

Specific gravity of wooden cylinder. . . . .

Specific gravity of alcohol by using the hydrometer. . . . .

CALCULATIONS

1. From the data of procedures (1) and (3), calculate the specific gravity of the metal cylinder.

2. From the data of procedures (1), (2), and (3), calculate the specific gravity of the alcohol.

3. From the data of procedures (4), (5), and (6), compute the specific gravity of the wooden cylinder.

4. Compute the per cent error of your measurements by comparing your results for the specific gravity of the metal cylinder and of the alcohol with the accepted values.

QUESTIONS

1. (a) Explain how you can obtain the volume of an irregular solid insoluble in water. (b) How can you obtain the weight of an equal volume of water?

2. (a) Why does a block of wood apparently lose more than its entire weight in air, when completely submerged in water? (b) How is this made possible?

3. (a) What becomes of the lost weight of an object when immersed in a liquid? (b) How is this apparent loss of weight explained?

4. Suppose there were a bubble of air on the bottom of the metal cylinder immersed in water, how would this affect the calculations of the density of the metal?

5. A piece of cork which weighs 25 grams in air and has a specific gravity of 0.25 is attached to a lead sinker which weighs 226 grams in air. What will be the apparent weight of the two solids when they are both immersed in water?

16

BOYLE'S LAW

One of the important properties of a gas is that it always tends to expand until it completely fills the vessel in which it is placed, and thus the pressure it exerts depends on the volume it occupies. To describe fully the condition of a gas it is necessary to give not only the volume but also the temperature and pressure, because they are all interrelated. It is the purpose of this experiment to study Boyle's law, that is, to show that the product of the pressure and the volume of a given mass of gas remains constant if the temperature is kept constant.

THEORY

The condition of a gas is completely determined by three variables: pressure, volume, and temperature. For a given amount of gas, if two of the variables are given, the third becomes known from the gas laws connecting these variables. Boyle's law states that if the temperature is kept constant, the volume of a given mass of gas varies inversely as the pressure. This means that for a constant temperature, the product of the volume and the pressure of a given amount of gas is constant. Thus

$$PV = \text{constant}$$

or

$$P_1V_1 = P_2V_2$$

where V_1 is the volume of a given mass of gas at pressure P_1, and V_2 is the volume at pressure P_2.

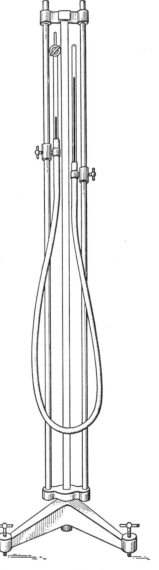

The experimental test of Boyle's law consists in observing a series of different volumes, measuring the corresponding pressures, and observing how nearly constant the product of the two remains. The apparatus is made up of two glass tubes of uniform bore connected by a flexible rubber tubing and mounted on a supporting frame to which a scale is attached (see Fig. 19). The apparatus is partially filled with mercury. One of the glass tubes is provided with a stopcock; the air upon which observations are made is confined in this tube. The other tube is open to the atmosphere and can be raised or lowered, thus changing the height of the mercury column which confines the air. The difference in height of the mercury in the two tubes causes a pressure to be exerted on the gas trapped in the closed tube. Suppose this is called a partial pressure. Then the total pressure is made up of the sum of this partial pressure and the atmospheric pressure, since the open tube is open to the atmosphere. If the height of the mercury in the open tube is less than that in the closed tube, then the total pressure is less than the atmospheric pressure.

The total pressure P acting on the confined air is given by

$$P = A + (h_2 - h_1)$$

where P is the total pressure; A is the atmospheric pressure, or the reading of the barometer; h_2 is the level of the mercury in the open tube; and h_1 is the level of the mercury in the closed tube. All values of pressure are expressed in centimeters of mercury.

APPARATUS

1. Boyle's law apparatus.
2. Barometer.
3. Centigrade thermometer.

PROCEDURE

1. Record the readings of the barometer and of the thermometer.

2. The apparatus has already been adjusted by the instructor. With the stopcock open, the level of the mercury was adjusted until a volume of air was enclosed which was equal to about half the volume of the tube.

Fig. 19. Boyle's Law Apparatus

Then the stopcock was closed. Under these conditions, the enclosed air is at atmospheric pressure and the level of the mercury is the same in both tubes. Do not touch the stopcock at all. Begin the experiment by adjusting the open tube so that the level of the mercury is the same in both tubes, and the enclosed air is thus at atmospheric pressure. Record the level of the top of the closed tube and the level of the mercury column in the closed tube and the open tube.

3. Decrease the pressure on the gas trapped in the closed tube by lowering the open tube as far as the instrument will permit. Allow it to remain in this position for a few minutes to test for a leak. If there is any leakage in the apparatus, consult the instructor. Record the level of the mercury column in the closed tube and the open tube.

4. Vary the pressure in approximately equal steps from the smallest to the largest value that can be obtained, making at least 10 different observations. Record the level of the mercury column in each tube for each setting. After changing the level, allow a minute or two before taking readings to permit the air to reach temperature equilibrium. Do not handle the closed tube or cause the enclosed air to be heated or cooled in any way.

DATA

Barometer reading...
Room temperature...
Level of the top of the closed tube, h_3...

MERCURY LEVEL		DIFFERENCE IN LEVELS $h_2 - h_1$	VOLUME OF AIR $h_3 - h_1$	TOTAL PRESSURE	PV	$1/V$
CLOSED TUBE h_1	OPEN TUBE h_2					

CALCULATIONS

1. Compute the value of $h_2 - h_1$ for each setting.

2. Compute the value of P, the total pressure on the confined air, for each observation taken. Express the result in centimeters of mercury. NOTE: In making the computations, for these and the following calculations, use three significant figures in the numbers representing the pressure, the volume, and the reciprocal of the volume. In calculating the product, use four significant figures.

3. Calculate the volume of the enclosed air for each observation. NOTE: Since the tube is of uniform bore, the volume of the tube is proportional to the length, hence the readings of the length of the closed tube may be taken as a measure of the volume of the enclosed air. This will be given by $h_3 - h_1$.

4. Calculate the product PV for each pressure.

5. Calculate the value of $1/V$ for each volume.

6. Plot a curve using the values of the pressure as abscissas and the corresponding values of the volume as ordinates. Use an entire sheet of graph paper for the curve. Read the instructions on plotting graphs in the introduction.

7. Plot a second curve using the values of the pressure as abscissas and the corresponding values of $1/V$ as ordinates. Use an entire sheet of graph paper for the curve.

QUESTIONS

1. Show how your results and curves verify Boyle's law. Explain the shape of the curves.

2. Explain how an error is introduced into the experiment when the room temperature changes.

3. How does the difference in height of the mercury in the two tubes cause it to exert a pressure on the enclosed air?

4. Does Boyle's law hold accurately at any temperature or pressure, such as a very high or very low one? Explain.

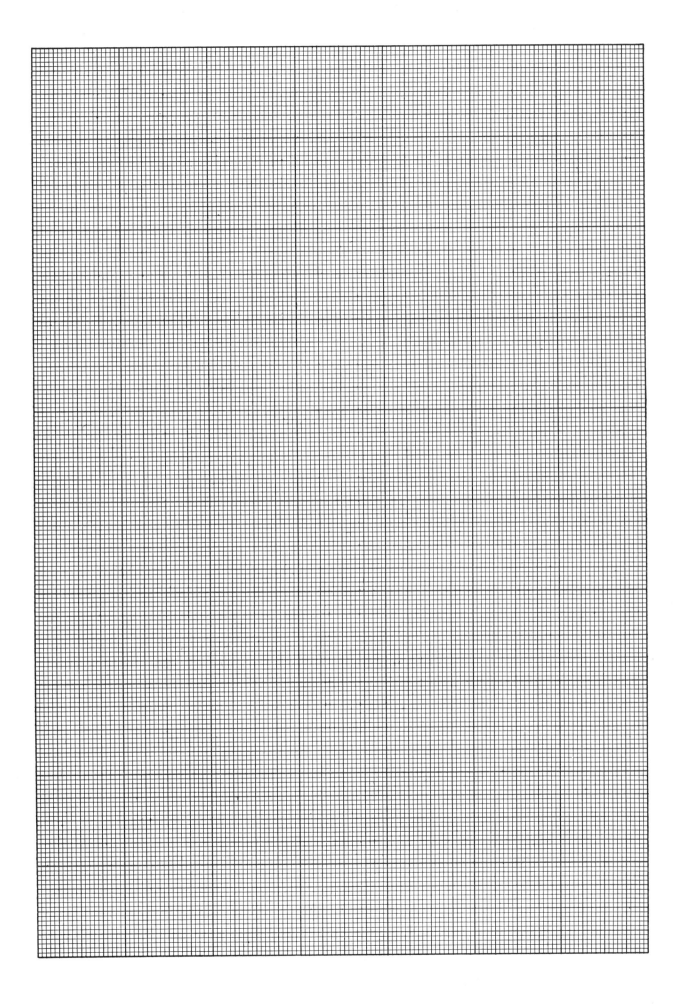

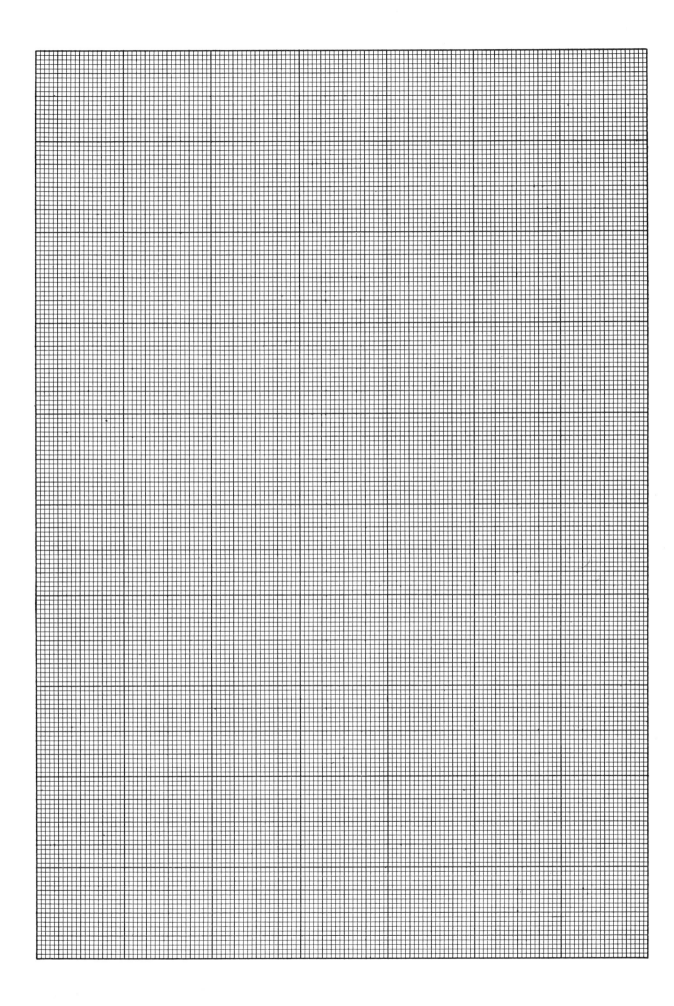

17

SIMPLE HARMONIC MOTION

Simple harmonic motion is one of the most common types of motion found in nature, and its study is therefore very important. Examples of this type of motion are found in all kinds of vibrating systems, such as water waves, sound waves, the rolling of ships, the vibrations produced by musical instruments, and many others. The object of this experiment is to study the vibrating spring as a type of simple harmonic motion; in particular, to determine the forces exerted by the spring when it is at different distances from its position of equilibrium, and to determine the periodic time of the vibrating spring.

THEORY

A rigid body is a body that does not change its shape. No actual body is perfectly rigid, hence any real body will be distorted when a force is applied to it. An elastic body is a body that changes in size or shape upon the application of a distorting force but returns to its original condition upon the removal of that force. The elastic limit is the greatest distortion a body can undergo and yet return to its original shape. Hooke's law of elasticity states that within the elastic limit of a substance, the stress is proportional to the strain. By the strain is meant the change of volume or of shape of a body, measured by the relative deformation, such as the stretch per unit length. The stress is the restoring force per unit area over which the force acts. In this experiment the elasticity of a spring is tested by measuring the elongation produced by different loads added to the spring. The force which tends to bring the spring back to its position of equilibrium is the restoring force and is the same as the suspended load, when the spring is at rest.

When an elastic body is distorted by an external applied force, a restoring force is produced in the body which is proportional to the distortion. If the applied force is removed, the restoring force will bring the body back to its equilibrium position. But the inertia of the body will carry it beyond the position of equilibrium, and thus a restoring force will be produced in the opposite direction. This force first brings the body to rest, and then brings it back to the equilibrium position. The action is repeated and the body executes a type of vibration known as simple harmonic motion.

Simple harmonic motion is motion in which the acceleration and the restoring force are at all times proportional to the displacement of a vibrating body from the position of equilibrium and are directed toward that point. It may be thought of as the projection of uniform circular motion upon the diameter of a circle. A body, then, executes simple harmonic motion when the resultant force F acting on it is proportional to the displacement x of the body from its equilibrium position and in the opposite direction to this displacement. The relation between the force and displacement is

$$F = -kx$$

In the case of a vibrating spring, the factor of proportionality k is known as the force constant of the spring; this is the force, expressed in dynes, which will produce an elongation of one centimeter in the spring.

The amplitude of the vibration is the maximum distance that the vibrating body moves from its position of equilibrium. The displacement is the distance of the body from its normal position of rest at any instant. The period is the time for one complete vibration, or the time it takes the body to swing from its maximum displacement on one side, to the other side, and back again. If the vibration is that of a mass suspended from a spring, the period is given by

$$T = 2\pi\sqrt{\frac{m}{k}}$$

where T is the period in seconds; k is the force constant of the spring expressed in dynes per centimeter; and m is the mass in grams of the vibrating system, which is made up of the suspended mass plus a part of the mass of the spring, since the spring itself is also vibrating. It is found by analysis that one third of the mass of the spring must be added to the mass of the suspended weight, in calculating the value of m used in the equation.

79

APPARATUS

1. Spring (cylindrical type).
2. Support for suspending the spring.
3. Set of hooked weights (100, 200, 200, 500 grams).
4. Stop watch or stop clock.
5. Upright meter stick with a movable index.
6. Equal arm balance and weights.

PROCEDURE

1. Weigh the spring and record the weight.

2. Suspend the spring from the support. Using the vertical meter stick, observe the position of the lower end of the spring and record the reading.

3. Suspend 100 grams from the spring and again record the position of the lower end of the spring.

4. Repeat procedure (3) with loads of 200, 300, 400, and 500 grams suspended from the spring. Record the position of the lower end of the spring in each case.

5. Suspend a mass of 200 grams from the spring, displace it about 5 centimeters from its position of equilibrium, and set it into vibration. Using a stop watch, measure the time for 50 complete vibrations of the mass, and record it.

6. Repeat procedure (5), again using a mass of 200 grams, but displacing it about 10 centimeters from its position of equilibrium and setting it into vibration. Again record the time for 50 complete vibrations.

7. Suspend a mass of 500 grams from the spring, displace it about 5 centimeters from its position of equilibrium, and set it into vibration. Record the time for 50 complete vibrations.

DATA

Weight of the spring...

Force constant of the spring...

MASS SUSPENDED FROM THE SPRING	SCALE READING	ELONGATION
0 GM.		
100 GM.		
200 GM.		
300 GM.		
400 GM.		
500 GM.		

MASS SUSPENDED FROM THE SPRING	MASS OF THE VIBRATING SYSTEM	AMPLITUDE OF VIBRATION	TIME FOR 50 VIBRATIONS	PERIOD		PER CENT DISCREPANCY
				EXPERIMENTAL VALUE	CALCULATED VALUE	
200 GM.		5 CM.				
200 GM.		10 CM.				
500 GM.		5 CM.				

CALCULATIONS

1. From the data of procedures (2–4) determine the elongation produced by each load by subtracting the zero reading from the reading corresponding to each load.

2. Plot a curve using the values of the elongation as ordinates and the corresponding total force as abscissas.

3. Using the value of the elongation obtained with the 500-gram load, calculate the force constant of the spring.

4. From the data of procedures (5–7) calculate the experimental value of the period, or the time of one complete vibration, for each set of observations.

5. Using the equation given in the theory, calculate the value of the period for each of the two masses used. The equivalent mass of the vibrating system to be used in the equation is equal to the mass suspended from the spring plus one third of the mass of the spring.

6. Calculate the per cent discrepancy between the experimental values of the period and the calculated values.

QUESTIONS

1. (a) At which point in its path does the mass have the greatest acceleration? (b) Where does it have the greatest velocity? (c) Where does it have its least acceleration? (d) Where does it have its least velocity?

2. Is the motion of the piston in a one-cylinder steam engine simple harmonic? Explain.

3. (a) What does your curve show about the dependence of the elongation upon the applied force? (b) Show how this verifies Hooke's law for your spring.

4. (a) If it takes a force of 500 dynes to stretch a spring 2 centimeters, what force is needed to stretch the spring 5 centimeters? (b) How much work is done in stretching the spring 5 centimeters?

5. What percentage error is introduced in the calculated value of the period of vibration, for the 200-gram load and the 500-gram load respectively, if the mass of the spring is neglected?

6. If the addition of an unknown weight in procedure (5) had doubled the period, compute the amount of the weight that was added.

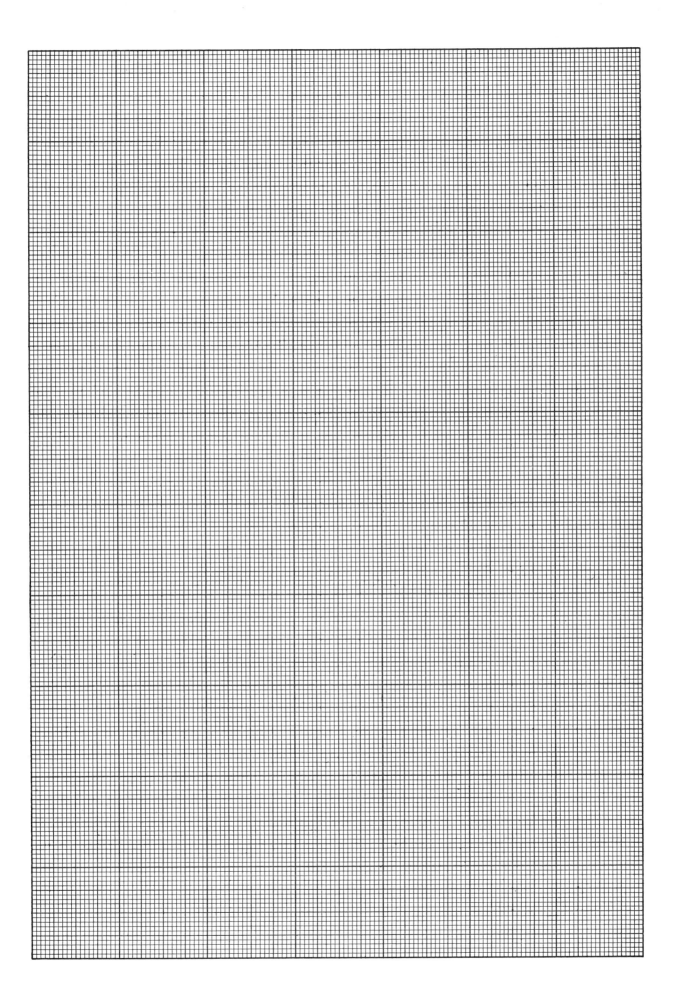

18

STANDING WAVES IN STRINGS

The general appearance of waves can be shown by means of standing waves in a string. This type of wave is very important because most of the vibrations of bodies, such as the prongs of a tuning fork or the strings of a piano, are standing waves. The purpose of this experiment is to study the relation between stretching force and wave length in a vibrating string; to determine the frequency of a string vibrator by means of standing waves.

THEORY

Standing waves, or stationary waves, are produced by the interference of two wave trains of the same wave length, velocity, and amplitude traveling in opposite directions through the same medium. The necessary conditions for the production of standing waves can be met in the case of a stretched string by having a train of waves, set up by some vibrating body, reflected at the end of the string and then interfere with the oncoming waves.

A stretched string has many modes of vibration. It may vibrate as a single segment; then its length is equal to one half the wave length of the vibrations produced. It may also vibrate in two segments with a node at each end and one in the middle; then the wave length of the vibrations produced is equal to the length of the string. It may also vibrate in a larger number of segments. In every case the length of the string is some whole number of half wave lengths.

When standing waves are produced, a condition of resonance exists between the vibrating body and the string, that is, the frequency of vibration of the body is the same as the frequency of that particular mode of vibration of the string. Corresponding to this frequency, there is a particular wave length λ such that

$$V = n\lambda$$

where n is the frequency and V is the velocity of the wave in the string. This velocity is given by

$$V = \sqrt{\frac{F}{d}}$$

where F is the tension in dynes and d is the mass per unit length of the string in grams per centimeter. If the tension is varied, there will be a change in the velocity of the wave, and hence in the wave length, if the frequency remains the same; thus a different mode of vibration will be produced. Then the conditions for the vibration of the string in parts will be fulfilled, and several resonant points will be found, as the tension is varied.

In this experiment standing waves are set up in a stretched string by the vibrations of an electrically driven string vibrator operated by a 60-cycle alternating current. The arrangement of the apparatus is shown in Fig. 20. Since the blade of the vibrator is attracted towards the pole face once during each half cycle, its frequency will be double that of the supply current, or 120 vibrations per second. The tension in the string is measured by the masses suspended over the pulley by means of a weight hanger and is altered by changing these masses. Since the distance L between consecutive nodes is equal to half a wave length λ, the equation for the frequency of vibration, $n = \dfrac{V}{\lambda}$, becomes

$$n = \frac{1}{2L}\sqrt{\frac{F}{d}}$$

The relation between the wave length and the tension is

$$\lambda = \frac{1}{n}\sqrt{\frac{F}{d}}$$

These relations between the wave length, the tension, and the length of the vibrating segment apply to each mode of vibration of the string, where L in each case is the length of one vibrating segment corresponding to a particular tension.

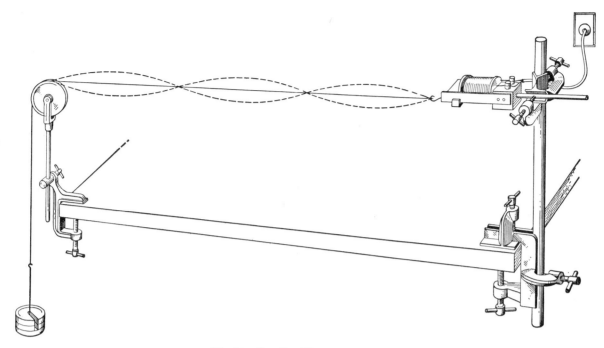

Fig. 20. Standing Waves in a String

APPARATUS

1. Electrically driven string vibrator.
2. Source of 110-volt, 60-cycle A.C.
3. String.
4. Triple-beam balance or analytical balance.

5. Meter stick.
6. Weight hanger.
7. Set of slotted weights.
8. Pulley.

PROCEDURE

1. Measure the length of a piece of string over one meter long of the same kind and thickness as the one to be used in the experiment, but free from knots. Weigh this measured length of the string.

2. Suspend the string with the loops from the vibrator, over the pulley, which is mounted in a clamp about 100 centimeters away, and attach the weight hanger to it.

3. Connect the vibrator directly to a 110-volt, 60-cycle outlet and switch the current on. Vary the tension by adding weights to the weight hanger until the string vibrates in two segments. Adjust the tension, by adding or removing small weights, until the loops formed are of maximum width. Measure the distance from the point where the string is attached to the vibrator, to the point directly over the center of the pulley. Record this length of the vibrating string, the number of segments, the tension, and the length of one vibrating segment.

4. Take a series of observations with different tensions, so adjusted as to make the string vibrate in 3, 4, 5, 6, 7, and 8 segments. To make the string vibrate with a larger number of segments, the tension has to be decreased. In each case, adjust the tension carefully so as to produce loops of the maximum width. Record the number of segments, the tension, and the length of one vibrating segment, for each set of measurements.

DATA

Length of string. . . . .

Mass of string. . . . .

Mass per unit length. . . . .

Total length of vibrating string. . . . .

Average value of the frequency. . . . .

Per cent error. . . . .

NAME_____ SECTION_____ DATE_____ EXPERIMENT EIGHTEEN

NUMBER OF SEGMENTS	TENSION		LENGTH OF ONE SEGMENT	WAVE LENGTH	SQUARE ROOT OF TENSION	FREQUENCY
	GRAMS	DYNES				
2						
3						
4						
5						
6						
7						
8						

CALCULATIONS

1. Determine the mass per unit length of the string; express it in grams per centimeter.

2. Calculate the tension in dynes for each observation.

3. Calculate the wave length in centimeters for each observation.

4. Compute the frequency of vibration for each case, from your data.

5. Calculate the average value of the frequency obtained from your experiment and compare it with the known frequency, 120 vibrations per second, by calculating the per cent error.

6. Compute the velocity of the wave in the string when it vibrates in three segments.

7. Compute the square root of the tension for each observation, from your data in column 2. Plot a curve using the square root of the tension as abscissas and the wave length as ordinates. Use an entire sheet of graph paper for the curve.

QUESTIONS

1. Explain the shape of the curve and state what it shows.

2. What is meant by resonance?

3. Upon what physical properties do (a) the loudness, (b) the pitch, and (c) the quality of a musical note depend?

4. A copper wire one meter long and weighing 0.01 gram per centimeter vibrates in two segments when under a tension of 250 grams. What is the frequency of this mode of vibration?

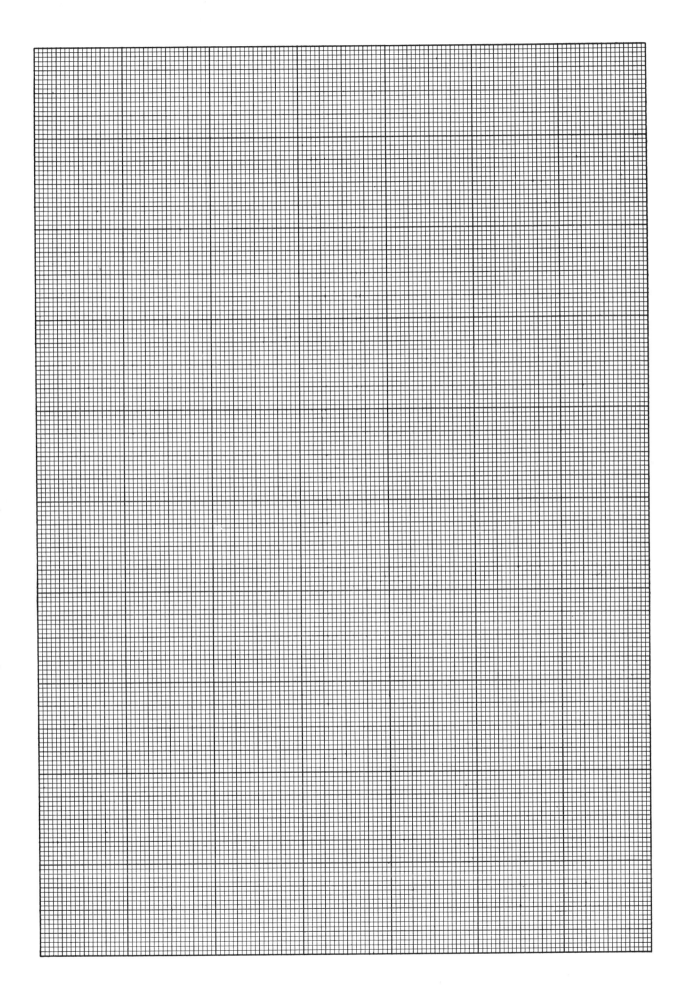

19

THE SONOMETER

A stretched string which is set into vibration will emit a musical note, the frequency of which is determined by the length of the string, the mass per unit length, and the tension. By varying any one of these quantities, the frequency may be changed. The purpose of this experiment is to determine (1) how the frequency of a vibrating string varies with its length when the tension is kept constant, (2) how the frequency of a vibrating string varies with the tension in the string when its length is kept constant, and (3) how the frequencies of two strings of the same length and material and under the same tension depend on their cross-sectional areas.

THEORY

The frequency, or number of vibrations per second, of the fundamental of a stretched string depends upon the length of the string, the tension, and the mass per unit length. The relation between these quantities is

$$n = \frac{1}{2L}\sqrt{\frac{T}{m}}$$

where n is the frequency of the note emitted in vibrations per second, L is the length of the vibrating segment in centimeters, T is the tension in dynes, and m is the mass per unit length of the string expressed in grams per centimeter.

In this experiment, the above relation will be tested by the use of a sonometer. This device consists of a resonant case provided with wires which may be stretched; the tension on the wires, or the stretching force, can be easily measured. Adjustable bridges are provided so that the lengths of the vibrating strings may be varied and measured. The general appearance of a sonometer is shown in Fig. 21.

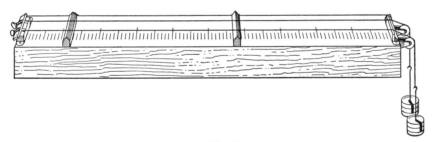

Fig. 21. The Sonometer

The experimental work consists in tuning the sonometer to several tuning forks of known frequencies, so that the law expressed by the relation given above may be tested. Thus the variation of the frequency of a vibrating string with stretching force may be studied, as well as the variation of frequency with length. Finally, the effect of the mass per unit length may be shown by using two wires of different diameters.

To detect when the wire and the fork are in unison, the two may be sounded alternately, making adjustments on the length of the wire until beats are observed. Then the two are sounded simultaneously and the adjustments are continued until the beats disappear. Unison may also be tested by placing the tip of the vibrating tuning fork on the top of the resonance board and noting whether the string is set into sympathetic vibration. Another method is to place a very small paper rider on the wire at the center of the vibrating segment. When the tip of the vibrating tuning fork is placed on the top of the resonance board, the rider will jump off if the string is in resonance with the tuning fork.

APPARATUS

1. Sonometer with two steel wires of different diameters.
2. Four tuning forks of different pitches (such as 256, 320, 384, and 512 vibrations per second).
3. Meter stick.
4. Rubber hammer.
5. Micrometer calipers.
6. Card giving the mass per unit length of the wires.

PROCEDURE

1. Adjust the tension in the string of smaller diameter to 4 kilograms. Vary the length of the string by means of the sliding bridge until its frequency is the same as that of the tuning fork of lowest pitch. Record the length of the string and the frequency of the tuning fork.

2. Repeat procedure (1) with the other three tuning forks. Record the length of the string and the frequency of the tuning fork in each case.

3. Adjust the tension in the string of smaller diameter to 5 kilograms. Vary the length of the string by means of the sliding bridge until its frequency is the same as that of the tuning fork of highest pitch. Keeping the length fixed, reduce the tension gradually until the frequency of the string is the same as that of the tuning fork of the next lower pitch. Record the length of the string, the tension, and the frequency of the tuning fork.

4. Repeat procedure (3) with the other two tuning forks. Record the value of the tension and the frequency of the tuning fork in each case.

5. Adjust the tension in both strings to 5 kilograms. Vary the length of one of the strings until its frequency is the same as that of the tuning fork of lowest pitch. Repeat this adjustment for the second string. Record the lengths of both strings and the frequency of the tuning fork.

6. Using the micrometer calipers, measure the diameter of each string and record the values.

DATA

Diameter of smaller wire..

Diameter of larger wire...

Mass per unit length of smaller wire...

Mass per unit length of larger wire..

PITCH OF TUNING FORK	LENGTH OF VIBRATING STRING	TENSION	DIAMETER OF WIRE	SQUARE ROOT OF TENSION	RECIPROCAL OF LENGTH OF THE STRING

CALCULATIONS

1. Using the values of the tension and length observed in procedure (1) and the given value of the mass per unit length of the wire, calculate the frequency of the fundamental of the string by means of the relation given in the theory. Compare the calculated value of the frequency with that of the tuning fork used, by finding the per cent error.

NAME_____, SECTION_____ DATE_____

2. From the data of procedures (1) and (2) calculate the reciprocals of the length of the string. Plot a curve using these reciprocals as abscissas and the corresponding frequencies as ordinates. What does this curve show about the way the frequency of a string under constant tension depends on the length of the string?

3. From the data of procedures (3) and (4) calculate the square roots of the tension. Plot a curve using the square roots of the tension as abscissas and the corresponding frequencies as ordinates. What does this curve show about the dependence of the frequency of a string of constant length on the tension in the string?

4. From the data of procedures (5) and (6) show how the lengths of two strings compare with the cross-sectional areas, if the strings vibrate at the same frequency, if they are under the same tension, and are made of the same material.

QUESTIONS

1. Upon what physical properties do (a) the loudness, (b) the pitch, and (c) the quality of a musical note depend?

2. What is meant by beats?

3. A wire weighing 0.003 gm./cm. and 50 cm. long is vibrating 200 times per second. What must be the tension in grams?

4. If the first overtone of a stretched string 75 cm. long has a frequency of 200 vibrations per second, when the string is stretched by a weight of 4 kilograms, what is the mass per unit length of the vibrating string?

5. Two wires equal in length and made of the same material are subjected to tensions in the proportion of 1 to 4, the one under the greater tension being the thicker wire. If they vibrate at the same frequency, how do their diameters compare?

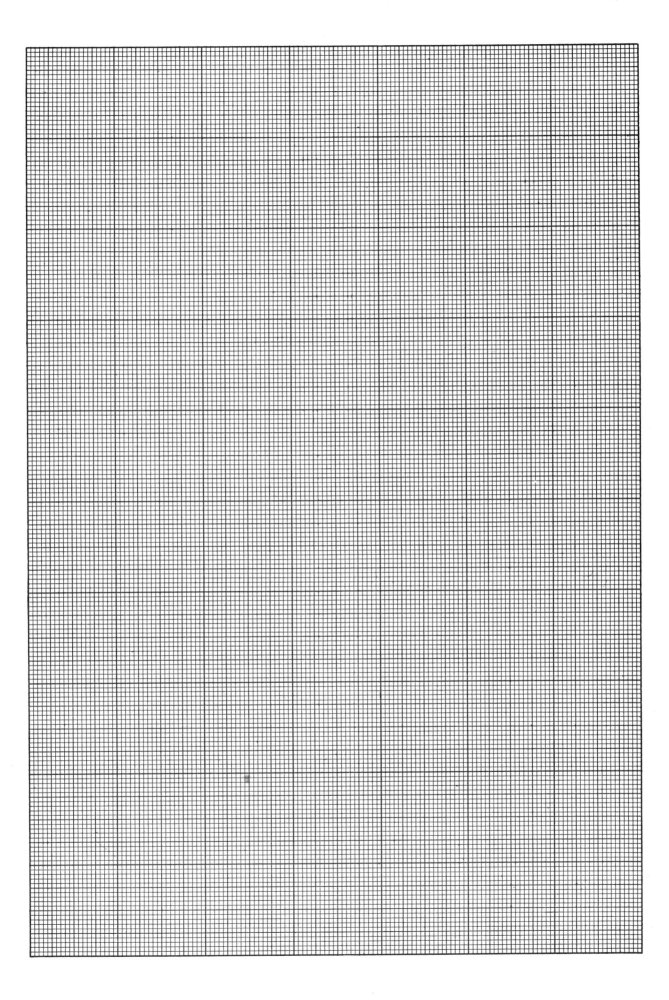

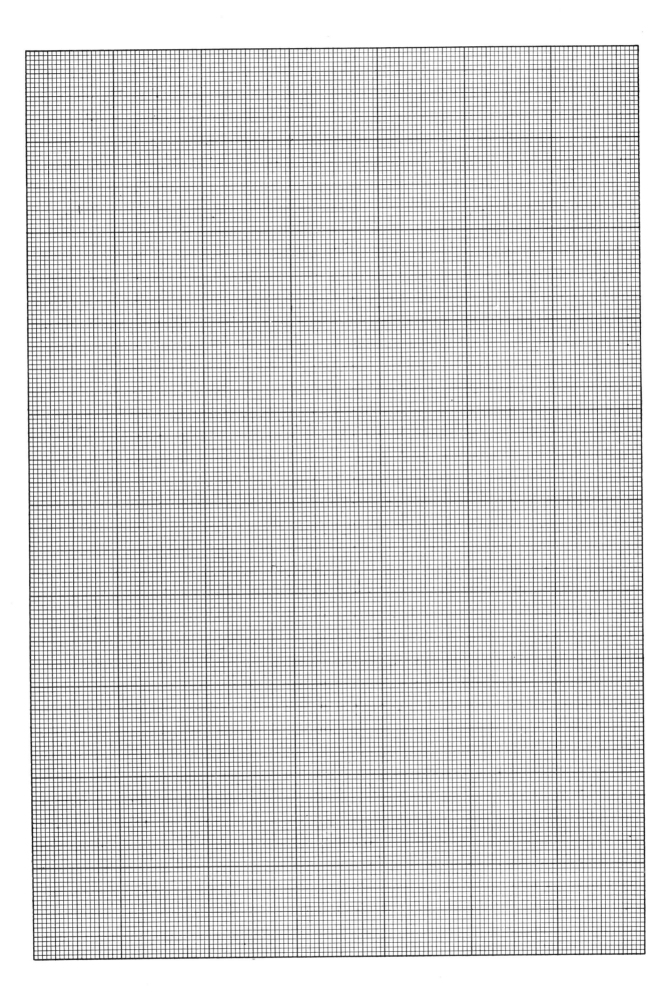

20
RESONANCE OF AIR COLUMNS

The velocity with which a sound wave travels in a substance may be determined if the frequency of the vibration and the length of the wave are known. In this experiment the velocity of sound in air will be found by using a tuning fork of known frequency to produce a wave length in air which can be measured by means of a resonating air column. The purpose of the experiment then is to determine the wave lengths in air of sound waves of different frequencies by the method of resonance in closed pipes and to calculate the velocity of sound in air from these measurements.

THEORY

If a vibrating tuning fork is held over a tube, open at the top and closed at the bottom, it will send air disturbances, made up of compressions and rarefactions, down the tube; these disturbances will be reflected at the closed end of the tube. If the length of the tube is such that the returning disturbances are in phase with those being sent out by the tuning fork, then resonance takes place. This means that the disturbances reinforce each other and produce a louder sound.

Thus, when a tuning fork is held over a tube closed at one end, resonance will occur if standing waves are set up in the air column with a node at the closed end and a loop near the open end of the tube. This can take place if the length of the tube is very nearly an odd number of quarter wave lengths of the sound waves produced by the fork. Hence resonance will occur when $L = \frac{1}{4}\lambda, \frac{3}{4}\lambda, \frac{5}{4}\lambda$, etc., where L is the length of the tube and λ is the wave length of the sound waves in air. It should be noted, however, that the center of the loop is not exactly at the open end of the tube, but is outside of it by a small distance which depends on the wave length and on the diameter of the tube. However, the distance between successive points at which resonance occurs, when the length of the tube is changed, gives the exact value of a half wave length.

In this experiment a closed pipe of variable length is obtained by changing the level of the water contained in a glass tube. The length of the tube above the water level when resonance occurs gives the length of the vibrating air column.

The resonance apparatus used in this experiment (see Fig. 22) consists of a glass tube 110 cm. long, sealed into a brass cup at the bottom, and mounted on a heavy tripod base. A brass supply tank, which is connected with the bottom of the glass tube by a rubber hose, is attached to the support rod by means of a clamp which permits rapid adjustment. A tuning fork clamp is mounted on the support rod directly above the glass tube.

The relation between the velocity of sound, the frequency, and the wave length is given by the wave equation

$$V = n\lambda$$

where V is the velocity of sound in air, in centimeters per second, n is the frequency, or the number of vibrations per second, and λ is the wave length of the sound wave in air, measured in centimeters. From the above relation, the velocity can be calculated if the frequency is known and the wave length is measured.

The velocity of sound in air is 331.4 meters per second at 0°C. At higher temperatures, the velocity is slightly higher. The relation is given by the expression

$$V_t = 331.4 + 0.6t$$

where V_t is the velocity at t°C., in meters per second. This means that the velocity increases 0.6 meter per second for each degree Centigrade rise in temperature.

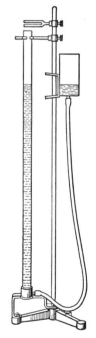

Fig. 22. Resonance Tube Apparatus

APPARATUS

1. Resonance tube apparatus.
2. Two tuning forks of different pitches (such as 512 and 640 vibrations per second).
3. Meter stick.
4. Rubber hammer.
5. Centigrade thermometer.

PROCEDURE

1. Adjust the level of the water in the glass tube by raising the supply tank, until the tube is nearly full of water. Clamp the tuning fork of higher frequency about 2 cm. above the tube and in such a manner that the prongs will vibrate vertically.

2. Determine the shortest tube length for which resonance is heard. Start the tuning fork vibrating by striking it gently with the rubber hammer. Slowly lower the water level while listening for resonance to occur. At resonance, there is a sudden increase in the intensity of the sound when the air column is adjusted to the proper length. When the approximate length for resonance has been found, run the water level up and down near this point, until the position for maximum sound is found. Measure and record the length of the resonating air column to the nearest millimeter. Make two additional determinations of this length by changing the water level and locating the position for maximum sound again. Record these two readings also.

3. Repeat procedure (2) with the same tuning fork to locate the second position at which resonance occurs. Make three independent determinations of this length and record the readings to the nearest millimeter.

4. Repeat procedures (2) and (3) for the tuning fork of lower frequency.

5. Record the temperature of the room and the frequency of each tuning fork.

DATA

Room temperature. . . . .

Calculated value of the velocity of sound in air (average). . . . .

Known value of the velocity of sound at room temperature. . . . .

Per cent error. . . . .

FREQUENCY OF TUNING FORK	FIRST POSITION OF RESONANCE				SECOND POSITION OF RESONANCE				WAVE LENGTH	VELOCITY OF SOUND IN AIR
	1	2	3	AVERAGE	1	2	3	AVERAGE		

CALCULATIONS

1. For each length of resonating air column calculate the average of the three readings taken.

2. For each tuning fork determine the value of the wave length of its sound wave in air from the lengths of the resonating air column.

3. For each tuning fork calculate the velocity of sound in air from the frequency stamped on the fork and the wave length found in calculation (2). Find the average of these two values.

4. Calculate the velocity of sound in air at room temperature from the known value of the velocity of sound at 0°C.

5. Compare the average value of the velocity of sound as found in calculation (3) with the known value as found in calculation (4) by finding the per cent error.

QUESTIONS

1. Suppose that in this experiment the temperature of the room had been lower, what effect would this have had on the length of the resonating air column for each reading? Explain.

2. (a) How would an atmosphere of hydrogen affect the pitch of an organ pipe? (b) How would it affect the pitch of a tuning fork? Explain.

3. An observer measured an interval of 10 seconds between seeing a lightning flash and hearing the thunder. If the temperature of the air was 20°C., how far away was the source of sound?

4. A tuning fork rated at 128 vibrations per second is held over a resonance tube. What are the two shortest distances at which resonance will occur at a temperature of 20°C.?

5. A vibrating tuning fork is held over a resonance tube, and resonance occurs when the surface of the water in the tube is 10 cm. below the fork. Resonance occurs again when the water is 26 cm. below the fork. If the temperature of the air is 20°C., calculate the frequency of the tuning fork.

21
COEFFICIENT OF LINEAR EXPANSION

Most substances expand with an increase of temperature. It is found that the change in length of a solid is proportional to the original length and to the change in temperature. The factor of proportionality, which is called the coefficient of linear expansion, depends on the material of which the solid is made. It is the purpose of this experiment to determine the coefficient of linear expansion of several metals.

THEORY

The coefficient of linear expansion of a substance is the change in length of each unit of length when the temperature is changed one degree. The coefficient α may be expressed by the relation

$$\alpha = \frac{L_2 - L_1}{L_1(t_2 - t_1)}$$

where L_1 is the original length in centimeters at the temperature t_1 degrees Centigrade, and L_2 is the length at the temperature t_2.

The apparatus consists of a metal rod which is placed in a brass jacket through which steam may be passed. The temperature of the rod is measured by a thermometer inserted in the jacket. One end of the rod is fixed and the other end is allowed to move. A micrometer screw, which may be adjusted to make contact with the movable end, is used to measure the change in length.

In determining the coefficient of linear expansion of a metal rod, the length of the rod is measured at room temperature. The rod is then placed in the brass tube of the apparatus and the initial reading of the attached micrometer screw is taken. Steam is then run through the tube, and the increase in length is measured by means of the micrometer screw. The supports of the apparatus carry binding posts for connecting an electric bell or a buzzer so as to indicate the exact point of contact of the screw. The coefficient of linear expansion is finally calculated from the above relation.

APPARATUS

1. Coefficient of linear expansion apparatus.
2. Boiler and tripod stand.
3. Bunsen burner.
4. 0–100°C. thermometer.
5. Rubber tubing.

6. Meter stick.
7. Dry cell.
8. Electric bell or buzzer.
9. Three metal rods: aluminum, copper, and iron.

PROCEDURE

1. Measure the length of the aluminum rod with the meter stick to 0.1 mm. at room temperature. Record the length and the temperature.

2. Adjust the rod in the brass tube and record the setting of the micrometer screw for the rod at room temperature. Make sure that one end of the rod is touching the fixed end of the apparatus and the other end is facing the micrometer screw, but not touching it. Carefully turn the micrometer screw until the bell begins to ring, showing that the screw has made contact with the rod. Record the setting of the micrometer screw.

3. Turn the micrometer screw back several millimeters to allow room for the expansion of the rod. Pass steam through the brass tube. When the rod has ceased to expand, carefully turn the micrometer screw until the bell begins to ring, showing that the screw has made contact with the rod. Record the setting of the micrometer screw. The temperature of the steam is 100°C. at normal pressure.

4. Repeat procedures (1–3) for the copper rod.

5. Repeat procedures (1–3) for the iron rod.

DATA

	ALUMINUM	COPPER	IRON
ROOM TEMPERATURE			
LENGTH OF ROD AT ROOM TEMPERATURE			
SETTING OF MICROMETER SCREW AT ROOM TEMPERATURE			
SETTING OF MICROMETER SCREW AT 100°C.			
CHANGE OF LENGTH OF THE ROD			
COEFFICIENT OF LINEAR EXPANSION			
VALUE OF THE COEFFICIENT OF LINEAR EXPANSION FROM TABLE V, APPENDIX			
PER CENT ERROR			

CALCULATIONS

1. Compute the change in length of each rod in centimeters from the two readings of the micrometer screw.

2. Calculate the coefficients of linear expansion of aluminum, copper, and iron from your data.

3. Compare your results with those given in Table V, Appendix, and find the per cent error.

NAME⎯⎯⎯⎯⎯⎯⎯⎯⎯⎯⎯⎯⎯⎯⎯⎯⎯⎯⎯⎯ SECTION⎯⎯⎯⎯⎯ DATE⎯⎯⎯⎯⎯⎯⎯⎯ EXPERIMENT TWENTY-ONE

QUESTIONS

1. Why must the increase in length of the rod be measured so carefully although the length itself can be determined by using an ordinary meter stick?

2. A compound bar made of an aluminum strip and an iron strip fastened firmly together is heated. Explain what happens to the shape of the bar.

3. When an ordinary mercury thermometer is placed in hot water, its reading drops at first, but quickly rises again. Explain why.

4. Why is the numerical value of the coefficient of linear expansion different when expressed in Fahrenheit degrees from what it is when expressed in Centigrade degrees?

5. The Golden Gate Bridge in San Francisco Bay is 4200 feet long. Compute the total expansion of the bridge as the temperature changes from $-20°C$. to $+40°C$. The coefficient of linear expansion for steel is given in Table V, Appendix.

22

SPECIFIC HEAT

To raise the temperature of a body from a given initial temperature t_1 to a final temperature t_2 requires a total quantity of heat which depends on the mass of the body, the specific heat of the material of which the body is composed, and the temperature difference. The process of measuring quantities of heat is called calorimetry. The purpose of this experiment is to determine the specific heat of one or more metals by the method of mixtures.

THEORY

The measurement of heat quantities is carried on by what is known as the method of mixtures. This makes use of the principle that when a heat interchange takes place between two bodies initially at different temperatures, the quantity of heat lost by the warmer body is equal to that gained by the cooler body, and some intermediate equilibrium temperature is finally reached. This is true provided no heat is gained from or lost to the surroundings.

The specific heat of a substance is the number of calories required to raise the temperature of one gram of the substance one degree Centigrade. If strict attention is paid to the correct usage of units, this definition of specific heat is actually the definition of the thermal capacity of a substance; then the specific heat of a substance would be defined as the ratio of the thermal capacity of the substance to the thermal capacity of water. The vessel in which the heat interchange takes place is called the calorimeter. The product of the mass of the calorimeter and its specific heat is called its water equivalent. This quantity must be included in any computations involving an interchange of heat. The water equivalent of a body is the mass of water which would require the same amount of heat as the body in order to raise the temperature through one degree Centigrade.

The experimental determination of the specific heat of a metal by the method of mixtures consists in dropping a known mass of the metal at a known high temperature into a known mass of water at a known low temperature. The equilibrium temperature is then measured. The heat absorbed by the water, calorimeter, and stirrer is equal to the heat lost by the metal. The unknown specific heat is computed from the following equation

$$Ms\ (t - t_2) = (m + m_1 s_1 + m_2 s_2)\ (t_2 - t_1)$$

where M is the mass of the metal in grams; s is the specific heat of the metal; t is the initial temperature of the metal; t_2 is the equilibrium temperature; t_1 is the initial temperature of the water and calorimeter; m is the mass of the cold water; $m_1 s_1 + m_2 s_2$ is the water equivalent of the calorimeter and stirrer; m_1 is the mass and s_1 is the specific heat of the calorimeter; m_2 is the mass and s_2 is the specific heat of the stirrer.

The initial temperature of the cold water should be as much below room temperature as the equilibrium temperature will be above it, so as to balance out errors due to losses of heat by radiation.

APPARATUS

1. Calorimeter and stirrer.
2. Boiler and tripod stand.
3. Bunsen burner.
4. Equal arm balance and set of weights.

5. One 0–100°C. thermometer.
6. One 0–50°C. thermometer
7. Aluminum cylinder.
8. Lead cylinder.

PROCEDURE

1. Weigh the calorimeter and the stirrer separately.

2. Weigh the aluminum cylinder and then lower it into the boiling water by means of a thread.

3. Pour cold water (about 3 degrees below room temperature) into the calorimeter until it is half filled. Then weigh the calorimeter with the stirrer.

4. Replace the calorimeter in the outer calorimeter jacket and record the temperature of the water. Then quickly transfer the aluminum cylinder from the heater to the calorimeter without splashing any water. Stir the water and record the equilibrium temperature. Record the temperature of the boiling water.

5. Repeat procedures (2), (3), and (4) for the lead cylinder.

101

DATA

Weight of calorimeter...

Weight of stirrer..

Specific heat of calorimeter...

Specific heat of stirrer...

	DATA FOR ALUMINUM CYLINDER	DATA FOR LEAD CYLINDER
WEIGHT OF CYLINDER		
WEIGHT OF CALORIMETER WITH STIRRER AND COLD WATER		
WEIGHT OF COLD WATER		
INITIAL TEMPERATURE OF COLD WATER		
TEMPERATURE OF BOILING WATER		
EQUILIBRIUM TEMPERATURE		
CALCULATED SPECIFIC HEAT		
SPECIFIC HEAT FROM TABLE VI, APPENDIX		
PER CENT ERROR		

CALCULATIONS

1. Calculate the specific heat of aluminum from the data of procedures (1–4).

2 Calculate the specific heat of lead from the data of procedure (5).

3. Compare your results for the specific heats with those given in Table VI, Appendix, and find the per cent error.

QUESTIONS

1. What is the purpose of starting with the temperature of the water lower than room temperature and ending about the same amount above room temperature?

2. How would the computed value of the specific heat be affected if some boiling water were carried over with the metal?

3. What will be the biggest source of error if too much water is used?

4. What is meant by the water equivalent of a body?

5. A platinum ball weighing 100 grams is removed from a furnace and dropped into 400 grams of water at 0°C. If the equilibrium temperature is 10°C. and the specific heat of platinum is 0.04, what must have been the temperature of the furnace? Neglect the effect of the mass of the calorimeter.

23

HEAT OF FUSION AND HEAT OF VAPORIZATION

To change a unit mass of a liquid to vapor without changing the temperature requires a certain amount of heat. This same heat is released when a unit mass of the vapor condenses with no change in temperature. In a similar manner, to change a unit mass of a solid to the liquid state without changing the temperature requires a certain amount of heat. This same heat is released when a unit mass of the liquid solidifies with no change in temperature. The object of this experiment is to determine the heat of fusion of ice and the heat of vaporization of water by the method of mixtures.

THEORY

The heat of fusion of a substance is the amount of heat required to change a unit mass of the substance from the solid to the liquid state without a change in temperature. The temperature at which this change takes place is called the melting point.

The heat of vaporization of a substance is the amount of heat required to change a unit mass of the substance from the liquid to the vapor state without a change in temperature. The temperature at which this change takes place is called the boiling point.

In doing heat experiments where the quantity of heat added to or taken from a substance is to be determined, the range of temperature should be equally above and below room temperature, so that the amount of heat absorbed from the surroundings during the course of the experiment will be approximately equal to the amount of heat radiated to the surroundings.

The experimental determination of the heat of fusion of ice and of the heat of vaporization of water is made by the method of mixtures. This makes use of the principle that when a heat interchange takes place between two bodies initially at different temperatures, the quantity of heat lost by the warmer body is equal to that gained by the cooler body, and some intermediate equilibrium temperature is finally reached. This is true provided no heat is gained from or lost to the surroundings.

In determining the heat of fusion of ice, a few small pieces of ice are placed, one by one, into a calorimeter containing water. As the ice melts, heat is absorbed from the water and calorimeter until the mixture comes to a final equilibrium temperature. The heat absorbed by the ice in melting plus the heat absorbed by the ice water produced is equal to the heat lost by the warm water, calorimeter, and stirrer. The working equation is

$$ML_f + M(t_2 - 0) = (m + m_1s_1 + m_2s_2)(t_1 - t_2)$$

where M is the mass of ice, in grams; L_f is the latent heat of fusion of ice; t_2 is the equilibrium temperature; t_1 is the initial temperature of the water and calorimeter; m is the mass of warm water; $m_1s_1 + m_2s_2$ is the water equivalent of the calorimeter and stirrer; m_1 is the mass and s_1 is the specific heat of the calorimeter; m_2 is the mass and s_2 is the specific heat of the stirrer.

The heat of vaporization of water is determined in a similar manner by the method of mixtures. A quantity of steam is passed into a known mass of cold water in a calorimeter, where it condenses and raises the temperature of the water. The heat lost by the steam in condensing plus the heat lost by the condensed steam is equal to the heat absorbed by the cold water, calorimeter, and stirrer. The working equation is

$$ML_v + M(100 - t_2) = (m + m_1s_1 + m_2s_2)(t_2 - t_1)$$

where M is the mass of steam in grams; L_v is the latent heat of vaporization of water; t_2 is the equilibrium temperature; t_1 is the initial temperature of the water and calorimeter; m is the mass of cold water; $m_1s_1 + m_2s_2$ is the water equivalent of the calorimeter and stirrer.

APPARATUS

1. Calorimeter and stirrer.
2. Steam generator on stand.
3. Water trap.
4. Rubber tubing.
5. Bunsen burner.
6. Equal arm balance and set of weights.
7. One 0–100°C. thermometer.
8. One 0–50°C. thermometer.
9. Ice.
10. Paper towels.

PROCEDURE

1. Weigh the calorimeter and the stirrer separately.

2. Fill the calorimeter half full of water about 10 degrees above room temperature and weigh it along with the stirrer. Replace it in the outer calorimeter jacket and record the temperature of the water.

3. Dry some small pieces of ice on a paper towel and add them to the water without touching the ice with the fingers, so as not to melt it. Add the ice until the temperature is about 10 degrees below room temperature, keeping the mixture well stirred. Record the equilibrium temperature, when the ice is entirely melted. Weigh the calorimeter with its contents again, but without the thermometer.

4. Fill the calorimeter three quarters full of water about 15 degrees below room temperature and weigh it along with the stirrer. Replace it in the outer calorimeter jacket.

5. Adjust the steam generator so that the steam passes through the water trap and flows freely from the steam tube. Record the temperature of the cold water and quickly immerse the steam tube. Allow the steam to pass in and condense until the temperature of the water is about 15 degrees above room temperature, stirring continuously. Remove the steam tube and record the equilibrium temperature. Weigh the calorimeter with its contents again, but without the thermometer.

DATA

Weight of calorimeter..

Weight of stirrer..

Specific heat of calorimeter..

Specific heat of stirrer..

HEAT OF FUSION

Weight of calorimeter and stirrer...

Weight of calorimeter, stirrer, and water...

Weight of water..

Initial temperature of water..

Equilibrium temperature..

Weight of calorimeter, stirrer, water, and melted ice................................

Weight of ice..

Calculated heat of fusion of ice..

Accepted value of heat of fusion of ice...

Per cent error...

HEAT OF VAPORIZATION

Weight of calorimeter and stirrer...

Weight of calorimeter, stirrer, and water...

Weight of water..

Initial temperature of water..

Equilibrium temperature..

Weight of calorimeter, stirrer, water, and condensed steam..........................

Weight of steam..

Calculated heat of vaporization of water..

Accepted value of heat of vaporization of water.....................................

Per cent error...

CALCULATIONS

1. From the data of procedures (1–3) compute the heat of fusion of ice.

2. From the data of procedures (4–5) compute the heat of vaporization of water.

3. Compare your results for the heat of fusion and the heat of vaporization with the known values by finding the per cent error.

QUESTIONS

1. Discuss the principal sources of error in this experiment.

2. Why is it necessary to stir the mixtures?

3. What error would have been introduced if the ice were not dry?

4. (a) What is the purpose of the water trap in determining the heat of vaporization? (b) How would its absence have affected the results?

24
GAS LAWS

In order to specify fully the condition of a gas it is necessary to know its pressure, volume, and temperature. These quantities are interrelated, being connected by the general gas law, so that if any two of them are known, the third is determined by the mathematical relation between them. The purpose of this experiment is to study two of the gas laws; that is, to study the relation between the volume and the total pressure of a given mass of gas, when the temperature is kept constant; and to investigate the variation of the volume of a given mass of gas with changes in its temperature, when the pressure is kept constant.

THEORY

In studying the behavior of a gas under different conditions of pressure, temperature, and volume, it is convenient to keep one of these constant and to vary the other two. Thus, if the temperature is kept constant, one obtains the relation between the pressure and the volume; if the pressure is kept constant, one gets the relation between the temperature and the volume.

Boyle's law states that when the temperature is kept constant, the volume of a given mass of gas varies inversely as the pressure. This law may be expressed algebraically thus

$$PV = \text{constant}$$
or
$$P_1 V_1 = P_2 V_2$$

where V_1 is the volume at pressure P_1 and V_2 is the volume at pressure P_2. Thus, when a gas is compressed at constant temperature, the product of the pressure and the volume is a constant.

Charles' law states that if the pressure is kept constant, the volume of a given mass of gas varies directly as the absolute temperature. The relation between the volume and the temperature is given by the equation

$$V = V_o(1 + \beta t)$$

where V_o is the volume of the gas at 0°C., V is the volume at some other temperature t, and β is the coefficient of volume expansion. If the temperature is expressed on the absolute scale, the equation becomes

$$\frac{V_1}{T_1} = \frac{V_2}{T_2}$$

where V_1 is the volume at temperature T_1 and V_2 is the volume at temperature T_2.

The general gas law gives the complete relation between the pressure, the volume, and the temperature of a given mass of gas. These are related according to the equation

$$\frac{P_1 V_1}{T_1} = \frac{P_2 V_2}{T_2}$$

where the symbols are the same as before, and the temperature is expressed on the absolute scale. Although these gas laws refer to an ideal gas, they hold accurately for air within the temperature and pressure ranges to be used in this experiment.

In studying these gas laws, a small quantity of air is confined in a capillary tube by means of a column of mercury, and the pressure or the temperature of the gas is varied. The tube is open to the atmosphere above the mercury column and it is mounted so that it may be turned into various positions (see Fig. 23). The pressure exerted on the confined air may be varied by changing the angle between the tube and the horizontal. When the open end is up, the total pressure is the sum of the atmospheric pressure and that due to the column of mercury. When the open end is down, the total pressure is the atmospheric pressure minus that due to the mercury. The total pressure P acting on the confined air is given by

$$P = A + (h_2 - h_1)$$

where P is the total pressure; A is the atmospheric pressure, or the reading of the barometer; h_2 is the vertical distance from the top of the table to the open end of the mercury column; and h_1 is the vertical distance from the top of the table to the closed end of the mercury column. All values of pressure are expressed in centimeters of mercury. When h_2 is greater than h_1, the quantity $(h_2 - h_1)$ is positive, and the pressure inside the tube is greater than the atmospheric pressure; this is the case shown in Fig. 23. When the tube is horizontal, $h_2 = h_1$,

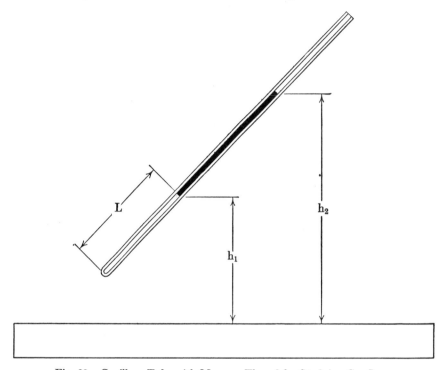

Fig. 23. Capillary Tube with Mercury Thread for Studying Gas Laws

and the pressure in the confined air is the same as the atmospheric pressure. When the closed end of the tube is higher than the open end, then h_2 is less than h_1, and the quantity $(h_2 - h_1)$ is negative; then the pressure inside the tube is less than the atmospheric pressure.

The volume of the confined air is equal to the cross-sectional area of the capillary tube times the length of the air column. Since the cross-sectional area is constant, the volume of the gas is proportional to the length L of the air column and may be expressed in terms of L.

APPARATUS

1. Capillary tube with mercury thread.
2. Support rod and swivel clamp.
3. Upright meter stick with a movable index.
4. 30 centimeter scale.
5. Small steel scale.
6. Thermometer (0–110°C.).

7. Pyrex beaker.
8. Ring clamp.
9. Bunsen burner.
10. Stirrer.
11. Barometer.

PROCEDURE

1. Record the reading of the mercury barometer.

2. Clamp the capillary tube in a vertical position with the open end up. Avoid jarring the tube, since the mercury thread is easily broken and the tube cannot be used with a broken mercury thread.

3. Measure the length L of the confined column of air to the nearest tenth of a millimeter and record it.

4. Measure the vertical distance from the table top to each end of the mercury column. Designate the distance to the enclosed end of the mercury column by h_1 and the distance to the open end by h_2. Record both readings.

5. Rotate the capillary tube through an angle of about 30° and repeat the measurements of procedures (3–4).

6. Repeat procedure (5), rotating the tube so that it makes angles of about 60, 90, 120, 150, and 180 degrees with the vertical, so that in the last position the tube is again vertical, but with the open end down. Record the values of L, h_1, and h_2 for each of these positions.

7. Clamp the capillary tube in a vertical position, with the open end up, leaving room underneath for the beaker and the Bunsen burner. Attach the thermometer and the steel scale to the capillary tube by means of clips, so that the bulb of the thermometer comes about the middle of the enclosed air column.

8. Record the reading of the thermometer and the position of the top and bottom of the air column to the nearest tenth of a millimeter.

9. Pour water into the beaker until half full, place it in the ring clamp, and adjust it so that the entire air column is just immersed. Put some cracked ice into the beaker and stir the water until the temperature is about 0°C. Record the exact temperature and the position of the top of the air column.

10. Remove the pieces of ice from the beaker. Place the Bunsen burner under the beaker and start heating the water. When the temperature of the water is about 20°C., remove the burner and stir the water. Record the exact temperature and the position of the top of the air column.

11. Continue heating the water and repeat procedure (10) for temperatures of 40, 60, 80, and 100 degrees. Record the exact temperature and the position of the top of the air column in each case.

DATA

Reading of the mercury barometer...

Value of the absolute zero from the graph...

Accepted value of the absolute zero...

Per cent discrepancy..

POSITION OF THE TUBE	LENGTH OF AIR COLUMN	DISTANCE FROM TABLE TO OPEN END OF MERCURY COLUMN	DISTANCE FROM TABLE TO ENCLOSED END OF MERCURY COLUMN
0°			
30°			
60°			
90°			
120°			
150°			
180°			

POSITION OF THE TUBE	HEIGHT OF MERCURY COLUMN	PRESSURE ON THE ENCLOSED AIR	VALUE OF $1/L$	PRODUCT $P \times L$
0°				
30°				
60°				
90°				
120°				
150°				
180°				

TEMPERATURE OF CONFINED AIR	POSITION OF TOP OF AIR COLUMN	POSITION OF BOTTOM OF AIR COLUMN	LENGTH OF AIR COLUMN

CALCULATIONS

1. Compute the value of $h_2 - h_1$ for each position of the capillary tube; this represents the vertical height of the mercury column.

2. Compute the value of P, the total pressure on the confined air, for each position of the capillary tube. NOTE: In making the computations, use only three significant figures in the numbers representing volume and pressure, and carry the product to four significant figures.

3. Calculate the value of $1/L$ for each value of L.

4. Calculate the product of P and L for each set of readings.

5. Plot a curve using the values of P as abscissas and the corresponding values of L as ordinates.

6. Plot another curve using the values of P as abscissas and the corresponding values of $1/L$ as ordinates.

7. From the observations of procedures (8–11), compute the length of the confined air column for each of the temperatures observed.

8. Plot a curve using the values of the temperature as abscissas and the corresponding values of the length of the confined air column as ordinates. This curve will show the relation between the volume of a gas and its temperature, when the pressure is kept constant. To obtain more accurate results, construct the graph of the data using as large a scale as possible; that is, utilize the whole sheet of graph paper and extend the line only to 0°C.

9. From your graph, determine the value of the absolute zero on the Centigrade scale; that is, calculate the temperature at which your graph predicts that the volume of the confined air would be zero. This may be done by means of a simple proportion, since the curve is a straight line. Compare your result with the accepted value by calculating the per cent discrepancy.

QUESTIONS

1. Suppose there were an air bubble in the mercury column of your apparatus; what effect would it have on your results?

2. Why does the value of $h_2 - h_1$ and not the actual length of the mercury column determine the additional pressure due to the mercury?

3. Explain how an error is introduced into the experiment if the room temperature changes.

4. Is it necessary to measure the angle that the capillary tube makes with the vertical very accurately? Explain.

5. What would be the length of the column of air in the capillary tube if its temperature were reduced to $-30°C.$? Assume that the tube is upright with the open end up.

6. A spherical basketball 10 inches in diameter is pumped up to a pressure of 44.1 pounds per square inch. If the normal atmospheric pressure is 14.7 pounds per square inch, what volume of air at this pressure is pumped into the ball?

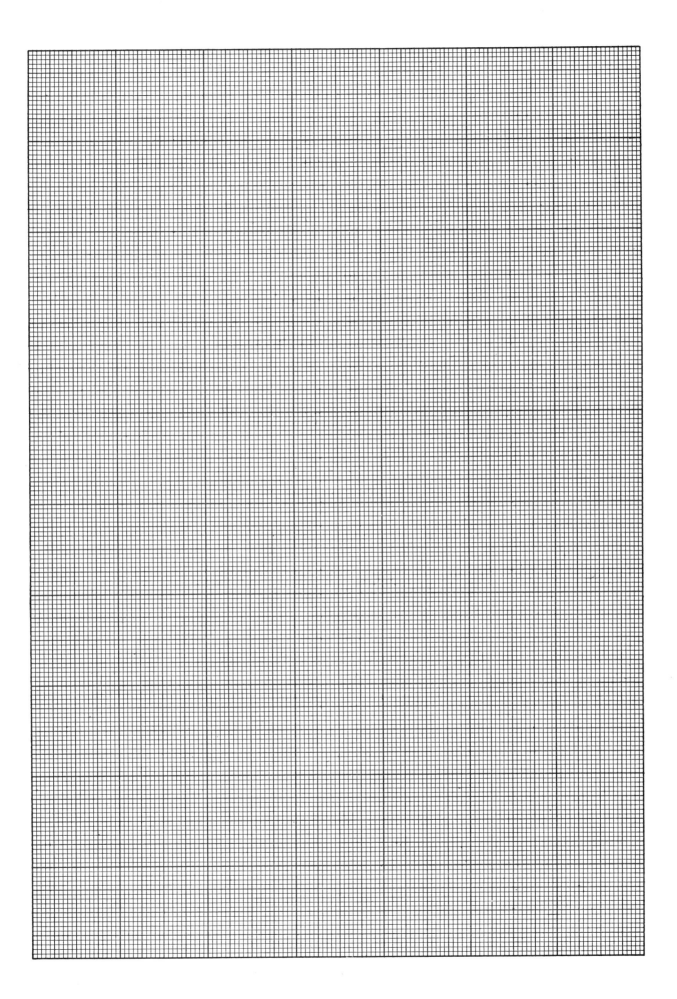

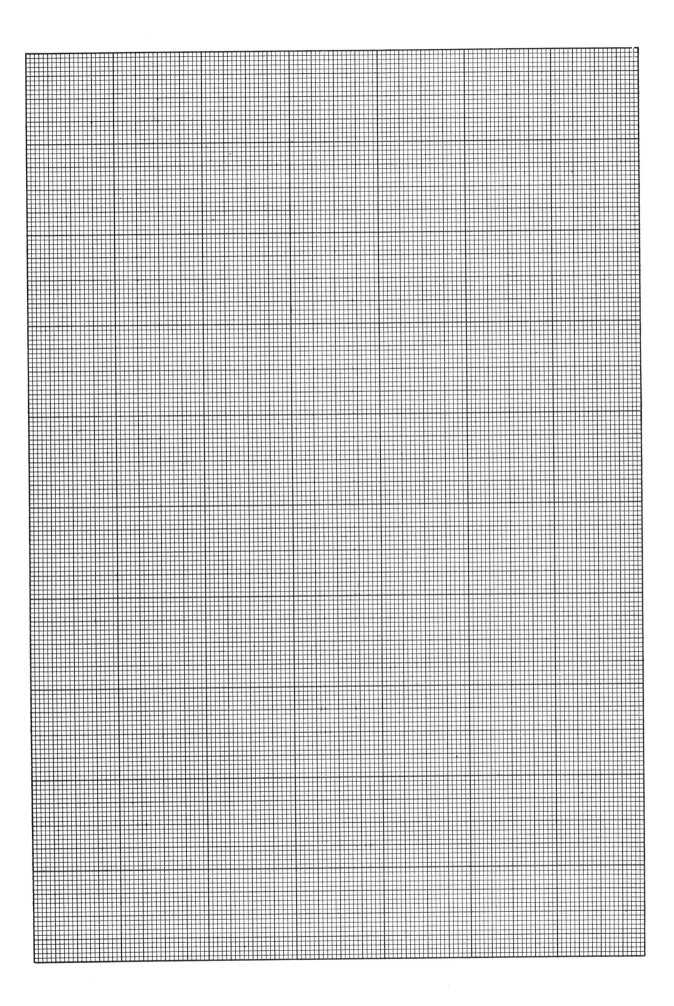

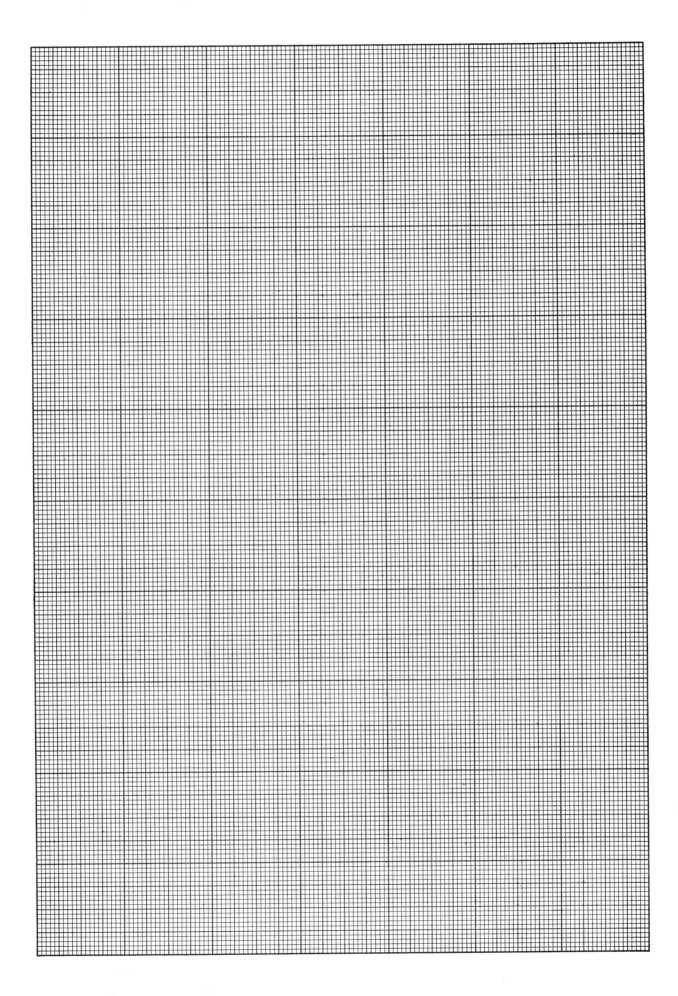

25

AIR THERMOMETER

All gases have very nearly the same coefficient of expansion, within certain limits; hence it is reasonable to expect the use of a gas as a thermometric substance. While the gas thermometer is not very practical for everyday use, still it forms the basis of the absolute temperature scale and is important as an instrument of calibration. In fact, the constant volume hydrogen thermometer is the standard thermometer in terms of which other types of thermometers are calibrated. The purposes of this experiment are to determine the pressure coefficient of air at constant volume by the use of a constant volume gas thermometer and to locate absolute zero on the Centigrade scale.

THEORY

Whenever heat is applied to a confined mass of gas, the temperature of the gas will rise and there will be an increase either in the volume or in the pressure of the gas, or in both. If the volume of the container remains fixed, as the temperature is raised, then the pressure will rise; if the pressure is to be kept fixed, then the volume of the container must be gradually increased at such a rate as to maintain the same pressure, as the temperature is raised. The corresponding coefficients of expansion are called the pressure coefficient and the volume coefficient respectively.

If the volume of a given mass of gas is kept constant, the pressure varies directly as the absolute temperature. This means that the change in pressure is directly proportional to the change in temperature within wide limits. The relation is expressed thus

$$p_t = p_o(1 + \beta t)$$

where p_t is the pressure at $t°$C., p_o is the pressure at 0°C., and β is a constant known as the pressure coefficient of the gas at constant volume. Solving the above equation for β, it is found that

$$\beta = \frac{p_t - p_o}{p_o t}$$

Thus the pressure coefficient of a gas at constant volume is the change in pressure per unit pressure per degree change of temperature. The pressure coefficient is very nearly the same for all gases and is equal to $\frac{1}{273}$, or to 0.00366 per degree Centigrade. This means that the pressure will increase by $\frac{1}{273}$ of its value at 0°C. when the temperature increases 1°C. It should be noted that this value of β applies only when the original temperature is 0°C.

The change in pressure of a gas at constant volume is used as a means of measuring temperature in the air thermometer. This consists of a glass bulb filled with dry air and connected by a thin glass tube to one arm of a flexible U-tube filled with mercury (see Fig. 24). The other arm of the U-tube is an open glass tube which may be raised or lowered to adjust the levels of the mercury. The volume of the enclosed air is kept constant by adjusting the mercury level to a fixed line on the side of the tube connected to the air bulb. The bulb is immersed in water contained in a metal can or a beaker, and the temperature of the confined air is varied by heating the water bath. The variation of pressure with temperature is studied by measuring the pressure of the enclosed air at different temperatures. The pressure exerted by the air in the bulb may be calculated from the barometric reading and the difference in levels of the mercury in the two arms of the U-tube. If the level of the mercury in the open tube is higher than in the closed tube, then the difference in levels is added to the value of the atmospheric pressure to ob-

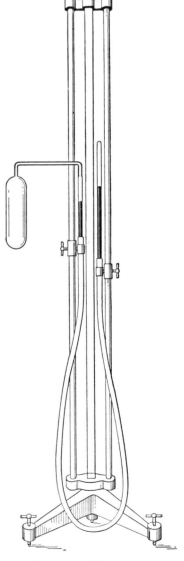

Fig. 24. Air Thermometer

tain the total pressure. If it is lower, then the difference in levels is subtracted from the value of the atmospheric pressure.

APPARATUS

1. Air thermometer.
2. Large metal can or Pyrex beaker.
3. Bunsen burner.
4. Thermometer (0–110°C.).

5. Barometer.
6. Stirrer.
7. Ice.

PROCEDURE

1. Place the bulb of the air thermometer in the metal can and fill the can with ice and water until the bulb is entirely covered. Watch the motion of the mercury in the U-tube and make sure it does not spill over into the glass bulb. This may be prevented by lowering the adjustable side of the U-tube. Also be careful that the mercury is not spilled from the open tube.

2. Adjust the open tube until the mercury level reaches the constant volume mark and wait for temperature equilibrium to be reached. Keep the mercury level at the constant volume mark until equilibrium is established, when the pressure remains constant. Stir the water well and record its temperature. Record the heights of the mercury levels in both arms of the U-tube.

3. Remove the ice and add enough water to cover the bulb. Heat the water slowly until its temperature is about 10°C. Remove the Bunsen burner and stir the water well. Keep the mercury on the side of the air bulb at the same level as in procedure (2) by raising the adjustable side of the U-tube. When equilibrium has been reached, record the temperature of the water and the height of the mercury in the open tube.

4. Repeat procedure (3), raising the temperature of the water in steps of about 10°, until the boiling point of the water is reached.

5. When the experiment is completed, lower the open tube to its original position in procedure (2), so that as the water cools, the mercury will not spill over into the glass bulb.

6. Take the barometer reading and record it.

DATA

Barometer reading...

Height of mercury in the closed tube...

Pressure coefficient of air at constant volume...

Accepted value of pressure coefficient...

Per cent discrepancy..

Value of the absolute zero from the graph..

Accepted value of the absolute zero...

Per cent discrepancy..

HEIGHT OF MERCURY IN THE OPEN TUBE	PARTIAL PRESSURE	TOTAL PRESSURE	TEMPERATURE OF THE BULB

CALCULATIONS

1. For each temperature calculate the partial pressure exerted on the air in the bulb by the difference in levels of the mercury column.

2. For each temperature calculate the total pressure in centimeters of mercury exerted on the air in the bulb by including the value of the atmospheric pressure.

3. Plot a curve using the values of the temperature as abscissas and the values of the total pressure as ordinates. To obtain more accurate results, construct the graph of the data using as large a scale as possible; that is, utilize the whole sheet of graph paper and extend the line only to 0°C.

4. From your graph compute the pressure coefficient of air at constant volume. Compare your result with the accepted value by calculating the per cent discrepancy.

5. From your graph determine the value of the absolute zero on the Centigrade scale; that is, calculate the temperature at which your graph predicts that the pressure would be zero. This may be done by means of a simple proportion, since the curve is a straight line. Compare your result with the accepted value by calculating the per cent discrepancy.

QUESTIONS

1. Mention two sources of error in this experiment and indicate how they might be eliminated.

2. What conclusion do you draw from the shape of your curve?

3. In an air thermometer like the one used in this experiment, the level of the mercury in the open tube is 20 cm. higher than that in the closed tube when the bulb is at 0°C. At what temperature will the level in the open tube be 40 cm. higher than in the closed tube? Assume standard atmospheric pressure.

4. A constant volume gas thermometer indicates an absolute pressure of 50.0 cm. of mercury at 0°C. and 68.3 cm. of mercury at 100°C. At what temperature will it read an absolute pressure of 56.1 cm. of mercury?

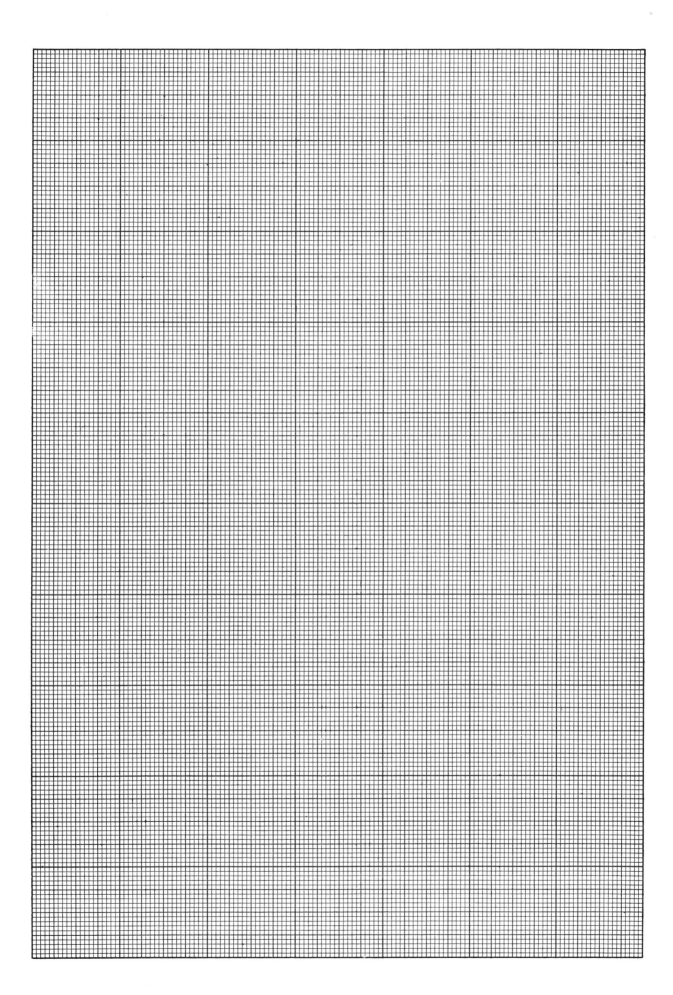

26
MAGNETIC FIELDS

A great deal can be learned about the action of magnets and the nature of magnetic forces by studying the space surrounding the magnets and plotting magnetic lines of forces. The purpose of this experiment is to study the magnetic field around a permanent magnet; in particular, to map the resultant field due to the magnetism of the earth and a permanent magnet.

THEORY

Magnetism is the property possessed by certain substances of attracting pieces of iron, nickel, or cobalt, and certain alloys. The poles of a magnet are regions where the magnetic properties are concentrated. Those poles which are attracted toward the north magnetic pole of the earth are called north poles, and those which are attracted toward the south magnetic pole are called south poles. Experiments show that like poles repel each other and unlike poles attract each other.

The region surrounding a magnet is called the magnetic field; it is the region in which magnetic forces due to the magnet are noticeable. The intensity of the magnetic field at any point is the force per unit north pole placed at that point. The direction of the magnetic field is the direction in which the north pole of a compass needle points, if placed at that point. A line whose direction at any point is the same as the direction of the magnetic field at that point is called a line of force. Magnetic lines of force, then, are imaginary lines which show the direction of the magnetic field or the direction in which a single north pole would travel if placed at that point. The magnetic field at any point near a magnet placed in the earth's magnetic field will be the resultant, or the vector sum, of the field due to the magnet alone and that due to the earth itself.

APPARATUS

1. Bar magnet.
2. U-magnet.
3. One 10-mm. compass.

4. Several large sheets of paper.
5. Four nonmagnetic weights.

PROCEDURE

1. Using the small compass, determine the north-south magnetic direction of the earth, for the location of your experiment; keep the magnets and all iron bodies far away from the compass.

2. Place the long edge of a large sheet of paper on the table, parallel to this direction, and anchor the ends by nonmagnetic weights.

3. Place the bar magnet in the center of the paper with its south pole pointing north. Outline the magnet on the paper; indicate its polarity and the direction of the earth's field.

4. Place the small compass near the north pole of the magnet and make a dot at each end of the needle. Do not use a pencil which is encased in metal, unless you are sure it does not affect the compass needle.

5. Move the compass forward until its south pole is exactly over the dot previously made at the north pole and make another dot at the north pole.

6. Repeat procedure (5) until the series of dots reaches the south pole of the large magnet or the edge of the paper.

7. Draw a smooth curve through the points and indicate the direction of the line of force by means of an arrow.

8. In a similar manner trace 10 or 12 lines of force, thus mapping the field of the magnet. Take points about 0.5 cm. apart near the ends of the magnet and 2 cm. apart near the middle, and repeat procedures (4–7). Draw enough lines of force to give a picture of the field over the entire paper.

9. There are two points, one near each end of the magnet, where the force of the earth's field is exactly equal and opposite to that of the magnet and the needle will have no tendency to turn in any particular direction.

These are called neutral points. Try to locate these points by tracing lines of force in their neighborhood very carefully.

10. Repeat procedures (1–9) using a new sheet of paper and a U-magnet.

QUESTIONS

1. Explain the similarity between this method of tracing lines of force and the use of iron filings sprinkled on a paper above the magnet.

2. Do lines of force represent lines along which the force on a unit pole is the same? Explain.

3. Do lines of force ever cross each other? Explain.

4. Mention two ways in which a bar of soft iron may be magnetized.

5. (a) What is meant by magnetic dip? (b) What is declination?

6. State Coulomb's law of force between magnetic poles.

7. The poles of a bar magnet have a strength of 200 electromagnetic units each and are 30 cm. apart. Calculate the magnitude and direction of the magnetic field strength at a point 30 cm. distant from each pole of the magnet.

27
OHM'S LAW

The most important principle in current electricity is that known as Ohm's law. This law, or some modification of it, is always used whenever it is necessary to calculate the current flowing in a circuit. If an electric charge is flowing through a conductor, we call this flow an electric current, and define it as the rate of flow of charge. A potential difference, or voltage, is necessary to make the current flow. It is found that the potential difference existing between the two ends of a conductor is directly proportional to the current flowing through the conductor. It is the object of this experiment to study Ohm's law and the laws relating to series and parallel direct current circuits.

THEORY

Ohm's law states that the value of the current in a conductor is equal to the voltage across the conductor divided by its resistance. Mathematically

$$I = \frac{E}{R} \quad \text{or} \quad E = RI$$

where E is the voltage across the conductor in volts, R is the resistance in ohms, and I is the value of the current in amperes.

When there is no source of electromotive force (e.m.f.) in a given portion of a circuit, the voltage between its ends is equal to the resistance times the current. When the circuit contains a source of e.m.f., as well as a resistance, then the current is obtained by dividing the total e.m.f. in the circuit by the total resistance.

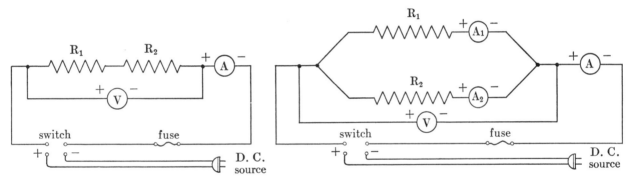

Fig. 25. Resistances in Series   Fig. 26. Resistances in Parallel

When resistances are connected in series (see Fig. 25), the current is the same throughout the circuit, while the sum of the voltage drops across the individual resistances is equal to the total applied voltage. The total resistance of the conductors in series is equal to the sum of the individual resistances. Thus

$$I = I_1 = I_2$$
$$E = E_1 + E_2$$
$$R = R_1 + R_2$$

When resistances are connected in parallel (see Fig. 26), the total current is equal to the sum of the currents through the individual resistances. The voltage is the same across each branch as well as across the whole group. The reciprocal of the total resistance is equal to the sum of the reciprocals of the individual resistances. Thus

$$I = I_1 + I_2$$
$$E = E_1 = E_2$$
$$\frac{1}{R} = \frac{1}{R_1} + \frac{1}{R_2}$$

In the above equations, I is the total current, I_1 is the current through resistance R_1, and I_2 is the current through resistance R_2. E is the voltage across the combination of resistances, E_1 is the voltage across R_1, and E_2 is the voltage across R_2.

APPARATUS

1. Tubular rheostat of about 400 ohms resistance.
2. Tubular rheostat of about 200 ohms resistance.
3. 110-volt D.C. supply.
4. D.C. ammeter (0–3 amperes).

5. D.C. voltmeter (0–150 volts).
6. One double pole, single throw switch with cord and plug.
7. Fuse.

PROCEDURE

CAUTION: Do not plug into the supply line or close the switch until your circuit has been approved by the instructor. The ammeter can be instantly and permanently ruined by an improper connection. Any changes in the circuit are to be made only after the plug has been pulled out. Have your circuit approved by the instructor every time you make any changes.

1. Connect the two rheostats in series, as shown in Fig. 25, with the ammeter and voltmeter properly connected in the circuit. Be sure that the fuse is included. Have your circuit approved by the instructor.

2. Plug into the 110-volt D.C. outlet and close the switch. Record the current through the circuit and the voltage drop across the series combination.

3. Open the switch. Connect the voltmeter across the two ends of R_1 without disturbing the rest of the circuit. Close the switch and record the voltage drop across R_1.

4. Repeat procedure (3) for R_2.

5. Connect the two rheostats in parallel, as shown in Fig. 26, with the ammeter at the point marked A and the voltmeter properly connected in the circuit. Be sure that the fuse is included.

6. Before closing the switch, have the circuit approved by the instructor. Record the voltage drop across the parallel combination and also the total current.

7. Open the switch. Connect the ammeter in the circuit at the point marked A_1 without disturbing the rest of the circuit. Close the switch and record the current through R_1.

8. Repeat procedure (7) for R_2.

DATA

	CURRENT (AMPERES)			VOLTAGE (VOLTS)			RESISTANCE (OHMS)		
	I	I_1	I_2	E	E_1	E_2	R	R_1	R_2
SERIES CONNECTION									
PARALLEL CONNECTION									

CALCULATIONS

1. Compute the values of the two resistances of the series connection and also the value of the total resistance by the application of Ohm's law, i.e. from the measured values of the current and the voltage drops in the data of procedures (2–4).

2. Calculate the values of the two resistances of the parallel connection and also of the total resistance by the application of Ohm's law, i.e. from the measured values of the currents and the voltage drop in the data of procedures (6–8).

3. Compute the value of the total resistance of the parallel combination by the application of the equation for parallel circuits, using the values of the resistances calculated in (1).

QUESTIONS

1. Show how your results check the formulas for the current, voltage, and resistance in series and parallel circuits.

2. In determining resistance by the ammeter-voltmeter method, why is it important to read both instruments simultaneously?

3. The resistance included between two points in a circuit is 10 ohms. How much resistance must be placed in parallel to make the total resistance 4 ohms?

4. A lamp whose resistance is 60 ohms and one whose resistance is 40 ohms are connected in parallel to a 120-volt line.   (a) What is the resistance of the combination?   (b) What is the current in each lamp?   (c) What would be the current if they were connected in series?   (d) What would then be the voltage drop across each lamp?

5. A lamp is connected to a 120-volt line.   When the switch is first turned on and the filament is cold, the current through the lamp is 8 amperes, but this drops quickly to 0.5 ampere when the filament is hot.   What is the per cent increase in resistance relative to the cold resistance due to the change in temperature?

6. Draw the circuit diagrams of the connections in procedures (1) and (5).

28
THE WHEATSTONE BRIDGE

The most convenient, and also the most accurate, method of measuring resistances of widely different values is by means of the Wheatstone bridge. The purpose of this experiment is to learn to use the slide wire and the box form of Wheatstone bridge and to measure the resistance of several metallic conductors, both individually and in series and parallel arrangements.

THEORY

A Wheatstone bridge is a circuit consisting of four resistors arranged as shown in Fig. 27. It is used for finding the value of an unknown resistance by comparing it with a known one. Three known and adjustable resistances are connected with the unknown resistance, a galvanometer, a dry cell, and a key, as shown in Fig. 27.

For a condition of balance no current flows through the galvanometer. Hence the current through R_1 is the same as the current through R_2, and the current through R_3 is the same as that through R_4. Also the potential drop across R_1 is equal to that across R_3

$$i_1 R_1 = i_2 R_3$$

Similarly, the potential drop across R_2 is equal to that across R_4

$$i_1 R_2 = i_2 R_4$$

Dividing the first equation by the second, one finds the relation

$$\frac{R_1}{R_2} = \frac{R_3}{R_4}$$

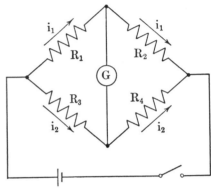

Fig. 27. The Wheatstone Bridge
Circuit Balanced

Therefore, if three of the resistances are known, the fourth may be calculated by using the above relation.

In the box form of the bridge, the resistances R_3 and R_4 appear as the ratio arms. In the slide wire form of the bridge, as shown in Fig. 28, the resistances R_3 and R_4 are replaced by the uniform wire AB with a sliding contact key at C. Since the wire is uniform, the resistances of the two portions are proportional to the lengths, hence the ratio R_3/R_4 is equal to the ratio AC/CB. If R_1 is represented by a variable known resistance R, and R_2 by the unknown resistance X, the relation becomes

$$\frac{R}{X} = \frac{AC}{CB}$$

From this the value of X may be calculated.

It is found that the resistance of a conductor depends on the material, the length, the area of cross section, and the temperature. For constant temperature, the resistance is given by

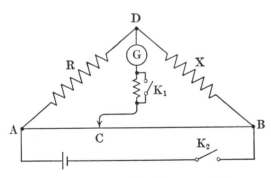

Fig. 28. The Slide Wire Wheatstone Bridge

$$R = \rho \frac{L}{A}$$

where R is the resistance in ohms, L is the length in centimeters, and A is the area of cross section in square centimeters. The proportionality factor ρ is known as the specific resistance, which is constant for a given temperature and depends only on the material used. Thus, the specific resistance of a substance is the resistance per centimeter of length when the cross section is one square centimeter.

In order to find ρ it is only necessary to measure the resistance of a measured length of wire of known diameter. The specific resistance is then calculated from the above equation.

APPARATUS

1. Slide wire form of Wheatstone bridge.
2. Box form of Wheatstone bridge.
3. Dry cell.
4. Galvanometer.
5. Standard decade resistance box calibrated in ohms.

6. Board with five coils of wire of unknown resistance.
7. Single pole, single throw switch.
8. Key.
9. 5000-ohm resistor.

PROCEDURE

1. Connect the slide wire form of the bridge as shown in Fig. 28. Let X be the unknown resistance of coil No. 1 and let R be the standard resistance box. Have the circuit approved by the instructor.

2. Measure the resistance of coil No. 1 with this bridge. To obtain a balance, set the sliding key in the center of the bridge wire and adjust the standard resistance until a minimum deflection of the galvanometer is observed. The sliding contact should be moved only when the contact edge is not touching the wire. To put a resistance in the circuit, a plug must be taken out of the resistance box.

3. For rough adjustments the galvanometer is connected in series with a high protective resistance. Leave the switch K_1 open. Set R equal to 10 ohms. Hold down key K_2 and then tap the contact key C. If the galvanometer shows a deflection, change the value of R and repeat. Continue this until the galvanometer shows a minimum deflection. Make the final adjustment by shifting the sliding key until no deflection is observed when the contact key C is tapped. Key K_2 should be held down only long enough to make the observation.

4. For the final adjustments, the protective resistance is short-circuited. When the galvanometer shows no deflection on tapping the contact key C, close the switch K_1. Now proceed with the adjustments, but do not shift the sliding key more than a fraction of a millimeter each time, until again the galvanometer shows no deflection. Record the setting of the standard resistance and of the sliding key.

5. Similarly measure the resistance of coils No. 2, 3, 4, and 5.

6. Measure the combined resistance of all the coils in series.

7. Connect coils 4 and 5 in parallel and measure their combined resistance.

8. Connect the box form of the bridge as shown in Fig. 27, making R_1 the unknown resistance of coil No. 1. R_2 is the standard known and adjustable resistance contained in the box. Measure the resistance of coil No. 1 by means of this bridge. Start with the dial set so that the ratio of the coils is 1 to 1. After an approximate balance is obtained, change the ratio step by step until the unknown resistance can be measured to four significant figures. Record the ratio of the coils and the setting of the standard resistance.

9. Repeat procedure (8) for coil No. 4.

DATA

TABLE I

MATERIAL	RESISTIVITY AT 20°C.
Copper	1.72×10^{-6} ohm-cm.
German Silver	33.0×10^{-6} ohm-cm.

TABLE II

COIL NO.	MATERIAL	GAUGE NO.	LENGTH IN METERS
1	Copper	22	10
2	Copper	28	10
3	Copper	22	20
4	Copper	28	20
5	German Silver	22	10

TABLE III

GAUGE NO.	DIAMETER IN CM.	AREA IN CM.^{2}
22	0.0644	0.00326
28	0.0321	0.00081

NOTE: The above data refer to a set of five coils supplied by Cenco. If some other set is used, the necessary data will be supplied by the instructor.

COIL NUMBER	R (OHMS)	AC (CM.)	CB (CM.)	X (OHMS)
1				
2				
3				
4				
5				
SERIES 1–5				
PARALLEL 4–5				

DATA FOR THE BOX FORM OF THE BRIDGE

COIL NUMBER	RATIO OF THE COILS	STANDARD RESISTANCE	X (OHMS)
1			
4			

CALCULATIONS

1. Compute the resistance of coils No. 1, 2, 3, 4, and 5 from the data of procedures (4–5).

2. Compute the resistance of all the coils in series from the data of procedure (6). Compare this value with the value to be expected from a series connection.

3. Compute the resistance of coils No. 4 and 5 in parallel from the data of procedure (7). Compare this value with the value to be expected from a parallel connection.

4. Calculate the specific resistance of the metals used from the data for coils No. 4 and 5. Compare your results with the accepted values by finding the per cent error.

5. Compare the values obtained with the slide wire bridge with those obtained with the box form of the bridge.

QUESTIONS

1. From your results show how the resistance is proportional to the length and inversely proportional to the area of cross section of a wire.

2. Why is the bridge method not adapted to measuring the hot resistance of an electric lamp?

3. Name three sources of error in using a slide wire bridge.

4. Why is it more accurate to set the sliding contact near the center of the bridge instead of near one end when the balance is obtained?

5. Assuming that there is an error of 1 mm. in locating the position of the contact on the slide wire, calculate the percentage error in determining the value of X when the contact was (a) at 50 cm., (b) at 5 cm. Suppose that $R = 10.0$ ohms in both cases, and $AB = 100.0$ cm.

6. Draw a diagram of the bridge as actually used in one of your measurements.

29
SPECIFIC RESISTANCE

It is found experimentally that if the temperature of a substance is kept constant, then the resistance depends upon its dimensions; it varies directly with the length of the wire and inversely as the cross-sectional area. The purpose of this experiment is to study some factors upon which resistance depends, and to determine the specific resistance of several metals.

THEORY

It is found that the resistance of a conductor depends on the material, the length, the area of cross section, and the temperature. For a constant temperature, the resistance is given by

$$R = \rho \frac{L}{A}$$

where R is the resistance of the conductor, in ohms, L is the length in centimeters, and A is the area of cross section in square centimeters. The proportionality factor ρ is known as the specific resistance, or resistivity, which is constant for a given temperature and depends only on the material used. Thus, the specific resistance of a substance is the resistance per centimeter of length when the cross section is one square centimeter.

In order to find ρ it is only necessary to measure the resistance of a measured length of wire of known diameter. The specific resistance is then calculated from the above equation. The resistance of each wire is measured by means of the slide wire form of Wheatstone bridge.

APPARATUS

1. Slide wire form of Wheatstone bridge.
2. Dry cell.
3. Galvanometer.
4. 5000-ohm resistor.
5. Standard decade resistance box calibrated in ohms.
6. Single pole, single throw switch.
7. Key.
8. Micrometer caliper.
9. Meter stick with caliper jaws.
10. Board with seven lengths of wire of unknown resistance. The board is about a meter long and the wires are mounted between binding posts. The first five lengths of wire consist of a single piece of copper wire. The sixth length is a piece of manganin wire, and the seventh length is a piece of nichrome wire.
11. Three short pieces of wire of the same diameter and material as the wires mounted on the board.

PROCEDURE

1. Measure the resistance of the first five lengths of wire mounted on the board by means of the Wheatstone bridge, making connections at the beginning of the first length and at the end of the fifth.

2. Connect the apparatus in the circuit of a Wheatstone bridge as shown in Fig. 29, where R is the resistance box and X is the unknown resistance. Before closing any switches, have the circuit approved by the instructor.

3. To obtain a balance, set the sliding key in the center of the bridge wire and adjust the standard resistance until a minimum deflection of the galvanometer is observed. The sliding contact should be moved only when the contact edge is not touching the wire.

4. For rough adjustments the galvanometer is connected in series with a high protective resistance. Leave the switch K_1 open. Set R equal to 10 ohms. Hold down key K_2 and then tap the contact key C. If the galvanometer shows a deflection, change the value of R and repeat. Continue this until the galvanometer shows a minimum deflection. Make the final adjustment by shifting the sliding key until no deflection is observed when the contact key C is tapped. Key K_2 should be held down only long enough to make the observation.

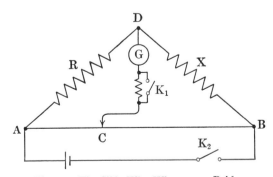

Fig. 29.   The Slide Wire Wheatstone Bridge

5. For the final adjustments the protective resistance is short-circuited. When the galvanometer shows no deflection on tapping the contact key C, close the switch K_1. Now proceed with the adjustments, but do not shift the sliding key by more than a fraction of a millimeter each time, until the galvanometer again shows no deflection. Record the setting of the standard resistance and of the sliding key.

6. Similarly measure the resistance of the sixth length of wire, which is a piece of manganin wire.

7. Measure the resistance of the seventh length of wire, which is a piece of nichrome wire.

8. Measure the length of each wire by means of the meter stick calipers, adjusting the caliper jaws so that they measure the distance between the binding posts where the wire is mounted.

9. The three short pieces of wire are of the same diameter and material as the wires mounted on the board. Measure the diameter of each piece of wire at four different points with the micrometer caliper. Record all four readings of the diameter of each wire, estimating to one tenth of the smallest scale division. The readings should be to 0.0001 centimeter.

10. In a similar manner, take and record four independent readings of the zero setting of the micrometer to 0.0001 centimeter. In your calculations be sure to properly include the algebraic sign of the zero correction.

DATA

WIRE	R OHMS	AC CM.	CB CM.	X OHMS	RESISTIVITY OHM–CM.	RESISTIVITY FROM TABLE VII, APPENDIX
COPPER						
MANGANIN						
NICHROME						

WIRE	MICROMETER READINGS					DIAMETER CM.	AREA CM.^{2}	LENGTH CM.
	1	2	3	4	AVERAGE			
COPPER								
MANGANIN								
NICHROME								
ZERO READING								

CALCULATIONS

1. Compute the average of the readings for the diameter of each wire, as well as for the zero reading of the micrometer. Calculate and record the diameter of each wire, properly corrected for the zero reading of the micrometer.

2. Compute the cross section of each wire in square centimeters.

3. Calculate the values of the resistances measured.

4. Compute the specific resistance for each metal used.

5. Look up the values of the specific resistances in Table VII, Appendix, and record them.

QUESTIONS

1. How does the resistance of a wire vary with the resistivity?

2. What would be the effect of a change of temperature on the resistivity?

3. How is the operation of the Wheatstone bridge affected by any changes in voltage of the cell used? Why?

4. What is the resistance of a copper bus bar 10 meters long and 0.3 × 0.3 cm. in cross section?

5. Calculate the resistance of 40 miles of No. 22 B and S gauge copper wire. The diameter of the wire is 0.0644 cm. The value of the specific resistance is given in Table VII, Appendix.

6. The temperature coefficient of resistance for copper is 0.00393 per degree Centigrade. Assuming room temperature to be 22°C., compute the specific resistance of copper at 0°C. from your measurements.

7. Assume that there was an error of 0.001 cm. in measuring the diameter of the copper wire used in the experiment. Calculate the error that this would introduce into your value of the specific resistance.

30

GALVANOMETER SENSITIVITY

The galvanometer forms the basis of practically all electrical measuring instruments. Hence it is very important to understand the working principle of the galvanometer and the type of measurements that can be made with it. It is the purpose of this experiment to measure the current, megohm, and voltage sensitivities of a galvanometer.

THEORY

A galvanometer is an instrument for measuring small electric currents. It consists essentially of a coil of fine wire mounted so that it can rotate in the field of a permanent magnet. When a current flows through the coil, it becomes an electromagnet. The field of the permanent magnet exerts a torque on the coil and makes it rotate until equilibrium is established between the torque due to the field and that exerted by a restoring spring or by the suspension of the coil. The angle of rotation is directly proportional to the current flowing through the coil, if the field of the permanent magnet is uniform in the region of the coil.

The sensitivity of a galvanometer is expressed in several ways. The current sensitivity is the current necessary to produce a deflection of one millimeter on a scale one meter distant. The megohm sensitivity is the resistance which has to be placed in series with the galvanometer coil to reduce the deflection to one millimeter on a scale one meter distant when a potential difference of one volt is applied across the combination. The voltage sensitivity is the voltage which must be impressed on the galvanometer terminals in order to produce a deflection of one millimeter on a scale one meter distant.

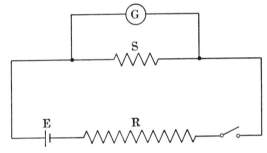

Fig. 30. Circuit for Measurement of Galvanometer Sensitivity

The galvanometer is connected with the high resistance, the shunt, the dry cell, and the key as shown in Fig. 30. The current through the galvanometer is given by

$$i = \frac{sE}{R(g + s)}$$

where E is the applied voltage, R is the high resistance, g is the resistance of the galvanometer, s is the shunt resistance, and i is the current through the galvanometer. The above expression is derived by the application of Ohm's law on the assumption that the joint resistance of the shunt and galvanometer is negligible in comparison with R.

APPARATUS

1. Reflecting galvanometer, mounted telescope, and scale.
2. Dry cell.
3. Key.
4. Meter stick.
5. 5000-ohm resistor.
6. Resistance box used as shunt (0–40 ohms).
7. D.C. voltmeter (0–3 volts).

PROCEDURE

1. Measure the voltage of the dry cell with the voltmeter and record it.

2. Connect the apparatus as shown in the diagram. Start with a low value of s (about one ohm). Have your circuit approved by the instructor. Close the key and observe the galvanometer deflection. Increase the value of the shunt resistance s, in small steps, until the deflection is almost full scale. Record the galvanometer deflection and the corresponding values of R and s.

3. Repeat procedure (2) taking a series of five readings and using different values of s, so that the galvanometer deflections range from a small value to the full-scale value.

4. Reverse the terminals of the cell and repeat procedure (3).

5. Measure the distance from the mirror of the galvanometer to the scale.

6. Record the resistance of the galvanometer.

DATA

Voltage of the dry cell. . . . .

Value of the high resistance. . . . .

Distance from mirror to scale. . . . .

Galvanometer resistance. . . . .

SHUNT RESISTANCE	GALVANOMETER DEFLECTION			GALVANOMETER CURRENT
	RIGHT	LEFT	AVERAGE	

CALCULATIONS

1. Calculate the average of the readings of the galvanometer deflection for each value of the shunt resistance.

2. Calculate the current through the galvanometer for each value of the shunt resistance. When comparing the galvanometer current with the corresponding galvanometer deflection, use the average of the readings of the galvanometer deflection.

3. Compute the current sensitivity, the megohm sensitivity, and the voltage sensitivity of the galvanometer, using the value of the current obtained for full-scale deflection.

138

QUESTIONS

1. How does the current through the galvanometer vary with the galvanometer deflection?

2. What is the object of reversing the terminals of the cell in procedure (4)?

3. Why must R be very large compared to the resistance of the galvanometer?

4. A galvanometer whose resistance is 125 ohms has a current sensitivity of 10^{-8} ampere. (a) What is its megohm sensitivity? (b) What is its voltage sensitivity?

5. A dry cell whose e.m.f. is 1.5 volts furnishes current to two resistances of 2 ohms and 10,000 ohms in series. Across the 2-ohm resistance is connected a galvanometer whose resistance is 150 ohms. The deflection produced on a scale 50 cm. from the mirror is 10 cm. Calculate the current through the galvanometer and the current sensitivity.

31

VOLTMETER AND AMMETER

It is extremely important to understand the operation of electrical measuring instruments, because they are constantly used in making electrical measurements. A galvanometer is an instrument for measuring very small electric currents. An ammeter, which measures large currents, is a galvanometer with a shunt resistance connected in parallel with it. A voltmeter, which measures voltage, is a galvanometer with a large series resistance. The purpose of this experiment is to convert a galvanometer into a voltmeter giving full-scale deflection for 3 volts and into an ammeter giving full-scale deflection for 3 amperes.

THEORY

A galvanometer is an instrument for measuring small currents. It consists essentially of a coil of fine wire mounted so that it can rotate in the field of a permanent magnet. When a current flows through the coil, it becomes an electromagnet. The field of the permanent magnet exerts a torque on the coil and makes it rotate until equilibrium is established between the torque due to the field and that exerted by a restoring spring, or by the suspension of the coil. The angle of rotation is directly proportional to the current flowing through the coil, if the field of the permanent magnet is uniform in the region of the coil.

A galvanometer may be converted into an ammeter by placing a suitable shunt in parallel with the coil to permit the flow of a larger current through the meter than the galvanometer coil will carry, and of such a value as to make the meter read in amperes. Similarly it may be converted into a voltmeter by placing a large resistance in series with the coil and calibrating the scale in volts to indicate the potential difference across the terminals of the meter.

Before a galvanometer can be converted into a voltmeter or ammeter, it is necessary to know the resistance of the coil and the galvanometer constant.

The resistance of the galvanometer is measured by a special method. A known e.m.f. V is connected in series with a large resistance R_1 and the coil, whose resistance is r, as shown in Fig. 31. The value of R_1 is so

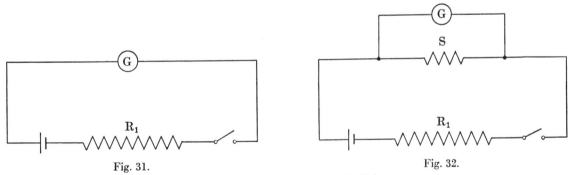

Fig. 31.   Fig. 32.

Circuits for Measuring the Resistance of a Galvanometer

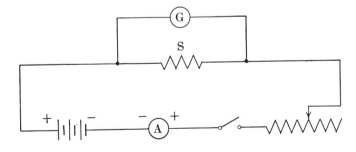

Fig. 33.   Circuit for Using a Galvanometer as an Ammeter

chosen that almost a full scale deflection d_1 is obtained. A shunt resistance S is now connected in parallel with r (see Fig. 32), the value of S being so chosen that the new deflection d_2 is about one half of d_1. The value of R_1

is then altered to R_2, so adjusted that the deflection is again d_1. By applying Ohm's law to these circuits it can be shown that the resistance r of the galvanometer is given by

$$r = S\left(\frac{R_1 - R_2}{R_2}\right)$$

The galvanometer constant, or current sensitivity, is the current in amperes necessary to produce a deflection of one scale division. Hence if the deflection produced by a certain current is multiplied by the galvanometer constant, the value of the current in amperes is obtained. The galvanometer constant K, then, is given by the relation

$$i_1 = Kd_1 = \frac{V}{R_1 + r}$$

where i_1 is the current through the coil producing the scale deflection d_1.

Let R be the series resistance which will convert the galvanometer into a voltmeter and r the resistance of the galvanometer. The current i flowing through the coil when a voltage V is applied across the terminals of the voltmeter will be

$$i = \frac{V}{R + r}$$

and will thus be proportional to V, since the resistances are constant. But the deflection d is also proportional to the current, $i = Kd$, where K is the constant of the galvanometer and d is the deflection in scale divisions. Thus

$$\frac{V}{R + r} = Kd \quad \text{or} \quad \frac{V'}{R + r} = Kd'$$

where now V' represents the range of the voltmeter, i.e. the full-scale reading, and d' is the number of divisions for full-scale deflection.

Let S be the shunt resistance which will convert the galvanometer into an ammeter (see Fig. 33) and r the resistance of the galvanometer. Also, let I_g be the current through the galvanometer, I_s the current through the shunt, and I the total current, or the current through the ammeter. Then, since r and S are in parallel, the current through the galvanometer is given by

$$I_g = I\frac{S}{r + S}$$

If the ammeter is to give a deflection of n divisions when I amperes pass through it, then $I_g = Kn$, and we get

$$I\frac{S}{r + S} = Kn$$

where I is the current through the ammeter for full-scale deflection of n divisions.

APPARATUS

1. Portable galvanometer.
2. D.C. voltmeter (0–3 volts).
3. D.C. ammeter (0–3 amperes).
4. Dry cell.
5. Decade resistance box (4000 ohms).
6. Decade resistance box (400 ohms).

7. Single pole, single throw switch.
8. Storage battery.
9. Tubular rheostat (about 30 ohms).
10. Piece of No. 28 copper wire about a foot long.
11. Wooden block with two binding posts.
12. Two short, heavy leads.

PROCEDURE

1. Measure the voltage of the dry cell with the voltmeter and record it.

2. Connect the dry cell in series with the resistance box, the galvanometer, and the switch, as shown in Fig. 31. Make the resistance R_1 equal to 3000 ohms.

3. Before closing the switch, have the circuit approved by the instructor. Now close the switch and record the galvanometer deflection d_1.

4. Open the switch. Connect the other resistance box in parallel with the galvanometer, as shown in Fig. 32, making S equal to 300 ohms, and leaving R_1 connected as before. Close the switch and record the value of the galvanometer deflection d_2.

142

5. Now decrease the value of R_1 in small steps, checking up on the galvanometer deflection each time, until the deflection is again exactly equal to d_1. This should be done carefully, and at no time should the value of R_1 be less than 1000 ohms. Record the final value of the resistance, calling it R_2.

6. Calculate the resistance of the galvanometer, r, and the galvanometer constant K, using the observed values of the deflections.

7. Calculate the series resistance R which will convert the galvanometer into a voltmeter giving full-scale deflection for 3 volts.

8. Connect the galvanometer in series with the calculated value of R, using the decade resistance box. This combination is now a voltmeter. Use it to measure the voltage of the dry cell, making sure that R is in series and that it is included in the circuit. Record this voltage.

9. Calculate the shunt resistance S which will convert the galvanometer into an ammeter giving 3 amperes for full-scale deflection. Compute the length of No. 28 copper wire which has the required resistance. Secure a piece of this wire and connect the correct length in parallel with the galvanometer. Make the connections on the binding posts mounted on the block provided for this purpose, connecting the short heavy leads directly to the galvanometer. Allow 0.01 ohm for the resistance of these leads. Make sure that all connections are tight. This combination is now an ammeter.

10. Connect your ammeter combination in series with the regular ammeter, the rheostat set with all of its resistance in the circuit, the switch, and the storage battery, as shown in Fig. 33. Before closing the switch, have your circuit approved by the instructor.

11. Close the switch. Adjust the rheostat until the standard ammeter reads 0.5 ampere. Record the reading of your ammeter. Now adjust the rheostat to make the standard ammeter read 1.0, 1.5, 2.0, and 2.5 amperes, recording the reading of your ammeter each time.

DATA

QUANTITIES	V	R_1	d_1	S	d_2	R_2	r	K
UNITS								
READINGS								

VOLTMETER

Resistance R for full-scale deflection of 3 volts. . . . .

Reading of this voltmeter for the voltage of the dry cell. . . . .

AMMETER

Shunt resistance S for full-scale deflection of 3 amperes. . . . .

Length of No. 28 copper wire required. . . . .

CURRENT IN STANDARD AMMETER	0.5 AMP.	1.0 AMP.	1.5 AMP.	2.0 AMP.	2.5 AMP.
READING OF GALVANOMETER USED AS AMMETER					

QUESTIONS

1. Calculate the series resistance R which will convert your galvanometer into a voltmeter reading 150 volts for full-scale deflection.

2. Calculate the shunt resistance S which will convert your galvanometer into an ammeter reading 0.3 ampere for full-scale deflection.

3. How should an ammeter be connected in a circuit?

4. How should a voltmeter be connected in a circuit?

5. A dry cell whose e.m.f. is 1.5 volts furnishes current to two resistances of 2 ohms and 16,000 ohms in series. Across the 2-ohm resistance is connected a galvanometer whose resistance is 200 ohms. The deflection produced is 10 scale divisions. Calculate the current through the galvanometer and the current sensitivity.

6. A certain 3-volt voltmeter requires a current of 10 milliamperes to produce a full-scale deflection. How may it be converted into a voltmeter with a range of 150 volts?

32

JOULE'S LAW. MECHANICAL EQUIVALENT OF HEAT

Whenever an electric current is flowing through a conductor, a certain amount of electrical energy is transformed into heat energy, just as mechanical energy may be transformed into heat energy by friction. The object of this experiment is to measure the mechanical equivalent of heat by the electrical method. The electrical energy used may be calculated by measuring the current, the voltage, and the time; while the number of calories liberated in the process is measured by means of a calorimeter.

THEORY

Energy exists in many forms and is measured in many different units. The purpose of this experiment is to find the ratio between the mechanical unit and the heat unit of energy. The ratio is found by using the electric current as a source of heat and equating the energy supplied by the current, expressed in mechanical units, to the same energy expressed in heat units.

Whenever a current flows through a conductor, a certain amount of heat is developed. The work done by the electric current is given by

$$W = VIt$$

where W is the work expressed in joules; V is the potential difference between the terminals of the conductor in volts; I is the current in amperes; and t is the time that the current flows in seconds. But, by Ohm's law

$$V = IR$$

so that the above relation becomes

$$W = I^2Rt$$

This relation is known as Joule's law of heating. Expressed in words, the law states that when an electric current flows through a pure resistance, the quantity of heat produced in the conductor is proportional to the time of current flow, to the resistance, and to the square of the current. In the above expression, W is the electrical energy dissipated in the conductor expressed in joules; I is the current in amperes; R is the resistance of the conductor in ohms; and t is the time of current flow in seconds.

From the principle of conservation of energy, whenever work is done in developing heat, the quantity of heat produced is always proportional to the work done. Thus

$$W = JH$$

where W is the work expressed in joules; H is the heat energy produced, in calories; and J is the mechanical equivalent of heat, which is the number of joules required to produce one calorie.

If the heat energy is used to raise the temperature of the water contained in a calorimeter, then

$$H = (m + m_1s_1 + m_2s_2)(t_2 - t_1)$$

where H is the heat energy produced in calories; m is the mass of water in grams; m_1 is the mass and s_1 is the specific heat of the calorimeter; m_2 is the mass and s_2 is the specific heat of the immersion heater; t_1 is the initial temperature of the water; and t_2 is the final temperature.

If the heat energy developed in a conductor is to be expressed in calories, then the mathematical statement of Joule's law becomes

$$H = \frac{I^2Rt}{4.186}$$

where H is the heat developed in the conductor.

APPARATUS

1. Immersion heater.
2. Calorimeter.
3. Thermometer (0–50°C.).
4. Stop watch or stop clock.
5. D.C. voltmeter (0–150 volts).
6. D.C. ammeter (0–3 amperes).
7. Equal arm balance and weights.
8. Tubular rheostat of about 100-ohms resistance.
9. Source of 110-volts D.C.

PROCEDURE

1. Weigh the immersion heater. Connect the immersion heater, along with the ammeter, voltmeter, fuse, and control rheostat, as shown in Fig. 34. Have the circuit approved by the instructor. Do not close the switch.

2. Weigh the empty calorimeter. Pour cold water (as cold as it will run from the tap) into the calorimeter until it is two thirds full. Replace the calorimeter in its container, and immerse the heater.

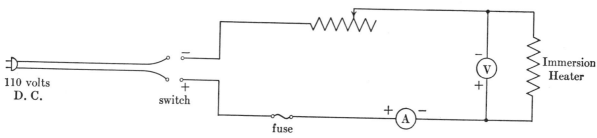

Fig. 34. Circuit for Measuring the Mechanical Equivalent of Heat

3. Do not close the switch unless the heater is immersed in water. Close the switch and adjust the current, by means of the control rheostat, to the value suggested by your instructor; then open the switch.

4. Stir the water; then measure its temperature, estimating to the nearest tenth of a degree.

5. Close the switch and start the stop watch at the same instant. Record the voltmeter and ammeter readings. Keep the current constant by means of the control rheostat. Record the voltage every minute, and use the average of the readings for the voltage. Use the heater as a stirrer and stir the water from time to time until the temperature of the water is about 10°C. above room temperature.

6. Open the switch and stop the watch at the same instant. Record the time. Continue to stir the water until the maximum temperature is reached. Record this temperature to the nearest tenth of a degree.

7. Weigh the calorimeter with the water, but without the immersion heater or thermometer.

DATA

Temperature of the room...

Weight of the immersion heater...

Specific heat of the immersion heater..

Weight of the empty calorimeter..

Specific heat of the calorimeter...

Current..

Initial temperature of the water...

Final temperature of the water...

Temperature rise...

Average voltage..

Time...

Weight of the calorimeter with water...

Weight of the water..

Electrical energy used...

Heat energy developed..

Calculated value of the mechanical equivalent of heat....................................

Value of the mechanical equivalent of heat from Table I, Appendix........................

Per cent error...

CALCULATIONS

1. Calculate the electrical energy used in joules and the heat energy developed in calories.

2. Compute the mechanical equivalent of heat. Compare your value with the accepted value by calculating the per cent error.

QUESTIONS

1. Discuss the principal sources of error in this experiment and justify the difference between your value of the mechanical equivalent of heat and the correct value.

2. Using your data, calculate how long it would take to heat the water from 20°C. to 100°C. by sending a current of 2 amperes through the same coil immersed in the water.

3. In question (2) how long would it take if a current of 4 amperes were used?

4. Give three examples of desirable heating effects of an electric current and three examples of undesirable ones.

5. State the factors on which the heating effect of an electric current depends and how it varies with each.

6. What must be the resistance of a coil of wire in order that a current of 2 amperes flowing through the coil may produce 1000 calories of heat per minute?

7. What is the purpose of starting with the temperature of the water lower than room temperature and ending about the same amount above room temperature?

33
ELECTROLYSIS

One of the important effects of an electric current is the chemical effect. Whenever an electric current is flowing through a conducting solution, certain chemical changes take place and the substance in solution is decomposed. The object of this experiment is to study the chemical action of an electric current and to determine the electrochemical equivalent of hydrogen and oxygen.

THEORY

Certain liquids have the property of conducting an electric current; these are called electrolytes. The most common of these are water solutions of acids, bases, or salts. When an electric current is passing through such a solution, certain chemical changes take place, and the process is called electrolysis. Thus electrolysis is the decomposition of a chemical compound by means of an electric current. The laws governing this phenomenon, Faraday's two laws of electrolysis, may be stated as follows:

1. The mass of a substance liberated in an electrolytic cell is proportional to the quantity of electricity passing through the cell; that is, to the current multiplied by the time during which the current flows.

2. When the same quantity of electricity is passed through different electrolytic cells, the masses of the substances liberated are proportional to their chemical equivalents. The chemical equivalent of a substance is equal to its atomic weight in grams divided by its valence.

The mass deposited, then, is proportional to the product of the current and the time. The constant of proportionality is called the electrochemical equivalent of a substance, which is the quantity deposited per second by a current of one ampere, or the quantity deposited by one coulomb of electricity. Hence the mass deposited is given by the relation

$$M = ZIt$$

where M is the mass in grams, I is the current in amperes, t is the time in seconds, and Z is the electrochemical equivalent in grams per coulomb.

In the decomposition of water by electrolysis, an electric current is passed through a cell containing a dilute solution of sulfuric acid. Hydrogen gas is liberated in one arm of the apparatus and oxygen gas in the other. The volumes of the gases formed when a known current flows for a known period of time are measured. The volumes under standard conditions of temperature and pressure may be calculated from the known conditions by application of the general gas law

$$\frac{P_o V_o}{T_o} = \frac{P_1 V_1}{T_1}$$

where P_o, V_o, and T_o refer to standard conditions, that is, the volume of a gas when the pressure is 76 cm. of mercury and the temperature is 0° Centigrade; P_1, V_1, and T_1 refer to any other set of conditions. In the above equation, however, the temperature must be expressed on the absolute scale. From the volume and the density of a gas, its mass may be calculated. Thus from the definition of density, we have

$$D = \frac{M}{V}$$

where D is the density in grams per cubic centimeter, M is the mass in grams, and V is the volume of the gas under standard conditions.

Finally, the electrochemical equivalent is obtained by solving the equation given above for Z.

APPARATUS

1. Electrolytic cell.
2. D.C. ammeter (0–1 ampere).
3. Tubular rheostat (about 200 ohms).
4. Switch.

5. Stop watch or stop clock.
6. Meter stick calipers.
7. Source of 110-volts D.C.
8. Barometer.

PROCEDURE

1. Connect the electrolytic cell in series with the ammeter, rheostat, and switch, as shown in Fig. 35. The electrodes are alike; hence either one may be used as anode. The ammeter should be connected on the range which shows one ampere full scale, or if this range is lacking, on the next higher range. Have the circuit approved by the instructor before closing the switch.

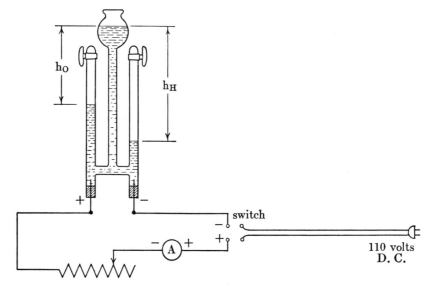

Fig. 35. Electrolysis of Water

2. Begin with all of the resistance of the rheostat in the circuit. Close the switch; then adjust the rheostat to produce a current of exactly 0.5 ampere. Now open the switch. Ask the instructor to let out the gases which have formed in the cell. The apparatus is now ready for operation.

3. Close the switch and start the stop watch at the same instant. Keep the current at exactly 0.5 ampere by means of the control rheostat.

4. Keep the current flowing until 50 c.c. of hydrogen have collected. Open the switch and stop the watch at the same instant. Record the exact time to the second.

5. Record the exact volumes of hydrogen and oxygen formed to 0.1 c.c.

6. Measure h_H and h_O with the meter stick calipers, and record the readings.

7. Record the barometric pressure.

8. Record the room temperature. Look up the value of the vapor pressure of water for this temperature and record it.

DATA

	CURRENT	TIME	h_H	h_O	h_H	h_O	BAROMETRIC PRESSURE	ROOM TEMP.	VAPOR PRESSURE OF WATER
UNITS					CM. HG	CM. HG			

	VOLUME	PRESSURE	VOLUME AT STANDARD TEMPERATURE AND PRESSURE	DENSITY	MASS	ELECTRO-CHEMICAL EQUIVALENT	VALUE OF Z FROM TABLE VIII, APPENDIX	% ERROR
UNITS								
HYDROGEN								
OXYGEN								

CALCULATIONS

1. Compute the values of h_H and h_O in cm. of mercury. The density of mercury is 13.6 grams per cubic centimeter.

2. Compute the pressure on the hydrogen; the value of h_H in cm. of mercury has to be added to the barometric pressure and the vapor pressure of water must be subtracted from the total. Similarly, compute the pressure on the oxygen.

3. Calculate the volume of the hydrogen and that of the oxygen under standard conditions (0°C. and 76.0 cm. of mercury) by using the general gas law.

4. Calculate the mass of the hydrogen and that of the oxygen.

5. Calculate the electrochemical equivalent for both hydrogen and oxygen. Compare your values with the known values in Table VIII, Appendix, by computing the per cent error.

QUESTIONS

1. Compute the time it would require a current of one ampere to liberate 22.4 liters of hydrogen under standard conditions of temperature and pressure.

2. How many grams of water would be decomposed by one coulomb?

3. Is the sulfuric acid used up in the process of the electrolysis of water? Explain.

4. An ammeter reading 0.5 ampere is connected in series with a coulomb-meter which deposits 1.50 grams of silver in 40 minutes. What is the percentage error of the reading of the ammeter?

5. A current flowing through copper sulfate and silver nitrate coulomb-meters connected in series deposits 0.200 gram of copper in 10 minutes. How much silver is deposited?

6. Assume a spoon has a total area of 20 square centimeters. It is to be coated with silver 0.01 mm. thick. The current is 0.05 ampere. Compute the mass of silver needed and the time required to deposit this amount of silver.

34

THE POTENTIOMETER

One of the most important instruments used in the electrical laboratory is the potentiometer, which is an instrument for measuring voltages, or potential differences. The potentiometer possesses a great advantage over the voltmeter because, under operating conditions, it draws no current from the source whose voltage is being measured and thus does not disturb the potential difference to be measured. The potentiometer is capable of very high precision and is very easy to handle. One of its most important uses is the calibration of electrical measuring instruments, such as voltmeters and ammeters. The purpose of this experiment is to study the slide wire form of the potentiometer and to measure several electromotive forces.

THEORY

The electromotive force (e.m.f.) of a cell is its terminal voltage when no current is flowing through it. The terminal voltage is the potential difference between the electrodes of a cell. A voltmeter cannot be used to measure the electromotive force of a cell accurately, because the voltmeter itself draws some current. For this purpose a potentiometer is used. This is a device for measuring the e.m.f. of a cell when no current is flowing. It employs a null method of measuring potential difference, so that when a balance is reached and the reading is being taken, no current is drawn from the source to be measured.

In this method a continuously variable potential difference is produced by sending a steady current from a storage battery through a uniform bare slide wire. The cell to be measured is connected through a galvanometer and a protective resistance to two points on the wire, in such a way that its e.m.f. opposes the potential difference in the wire. To obtain a condition of balance, one of the contacts is moved along the wire until no current flows through the galvanometer. The potential difference in this portion of the wire is now equal to the e.m.f. of the cell. This process is repeated with a standard cell. Since the wire is uniform, the length of the wire spanned is proportional to the potential drop. Thus the e.m.f. of any cell can be compared with that of a standard cell.

The circuit used in this experiment is shown in Fig. 36. E_s is the standard cell, E_x is the cell whose e.m.f. is to be measured. K_2 is the key which connects either cell in the circuit. G is the galvanometer, R_1 is the pro-

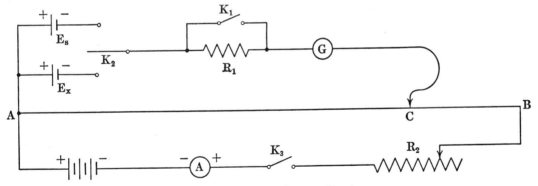

Fig. 36. The Potentiometer Circuit

tective resistance, and R_2 is the tubular rheostat. Since the electromotive force of the standard cell is equal to the potential drop in the length of the wire spanned for a condition of balance and the same is true for the unknown cell, the e.m.f.'s are proportional to the lengths of wire spanned. Thus

$$\frac{E_x}{E_s} = \frac{L_x}{L_s}$$

The unknown e.m.f. is then given by

$$E_x = E_s \frac{L_x}{L_s}$$

where E_x is the unknown e.m.f., E_s is the e.m.f. of the standard cell, L_x is the length of the wire (AC) used for the unknown cell, and L_s is the length of the wire used for the standard cell for a condition of balance.

157

APPARATUS

1. Slide wire potentiometer.
2. Galvanometer.
3. Protective resistance (5000 ohms).
4. Single pole, double throw switch.
5. 6 volt storage battery.
6. Tubular rheostat (about 20 ohms).

7. Standard cell.
8. Good dry cell, or a dry cell which tests 1.5 volts.
9. Old dry cell, or a dry cell which tests about 1.0 volt.
10. D.C. ammeter (0–1 ampere).
11. D.C. voltmeter (0–3 volts).
12. Two knife switches.

PROCEDURE

1. Connect the apparatus as shown in Fig. 36. R_1 is the protective resistance and R_2 is the tubular rheostat. Keep all switches open while connections are being made. Have your circuit approved by the instructor.

2. *Leave switch K_1 open.* Set R_2 for maximum resistance and then close switch K_3; adjust the rheostat so that the current through the wire is exactly 0.50 ampere. Keep this current constant throughout the experiment by means of the control rheostat.

3. Close switch K_2 in the direction to put the standard cell E_s into the circuit and find the setting of the contact point C for a position of balance. For rough adjustments the galvanometer is connected in series with a high protective resistance. Press the contact C. The galvanometer will probably deflect. Find a point C where there is no deflection.

4. For the final adjustments the protective resistance is short-circuited by a switch. When the galvanometer shows no deflection on pressing C, close switch K_1. Again locate C so that the galvanometer shows no deflection by moving the point of contact a very short distance each time. Closing K_1 increases the sensitivity of the galvanometer many times and allows point C to be located more accurately. Record the final setting of the contact point and the known value of the e.m.f. of the standard cell.

5. *Open the switch K_1.* Move K_2 in the direction to include the good dry cell instead of the standard cell. Repeat procedures (3–4) to measure the e.m.f. of the good dry cell. Record the setting of the contact point.

6. Again *open the switch K_1.* Replace the good dry cell by the old dry cell. Repeat procedures (3–4) to measure the e.m.f. of the old dry cell. Record the setting of the contact point.

7. Measure the terminal voltage of the good dry cell and of the old dry cell with the voltmeter and record the values. Do not measure the voltage of the standard cell with a voltmeter, because the current taken by the voltmeter will cause the cell to change so that it will no longer be standard.

8. Compute the e.m.f. of the good dry cell from the data of procedures (4) and (5).

9. Compute the e.m.f. of the old dry cell from the data of procedures (4) and (6).

DATA

KIND OF CELL	AC CM.	E.M.F. VOLTS	TERMINAL VOLTAGE VOLTMETER READING
STANDARD CELL			
GOOD DRY CELL			
OLD DRY CELL			

QUESTIONS

1. Compare the e.m.f. of the good dry cell with that of the old dry cell. Compare the terminal voltages. Explain these results.

2. If you use a meter wire of uniform cross section having a resistance of 5 ohms with a storage battery whose e.m.f. is 6 volts and whose internal resistance is 0.2 ohm, what resistance must be placed in series with the wire in order that the potential drop per millimeter shall be exactly 1 millivolt? This will be a direct reading potentiometer.

3. The voltage of the storage battery was not measured or used in the calculations. Why is the value of this voltage not needed?

4. The voltage of the unknown cell as indicated by the voltmeter should be less than that found by the potentiometer. Explain why.

5. A cell whose e.m.f. is 1.52 volts is connected to a voltmeter which records 1.48 volts. If the resistance of the voltmeter is 200 ohms, what is the internal resistance of the cell?

6. How can a potentiometer be made direct reading in volts on a slide wire?

35

MEASUREMENT OF CAPACITANCE BY THE BRIDGE METHOD

In many practical applications of electricity it is found necessary to increase the capacity of a conductor for storing an electric charge. The stored charge can then be used to obtain pulses of current for various purposes. This is done by using a condenser, which generally consists of two metal plates separated by an insulator. If a potential difference is applied to the plates, these will acquire equal and opposite charges, the value of the charge being proportional to the applied voltage. The factor of proportionality, which is characteristic of the particular condenser, is called the capacitance of the condenser. The object of this experiment is to study the bridge method for the comparison of capacitance and to check the laws of series and parallel connections of condensers.

THEORY

A condenser consists of two metal plates separated by an insulating material which is called a dielectric. A condenser is capable of storing an electric charge. When the plates are connected to two points between which there is a difference of potential, each plate will acquire an electric charge whose magnitude is proportional to the potential difference between the plates; the charges on the two plates are equal and opposite. The ratio between the quantity of charge on one plate of the condenser and the potential difference between the plates is a constant for a given condenser and is called the capacitance of the condenser. Thus

$$C = \frac{Q}{V}$$

where C is the capacitance in farads, Q is the quantity of electricity in coulombs, and V is the potential difference in volts. The farad is the unit of capacitance. A condenser has a capacitance of one farad if it acquires a charge of one coulomb when one volt is impressed across it. The farad is too large a unit for practical purposes, hence the microfarad, or millionth of a farad, is used as a practical unit.

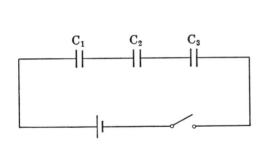

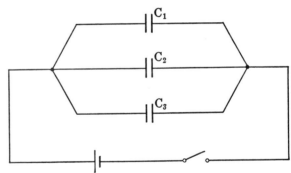

Fig. 37. Condensers in Series   Fig. 38. Condensers in Parallel

When condensers are connected in parallel (see Fig. 38), the total capacitance is equal to the sum of the individual ones. Thus

$$C = C_1 + C_2 + C_3$$

where C is the capacitance of the combination of condensers in parallel.

When condensers are connected in series (see Fig. 37), the reciprocal of the total capacitance is equal to the sum of the reciprocals of the individual ones. Thus

$$\frac{1}{C} = \frac{1}{C_1} + \frac{1}{C_2} + \frac{1}{C_3}$$

where C now represents the capacitance of the combination of condensers in series.

The capacitance of a parallel plate condenser is given by the expression

$$C = \frac{KA}{4\pi d}$$

where C is expressed in electrostatic units of capacitance. To get C in microfarads, the result has to be divided by 9×10^5. In the above expression, A is the area of one plate in square centimeters, d is the distance between the plates in centimeters, and K is the dielectric constant of the material between the plates. It is thus seen that the capacitance of a condenser varies directly with the dielectric constant of the insulator between the plates. Hence if one measures the capacitance of a parallel plate condenser with a dielectric such as mica between the plates and then measures the capacitance when the plates are separated by air of the same thickness as the mica, he will be able to determine the dielectric constant of the mica experimentally. In this case the ratio of the two capacitances is the same as the ratio of the dielectric constants.

In this experiment the capacitance of a condenser is measured in terms of the capacitance of a standard condenser and two known resistances by the bridge method. The connections as shown in Fig. 39 are the same as for the measurement of resistance with the Wheatstone bridge. A source of audio-frequency alternating current is used in place of the dry cell, and a telephone receiver is used as detector in place of the galvanometer. For a condition of balance the relation between the capacitances and the resistances is

$$\frac{C_1}{C_2} = \frac{R_2}{R_1}$$

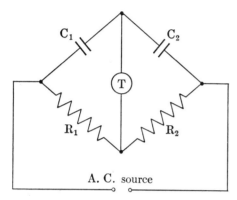

Fig. 39. Bridge Method of Comparing Capacitances

APPARATUS

1. Standard condenser (C_1).
2. Two unknown condensers (C_2 and C_3).
3. Two standard decade resistance boxes calibrated in ohms (about 400 ohms each).
4. Single pole, single throw switch.
5. Source of audio-frequency alternating current.
6. Telephone receiver.

PROCEDURE

1. Connect the apparatus as shown in Fig. 39. Use as C_1 the standard condenser. Measure the capacitance of C_2 by the bridge method. Use a known value of R_1, say 200 ohms, and vary R_2 until the sound heard in the telephone receiver is a minimum when the audio-frequency current is applied to the circuit. Record the values of C_1, R_1, and R_2.

2. Repeat procedure (1) for measuring the capacitance of C_3. Use as C_1 the same standard condenser, and use the same value of R_1. Record the new value of R_2 for the position of balance.

3. Measure the capacitance of C_2 and C_3 when they are connected in series. Again use as C_1 the standard condenser, and use the same value of R_1. Record the new value of R_2 for the position of balance.

4. Measure the capacitance of the combination of condensers C_2 and C_3 when they are connected in parallel. Use the same C_1 and R_1 as before. Record the value of R_2 for the position of balance.

DATA

CONDENSERS MEASURED	R_1	R_2	C_1	CALCULATED CAPACITANCE
C_2				
C_3				
C_2 AND C_3 IN SERIES				
C_2 AND C_3 IN PARALLEL				

CALCULATIONS

1. Compute the capacitance of C_2 from the data of procedure (1) and that of C_3 from the data of procedure (2).

2. Compute the capacitance of the combination of condensers C_2 and C_3 when they are connected in series, from the data of procedure (3).

3. Compute the capacitance of the combination of condensers C_2 and C_3 when they are connected in parallel, from the data of procedure (4).

QUESTIONS

1. Do the results you obtained experimentally for the series and parallel connections of condensers check the laws for such connections within experimental error?

2. What would be the effect on the capacitance of a parallel plate condenser if a sheet of glass were introduced between the plates?

3. Assuming that the charge on the condenser remains the same, what would be the effect on the potential difference between the plates of a parallel plate condenser, if a sheet of glass were introduced between the plates?

4. Which factor in the expression $C = \dfrac{KA}{4\pi d}$ is varied in the tuning condensers used in a radio set? Explain how this is done.

5. Three condensers with capacitances of 2, 3, and 5 microfarads respectively are joined in parallel. The combination is connected in series with a 5 microfarad condenser. What is the capacitance of the final arrangement?

6. A parallel plate condenser is made up of two circular plates separated by a sheet of mica. The plates have a diameter of 20 centimeters, and the mica is 0.1 millimeter thick and has a dielectric constant of 3. Calculate the capacitance of this condenser in microfarads.

36
MEASUREMENT OF CAPACITANCE BY THE BALLISTIC GALVANOMETER

There are two general methods of measuring capacitance. One involves the comparison of the capacitance of the unknown condenser with that of a standard condenser, and is similar in principle to the comparison of resistances by the Wheatstone bridge method. The other involves the use of the relation defining the capacitance of a condenser, that is, the ratio between the quantity of charge on the condenser and the potential difference between the plates. The quantity of charge is determined by the use of a ballistic galvanometer. The object of this experiment is to measure the ballistic constant of a galvanometer, to determine the capacitance of a condenser from the measurement of the charge with a ballistic galvanometer, and to check the laws of series and parallel connections of condensers.

THEORY

A condenser consists of two metal plates separated by an insulating material, which is called a dielectric. If the plates are connected to two points between which there is a difference of potential, the two plates will acquire equal and opposite charges, the magnitude of each charge being directly proportional to the applied voltage. This relation may be expressed in the form

$$Q = CV$$

where Q is the quantity of electricity in coulombs; V is the potential difference in volts; and C is a constant of proportionality known as the capacitance of the condenser. Thus the capacitance of a condenser is the ratio between the quantity of charge on one plate of the condenser and the potential difference between the plates. In the above expression, C is the capacitance in farads.

The farad is the unit of capacitance. A condenser has a capacitance of one farad if it acquires a charge of one coulomb when one volt is impressed across it. The farad is too large a unit for practical purposes; hence the microfarad, or millionth of a farad, is used as a practical unit.

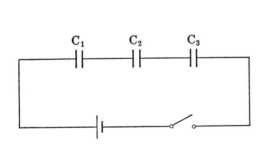

Fig. 40. Condensers in Series

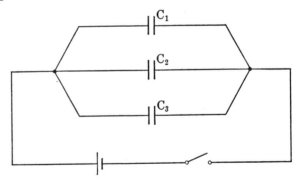

Fig. 41. Condensers in Parallel

When condensers are connected in parallel (see Fig. 41), the total capacitance is equal to the sum of the individual ones. Thus

$$C = C_1 + C_2 + C_3$$

where C is the capacitance of the combination of condensers in parallel.

When condensers are connected in series (see Fig. 40), the reciprocal of the total capacitance is equal to the sum of the reciprocals of the individual ones. Thus

$$\frac{1}{C} = \frac{1}{C_1} + \frac{1}{C_2} + \frac{1}{C_3}$$

where C now represents the capacitance of the combination of condensers in series.

The capacitance of a parallel plate condenser is given by the expression

$$C = \frac{KA}{4\pi d}$$

where C is in electrostatic units of capacitance; A is the area of one plate in square centimeters; d is the distance between the plates in centimeters; and K is the dielectric constant of the material between the plates. To get the capacitance in microfarads, the above result has to be divided by 9×10^5.

When a condenser is connected to a source of voltage, a charge is transferred from one plate to the other and the potential difference between the plates rises from the initial value zero to the final value of the impressed voltage. In transferring this charge work has to be done, and the total work done in this charging process is given by the expression

$$W = \tfrac{1}{2}QV$$

where W is the work done in joules; Q is the charge on the condenser in coulombs; and V is the potential difference between the plates in volts. This work done represents the energy of a charged condenser, or the amount of electrical energy stored in the condenser. This energy can also be expressed in the form

$$W = \tfrac{1}{2}CV^2$$

where W and V are the same as before, and C is the capacitance of the condenser in farads.

In this experiment the capacitance of a condenser is determined by measuring the charge on the condenser and the potential difference between its plates. The condenser is charged to a known voltage and then discharged through a ballistic galvanometer to measure the quantity of charge on the plates.

A ballistic galvanometer is used for the measurement of quantity of electricity. This type of galvanometer is so constructed that its suspended coil has a relatively large moment of inertia and a long period of vibration. As a result, when a condenser is discharged through such a galvanometer, the pulse of current produced rises through a maximum and decreases to zero in a time that is short compared to the period of oscillation of the suspended coil. Thus all the charge passes through the coil before it has been able to move appreciably, and the coil receives an impulsive torque. Instead of producing a steady deflection, this type of torque produces a throw; that is, the coil swings through an angle and then comes back to rest. The reading of the galvanometer, therefore, is the maximum deflection obtained and not a steady deflection as in the ordinary type of galvanometer.

It can be shown that this maximum deflection of the galvanometer is proportional to the quantity of electricity that has passed through the coil. Thus

$$Q = kd$$

where Q is the quantity of electricity; d is the maximum deflection; and k is known as the ballistic constant of the galvanometer. It will be observed that the ballistic constant is numerically equal to the quantity of electricity necessary to produce a unit scale deflection. If Q is expressed in microcoulombs and d in millimeters, then k will be expressed in microcoulombs per millimeter.

APPARATUS

1. Ballistic wall galvanometer.
2. Two unknown condensers.
3. A board on which are mounted eight $\tfrac{1}{2}$-microfarad condensers with individual switches, connected in parallel to two binding posts.
4. Single pole, double throw switch.
5. Two dry cells.

PROCEDURE

1. Connect the apparatus in the circuit as shown in Fig. 42, using the condenser board and one dry cell. Do not connect the cell until the instructor has checked your circuit. The galvanometer has already been adjusted and should be ready for use. If it is not, consult the instructor. Do not try to adjust it yourself.

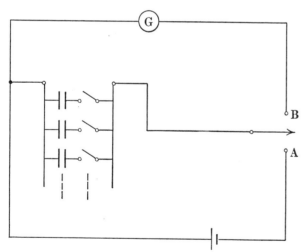

Fig. 42. Circuit for the Measurement of Capacitance

2. It will be observed that when the switch is closed in the direction A, the condenser is being charged by the dry cell, and when it is closed in the direction B, the condenser is discharged through the galvanometer. Connect the first condenser on the board in the circuit by closing the first switch on the condenser board.

Then close the triangular switch in the direction A, thus charging the condenser. Wait a few seconds for the condenser to become fully charged. Now close the switch in the direction B, thus discharging the condenser through the galvanometer. Observe the maximum deflection of the galvanometer, estimating the reading to a half millimeter. The first time this observation is made, it may be necessary to take two or three readings of the galvanometer deflection to practice catching the very end of the first throw of the galvanometer coil.

3. Connect the second condenser on the board in the circuit by closing the second switch on the condenser board. Repeat procedure (2), observing the maximum deflection of the galvanometer when two condensers are discharged. Keep on increasing the number of condensers connected in the circuit until all of the eight condensers are being used. Observe the maximum deflection of the galvanometer for each group when the condensers are discharged, and record the readings.

4. Replace the condenser board by one of the unknown condensers. Charge the condenser using one dry cell, then discharge it through the galvanometer. Observe the maximum deflection of the galvanometer, estimating the reading to a half millimeter.

5. Repeat procedure (4), using the same condenser but with two dry cells in series.

6. Repeat procedures (4) and (5), using the other unknown condenser.

7. Connect the two unknown condensers in parallel and charge them with only one dry cell. Then discharge them through the galvanometer and observe the deflection.

8. Connect the two unknown condensers in series and charge them, using two dry cells in series. Then discharge them through the galvanometer and observe the deflection.

DATA

	CAPACITANCE USED	CHARGING VOLTAGE	GALVANOMETER DEFLECTION	TOTAL CHARGE
1.	0.5 MFD.			
2.	1.0 MFD.			
3.	1.5 MFD.			
4.	2.0 MFD.			
5.	2.5 MFD.			
6.	3.0 MFD.			
7.	3.5 MFD.			
8.	4.0 MFD.			

CAPACITANCE USED	CHARGING VOLTAGE	GALVANOMETER DEFLECTION	TOTAL CHARGE	VALUE OF CAPACITANCE	CAPACITANCE CALCULATED FROM FORMULA
CONDENSER NO. 1	1.5 VOLTS				
CONDENSER NO. 1	3.0 VOLTS				
CONDENSER NO. 2	1.5 VOLTS				
CONDENSER NO. 2	3.0 VOLTS				
CONDENSERS 1–2 IN PARALLEL	1.5 VOLTS				
CONDENSERS 1–2 IN SERIES	3.0 VOLTS				

Ballistic constant of the galvanometer...

CALCULATIONS

1. Calculate the value of the total charge on the condensers used in procedures (2) and (3) by using the relation

$$Q = CV$$

where C is the capacitance in microfarads, V is the charging voltage in volts (the e.m.f. of each dry cell is 1.5 volts), and Q is the charge in microcoulombs.

2. Using the data of procedures (2) and (3) and the results of calculation (1), plot the galvanometer deflections along the x axis and the corresponding values of the charge along the y axis. Draw a straight line through the plotted points in such a way as to fit the points as closely as possible. This graph will be the calibration curve for the galvanometer. Calculate the slope of this straight line. This will be the value of the ballistic constant of the galvanometer in microcoulombs per scale division.

3. Using the values of the galvanometer deflections obtained in procedures (4) to (8), read the corresponding values of the total charge in microcoulombs from your graph.

4. From the data of procedures (4) and (5) plot the voltage along the x axis and the corresponding values of the charge along the y axis. Draw a straight line through the origin, and as nearly as possible through the two plotted points. Determine the slope of this line. The value of the slope is the capacitance of the condenser in microfarads.

5. Repeat calculation (4) using the data of procedure (6) and plotting the points on the same graph paper, using the same axes.

6. From the data of procedure (7), determine the capacitance of the two unknown condensers in parallel by dividing the charge on the condensers by the charging voltage.

7. Calculate the capacitance of the two unknown condensers in parallel by using the formula for condensers in parallel and the values of the individual capacitances obtained before. Compare this value with the one obtained in calculation (6).

8. From the data of procedure (8) determine the capacitance of the two unknown condensers in series by dividing the charge on the condensers by the charging voltage.

9. Calculate the capacitance of the two unknown condensers in series by using the formula for condensers in series and the values of the individual capacitances obtained before. Compare this value with the one obtained in calculation (8).

QUESTIONS

1. Do the results you obtained experimentally for the series and parallel connections of condensers check the laws for such connections within experimental error?

2. A condenser is charged by a 45-volt battery and is then discharged through a galvanometer whose ballistic constant is 1.5 microcoulombs per scale division. The galvanometer deflection produced is 20 divisions. What is the capacitance of the condenser?

3. Two condensers with capacitances of 4 and 5 microfarads respectively are connected in parallel. The combination is connected in series with a 3 microfarad condenser. What is the total capacitance of the final arrangement?

4. Which factor in the expression

$$C = \frac{KA}{4\pi d}$$

is varied in the tuning condensers used in a radio set? Explain how this is done.

5. A parallel plate condenser is made up of two circular plates separated by a thin sheet of mica. The plates have a diameter of 18 centimeters, and the mica is 0.2 millimeter thick and has a dielectric constant of 5.7. Calculate the capacitance of the condenser in microfarads.

6. Compute the energy in joules in one of your standard condensers on the condenser board when it is charged with one dry cell. What happens to this energy when the condenser is discharged through the galvanometer?

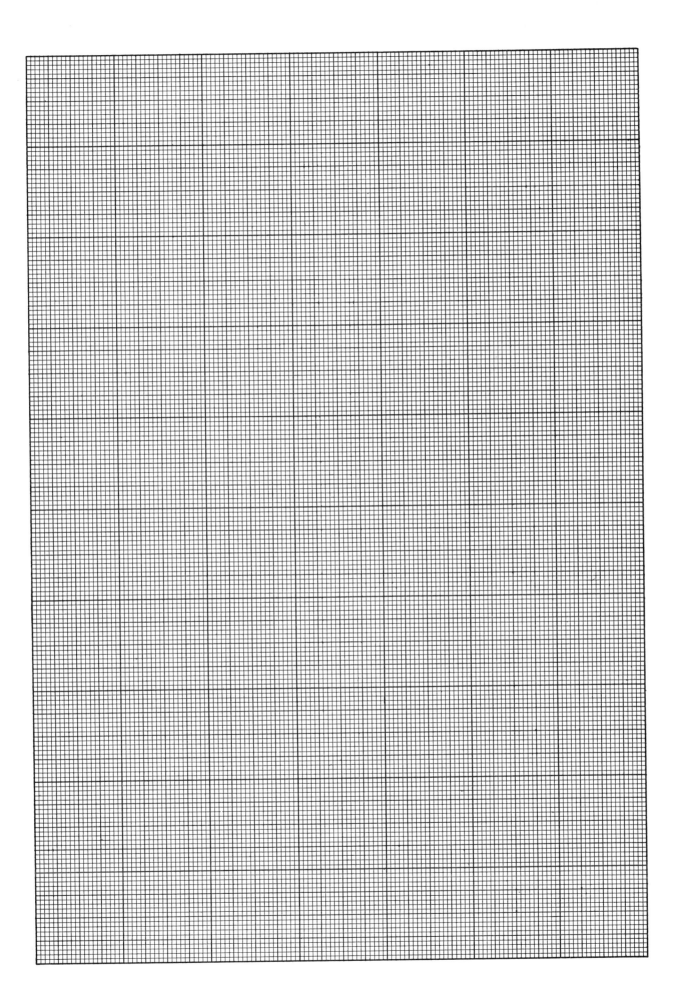

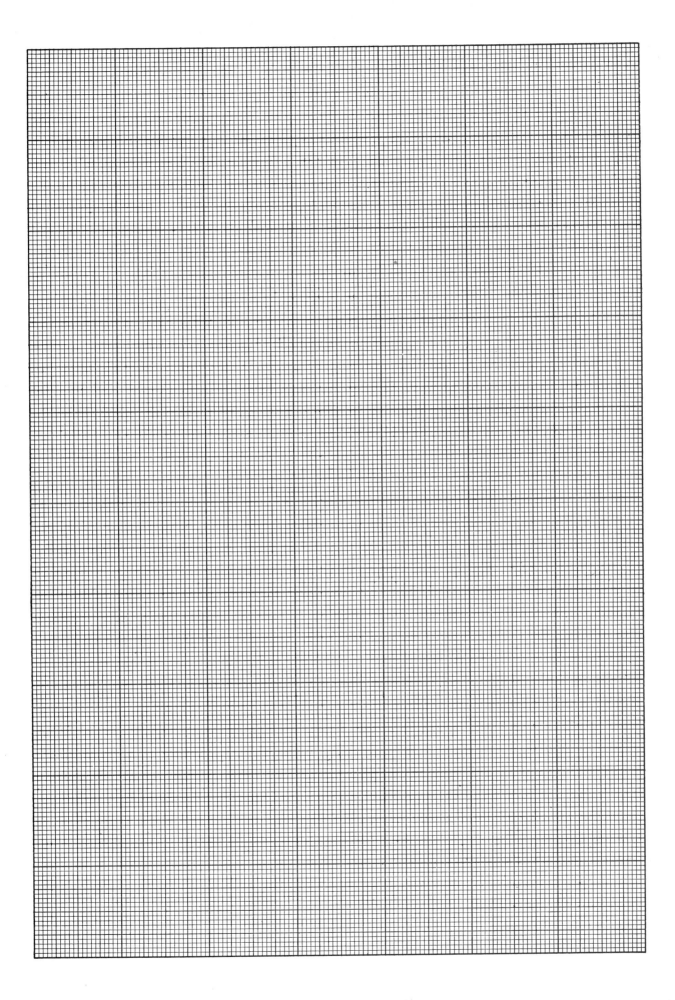

37

ELECTROMAGNETIC INDUCTION

The production of induced currents is one of the most important branches of the study of electricity, since it forms one of the foundations of the electrical industry. The present experiment deals with some of the fundamental principles involved. The work is largely qualitative, so that a complete record of the observations must be kept. The object of the experiment is to study the laws of electromagnetic induction, Lenz's law, and the general features of a magnetic circuit.

THEORY

An electromotive force is induced in a coil of wire whenever there is a change in the magnetic flux passing through the coil. The induced e.m.f. is proportional to the rate of change of flux passing through the coil and to the number of turns in the coil. The induced e.m.f. is given by the expression

$$E = \frac{N\phi}{t} \times 10^{-8}$$

where E is the average value of the induced e.m.f. in volts; N is the number of turns of wire in the coil; ϕ is the change of flux in electromagnetic units, that is, in maxwells; and t is the time in seconds in which the change of flux takes place.

A more accurate expression for the induced e.m.f. is

$$E = -N\frac{d\phi}{dt} \times 10^{-8}$$

where E is the instantaneous value of the induced e.m.f. in volts, and the symbol $\frac{d\phi}{dt}$ denotes the time rate of change of flux, using the calculus notation.

An e.m.f. can be produced by the relative motion between an electric circuit and a magnetic field, or by any other method by which a change in the magnetic flux passing through the coil may be produced. Thus, a magnet may be moved relative to a coil, or a coil may be moved relative to a magnet. But the magnetic field may be produced by a coil of wire through which a current is flowing; and so this coil may be moved relative to another coil, in which case an e.m.f. will be induced in the second coil. Or the current may be changing in the first coil; this will produce a change in the magnetic flux passing through both coils, and therefore an e.m.f. will be induced in the second coil, and another one, or back e.m.f., will also be induced in the first coil.

Lenz's law states that the induced current in any circuit is always in such a direction that its magnetic effect opposes the change of conditions by which it is produced. The statement of the law refers to the direction of the magnetic field due to the induced current. The relation between the magnetic field and the direction of the current is given by the right-hand thumb rule: when the fingers of the right hand curl around the coil in the same direction as the current is flowing, the thumb points in the direction of the magnetic field produced by the current in the coil.

A transformer consists of two coils of wire wound on the same core of laminated iron. One coil, the primary, is connected to the supply mains; the other coil, the secondary, is separated electrically from the primary. The following relation exists between the primary and secondary e.m.f.'s

$$\frac{E_1}{E_2} = \frac{N_1}{N_2}$$

where E_1 is the primary e.m.f., or the voltage applied to the primary coil; E_2 is the e.m.f. induced in the secondary coil; N_1 is the number of turns in the primary coil; and N_2 is the number of turns in the secondary coil.

APPARATUS

1. Primary coil of about 100 turns of copper wire.
2. Secondary coil of about 1000 turns of copper wire.
3. U-shaped piece of iron.
4. Straight piece of iron.
5. Galvanometer.

6. D.C. ammeter (0–2 amperes).
7. 6-volt storage battery.
8. A double pole, double throw reversing switch.
9. Rheostat (0–7 ohms).
10. Permanent bar magnet.

PROCEDURE

1. Connect the secondary coil to the galvanometer. Thrust the N-pole of the magnet into the coil. Record the magnitude and direction of the deflection of the pointer, for a fast speed of motion and for a slow speed. Observe whether the deflection is to the left or to the right; a deflection of the pointer to the right means that the current enters the galvanometer at its + terminal. Determine the direction of the current induced in the coil by noting the direction of the current through the galvanometer and the direction in which the coil is wound.

2. Repeat procedure (1) withdrawing the N-pole from the coil, after having inserted it as in (1). Observe the direction of the current induced in the coil when the N-pole is being withdrawn.

3. Repeat procedures (1) and (2) using the S-pole of the magnet.

4. Connect the primary coil in series with the rheostat, the ammeter, the double pole, double throw reversing switch, and the storage battery, as shown in Fig. 43. Have the circuit approved by the instructor. Mount

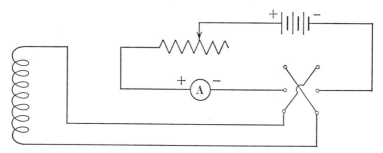

Fig. 43. Primary Circuit Used in Studying Electromagnetic Induction

the two coils in a complete square of iron, made up of the U-piece and the straight piece. Using a current of 0.2 ampere through the primary, observe and record the magnitude and direction of the deflection when the primary circuit is opened and when it is closed. Repeat the observations using primary currents of 0.4, 0.6, 0.8, and 1.0 ampere.

5. Using a current of one ampere, observe the effect of reversing the current in the primary. Notice the direction of the induced current when the primary circuit is opened and when it is closed.

6. Keep the current through the primary at some constant value, say 0.5 ampere. Observe the galvanometer deflection upon opening and closing the primary circuit, using the complete square of iron.

7. Repeat procedure (6) using the open U-piece only.

8. Repeat procedure (6) using no iron at all.

9. Repeat procedure (8) placing the two coils twice as far apart as in (8).

10. Plot the data of procedure (4) using primary currents as abscissas and galvanometer deflections as ordinates.

DATA

	DIRECTION OF CURRENT	GALVANOMETER DEFLECTION	
		SLOW MOTION	FAST MOTION
N-POLE INTO THE COIL			
N-POLE OUT			
S-POLE INTO THE COIL			
S-POLE OUT			

PRIMARY CURRENT	DIRECTION OF SECONDARY CURRENT		GALVANOMETER DEFLECTION		MAGNETIC CIRCUIT
	OPENING	CLOSING	OPENING	CLOSING	
0.2 AMP.					COMPLETE SQUARE OF IRON
0.4 AMP.					COMPLETE SQUARE OF IRON
0.6 AMP.					COMPLETE SQUARE OF IRON
0.8 AMP.					COMPLETE SQUARE OF IRON
1.0 AMP.					COMPLETE SQUARE OF IRON
0.5 AMP.					COMPLETE SQUARE OF IRON
0.5 AMP.					OPEN U-PIECE ONLY
0.5 AMP.					NO IRON
0.5 AMP.					NO IRON, DOUBLE DISTANCE BETWEEN COILS

QUESTIONS

1. How does the experiment verify Lenz's law?

2. Show how the laws of electromagnetic induction were verified.

3. Discuss the essentials of a good magnetic circuit from the observations of procedures (6–9).

4. Name three practical applications of electromagnetic induction.

5. By using Lenz's law, how can you predict the direction of flow of current in a secondary coil when the current in the primary is turned on? Assume a direction for the primary current and assume that the two coils are placed parallel to each other.

6. (a) Can an induced e.m.f. be present in a circuit without an induced current flowing? (b) Can an induced current flow without an induced e.m.f.?

7. A magnet which includes 5000 lines of force is pulled out of a coil of 200 turns of wire which closely surrounds it, in one tenth of a second. Find the induced e.m.f. in volts, assuming that the lines of force are all cut by the coil.

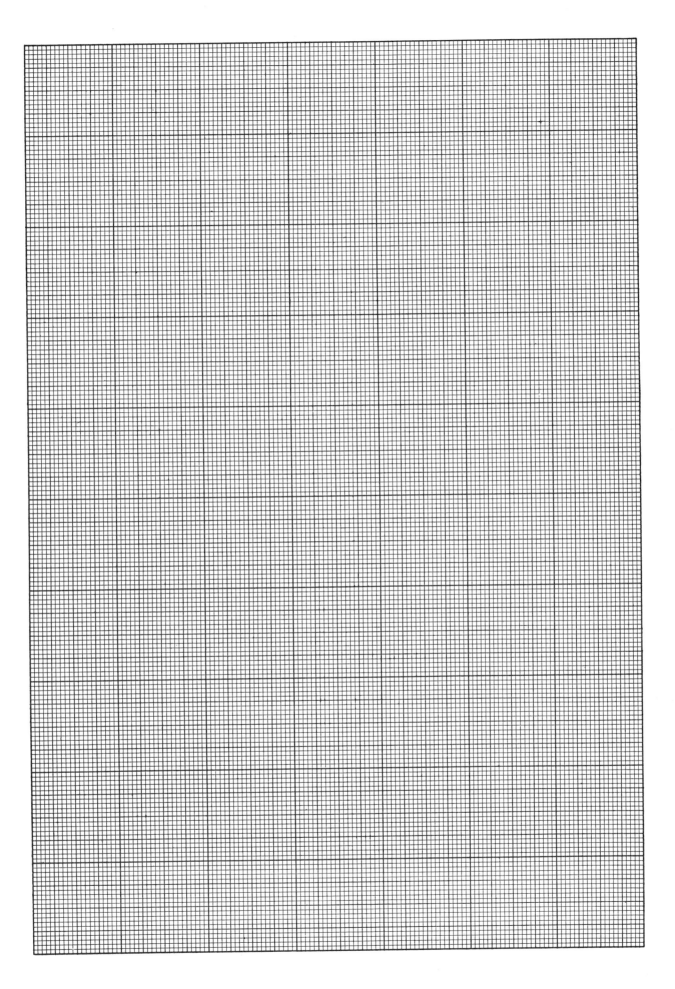

38

ELEMENTARY PRINCIPLES OF THE GENERATOR

The electric generator has revolutionized modern industry by furnishing us with a source of cheap electricity. Its operation is based upon the principles of electromagnetic induction, by which it is possible to transform mechanical energy directly into electrical energy. Thus the enormous energy of steam engines, gas engines, and water wheels can now be transformed into electricity which can be conveniently used in motors to turn all kinds of machinery. It is the purpose of this experiment to study a simple alternating current generator and to investigate the variation of the electromotive force induced in a coil of wire as it is rotated in a uniform magnetic field.

THEORY

A generator is a machine for converting mechanical energy into electrical energy. It is a machine which is driven mechanically by an engine or a turbine and which is capable of sending an electric current through a circuit connected to it.

The essential parts of a generator are the magnetic field, the armature, and some device, such as slip rings or a commutator, for connecting the armature to the external circuit. The magnetic field is produced by permanent magnets or by electromagnets. The armature consists of a rotating coil wound on a soft iron core to obtain an intense and uniform field. As the armature rotates, its conductors cut lines of force and an electromotive force is induced in them.

A simplified diagram of a generator is shown in Fig. 44 in which a rectangular coil of wire *ABCD* is mounted on a longitudinal axis *OO'* between the magnetic poles N and S. The two ends of the coil are connected to two

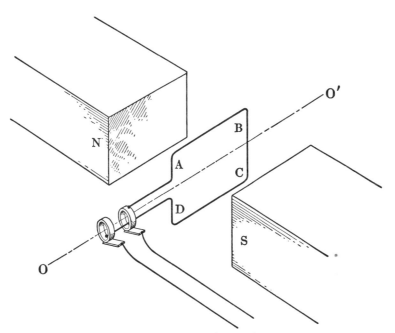

Fig. 44. Principle of a Simple Generator

insulated rings mounted on the axis and rotating with the coil. Two blocks of carbon, called brushes, press against these rings as they rotate and provide electrical contact with the external circuit.

A cross section of the coil is represented in Fig. 45. The e.m.f. induced in the coil will be zero at the position *AD*, or when the angle θ is zero, because at that instant the conductors are moving in a direction parallel to the magnetic field. The e.m.f. will be at a maximum when θ is 90°, because at that instant the conductors are moving in a direction perpendicular to the magnetic field and hence they are cutting lines of force at the maximum rate.

175

The principle on which a generator operates is that the relative motion of a conductor and of a magnetic field produces an electromotive force in the conductor.

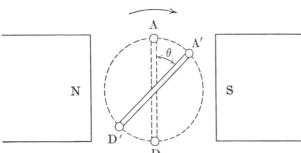

Fig. 45. Armature Coil Rotating in a Uniform Magnetic Field

According to Faraday's law of induction, an electromotive force is induced in a coil of wire whenever there is a change in the magnetic flux passing through the coil. The induced e.m.f. is proportional to the rate of change of flux passing through the coil and to the number of turns in the coil. The induced e.m.f. is given by the expression

$$E = \frac{N\phi}{t} \times 10^{-8}$$

where E is the average value of the induced e.m.f. in volts; N is the number of turns of wire in the coil; ϕ is the change of flux in electromagnetic units, that is, in maxwells; and t is the time in seconds in which the change of flux takes place.

The direction of the current induced in a wire can be determined by using Lenz's law. This law states that the induced current in any circuit is always in such a direction that its magnetic effect opposes the change of conditions by which it is produced.

A more accurate expression for the induced e.m.f. is

$$E = - N \frac{d\phi}{dt} \times 10^{-8}$$

where E is the instantaneous value of the induced e.m.f. in volts, and the symbol $\frac{d\phi}{dt}$ denotes the time rate of change of flux, using the calculus notation.

If a coil is rotated at constant angular velocity in a uniform magnetic field, the e.m.f. is given by

$$E = E_m \sin \omega t$$

where E is the instantaneous value of the induced e.m.f.; E_m is the maximum value of the e.m.f.; ω is the angular velocity; and t is the time in seconds. The above relation may also be written

$$E = E_m \sin \theta$$

where θ is the angle through which the plane of the coil is displaced from a position at right angles to the field.

Therefore, if the coil in this simple form of a generator is rotated at a constant speed, the induced e.m.f. is at any instant proportional to sin θ. During the first half revolution, the e.m.f. will be in one direction, or positive, while during the second half revolution, it will be in the opposite direction, or negative. This simple form of generator is an alternating current (or A.C.) generator.

By using a model generator, it can be easily shown that the curve of the induced e.m.f. has the form of a sine wave. The model generator used in this experiment is illustrated in Fig. 46. It consists of a flat, rectangular coil mounted so that it can rotate in a uniform magnetic field. The field is produced by two sets of permanent horseshoe magnets. The coil can be rotated in equal steps by means of a spring and ratchet mechanism. The spring provides a constant torque, while a ratchet wheel and a stop

Fig. 46. The Model Generator

allow the coil to rotate through a ten degree interval each time the ratchet is released. The terminals of the coil are connected by means of slip rings and brushes to a pair of binding posts.

If the coil is rotated through a series of small equal angles, the induced e.m.f.'s can be measured by connecting the coil to a ballistic galvanometer. As the coil is rotated, the galvanometer deflection produced in each step is proportional to the quantity of electricity passing through the galvanometer. But the quantity of electricity is proportional to the induced e.m.f. Hence the galvanometer deflection is proportional to the induced e.m.f., and it may be taken as a measure of the e.m.f. induced in the coil in each of the intervals. Since the e.m.f. produced in a generator is proportional to the rate of cutting lines of force, the model generator shows the relative values of the e.m.f.'s which would be produced at any position of the coil if it were rotated with uniform speed.

APPARATUS

1. Model generator.
2. Ballistic wall galvanometer.

3. Resistance box used as shunt (0–40 ohms).

PROCEDURE

1. Connect the armature terminals of the model generator to the ballistic galvanometer, and then connect the resistance box in parallel with the galvanometer, as shown in Fig. 47. Set the armature coil in the position for maximum induced electromotive force, that is, with the plane of the coil parallel to the direction of the magnetic field. Adjust the shunt resistance so that the maximum deflection of the galvanometer is about 20 divisions when the coil is rotated through a ten degree interval.

2. Begin your observations with the armature coil set at right angles to the magnetic field. Rotate the coil through a ten-degree interval and observe the maximum deflection of the galvanometer. Take observations of the galvanometer deflection for each ten-degree movement of the coil over one complete revolution. Reset the spring after every second rotation of the coil, to make sure that the spring tension remains the same, and therefore the speed of rotation of the coil remains

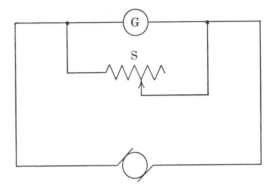

Fig. 47. Circuit for the Model Generator

the same. Record the galvanometer deflection observed for each movement of the coil. Notice that the deflection of the galvanometer corresponds to the position of the coil at the middle of its movement.

CALCULATIONS

1. Plot a curve, putting the angular displacements of the coil along the x axis and the galvanometer deflections along the y axis. Notice that some of the deflections are positive and some are negative; hence the x axis should be chosen in the middle of the paper. The scales on the two axes should be so chosen as to utilize, as nearly as possible, the whole sheet of graph paper. Draw a smooth curve through the plotted points, using a solid line for this part of the graph.

2. Look up the value of sin θ in the trigonometric tables in the Appendix for each angular displacement of the coil, and record the values. Multiply each of these by the maximum galvanometer deflection for the corresponding half cycle; that is, multiply the positive values of sin θ by the maximum positive deflection and the negative values by the maximum negative deflection.

DATA

SETTING OF THE COIL	GALVANOMETER DEFLECTION	SIN θ	PRODUCT OF THE MAXIMUM DEFLECTION AND SIN θ
0°			
10°			
20°			
30°			
40°			
50°			
60°			
70°			
80°			
90°			
100°			
110°			
120°			
130°			
140°			
150°			
160°			
170°			
180°			
190°			
200°			
210°			
220°			
230°			
240°			
250°			
260°			
270°			
280°			
290°			
300°			
310°			
320°			
330°			
340°			
350°			
360°			

3. Plot a second curve on the same sheet of graph paper, using the same axes. Put the angular displacements of the coil along the x axis and the product of the maximum deflection and sin θ along the y axis. Draw a smooth curve through the plotted points, using a dotted line for this part of the graph. This one is a sine curve. Notice how it compares with the other curve.

QUESTIONS

1. Suppose that the resistance of the coil of the model generator were doubled, while the size, shape, and number of turns remained the same. (a) How would this affect the electromotive force produced in the coil? (b) How would it affect the galvanometer deflection? Explain.

2. Compare the power required to drive a generator on open circuit with no current in the armature with the power required to drive a loaded generator. Explain the difference.

3. Referring to Fig. 44, assume that the coil $ABCD$ is rotating clockwise around the axis OO', looking at the coil in the direction OO'. Predict the direction of flow of the induced current at the instant when the coil has rotated through an angle of 90° from the position shown in the figure.

4. The current induced in the coils of an armature is always an alternating current. Sometimes it is desired to change the A.C. developed in the armature to current which always flows in the same direction in the outside circuit, i.e. to change the generator into a direct current generator. Explain how this is accomplished by using a commutator.

5. A coil is composed of 50 turns of wire and has an area of 100 square centimeters. Assume that it is rotated at the rate of 180 revolutions per minute in a uniform magnetic field of 1000 lines per sq. cm. Calculate the average electromotive force in volts induced in the coil over a quarter of a cycle beginning with the plane of the coil perpendicular to the field.

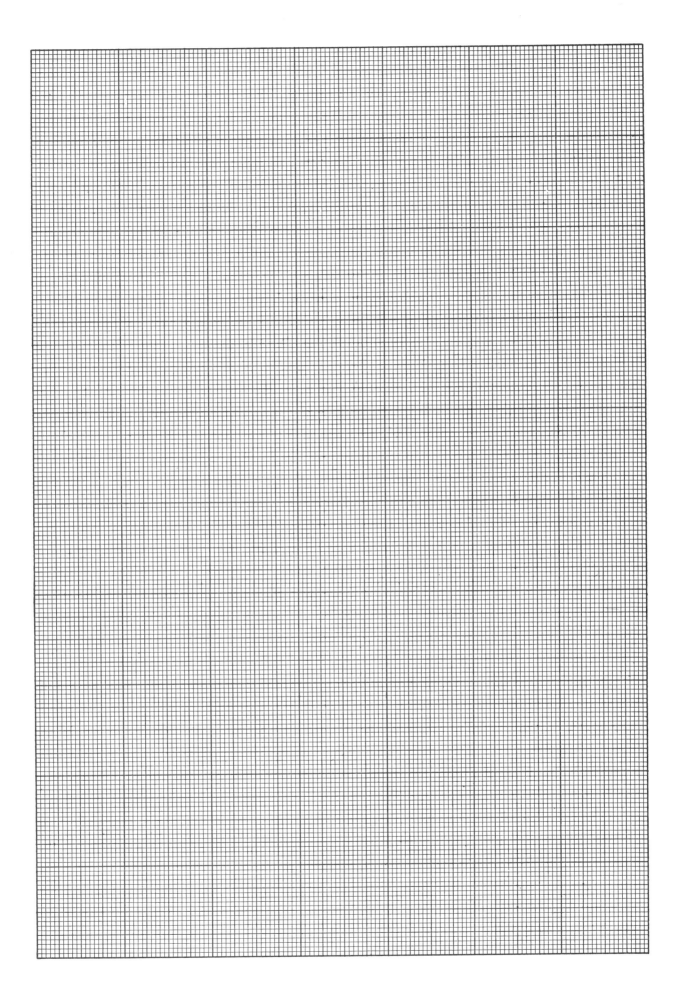

39

ALTERNATING CURRENT

Whenever an electric current is flowing through a conductor, certain effects are produced, such as heating effects, magnetic effects, and chemical effects. An electric current may be either a direct current, that is, one which is always flowing in one direction; or it may be an alternating current, that is, one whose direction is continually changing. The purpose of this experiment is to study the effects associated with the passage of a direct current and compare them with the effects of an alternating current.

THEORY

An alternating current is one whose direction is continually changing; the current rises from zero to a maximum value, decreases to zero, then rises to a maximum value in the opposite direction, and finally decreases to zero again. Each of these series of variations is known as a cycle, and the number of cycles per second is known as the frequency of the alternating current. The heating effect of an alternating current is used to define the effective value of an alternating current. If an alternating current passing through a pure resistance produces the same heating effect as a direct current of one ampere, then the alternating current is said to have an effective value of one ampere. Similarly, an alternating voltage has an effective value of one volt when it will develop an alternating current of one ampere in a pure resistance of one ohm.

The chemical effects of an electric current are produced in the process known as electrolysis. This is the passage of electricity through a liquid with the chemical changes connected with it. An electrolyte is a liquid which permits an electric current to flow through it and is decomposed by the current. If the electrolyte is a solution of a metallic salt, the salt will be decomposed and the metal will be deposited upon the cathode. In electrolysis direct current must be used, for if an alternating current is used, the polarity of the cell is continually changing, and hence the metal deposited in one half of a cycle will be removed during the second half.

An electric current also produces a magnetic effect. If a wire is held over a balanced magnetic needle and parallel to it, the needle will be deflected when an electric current flows through the wire; the direction in which the needle will be deflected depends on the direction of the current. This means that there is a magnetic field around a conductor carrying an electric current, and hence a magnet placed in this field will experience a force. On the other hand, a wire carrying a current and located in a magnetic field is also acted upon by a force. This is a consequence of the law of action and reaction. The force is proportional to the flux density of the field, to the current, and to the length of the wire placed in the field. The direction of the force is perpendicular to both the direction of the field and that of the current.

If a pure inductance is included in a D.C. circuit, it has no effect in limiting the current in the circuit. However, if it is introduced in an A.C. circuit, the value of the current flowing through the circuit will be reduced, because a counter electromotive force is produced in the inductance by the variation of the electric current; this counter e.m.f. has to be subtracted from the applied e.m.f. in calculating the current flowing through the circuit, and thus the current is reduced.

APPARATUS

1. Coil of copper wire with removable iron core.
2. Source of 110-volts D.C.
3. Source of 110-volts A.C.
4. Bank of four 1-microfarad condensers.
5. D.C. ammeter (0–2 amperes).
6. A.C. ammeter (0–2 amperes).
7. Lamp bank with two lamps, one large and one small.
8. One carbon filament lamp of about 60 watts.
9. One 2-watt neon glow lamp.
10. Electrolytic cell (copper sulfate solution, nickel electrode, copper electrode).
11. One double pole, double throw switch with fuses, cords, and plugs, one for A.C. and one for D.C.
12. Horseshoe magnet.

PROCEDURE

CAUTION: All wiring connections are to be made *before* plugging into the supply line. Any changes in the circuit are to be made *only after* the plug has been pulled out. Have the circuit approved by the instructor *before* plugging into the supply line every time a change in the circuit is made.

1. Connect in series the lamp bank, the D.C. ammeter, and the switch, as shown in Fig. 48. Plug into the 110-volt D.C. outlet, close the switch on the D.C. side, and record the current drawn by each lamp. Notice the brightness of the lamps.

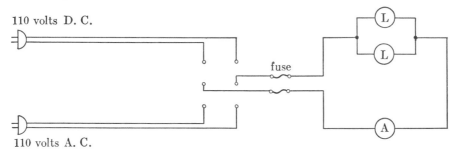

Fig. 48. Circuit for Showing the Heating Effect of an Electric Current

2. Repeat procedure (1) using the 110-volt A.C. outlet. Use the A.C. ammeter in the circuit this time. Again notice the brightness of the lamps for the same effective value of the current as in (1).

3. Connect in series the lamp bank, the D.C. ammeter, the electrolytic cell, and the switch, as shown in Fig. 49. Adjust the polarity of the cell so that the nickel electrode is the cathode. Plug into the 110-volt

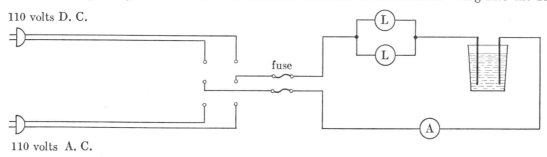

Fig. 49. Circuit for Showing the Chemical Effect of an Electric Current

D.C. outlet, and close the switch on the D.C. side. After the current has passed through the cell for several minutes, open the switch, pull out the D.C. plug, and examine the electrodes. Record their appearance.

4. Repeat procedure (3) reversing the polarity of the cell. Notice what happens to the copper deposited on the nickel.

5. Repeat procedure (3) using A.C. Include the A.C. ammeter in the circuit. Record the result.

6. Approach the horseshoe magnet carefully to the carbon filament lamp connected to the D.C. line. Notice what happens to the filament as the magnet approaches the lamp and record the results.

7. Repeat procedure (6) using A.C.

8. Connect in series the lamp bank, the D.C. ammeter, the coil with the iron core, and the switch. Plug into the 110-volt D.C. outlet and close the switch on the D.C. side. Observe the magnetic strength of the coil

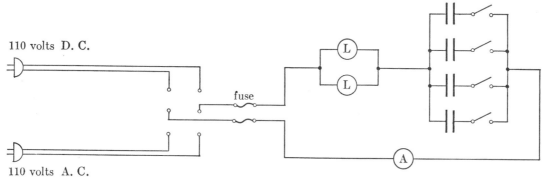

Fig. 50. Circuit Including Condensers

and the current in the circuit with the iron core in the coil, and with the iron core removed. Test the polarity of the ends of the coil with the horseshoe magnet.

9. Repeat procedure (8) using A.C.

182

10. Connect in series the lamp bank, the D.C. ammeter, the condenser bank, and the switch, as shown in Fig. 50. Have the switches on the condenser bank closed. Plug into the 110-volt D.C. outlet and close the switch on the D.C. side. Notice the result. Open the switch and pull out the plug. Now short-circuit the condensers and notice what happens.

11. Repeat procedure (10) using A.C. and the small lamp. Notice the effect of changing the capacity from one to four microfarads in steps of one microfarad.

12. Connect the neon glow lamp first to the D.C. line and then to the A.C. line. Observe the appearance of the lamp in each case.

QUESTIONS

1. Summarize your results briefly, comparing the behavior of the various circuits used on A.C. and D.C.

2. Explain the differences observed.

3. Draw the circuit diagram for procedure (8).

4. When the condenser bank was short-circuited in procedure (10), was there any evidence that the condensers were charged? Explain the result by comparing the action of a condenser when placed in a D.C. circuit with the action when placed in an A.C. circuit.

5. (a) What principle is illustrated by procedure (6)? (b) Name two practical devices based on this effect.

40

VACUUM TUBE CHARACTERISTICS. DIODE

When metals are raised to a high temperature, they emit electrons. This emission of electrons from hot bodies forms the basic principle of the operation of the thermionic vacuum tube, which is perhaps the most important single electrical device. The two-element vacuum tube consists of a filament and a plate. The filament emits electrons when heated by an electric current. If the potential of the plate is made positive with respect to the filament, an electron current flows from filament to plate. The purpose of this experiment is to determine how the plate current varies with a change of plate voltage when the filament temperature is kept constant.

THEORY

A vacuum tube consists of two or more elements sealed in an evacuated glass bulb. The simplest type of vacuum tube is the diode, which consists of two elements, a filament and a plate. The filament is a wire, usually made of tungsten, which is heated by the passage of an electric current and becomes a source of electrons. The plate is a thin piece of metal surrounding the filament. The emission of electrons by a hot body is known as thermionic emission. The rate at which electrons are emitted by the filament increases as the temperature is raised. When a potential is applied to the plate, positive with respect to the filament, the electrons given off by the filament are attracted to the plate, and they constitute the plate current. The plate current is not proportional to the potential difference between filament and plate. The particular way in which the plate current varies with the plate voltage is called the plate characteristic of the tube.

The magnitude of the plate current in the tube may be limited by two factors: the rate of emission of electrons by the filament, and the space charge. The space charge is an accumulation of electrons near the filament, which retards the flow of electrons from the filament to the plate, since it repels the electrons trying to leave the filament. If the temperature of the filament is kept constant and the plate potential is gradually increased, the space charge will be attracted to the plate and more electrons will be emitted. It will be found that raising the potential of the plate increases the current only up to a certain point, when all of the electrons emitted by the filament at that temperature are driven to the plate. This maximum plate current obtainable at a given filament temperature is called the saturation current.

Since the electrons have a negative charge, a current can flow only when the plate is positive with respect to the filament. Hence, if an alternating potential difference is applied between the filament and the plate, the plate current will be a pulsating direct current that flows only during one half a cycle. Under these conditions the diode is said to act as a rectifier, which means that it changes an alternating current into a direct current.

APPARATUS

1. Three-electrode vacuum tube (Type 6A5).
2. Radio tube socket.
3. D.C. voltmeter (0–150 volts).
4. D.C. ammeter (0–1.5 amperes).
5. D.C. milliammeter (0–100 milliamperes).
6. Filament rheostat (about 20 ohms).
7. Tubular rheostat (about 200 ohms).
8. 6-volt storage battery.
9. 110-volt D.C. supply.
10. One single pole, single throw switch.
11. One double pole, single throw switch with cord and plug.

PROCEDURE

1. Connect the tube in the circuit as shown in Fig. 51, keeping all switches open. In this experiment a three-element tube is used as a diode. Set the grid voltage at zero by connecting the grid directly to the negative terminal of the filament. This is done by attaching a wire to the appropriate binding posts. Have the circuit approved by the instructor.

2. Set R_1 at its maximum value. Close switch K_1 and adjust the filament current to 1.10 amperes by means of the control rheostat R_1. Keep this current constant. NOTE: The value of the filament current to be used applies only to tubes of type 6A5. In case a tube of a different type is used, the proper value will be suggested by the instructor.

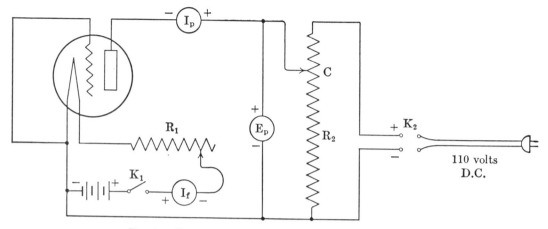

Fig. 51. Circuit for Measurements on Two-electrode Tubes

3. Plug into the 110-volt D.C. outlet and close switch K_2. Vary the plate voltage by moving the contact point C on the potential divider R_2. Set the plate voltage at zero. Record the value of the plate current.

4. Now set the plate voltage at 10 volts. Again record the value of the plate current.

5. Keep on increasing the plate voltage in steps of 10 volts, up to 110 volts, and record the corresponding values of the plate current.

6. Now adjust the filament current to 1.00 ampere by means of the control rheostat R_1. Keep this current constant.

7. Set the plate voltage at zero and record the value of the plate current.

8. Increase the plate voltage in steps of 10 volts up to 110 volts, and record the corresponding values of the plate current.

DATA

	FILAMENT CURRENT 1.1 AMPERES	FILAMENT CURRENT 1.0 AMPERE
PLATE VOLTAGE	PLATE CURRENT	PLATE CURRENT
0		
10		
20		
30		
40		
50		
60		
70		
80		
90		
100		
110		

9. Plot the plate characteristic of the diode on a full sheet of graph paper. Using the data of procedures (4–5) plot the values of the plate voltage along the x axis and the corresponding values of the plate current along the y axis. Indicate the position of each point on the graph by a small pencil dot. Then draw a *smooth* curve through the points. The curve does not necessarily have to pass through all the points, but it should have on the average as many points on one side of it as on the other.

10. Using the data of procedure (8), plot a second curve on the same graph paper and using the same coordinates and the same scale. This will be another plate characteristic curve of the diode, but for a different filament temperature.

QUESTIONS

1. Does a vacuum tube obey Ohm's law; i.e. is the plate current always proportional to the plate voltage?

2. (a) What is meant by a saturation current? (b) Why should there be saturation?

3. Why do the curves flatten out?

4. What do the curves show about the dependence of electron emission on the temperature of the filament?

5. Why is the tube evacuated?

6. Would the tube operate if the plate were made negative with respect to the filament? Explain.

187

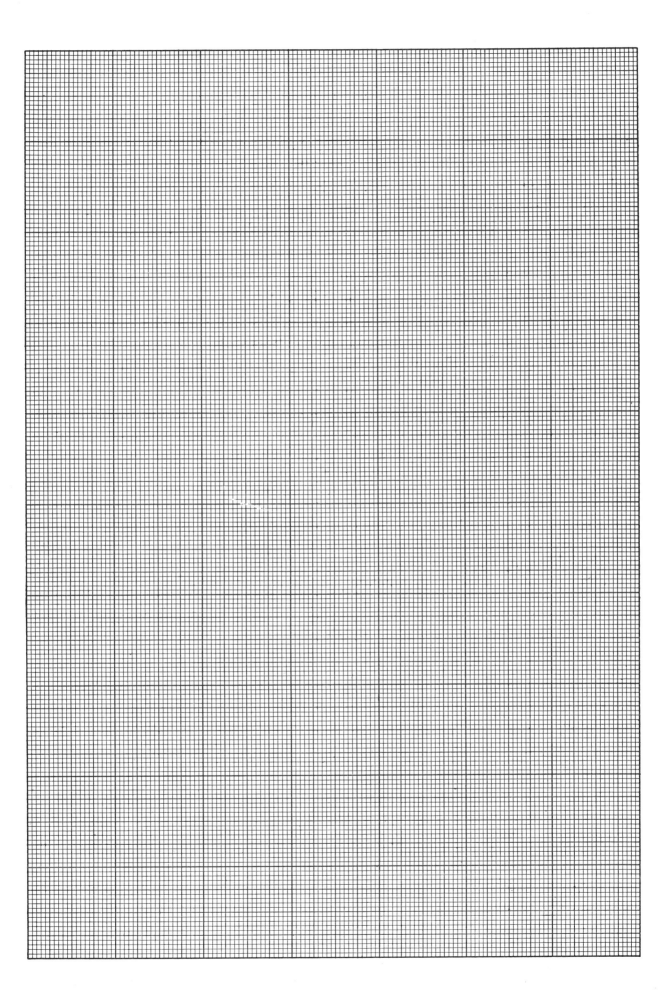

41

VACUUM TUBE CHARACTERISTICS. TRIODE

The importance of vacuum tubes in modern radios and all kinds of electronic devices is well known. The vacuum tube operates on the principle of the emission of electrons from hot bodies. The two-element vacuum tube consists only of a filament and a plate. In a three-element tube, or triode, a grid is added to control the plate current; this makes the tube an extremely useful device. The purpose of this experiment is to study how the plate current varies with a change of grid voltage and to determine the amplification factor of the tube.

THEORY

A triode is a vacuum tube composed of three elements: a filament, a plate, and a grid. The filament is a wire, usually made of tungsten, which is heated by the passage of an electric current and emits electrons. The plate is a thin piece of metal surrounding the filament. The grid consists of a fine wire mesh supported between the filament and the plate. When a potential is applied to the plate, positive with respect to the filament, the electrons given off by the filament are attracted to the plate, and they constitute the plate current. The purpose of the grid is to control the flow of current from the filament to the plate. As the potential between the grid and the filament is varied, there is produced a corresponding variation in the plate current. The way in which the plate current depends upon the grid potential, for a fixed plate potential, is known as the grid characteristic of the tube.

Since the grid is much closer to the filament than the plate is, a small change in grid potential produces a much greater change in plate current than the same change in plate potential would produce. Thus the triode can be used as a voltage amplifier, and one of the important characteristics of such a tube is the voltage amplification factor. The amplification factor of a tube, then, is defined as the ratio of the change in plate voltage to the change in grid voltage in the opposite direction such that the plate current remains unchanged. Thus

$$\frac{E_p'' - E_p'}{E_g' - E_g''} = \mu$$

where μ is the amplification factor, $E_g' - E_g''$ is the change in grid voltage, and $E_p'' - E_p'$ is the change in plate voltage needed to bring the plate current back to its original value.

APPARATUS

1. Three-electrode vacuum tube (Type 6A5).
2. Radio tube socket.
3. D.C. voltmeter (0–150 volts).
4. D.C. voltmeter (0–25 volts).
5. D.C. ammeter (0–1.5 amperes).
6. D.C. milliammeter (0–100 milliamperes).
7. Filament rheostat (about 20 ohms).
8. Tubular rheostat (about 200 ohms).
9. Tubular rheostat (about 1000 ohms).
10. 6-volt storage battery.
11. 110-volt D.C. supply.
12. Battery of dry cells (45 volts).
13. Two single pole, single throw switches.
14. One double pole, double throw reversing switch.
15. One double pole, single throw switch with cord and plug.

PROCEDURE

1. Connect the tube in the circuit as shown in Fig. 52, keeping all switches open. R_1 is the filament rheostat of about 20 ohms; R_2 is a rheostat of about 200 ohms used as potential divider to supply the plate voltage; R_3 is a rheostat of about 1000 ohms used as potential divider to supply the grid voltage. Have the circuit approved by the instructor.

2. Set R_1 at its maximum value. Close switch K_1 and adjust the filament current to 1.10 amperes by means of the control rheostat R_1. Keep this current constant throughout the experiment. NOTE: The values of the filament current, the plate voltages, and the grid voltages to be used apply only to tubes of type 6A5. In case a tube of a different type is used, the proper values will be suggested by the instructor.

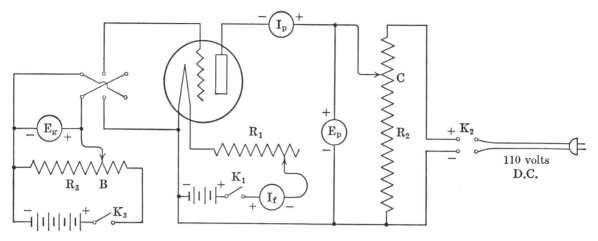

Fig. 52. Circuit for Measurements on Three-electrode Tubes

3. Plug into the 110-volt D.C. outlet and close switch K_2. Vary the plate voltage by moving the contact point C on the potential divider R_2. Set the plate voltage at 100 volts. Keep this voltage constant.

4. Close switch K_3. Close the reversing switch in the direction to apply negative voltage to the grid. Vary the grid voltage by moving the contact point B on the potential divider R_3. Set the grid voltage at zero. Record the value of the plate current.

5. Now set the grid voltage at -1.0 volt. Again record the value of the plate current.

6. Keep on varying the grid voltage in steps of one volt to -6.0 volts, and in steps of two volts to -20.0 volts. Record the corresponding values of the plate current.

7. Bring the grid voltage back to zero. Close the reversing switch in the direction to apply positive voltage to the grid. Vary the grid voltage from zero to $+5.0$ volts in steps of one volt, and record the corresponding values of the plate current.

8. Adjust the plate voltage to 50 volts. Repeat procedures (4–7).

9. With the plate voltage at 50 volts, adjust the grid voltage to -1.0 volt and record the value of the plate current. Now decrease the grid voltage to -3.0 volts, and then increase the plate voltage until the plate current is restored to its original value. Record the value of the plate voltage.

10. Plot the grid characteristic of the triode on a full sheet of graph paper. Using the data of procedures (4–7), plot the grid voltage along the x axis and the corresponding values of the plate current along the y axis. Draw a *smooth* curve through the points.

11. Using the data of procedure (8), plot a second curve on the same graph paper, using the same coordinates and the same scale. This will be another grid characteristic of the triode, but for a different plate voltage.

12. From the data of procedure (9) compute the amplification factor. This will be the amplification factor for a grid potential of -2.0 volts and a plate potential of about 55 volts.

NAME_____ SECTION_____ DATE_____ EXPERIMENT FORTY-ONE

DATA

GRID VOLTAGE	PLATE VOLTAGE 100 VOLTS	PLATE VOLTAGE 50 VOLTS
	PLATE CURRENT	PLATE CURRENT
5.0		
4.0		
3.0		
2.0		
1.0		
0.0		
−1.0		
−2.0		
−3.0		
−4.0		
−5.0		
−6.0		
−8.0		
−10.0		
−12.0		
−14.0		
−16.0		
−18.0		
−20.0		

DATA FOR THE AMPLIFICATION FACTOR

Original plate voltage $E_p' =$

New plate voltage $E_p'' =$

Plate current $I_p =$

Original grid voltage $E_g' =$

New grid voltage $E_g'' =$

QUESTIONS

1. Summarize briefly the results of the experiment, explaining the significance of the shape of the curves.

2. How does a positive voltage on the grid affect the plate current?

3. Mention three ways in which a triode may be used in a radio circuit.

4. In using vacuum tubes as amplifiers, it is necessary that the portion of the grid characteristic curve used be a straight line in order to prevent distortion of the signal. Explain why.

5. (a) Determine the amplification factor from the two grid characteristic curves for a plate current equal to that observed in procedure (9). (b) How does this value compare with that found in procedure (12)?

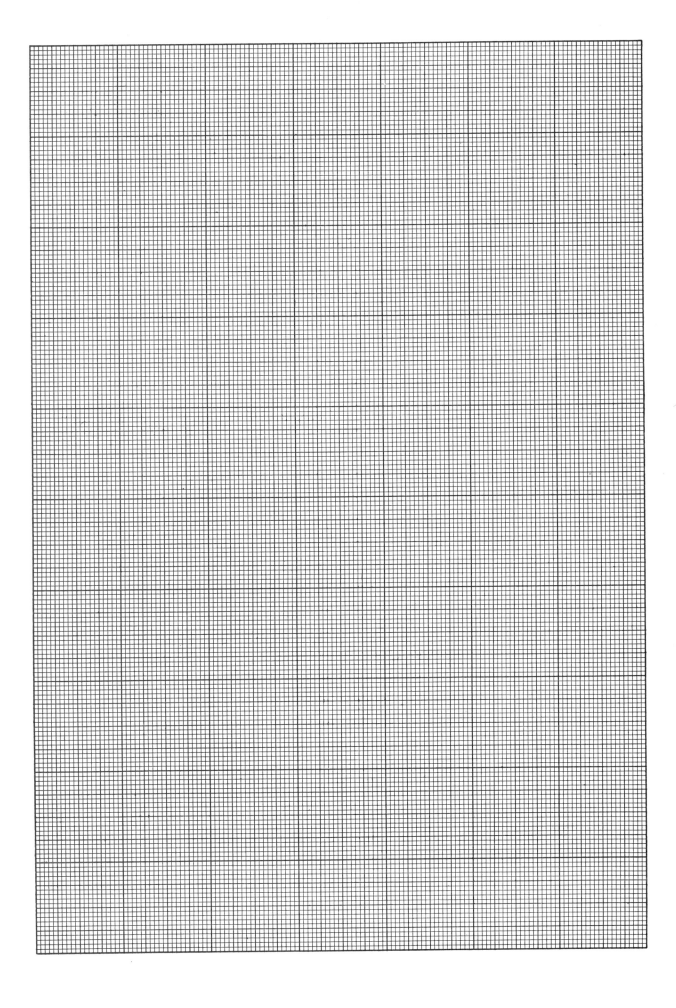

42
PHOTOMETRY

The measurement of the relative amounts of light given out by two sources is called photometry. One of the sources, which is taken as a standard, illuminates one side of a white screen, the other illuminates the other side. The distance of the screen from the two sources is varied until the intensity of illumination is the same on both sides. The object of this experiment is to study the Bunsen photometer, or the Lummer-Brodhun photometer, and its use in comparing the candle powers of several light sources.

THEORY

The candle power of a light source is a measure of the intensity of the source: it is the ratio of the visible light emitted by the source to that emitted by a standard candle which is arbitrarily chosen as the unit of candle power. Originally, the standard source was a candle made according to definite specifications. The light standards actually used now are certain incandescent lamps run at specified voltages.

The illumination of any surface is directly proportional to the candle power of the source of light illuminating it, and inversely proportional to the square of its distance from the light source. The foot-candle is the illumination produced on a surface placed one foot away from a source of one candle power, where the surface is perpendicular to the rays of light. The amount of light needed to produce a given illumination on any surface depends on the area of the surface. The amount of light falling on a surface whose area is one square foot, when the illumination is one foot candle, is called a lumen. Thus the lumen is the unit of light energy flow such that a lamp of one candle power emits light at the rate of 4π lumens.

The Bunsen photometer consists simply of a piece of white paper with a translucent spot at its center, provided with a convenient method of viewing both sides of the paper simultaneously. When the illumination is the same on both sides of the screen, the translucent spot will disappear, or at least will have the same appearance when viewed from either side. When this condition is fulfilled, the candle powers of the two lamps producing the illumination of the two sides of the paper are to each other as the square of their distances from the screen. Thus

$$\frac{C_1}{C_2} = \frac{d_1^2}{d_2^2}$$

where C_1 and C_2 are the candle powers of the lamps, and d_1 and d_2 are their respective distances from the screen. In this manner the candle power of any unknown lamp can be determined from that of a standard lamp.

The Lummer-Brodhun photometer, which is illustrated in Fig. 53, has an improved optical system and is

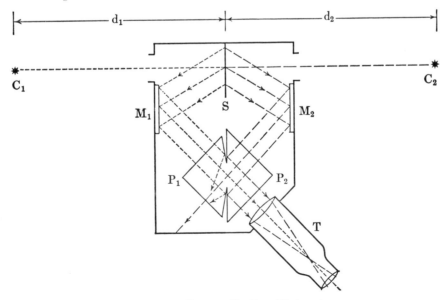

Fig. 53. The Lummer-Brodhun Photometer

widely used in accurate photometric work. Light from the two lamps of candle powers C_1 and C_2 is diffusely reflected by the white screen S to the mirrors M_1 and M_2, and from these through the prisms P_1 and P_2 to the viewing telescope T. The prisms P_1 and P_2 are two right-angle prisms with their hypotenuse faces in contact. A part of the hypotenuse face of one prism is ground away, so that the two prisms make contact only at the central part. Light incident on the contact face will be transmitted by both prisms, while light incident on that part of the hypotenuse face of either prism not in contact with the other prism will be totally reflected. Thus the light from C_1 is reflected by the screen S to the mirror M_1, then through the central portion of the prisms P_1 and P_2 to the viewing telescope. Similarly, the light from C_2 is reflected from the other side of the screen S to the mirror M_2, and is then totally reflected by the outer portion of the prism P_2 into the viewing telescope. The central portion of the field of view of the telescope will be illuminated by light from C_1, while the outer portion will be illuminated by light from C_2. When the entire field of view appears of uniform brightness, then the illumination is the same on both sides of the screen.

APPARATUS

1. Optical bench.
2. Bunsen photometer head or Lummer-Brodhun photometer head.
3. Standard lamp (16 candle power).
4. Rheostat for the standard lamp (about 200 ohms).
5. D.C. voltmeter (0–150 volts).
6. D.C. ammeter (0–1.5 amperes).
7. 110-volt D.C. supply.
8. One double pole, single throw switch with cord and plug.
9. 60-watt carbon filament lamp.
10. Tungsten filament lamps (25, 50, 75 watts).

PROCEDURE

1. Adjust the standard lamp, the photometer head, and the 60-watt carbon filament lamp, all to the same height on the optical bench; clamp the standard lamp at the zero point, and the 60-watt lamp at the 100 point of the optical bench. The standard lamp will be already connected with the ammeter, voltmeter, and control rheostat, as shown in Fig. 54. Plug into the 110-volt D.C. line and close the switch. Adjust the voltage of the standard lamp accurately to the rated voltage, by means of the control rheostat.

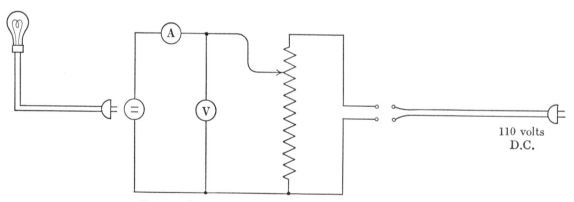

Fig. 54. Circuit for Measuring the Power Input to a Lamp

2. Move the photometer head back and forth until the translucent spot disappears, or at least has the same appearance when viewed from either side. Record the setting of the photometer head. Make four independent determinations of this setting, by moving the photometer head away from its setting and adjusting it again each time, and record the results. NOTE: In other types of photometers, the two sides of the screen can be viewed simultaneously, either directly or by means of mirrors or prisms. The observer sees the field of view divided into two portions. When the dividing line between the two portions of the field disappears, then the two sides of the screen are equally illuminated.

3. Repeat procedures (1–2) by using the standard lamp as C_1 and the 25-watt tungsten filament lamp as C_2.

4. Repeat procedures (1–2) by using the standard lamp as C_1 and the 50-watt tungsten filament lamp as C_2.

5. Repeat procedures (1–2) by using the standard lamp as C_1 and the 75-watt tungsten filament lamp as C_2.

NAME_____ SECTION_____ DATE_____ EXPERIMENT FORTY-TWO

DATA

Candle power of standard lamp...

Rated voltage of standard lamp...

| TYPE OF LAMP | SETTING OF PHOTOMETER HEAD | | | | | d_2 | d_1^2 | d_2^2 |
	1	2	3	4	AVERAGE d_1			
60-WATT, CARBON								
25-WATT, TUNGSTEN								
50-WATT, TUNGSTEN								
75-WATT, TUNGSTEN								

| TYPE OF LAMP | CANDLE POWER | LUMENS | EFFICIENCY | |
			CANDLE POWER PER WATT	LUMENS PER WATT
60-WATT, CARBON				
25-WATT, TUNGSTEN				
50-WATT, TUNGSTEN				
75-WATT, TUNGSTEN				

CALCULATIONS

1. Calculate the average of each set of readings taken. This represents the distance d_1 of the standard lamp from the screen in each case.

2. Using the average values of d_1, calculate the distance d_2 for each set of readings.

3. Compute the values of the squares of the distances d_1^2 and d_2^2.

4. Calculate the candle power of each lamp used.

5. Calculate in lumens the rate at which each lamp emits light energy.

6. Determine the efficiency of each of the four lamps in candle power per watt and in lumens per watt.

QUESTIONS

1. (a) Compare the efficiency of the carbon filament lamp with that of the 50-watt tungsten filament lamp. (b) Also compare the efficiency of the 25-watt lamp with that of the 75-watt lamp. (c) Explain these differences in efficiency.

2. (a) What is the significance of the ratio candle power per watt? (b) How does this ratio vary as the temperature of the filament is increased?

3. In this experiment have you proved the inverse square law?

4. What happens to the electrical energy input of a lamp which is not converted into visible light?

5. Why is the light from the tungsten filament lamp whiter than the light from the carbon lamp?

6. If the two lamps you were comparing had candle powers of 24 and 32 candles respectively, where would the screen have to be placed in order that the two sides be equally illuminated?

43
RAY TRACING

When a beam of light travels from one medium to another of different density, a part of the incident light energy is reflected. If the second medium is transparent, most of the light energy travels through the medium, but the rays are bent at the surface if the incident beam was not perpendicular to the surface; this bending of the rays of light is called refraction. The purpose of this experiment is to study the laws of reflection and refraction by tracing the paths of light rays.

THEORY

Reflection occurs whenever light strikes the surface of a medium whose optical density is greater than or less than that of the medium in which it is traveling. Regular reflection is the reflection taking place from a smooth surface, like a mirror, along a definite direction, determined by the direction of the incident ray. A single ray of light will proceed, after reflection, in a direction given by the law of reflection. This law states that when a ray of light is regularly reflected, the angle of incidence is equal to the angle of reflection; the incident ray, the normal, and the reflected ray all lie in one plane. The normal is the perpendicular to the surface at the point of reflection; the angle of incidence is the angle between the incident ray and the normal; the angle of reflection is the angle between the reflected ray and the normal.

A spherical mirror is a mirror whose surface is a portion of a sphere. If the surface of a concave spherical mirror is held facing a beam of parallel rays of light, the reflected rays will converge to a point. This point is the principal focus of the mirror. The focal length of the mirror is the distance from the mirror to the principal focus. The principal axis of the mirror is the line drawn from the center of the mirror to the center of curvature (the center of the sphere of which the mirror is a part).

Refraction is the bending of the rays of light in passing obliquely from one medium to another of different density (see Fig. 55). The direction in which a single ray of light will travel after refraction is given by the law of refraction. This law states that the ratio of the sine of the angle of incidence to the sine of the angle of refraction is constant, for any two given media, for light of any given wave length; the incident ray, the refracted ray, and the normal are all in the same plane. The angle of refraction is the angle between the refracted ray and the normal. The law of refraction may be stated mathematically

$$\frac{\sin i}{\sin r} = \frac{V_1}{V_2} = \mu$$

where

i = angle of incidence
r = angle of refraction
V_1 = velocity of light in the first medium
V_2 = velocity of light in the second medium
μ = index of refraction

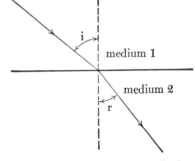

Fig. 55. Refraction at a Plane Surface

The index of refraction of a medium with respect to air is the ratio of the velocity of light in air to the velocity of light in the medium.

A lens is a piece of glass, or other transparent material, usually bounded by spherical surfaces, which is used to converge or diverge a beam of light. The principal axis of a lens is the line joining the centers of curvature of the surfaces of the lens. The principal focus is the point to which a beam of rays parallel to the principal axis converges. The focal length of a lens is the distance from the lens to the principal focus.

Whenever a ray of light passes from one medium into a second medium in which the velocity of light is greater, as when it passes from glass into air, the refracted ray is bent away from the normal. As the angle of incidence is increased, eventually the refracted ray will graze along the surface. The critical angle is the angle of incidence in the more highly refractive medium for which the angle of refraction is equal to 90°, and the refracted ray grazes along the surface. If the angle of incidence is made greater than the critical angle, then total reflection occurs at the boundary and no light is refracted.

199

APPARATUS

1. Light source, preferably with single straight tungsten filament, with converging lens to produce a parallel beam of light.
2. Drawing board.
3. Metal plate with 5 parallel slits.
4. Plane mirror.
5. Concave mirror.
6. Convex mirror.
7. Double concave lens.
8. Double convex lens.
9. 90° prism.
10. 60° prism.
11. 12-inch ruler.
12. Protractor.
13. Drawing compass.
14. White paper.

PROCEDURE

1. Arrange the apparatus so that five equally spaced narrow parallel rays of light cross the drawing board. Place a piece of white paper on the board and set the plane mirror perpendicularly on the paper, and oblique to the rays. Using a sharp pencil and a ruler, draw straight lines to indicate the position of the mirror and the paths of the incident rays and the reflected rays. Indicate the direction of the rays by means of arrowheads. NOTE: In these drawings, represent the actual paths of all rays of light by solid lines; represent virtual rays, which are prolongations of actual ray paths, by broken lines; and indicate optical surfaces by heavy solid lines.

2. Make a corresponding drawing for a concave spherical mirror (in this case using a cylindrical mirror). Set the mirror perpendicularly on the paper with the central ray striking the mirror normally. Trace the reflecting surface of the mirror on the paper and indicate the paths of the incident rays and the reflected rays. Locate the principal focus of the mirror. Locate the center of curvature of the mirror as follows: Draw any two chords and construct their perpendicular bisectors. The intersection of the two perpendicular bisectors is the center of curvature of the mirror.

3. Repeat procedure (2) using a convex mirror. Extend the diverging rays backward as dotted lines, and thus locate the principal focus. Also locate the center of curvature of the mirror.

4. Remove the converging lens from between lamp and slits, thus obtaining five divergent rays of light. Set the plane mirror on the paper normal to the central ray, and draw straight lines to indicate the position of the mirror and the paths of the incident and reflected rays. Extend the reflected rays backward as dotted lines, and thus locate the image of the lamp.

5. Repeat procedure (4) using the convex mirror.

6. Repeat procedure (4) using the concave mirror. In this case the reflected rays will converge in front of the mirror to form the image.

7. Replace the converging lens and again arrange the apparatus so that five parallel rays are produced. Set the convex lens on the paper perpendicular to the central ray. Trace the outline of the lens and the paths of the rays, paying particular attention to the condition near the principal focus. Draw also the rays reflected at the surface of the lens, but draw these in very lightly.

8. Repeat procedure (7) using the concave lens. Locate the principal focus by extending the refracted rays backward as dotted lines.

9. Set the 60° prism on the paper in such a way as to allow the rays to pass through the prism symmetrically, i.e. so that the path of the rays inside the prism is parallel to the base of the prism. Trace the prism and the paths of the rays. The emerging light is colored, but for the present ignore this and use the center of the beam. The angle between the direction of the incident ray and that of the emergent ray is called the angle of deviation. The angle between the two refracting faces of the prism is called the refracting angle.

10. Set the right angle prism so that a short face is perpendicular to the rays. Trace the prism and the paths of the rays.

NAME_____ SECTION_____ DATE_____

QUESTIONS

1. Why are the concave mirrors used in automobile headlights parabolic instead of spherical?

2. Under what conditions is the angle of refraction greater than the angle of incidence?

3. (a) What is the focal length of the concave mirror you used? _____

   (b) What is its radius of curvature? _____

   (c) What is the focal length of the convex mirror you used? _____

   (d) What is its radius of curvature? _____

   (e) What is the focal length of the convex lens you used? _____

   (f) What is the focal length of the concave lens you used? _____

   (g) What is the angle of deviation in procedure (9)? _____

4. What is meant by the spherical aberration of a mirror?

5. What is meant by the chromatic aberration of a lens?

44

MEASUREMENT OF THE FOCAL LENGTH OF LENSES

The formation of images by lenses is one of the most important studies in the field of optics. The purpose of this experiment is to observe the real images formed by various lenses and to verify the lens equation; in particular, to measure the focal length of some positive and negative lenses and the equivalent focal length of a combination of thin lenses.

THEORY

When a beam of rays parallel to the principal axis of a lens impinges upon a converging lens, it is brought together at a point called the principal focus of the lens. The distance from the principal focus to the center of the lens is the focal length of the lens; the focal length is positive for a converging lens and negative for a diverging lens. The relation between the object distance, p, the image distance, q, and the focal length, f, of a thin lens is given by the lens equation

$$\frac{1}{p} + \frac{1}{q} = \frac{1}{f}$$

The magnification produced by a lens, i.e. the linear magnification, is defined as the ratio of the length of the image to the length of the object. This is also equal to the ratio of the image distance to the object distance. Therefore

$$\text{Magnification} = \frac{q}{p}$$

The principal focal length of a converging lens may be determined by forming an image of a very distant object on a screen and measuring the distance from the screen to the lens. This distance will be the focal length, since the rays of light from a very distant object are very nearly parallel. A more accurate method of determining the focal length of a positive lens is to measure the image distance corresponding to a suitable and known object distance, and to calculate the focal length from the lens equation.

When two thin lenses are in contact, the equivalent focal length of the combination may be measured experimentally by one of the above methods. It may also be calculated in terms of the individual focal lengths. Thus

$$\frac{1}{f} = \frac{1}{f_1} + \frac{1}{f_2}$$

where f is the equivalent focal length of the lens combination, f_1 is the focal length of the first lens, and f_2 is the focal length of the second lens.

A concave lens by itself cannot form a real image, since it is a diverging lens, hence a different method must be used for measuring its focal length. This is done by placing the negative lens in contact with a positive lens of shorter and known focal length, measuring the equivalent focal length of the combination experimentally, and then using the equation for the equivalent focal length of two thin lenses in contact to solve for the focal length of the negative lens.

APPARATUS

1. Optical bench.
2. Illuminated object.
3. Lens holders.
4. Screen.

5. Two convex lenses, A and B (of about 20 cm. and 10 cm. focal length respectively).
6. One concave lens, C (of about -20 cm. focal length).
7. Metric ruler.

PROCEDURE

1. Measure the focal length of lens A directly by obtaining the image of a very distant object on the screen and measuring the image distance. The object may be a tree or a house about a block away.

2. Repeat procedure (1) for lens B.

3. Determine the focal length of lens A by the use of the lens equation. Place the illuminated object at one end of the optical bench; then place the screen at a distance of about five times the focal length of the lens. With the object and screen fixed, find the position of the lens for which a sharp, enlarged image is produced on the screen. Make sure that the object, lens, and screen all lie along the same straight line, the principal axis of the lens, and that they are all perpendicular to the axis. Record the position of the object, the lens, and the screen; record the measurements to one millimeter. Measure the size of the object and the size of the image; record these measurements to 0.5 millimeter.

4. Repeat procedure (3) using lens B.

5. Repeat procedure (3) using the combination of lenses A and B in contact.

6. Repeat procedure (3) using the combination of lenses B and C in contact.

DATA

LENSES	FOCAL LENGTH MEASURED DIRECTLY	OBJECT DISTANCE p	IMAGE DISTANCE q	SIZE OF OBJECT	SIZE OF IMAGE
A					
B					
A AND B					
B AND C					

LENSES	FOCAL LENGTH FROM LENS EQUATION	FOCAL LENGTH FROM EQUATION FOR LENSES IN CONTACT	MAGNIFICATION	
			$\dfrac{\text{SIZE OF IMAGE}}{\text{SIZE OF OBJECT}}$	$\dfrac{q}{p}$
A				
B				
A AND B				
B AND C				
C				

CALCULATIONS

1. Calculate the focal length of lens A from the data of procedure (3), and the focal length of lens B from the data of procedure (4). Compute the magnification produced in each case from the ratio of the size of the image to the size of the object and from the ratio of the image distance to the object distance.

2. Calculate the focal length of the combination of lenses A and B from the data of procedure (5). Compare the result with the value obtained from theory, using the formula for the focal length of two thin lenses in contact.

3. Calculate the focal length of the combination of lenses B and C from the data of procedure (6). By using this value for the focal length of the combination, compute the focal length of the negative lens C, using the formula for the focal length of two thin lenses in contact.

QUESTIONS

1. Draw the ray diagram for the optical arrangement of parts in procedure (3). Represent the object by a small arrow.

2. (a) What is meant by the spherical aberration of a lens? (b) How can this aberration be reduced in a simple lens?

3. What is a real image?

4. What is a virtual image?

5. In a film projection apparatus it is desired to produce pictures 12 feet wide on a screen 50 feet from the lens; the size of the picture on the film is one inch wide. What must be the focal length of the projecting lens used?

45

THE TELESCOPE

Combinations of lenses are used extensively in many kinds of optical instruments. It is instructive to see how such a combination operates in actual practice. As an example this experiment presents a method of constructing an astronomical telescope and an opera glass and of determining the magnifying power of a telescope.

THEORY

There are three main types of telescopes: the astronomical telescope, the terrestrial telescope, and the opera glass.

The astronomical telescope, which is the simplest type, consists of two lenses, the objective lens and the eyepiece. The objective lens is a positive lens of long focal length, which forms a real inverted image of a distant object in its focal plane. The eyepiece is a positive lens of short focal length used to magnify the image produced by the objective lens. The eyepiece is used as a magnifying glass, by means of which an enlarged virtual image is formed of an object placed just inside its focus. In this instance the object used is the image formed by the objective lens. The eye looks directly at the enlarged virtual image produced by the eyepiece.

In the terrestrial telescope the image produced by the objective lens is made erect by means of another positive lens. This lens is placed beyond the first image and at such a distance as to produce a real inverted image of it, so that the second image is erect. The eyepiece is used to magnify this image, as described above.

The opera glass is a telescope in which the eyepiece is a divergent lens. This lens is so placed that the rays from the objective lens strike it before they converge to form an image. Thus the image that would have been formed by the objective lens serves as the virtual object for the negative lens. After leaving this lens, the rays diverge as if they came from an enlarged virtual image. The distance between the two lenses is made equal to the difference of their focal lengths. This type of telescope has a small field of view, but it has the advantage that it is shorter than the other forms of telescope and gives an erect image of the distant object.

The magnifying power of an optical instrument is defined as the ratio of the angle subtended at the eye by the image of an object viewed through the instrument to the angle subtended at the eye by the object viewed directly.

APPARATUS

1. Optical bench.
2. One long focus convergent lens (about 25 cm.).
3. One short focus convergent lens (about 10 cm.).
4. One short focus divergent lens (about 18 cm.).
5. Lens holders.
6. Screen.
7. Illuminated object.

8. Actual telescope, e.g. one taken from a wall galvanometer.
9. Telescope magnification scale. This scale is made up of a strip of white paper two feet long with a series of thick black lines drawn horizontally across it at regular intervals of about two inches. The lines are numbered to facilitate counting.

PROCEDURE

1. Measure the focal length of the two convergent lenses directly by obtaining the image of a very distant object on the screen and measuring the image distance. The object may be a tree or a house about a block away. Record each focal length.

2. The focal length of a divergent lens cannot be measured directly, since a divergent lens by itself cannot form a real image. Hence a different method must be used. The negative lens is placed in contact with a positive lens of shorter and known focal length, the equivalent focal length of the combination is then measured experimentally, and finally the focal length of the negative lens is calculated by using the equation for the equivalent focal length of two thin lenses in contact. When two thin lenses are in contact, the equivalent focal length of the combination may be calculated in terms of the individual focal lengths. The equation to be used is

$$\frac{1}{f} = \frac{1}{f_1} + \frac{1}{f_2}$$

where f is the equivalent focal length of the lens combination, f_1 is the focal length of the first lens, and f_2 is the focal length of the second lens.

Place the divergent lens in contact with the short focus convergent lens. Measure the focal length of this combination of lenses directly, by obtaining the image of a very distant object on the screen and measuring the image distance. Finally calculate the focal length of the negative lens by using the equation for the equivalent focal length of two thin lenses in contact. The focal length of the short focus convergent lens was found in procedure (1).

3. Construct a simple astronomical telescope, using the long focus convergent lens as the objective lens, and the short focus convergent lens as the eyepiece. Special care must be taken to have the various optical parts at the same height and well lined up. In addition the lenses must be perpendicular to the optic axis of the system. Placing the illuminated object at one end of the table, focus on a screen the image produced by the objective lens. Mount the eyepiece on the other side of the screen at a distance of its own focal length from the screen. Note the distance between the lenses and then move both of them so that the eyepiece will be near the end of the optical bench, keeping the lenses the same distance apart.

4. Remove the screen and move the eyepiece slightly, adjusting it so that on looking through it you can see a sharp inverted image of the illuminated object.

5. In order to measure the magnifying power of your telescope, point it in the direction of the telescope scale. Look through the telescope with one eye and directly at the scale with the other. The magnified image of the scale will be superimposed on the unmagnified scale. Count the number of divisions of the scale as viewed directly which cover exactly one division of the magnified scale. This number gives the magnifying power of the telescope.

6. Construct an opera glass using the same lens for the objective as before, and the short focus divergent lens as the eyepiece. Placing the illuminated object at one end of the table, focus on a screen the image produced by the objective lens. Mount the eyepiece on the same side of the screen as the objective lens and at a distance from it equal to the difference of their focal lengths.

7. Remove the screen and adjust the eyepiece so that on looking through it you can see the largest clear and erect image that can be formed.

8. Determine the magnifying power of the opera glass as in procedure (5).

9. Study an actual telescope. Pull out the tube containing the eyepiece and cross hairs and determine the focal length of both the eyepiece and the objective lens.

10. Look at the sky through the eyepiece and adjust it until the cross hairs are sharply in focus.

11. Put the telescope together again and adjust it by focusing on some distant object until a sharp image is obtained. Adjust the eyepiece carefully until there is no parallax, that is, until there is no relative motion between the image and the cross hairs when the eye is shifted from side to side. Now the telescope is adjusted.

12. Determine the magnifying power of this telescope as in procedure (5).

DATA

Focal length of the long focus convergent lens..

Focal length of the short focus convergent lens...

Focal length of the short focus divergent lens..

Magnifying power of the astronomical telescope...

Magnifying power of the opera glass...

Focal length of the objective lens of the actual telescope.....................................

Focal length of the eyepiece of the actual telescope....................................

Magnifying power of the actual telescope...

QUESTIONS

1. If a telescope is accurately focused on a distant object, in what direction must the eyepiece be moved to focus on a near object? Explain.

2. (a) How does the terrestrial type of telescope differ from the astronomical telescope? (b) Explain how the change is accomplished.

3. What is meant by parallax?

4. Draw a ray diagram, approximately to scale, showing the illuminated object, the real image formed by the objective, and the virtual image formed by the eyepiece of your astronomical telescope. Represent the object by a small arrow.

5. The magnifying power of a telescope 24 inches long is equal to 15. Determine the focal length of the objective lens and that of the eyepiece. Assume that the telescope is focused on a distant object.

46

INDEX OF REFRACTION BY A PRISM SPECTROMETER

One of the important properties of light is the bending of its rays as it passes obliquely from one transparent substance into another. This effect is called refraction. The laws of refraction are used extensively in applied optics in the design of all kinds of optical instruments. The object of this experiment is to measure the refracting angle of a prism and the angle of minimum deviation by means of a spectrometer and to compute the index of refraction of the prism. Incidentally, the experiment introduces the student to a preliminary study of the spectrometer.

THEORY

The index of refraction of a medium with respect to air for any particular wave length of light is the ratio of the velocity of light in air to the velocity of light in the medium. The law of refraction states that the ratio of the sine of the angle of incidence to the sine of the angle of refraction is constant, for any two given mediums, for light of any given wave length; the constant is equal to the relative index of refraction of the two mediums.

If a beam of light passes through a prism, it will be deviated from its original course. The angle between the ray emerging from the prism and the original direction of the beam of light is called the angle of deviation. If the direction of the incident ray is varied, it is found that the magnitude of the deviation varies also, but that for one particular angle of incidence the angle of deviation becomes a minimum. The angle of minimum deviation occurs when the path of the ray through the prism is symmetrical; this means that the initial angle of incidence is the same as the final angle of refraction, as the ray emerges from the prism. Under these conditions, the index of refraction of the prism is given by the relation

$$\mu = \frac{\sin \frac{1}{2}(A + D)}{\sin \frac{1}{2}A}$$

where μ is the index of refraction, A is the refracting angle of the prism, and D is the angle of minimum deviation. In order to measure the angles A and D, a spectrometer is used.

A spectrometer (see Fig. 56) is an optical instrument for producing and analyzing spectra. It consists of four essential parts: a collimator, a prism, a telescope, and a divided circle. The collimator is a tube with a con-

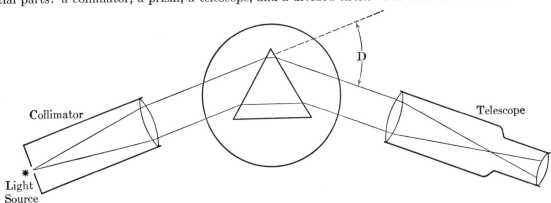

Fig. 56. Prism Spectrometer

verging lens at one end and a fine slit of adjustable width placed in the focal plane of the lens at the other end of the tube. The function of the collimator is to render the rays of light from the slit parallel by means of a lens. The prism deviates the rays of light and disperses them into a spectrum. The telescope consists of the objective lens, which brings the parallel rays of light to a focus in its focal plane, and the eyepiece, through which the image of the spectrum is viewed. If the light is all of one color, or monochromatic, a single image of the slit appears. The position of the image can be read by the setting of the telescope on the divided circle of the spectrometer. If a source of light containing several colors is used, several images of different color will appear side by side, each being an image of the slit formed by one component of the light.

CAUTION: Do not handle the spectrometer at all until the instructor has demonstrated its operation to you, for it is very easy to upset the adjustments and thus cause needless delay.

APPARATUS

1. Prism spectrometer.
2. Bunsen burner.

3. Rock salt.
4. Desk lamp.

PROCEDURE

1. The spectrometer should be already adjusted with the collimator and telescope properly focused and aligned, the prism mounted on the prism table, and the prism table leveled so that the refracting edge of the prism is parallel to the slit of the collimator. CAUTION: The spectrometer is easily thrown out of adjustment and even damaged beyond repair. Be extremely careful in handling it.

2. Set up a Bunsen burner in front of the slit of the spectrometer, and about three inches away from it. Put a small piece of rock salt on top of the burner, light the gas, and obtain a brilliant yellow flame.

3. Turn the refracting angle of the prism toward the collimator so that the edge of the prism divides the light, part falling on one face, part on the other.

4. Determine the direction of the light which is reflected from one face of the prism. Move the telescope into its path and view the slit through the eyepiece. The slit should be made as narrow as possible and yet remain visible in the telescope. Adjust the position of the telescope until the image of the slit falls on the intersection of the cross hairs.

5. Directly under the arm supporting the telescope is a clamping device which rotates with the arm and permits the telescope to be clamped to the base by means of a radial screw. A tangent screw on the telescope arm allows a fine adjustment of the setting of the telescope; however, the tangent screw is used only after the telescope has been clamped with the radial screw. Clamp the telescope by means of the radial screw and locate the position of the image of the slit by setting the intersection of the cross hairs exactly on the yellow line by means of the tangent screw. Record the setting of the telescope to the nearest minute of arc, reading the divided circle with the help of the vernier.

6. Repeat procedures (4–5) for the image from the other face of the prism.

7. Turn the prism table so that the path of the beam of light through the prism is approximately symmetrical. Move the telescope into the path of the refracted beam and adjust its position so that the image of the slit is roughly in the center of the field of view. Slowly turn the prism table in such a direction as to diminish the angle of deviation, until the deviation becomes a minimum. The test for this position is that any further motion of the prism table in the same direction will reverse the direction of motion of the slit image. In locating this position of minimum deviation, if the image moves out of the field of the telescope, the telescope must be moved so as to follow it. When the position of the prism for minimum deviation has been found, and the prism table set as near to it as possible, adjust the position of the telescope until the image of the slit falls on the intersection of the cross hairs. Record the setting of the telescope to the nearest minute of arc.

8. Ask the instructor to remove the prism from the spectrometer. Turn the telescope into line with the collimator and adjust its position until the image of the slit falls on the intersection of the cross hairs. Record the setting of the telescope to the nearest minute of arc. This is the setting of the telescope for the undeviated beam of light.

9. If white light is passed through the slit of the spectrometer, a continuous image showing all the colors of the spectrum may be seen through the telescope. After the prism has been replaced on the spectrometer by the instructor, examine the spectrum of the light from a tungsten lamp, noting the relative position of the different colors.

DATA

Setting of the telescope for the beam of light reflected from one face of the prism. . . . .

Setting of the telescope for the beam of light reflected from the other face of the prism. . . . .

Setting of the telescope for the refracted beam at minimum deviation. . . . .

Setting of the telescope for the undeviated beam of light. . . . .

Angle between the two reflected beams of light. . . . .

Refracting angle of the prism. . . . .

Angle of minimum deviation. . . . .

Index of refraction of the prism for the sodium *D* line. . . . .

NAME__________ SECTION__________ DATE__________ EXPERIMENT FORTY-SIX

CALCULATIONS

1. Compute the refracting angle of the prism from the data of procedures (5–6). The total angle between the two reflected beams is equal to twice the refracting angle. If the two settings of the telescope lie on either side of the zero of the divided circle, be sure to compute the angle between the two reflected beams properly.

2. Calculate the angle of minimum deviation from the data of procedures (7–8).

3. Calculate the index of refraction of the prism using the formula given in the theory. This will be the index of refraction for the sodium *D* line.

QUESTIONS

1. Explain why monochromatic light must be used in determining the angle of minimum deviation.

2. (a) Explain the spectrum produced when white light is used. (b) Which color is deviated most? (c) For which color does glass have the highest index of refraction? (d) For which color does it have the lowest?

3. Compute the velocity of light in glass in centimeters per second from your value of the index of refraction for yellow light and the known value of the velocity of light in vacuum.

47

ANALYSIS OF LIGHT BY A SPECTROSCOPE

Light is made up of many different colors, each of which has a definite wave length. When a beam of light is passed through a glass prism, it is broken up into a spectrum. Each chemical element produces its own characteristic spectrum, so that by analyzing the light given off by a substance, it is possible to identify the elements which it contains. The object of this experiment is to analyze light by means of a spectroscope and to study bright line spectra and continuous spectra.

THEORY

In general, light is made up of many component parts, each of which has a definite wave length corresponding to a definite color. When a beam of light is passed through a glass prism, it is refracted or bent from its original direction, and also dispersed into a spectrum. Dispersion occurs because the velocity with which different colors pass through the prism depends on their wave length; hence the index of refraction is different for each wave length, and the angle of deviation is also different.

Spectrum analysis is the decomposition of a beam of light into its constituents and the examination of the image so formed. A spectroscope is an optical instrument for producing and analyzing spectra. It consists of three essential parts: a collimator, a prism, and a telescope. The collimator is a tube with a converging lens at one end and a fine slit of adjustable width placed in the focal plane of the lens at the other end of the tube. The function of the collimator is to render the rays of light from the slit parallel by means of the lens. The prism deviates the rays of light and disperses them into a spectrum. The telescope consists of the objective lens, which brings the parallel rays of light to a focus in its focal plane, and the eyepiece, through which the image of the spectrum is viewed. If the light is all of one color, or monochromatic, a single image of the slit appears. If a source containing several colors is used, several images of different color will appear side by side, each being an image of the slit formed by one component of the light. The position of each image can be read off by the setting of the telescope on the divided scale of the spectroscope.

There are three main types of spectra: continuous, bright line, and absorption. A continuous spectrum is produced by light from an incandescent solid or liquid; it contains a continuous gradation of colors, merging with very gradual changes from red to violet. The bright line spectrum is produced by exciting an element in the gaseous state by means of an electric discharge or by heating; such a spectrum consists of bright lines, corresponding to light of definite colors, separated by dark spaces, the number and relative positions of the lines depending on the element used and the method of excitation employed. An absorption spectrum is produced when light from a source furnishing a continuous spectrum is passed through some cooler absorbing medium; the resulting spectrum is crossed by dark spaces or lines which form the absorption spectrum of the material.

Wave lengths of visible light are usually expressed in Angstrom units. One Angstrom unit is 10^{-8} centimeter. The principal lines in the helium spectrum are given in the following table:

HELIUM LINES

WAVE LENGTH IN ANGSTROM UNITS	COLOR
7065	red
6678	red
5876	yellow
5048	green
4922	blue-green
4713	blue
4471	deep blue
4388	blue-violet
4026	violet
3889	violet

215

The principal lines in the mercury spectrum are given in the following table:

MERCURY LINES

WAVE LENGTH IN ANGSTROM UNITS	COLOR
5790	yellow
5770	yellow
5461	green
4916	blue-green
4358	blue
4078	violet
4047	violet

In these spectra other fainter lines are also present, but these are the brightest and easiest to find.

APPARATUS

1. Spectroscope.
2. Mercury arc.
3. Helium tube.
4. Hydrogen tube.
5. Neon tube.
6. Bunsen burner.
7. Rock salt.
8. Desk lamp.
9. Storage battery.
10. Induction coil.
11. Holder for the discharge tubes.
12. Switch.

PROCEDURE

1. Study the helium spectrum. Place the stand containing the spectrometer tube in front of the spectroscope with the helium tube just outside the slit of the collimator tube. Connect the terminals of the helium tube to the secondary of the induction coil. Adjust the spectroscope so that the collimating tube is pointing directly at the discharge tube. Close the switch. CAUTION: Do not touch the discharge tube or high tension wires while the induction coil is in operation.

2. Adjust the position of the telescope until the first red line of the helium spectrum falls exactly on the intersection of the cross hairs of the telescope. Record the wave length, the color, and the setting of the telescope for this line; record the setting to the nearest minute of arc, reading the divided circle with the help of the vernier.

3. Repeat procedure (2) for the other lines of the helium spectrum, taking readings of the setting of the telescope for each of the lines that can be recognized. Do not try to adjust the prism and do not change its setting.

4. Repeat procedures (1–3) for the mercury spectrum.

5. Using the neon discharge tube, observe the spectrum. No measurements are necessary.

6. Repeat procedure (5) for the hydrogen tube.

7. Set up a Bunsen burner in front of the slit of the spectrometer, and about three inches away from it. Put a small piece of rock salt on top of the burner, light the gas, and obtain a brilliant yellow flame. Record the setting of the telescope for the sodium doublet.

8. Examine the spectrum of the light from a tungsten lamp. Record the setting of the telescope for the upper and lower limits of the visible spectrum.

NAME_____ SECTION_____ DATE_____ EXPERIMENT FORTY-SEVEN

DATA

SPECTRUM	COLOR	WAVE LENGTH	SETTING OF TELESCOPE	WAVE LENGTH FROM CALIBRATION CURVE
HELIUM				
MERCURY				
SODIUM				
VISIBLE				

CALCULATIONS

1. Draw a graph with wave lengths in Angstrom units as abscissas and the settings of the telescope as ordinates for the lines of the helium spectrum from the data of procedures (2–3). The smooth curve so obtained is the calibration curve of the instrument. This curve is obtained by plotting the scale readings of each of the known lines of an element against the corresponding wave length. From this curve the wave length of the lines observed in other spectra may be determined.

2. Measure the wave length of the sodium doublet by using the reading of the telescope in procedure (7) and reading off the wave length from the calibration curve. Compare your results with the known value (use 5893 Angstroms, the mean of 5890 and 5896, which are the wave lengths of the doublet).

3. From the calibration curve read off the wave lengths of the mercury lines by using the readings of the telescope obtained in procedure (4); tabulate the results. How do these values compare with the known values?

4. From the data of procedure (8) and the calibration curve determine the range of the visible spectrum in Angstrom units.

QUESTIONS

1. Compare the appearance of the bright line spectrum with that of the continuous spectrum and explain the difference.

2. Compare your results for the range of the visible spectrum with the known values.

3. Of what use is the calibration curve and why is it needed?

4. Explain how the Doppler effect may be adapted to light waves in determining the speed of stars toward the earth or away from the earth.

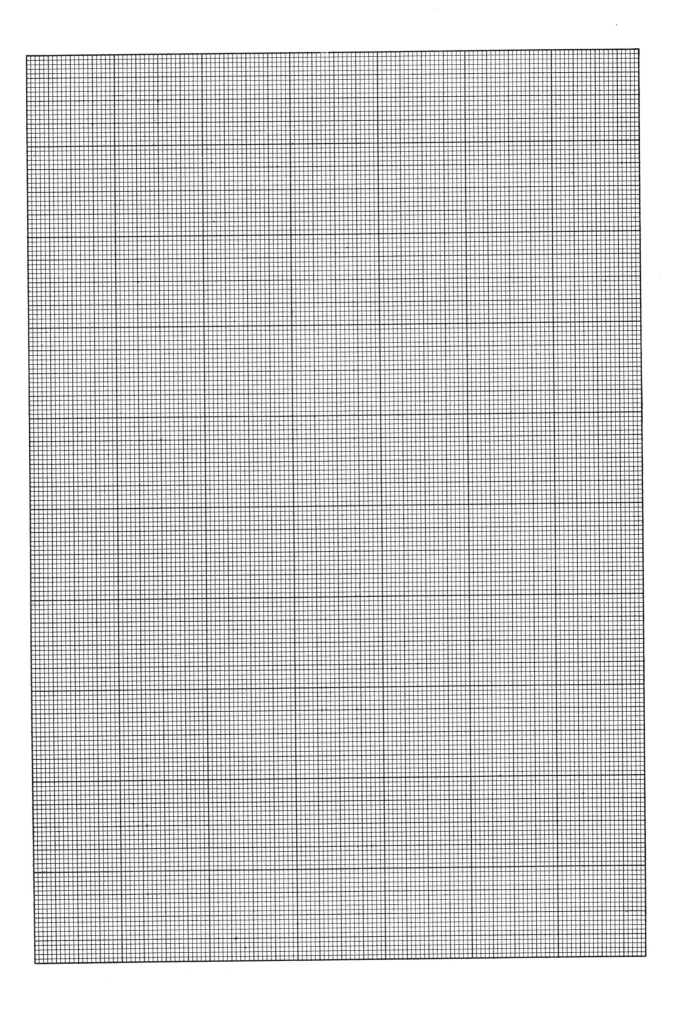

48

THE DIFFRACTION GRATING

The diffraction grating is one of the most important optical instruments. It is one of the simplest devices for producing spectra and for measuring wave lengths of light. The object of this experiment is to measure the wave lengths of certain lines in the mercury spectrum by means of the diffraction grating.

THEORY

The diffraction grating provides the simplest and most accurate method for measuring wave lengths of light. It consists of a very large number of fine, equally spaced parallel slits. There are two types of diffraction gratings: the reflecting, and the transmitting type. The lines of the reflection grating are ruled on a polished metal surface; the incident light is reflected from the unruled portions. The lines of the transmission grating are ruled on glass; the unruled portions of the glass act as slits. Gratings usually have about 10,000 to 20,000 lines per inch. The grating used in this experiment is a transmission grating replica.

The principles of diffraction and interference are applied to the measurement of wave length in the diffraction grating. Let the broken line in Fig. 57 represent a magnified portion of a diffraction grating. Let a beam of parallel monochromatic light, originally from the same source and having passed through a slit, impinge upon the grating from the left. By Huygens' principle, the light spreads out in every direction from the apertures of the grating, each of which acts as a separate new source of light. The envelope of the secondary wavelets determines the position of the advancing wave. In the figure are seen the instantaneous positions of several successive wavelets after they have advanced beyond the grating. Lines drawn tangent to these wavelets connect points which are in phase; hence they represent the new wave fronts. One of these wave fronts is tangent to wavelets which have all advanced the same distance from the slits, and the wave front formed is thus parallel to the original wave front. A converging lens placed in the path of these rays would form the central image. Another wave front is tangent to wavelets whose distances from adjacent slits differ by one

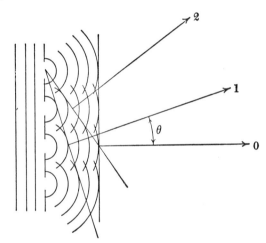

Fig. 57. The Diffraction Grating

wave length. This wave front advances in the direction 1 and forms the first order spectrum. The next wave front is tangent to wavelets whose distances from adjacent slits differ by two wave lengths. This wave front advances in the direction 2 and forms the second order spectrum. Spectra of higher orders will be formed at correspondingly greater angles.

The wave length of the light is given by the grating equation

$$n\lambda = d \sin \theta$$

where λ is the wave length of the light, in centimeters; n is the order of the spectrum, i.e. the first image, the second image, etc., formed on either side of the central image; d is the distance between the lines on the grating in centimeters; and θ is the angle of deviation from the original direction of the light. The angle θ is measured directly, while the grating constant d is calculated from the number of lines per inch ruled on the grating. If the light is all of one color (monochromatic), a single image of the slit will appear in each order of the spectrum. But if the light is not monochromatic, there will be as many images of the slit in each order as there are different wave lengths in the light from the source, the diffracting angle for each wave length being given by the above equation. The wave length of visible light is usually expressed in Angstrom units. One Angstrom unit is 10^{-8} centimeter.

The arrangement used in this experiment is shown in Fig. 58. Light from the mercury arc passes through a narrow slit and falls on the grating. The observer looks through the grating in the direction of the mercury arc

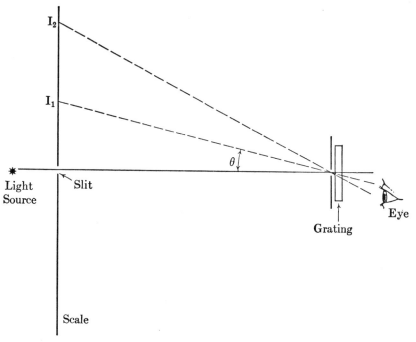

Fig. 58. Optical System for the Diffraction Grating

and sees the central image and the diffracted beams which make up the spectra on either side of the central image. The meter stick should be mounted horizontally and perpendicular to the central ray. The grating should be mounted parallel to the scale about 50 cm. away from it and with the grating rulings parallel to the slit.

APPARATUS

1. Diffraction grating.
2. Grating holder.
3. Slit.
4. Rider for locating the images
5. Two meter sticks.

6. Mercury arc.
7. Source of 110-volt D.C.
8. Tungsten lamp.
9. Stand and clamps for mounting the meter stick and the grating.

PROCEDURE

1. The grating spectrometer will be already adjusted with the grating rulings parallel to the slit, and the plane of the grating and the scale both perpendicular to the central ray. CAUTION: The spectrometer, grating, and mercury arc are all easily thrown out of adjustment and even damaged beyond repair. Be extremely careful in handling them.

2. Look through the diffraction grating in the direction of the mercury arc. Keep your eye several inches away from the grating. The lens of the eye will focus the beam emerging from the grating on the retina of the eye. You will see the source, which will be the central image, and the virtual images of the source on either side, which constitute the first and second order spectra. Look in the direction of the first order spectrum so that the violet line of the right-hand first order spectrum appears centered in the aperture on the grating. Slide the meter stick rider until it coincides exactly with the violet line. Record the position of the rider to one millimeter.

3. Repeat procedure (2) for the blue, green, and yellow lines of the spectrum. You will see two yellow lines very close together; record the one of longer wave length, or on the side away from the central image.

4. Repeat procedure (2) for the same four lines for the left-hand first order spectrum.

5. Repeat procedure (2) for the same four lines for the left-hand second order spectrum.

6. Repeat procedure (2) for the same four lines for the right-hand second order spectrum. Record the distance of the slit from the grating and the number of lines per inch stated on the grating.

7. Examine the continuous first order spectrum produced by the light from a tungsten lamp, noting the relative position of the different colors. Observe the continuous spectrum of the second order, noting the width of the colored bands as compared with the first order.

DATA

Number of lines per inch on the grating...

Grating constant in centimeters..

Distance of the slit from the grating...

The brightest lines in the visible spectrum of mercury are given in the following table:

Mercury Lines

WAVE LENGTH IN ANGSTROM UNITS	COLOR
5790	yellow
5461	green
4358	blue
4047	violet

MERCURY LINES		POSITION OF RIDER			CALCULATED VALUES				
WAVE LENGTH ANGSTROM UNITS	COLOR	RIGHT	LEFT	AVERAGE DISTANCE FROM THE SLIT	TAN θ	θ	SIN θ	COMPUTED WAVE LENGTH	PER CENT DEVIATION
FIRST ORDER SPECTRA									
5790	YELLOW								
5461	GREEN								
4358	BLUE								
4047	VIOLET								
SECOND ORDER SPECTRA									
5790	YELLOW								
5461	GREEN								
4358	BLUE								
4047	VIOLET								

CALCULATIONS

1. Compute the average distance of the rider from the slit for each of the four lines of the first order spectrum measured.

2. Evaluate tan θ, θ, and sin θ for each line. Tan θ can be obtained by dividing the average distance of the rider from the slit by the distance of the slit from the diffraction grating. The values of θ and sin θ can be obtained from tables of trigonometric functions.

3. Compute the wave length of each line, using the grating constant d computed from the number of lines per inch stated on the grating and applying the grating equation.

4. Calculate the per cent deviation of the computed values of the wave lengths from the known values.

5. Repeat calculations (1–4) for the second order spectra.

NAME_____ SECTION_____ DATE_____ EXPERIMENT FORTY-EIGHT

QUESTIONS

1. (a) Discuss the difference between the continuous spectrum obtained with a grating and one obtained with a prism. (b) Which color is deviated most in each case? Why?

2. Why does a grating produce several spectra, while a prism produces only one?

3. Why are the higher order spectra more accurate than the first order spectrum in determining wave lengths of light?

4. A monochromatic beam of light impinges normally on a grating and forms an image of the slit 10 cm. from the central image on a screen. The screen is 50 cm. from the grating and is set parallel to it. The grating has 10,000 lines per inch. What is the wave length of the light?

5. A grating having 15,000 lines per inch is mounted as in the experiment and produces a spectrum of the mercury arc. What is the angle between the first order green line and the second order green line?

49

INTERFERENCE OF LIGHT

One of the important methods of measuring the wave length of light is to allow monochromatic light to be reflected from the two surfaces of a very thin film of varying thickness. The light reflected from the surfaces of the film will produce interference fringes, and from the dimensions of the film and the number of fringes, the wave length of the light can be evaluated. The object of this experiment is to study the interference of light and to measure the wave length of the yellow light from a sodium flame.

THEORY

Interference is the effect produced when two or more vibrations or trains of waves are superimposed so as to strengthen or to neutralize one another, the magnitude of the effect depending on the relative phases of the components. Interference of light will be produced when a beam of monochromatic light is divided into two beams, one of which travels a longer distance than the other, and the two beams are then superimposed. When the two beams are reunited, they will produce darkness wherever the path difference is an odd number of half wave lengths of light, and they will produce a bright spot wherever the path difference is any number of whole wave lengths of light. A method of producing interference is to allow monochromatic light to fall upon two pieces of plate glass placed at a very small angle to each other (see Fig. 60). Light will be reflected from each of the glass surfaces. The light reflected from the lower surface of the upper plate and the light reflected from the upper surface of the lower plate will interfere. The second reflected beam will travel a longer distance, namely across the air film and back. Since the air film varies regularly in thickness, the interference pattern produced will consist of a series of parallel bright and dark lines which are called interference fringes.

The wave length of the yellow light from a sodium flame may be determined by using interference fringes. At any place where the path difference is a whole number of full wave lengths, the two reflected rays will be in phase and the spot will be bright. Where the path difference is an odd number of half wave lengths, the spot will be dark. Thus, from one bright fringe to the next one, the difference in path increases by one whole wave length of light. This means that the thickness of the air film increases by one half of a wave length of light in this distance, since the light goes across the film and back. But in the entire length L of the air film (see Fig. 59), its thickness increases from zero to T, the thickness of the thin strip of steel which separates the glass plates at one end. Therefore, at the thick end of the air film the path difference is $2T$. The total number of wave lengths contained in this distance is $2T/\lambda$; but this is also the total number of bright fringes in the air film, or nL, where n is the number of bright fringes per centimeter. Hence the wave length λ is given by the expression

$$\lambda = \frac{2T}{nL}$$

where T is the thickness of the steel strip in centimeters, L is the length of the air film, and n is the number of bright fringes per centimeter.

APPARATUS

1. Bunsen burner.
2. Rock salt.
3. Two plane parallel glass plates and a board for mounting them.
4. Mirror, lens, and supporting stand.
5. Thin strip of steel.
6. Centimeter scale.
7. Micrometer caliper.

PROCEDURE

1. Measure the thickness of the thin strip of steel with the micrometer caliper and record the reading.

2. Be sure that the glass plates are clean. Be careful not to get finger marks on the surfaces which are to be placed together. Carefully **lay one glass plate** down flat upon the other with the best surfaces in contact, and

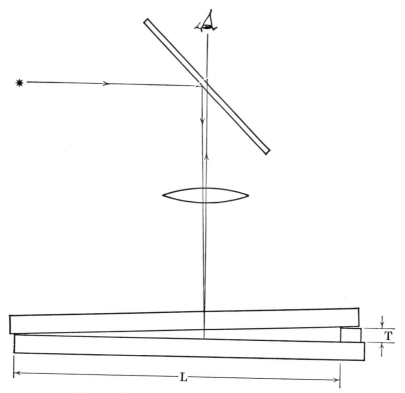

Fig. 59. Apparatus for Viewing Interference Fringes

so that the upper plate projects slightly at the thin end of the air film. Separate them at the other end by the thin steel strip, placing the edge of the strip parallel to the ends of the glass plates.

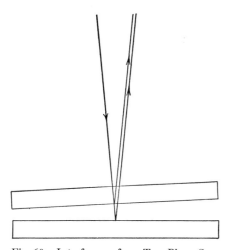

Fig. 60. Interference from Two Plane Surfaces

3. Measure the length L of the air film, i.e. the distance between the edge of the steel strip and where the two plates rest on each other, and record this reading.

4. Place the supporting stand, with the mirror set at 45° and the lens, over the center of the wedge shaped air film (see Fig. 59). Place a small piece of rock salt on the Bunsen burner. Light the burner and place it at a convenient distance opposite the mirror. The image of the flame, when viewed through the small hole in the mirror, should be parallel to the length of the air film. The lens is used to magnify the fringes; the pinhole in the mirror is placed at the focus of the lens.

5. Observe the interference fringes. They consist of a series of dark parallel lines across the image of the yellow flame and are perpendicular to the length of the air film. Lay the centimeter scale flat upon the upper plate, so that the edge of the scale is perpendicular to the fringes. Looking through the lens, count the number of dark fringes in two centimeters of length, estimating to tenths of a fringe. Record this reading.

6. Repeat procedure (5) making a second determination of the number of dark fringes in two centimeters of length, and record the reading.

DATA

Thickness of the thin strip of steel. . . . .

Length of the air film. . . . .

Number of fringes in two centimeters of length:. . . . .

    First reading. . . . .

    Second reading. . . . .

    Average. . . . .

Number of fringes per centimeter of length...

Wave length of yellow light from sodium flame...

Per cent error...

CALCULATIONS

1. Compute the number of fringes per centimeter, using the average of the two readings taken.

2. Using the formula given in the theory, calculate the wave length of the yellow light from the sodium flame. Express your result in Angstrom units. (1 Angstrom = 10^{-8} cm.)

3. Compare your result with the known value, taking the average wave length of the sodium doublet as 5893 Angstroms, and compute the per cent error of your determination.

QUESTIONS

1. (a) Explain how the method used in this experiment could be employed to test whether a surface is optically plane or not. (b) What would be the shape of the fringes if a spherical surface were placed in contact with a flat surface?

2. Explain why it sometimes occurs that the fringes run diagonally across the plates.

3. Suppose that white light were used to produce the interference fringes in the experiment. What would be the appearance of the fringes produced?

4. Two plane glass plates touch at one edge and are separated at the opposite edge by a strip of tinfoil. The air wedge is examined with sodium light reflected normally from its two surfaces, and 35 dark interference fringes are observed. Compute the thickness of the tinfoil.

5. How is this experiment evidence for a wave theory of light? Explain.

50

POLARIZED LIGHT

Experiments on interference and diffraction show that light is composed of waves, but they do not offer any evidence as to whether these waves are transverse or longitudinal. However, experiments on polarization show that light waves must be transverse waves. The purpose of this experiment is to study some of the fundamental phenomena of polarized light.

THEORY

Light waves consist of transverse electromagnetic vibrations which travel with finite velocity. The electric vibrations and the magnetic vibrations are perpendicular to the direction of propagation of the light, and also perpendicular to each other. In ordinary light, the electric vibrations occur in all directions, in a plane perpendicular to the direction of propagation; this light is unpolarized. It is possible to produce plane polarized light, that is, light in which the electric vibrations all occur in some one direction perpendicular to the ray of light. In this case the electric vibrations are all restricted to a single plane.

Light may be plane polarized by reflection from a nonconducting reflector or by passing through a doubly refracting crystal. When light is reflected from the surface of a nonconductor, it is partially polarized. For a certain angle of incidence, it is almost completely polarized. This angle is known as the polarizing angle, and for a piece of flat unsilvered glass it is about 57°. The refracted beam is found to be partially polarized in a direction at right angles to that of the reflected beam.

A doubly refracting crystal, like calcite, has the property of dividing a beam of ordinary light which passes through it into two polarized beams of light. In each of these beams the direction of vibration of the light is in a single plane, the two planes of vibration being perpendicular to each other. Some crystals have also the property of absorbing one of these beams and transmitting the other, so that the transmitted light becomes plane polarized. Tourmaline is a crystal of this type.

Natural crystals are usually too small to be used in an experiment where a wide beam of polarized light is needed; for this purpose, Polaroid sheets are used. In a Polaroid, very minute crystals are distributed uniformly and densely in a cellulose film which is mounted between two glass plates. The individual crystals are needle shaped and submicroscopic in size, and are turned so that their axes are parallel by stretching the film before it is mounted on glass. Polaroids produce polarized light in the same manner as described above for natural crystals.

APPARATUS

1. Two Polaroid disks, each mounted in a holder in which it can rotate.
2. Optical bench.
3. Light source with lens to produce a parallel beam of light.
4. Desk lamp.
5. Photronic cell connected to a microammeter.
6. Calcite crystal.
7. Pile of thin glass plates.
8. Black glass mirror.
9. Piece of cellophane.
10. Thin piece of mica.
11. Unannealed glass plate.
12. Annealed glass plate.
13. Piece of celluloid.

PROCEDURE

1. Place the light source at one end of the optical bench. Place the photronic cell at the other end of the optical bench, and in such a position as to receive the light. Place one of the Polaroid disks on the optical bench and in front of the photronic cell, so that the light has to pass through it to get to the cell. This Polaroid is the analyzer. Rotate the analyzer and notice the reading of the microammeter. If the microammeter goes off scale, decrease the size of the beam of light by placing a diaphragm in front of the condensing lens, regulating the size of the beam so that the microammeter reads nearly full scale. The light coming directly from the lamp is unpolarized. The intensity of the light transmitted by the analyzer should be nearly independent of the angle that its axis makes with the vertical.

2. Place the second Polaroid disk on the optical bench in front of the lamp and about four inches away from it, and in such a position that all the light passes through it. This is the polarizer. Place it with its axis in the vertical direction.

3. Now rotate the analyzer and take readings of the microammeter for different settings of the analyzer. Begin with the axis vertical and take readings of the microammeter for angles 0, 10, 20, 30 degrees, etc., up to 180 degrees. You will observe that the intensity of the light transmitted by the analyzer depends upon the angle between the axis of the analyzer and that of the polarizer.

4. Remove the photronic cell. Allow the light to pass through both Polaroids, leaving a space of about six inches between them. Set the two Polaroids for extinction, i.e. so that the minimum amount of light passes through them. Now place a piece of cellophane in the space between the Polaroids, look at the cellophane through the analyzer, and observe the field of view. Fold the cellophane into several thicknesses and observe the effect on the color produced.

5. Place a thin piece of mica in the space between the Polaroids, look at the mica through the analyzer, and observe the field of view.

6. Repeat procedure (5) using the unannealed glass plate.

7. Repeat procedure (5) using the annealed glass plate.

8. Repeat procedure (5) using a piece of celluloid. Twist the celluloid slightly out of shape and observe the regions where strains are produced.

9. Remove the polarizer from the optical bench. Place the black glass mirror in a holder on the optical bench and allow the unpolarized light from the lamp to fall on it. Rotate the mirror holder so as to make the angle of incidence about 55°. Observe the light reflected from the mirror by looking at it through a Polaroid. By rotating the Polaroid, notice whether the reflected light is polarized.

10. Repeat procedure (9) using a pile of thin glass plates as the mirror. Determine whether the reflected light is polarized, and also whether the transmitted light is polarized.

11. Make a dot on a piece of paper. Place a calcite crystal over the dot and look through it. You will observe two images. Rotate the crystal and notice what happens to the two dots. Now look at the dots through the calcite and a Polaroid. Rotate the Polaroid and notice the result. The two dots represent two beams of light coming from the calcite crystal. Determine whether these two beams are polarized and find the relative direction of vibration of the two beams.

12. If the sun is shining, look at the blue light from the sky through the analyzer. Notice particularly the light coming from a direction roughly perpendicular to the sun's direction. Determine whether this light is polarized.

DATA

SETTING OF THE ANALYZER	MICROAMMETER READING	SETTING OF THE ANALYZER	MICROAMMETER READING
0°		100°	
10°		110°	
20°		120°	
30°		130°	
40°		140°	
50°		150°	
60°		160°	
70°		170°	
80°		180°	
90°			

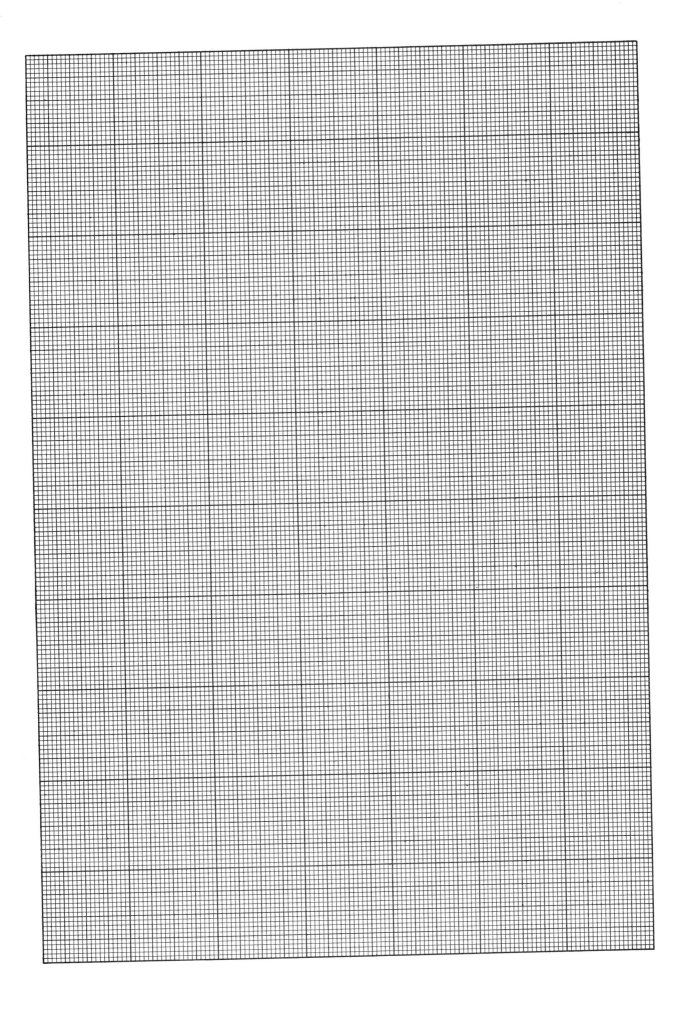

CALCULATIONS

1. The percentage polarization is given by the expression

$$P = 100 \frac{I_{max} - I_{min}}{I_{max} + I_{min}}$$

where P is the percentage polarization, I_{max} is the largest value of the microammeter reading observed, and I_{min} is the smallest value observed.

Calculate the percentage polarization from your readings in procedure (3).

2. Plot a graph using the microammeter readings as ordinates and the values of the angles as abscissas.

QUESTIONS

1. Explain the difference between transverse waves and longitudinal waves.

2. What is meant by a plane polarized beam of light?

3. Mention some of the uses of polarized light.

4. (a) Describe the construction of a nicol prism. (b) Explain how it produces a polarized beam of light.

51

THE GEIGER COUNTER

The perfection of the Geiger counter and the manufacture of radioisotopes in the atomic pile have provided the tools with which to perform new experiments in college physics. These experiments will make the study of atomic physics meaningful and tangible to the student. This experiment contains a discussion of the methods of measuring radioactive radiations and is designed to acquaint the student with the operation of the Geiger counter. It is the purpose of this experiment to determine the characteristic curve and the proper operating voltage of a Geiger tube.

THEORY

The study of atomic energy begins with a careful study of radioactivity. This study will eventually acquaint the student with the important peacetime uses of the products of atomic energy. In radioactivity we are dealing with the changing of one element into another, called *the transmutation of elements*. A substance which is radioactive is continually giving off penetrating radiations, and in the process the radioactive element is transformed into a new element. In natural radioactivity, this process goes on of its own accord. In artificial radioactivity, radioactive substances are produced artificially by bombarding even nonradioactive substances with high energy particles and producing various nuclear transformations.

The radiations from radioactive substances cause fluorescence, affect photographic plates, and produce ionization in air. Some of the radiations are extremely penetrating, and they produce physiological effects similar to those of X rays, but even more pronounced. However, a person cannot detect the presence of any of these radiations by his unaided senses. Special instruments must be used to measure the effects produced by the rays. Then each effect may be correlated with the intensity of the radiation being measured.

The penetrating radiations given off by radioactive substances may be detected and measured in several ways. These are by the use of a photographic plate, a gold-leaf electroscope, an ionization chamber, a Wilson cloud chamber, or a Geiger-Müller counter.

One method of measurement is to use a *photographic plate*. The rays that penetrate the sensitive emulsion produce a latent image that can be developed. The density of the film is a measure of the intensity of radiation. The *Wilson cloud chamber* is another instrument used to study penetrating radiation. The cloud chamber works on the principle that when air saturated with water vapor is expanded suddenly, the cooling effect causes the formation of a cloud of tiny water drops. Drops of water form around dust particles or any ionized particles present in the chamber. When a ray of penetrating radiation passes through the chamber, it produces ions along its path. The air is then suddenly expanded and liquid droplets are formed on the ions. These water drops appear momentarily as a white line which may be seen or photographed.

Still another method of measurement is to use an *ionization chamber* connected to a *gold-leaf electroscope*. When a gas is exposed to radioactive radiations, it becomes ionized, and the amount of ionization produced is a measure of the intensity of the rays. The ionization chamber consists of a closed metal box, with a thin aluminum or celluloid window, and containing an insulated metal electrode to which the electroscope is connected. The electroscope is charged by applying a sufficient voltage to the leaf system to make the gold leaf deflect to a convenient angle. If some penetrating radiation enters the chamber, it will ionize the gas in the chamber, producing an equal number of positive and negative ions. These ions separate under the influence of the electric field, the positive ions going in one direction and the negative ions in the other. The flow of ions constitutes an electric current which discharges the electroscope. The rate at which the electroscope discharges is proportional to the intensity of the radiation which entered the ionization chamber.

The *Geiger-Müller counter* is one of the most important instruments of modern physics, giving us the most convenient method of measuring penetrating radiation. A Geiger counter consists of a metal tube fitted inside a thin-walled glass cylinder, with a fine tungsten wire stretched along the axis of the tube. The arrangement is illustrated in Figure 61. The cylinder contains a gas such as air or argon at a pressure of about 10 centimeters of mercury. A difference of potential of about 1000 volts is applied between the wire and the metal cylinder, the positive voltage being applied to the wire and the negative to the cylinder. This difference of

233

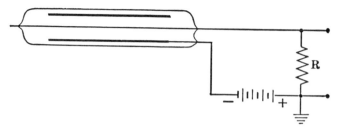

Fig. 61. The Geiger Counter; Schematic Diagram.

potential is slightly less than that necessary to produce a discharge. When any ionizing radiation, such as a high-speed particle from a radioactive source, enters the tube, ions will be produced by the freeing of electrons from the gas molecules. These ions are accelerated by the electric field and produce more ions by collision. The process repeats itself, and the ionization current is rapidly built up. However, the current drops to zero just as rapidly. As the current flows through the external resistance R, it produces a potential drop across R and this causes the net voltage across the tube to fall below the extinction voltage. The current then ceases to flow. But this sudden pulse of current, which produces a sudden pulse of voltage across R, can be amplified by means of radio tubes and be made to operate a mechanical counter or to produce a click on a loudspeaker. In this manner the passage of a single particle through the counter can be registered.

The electrical pulses from the Geiger tube are usually fed to a counting circuit. In some instruments the individual pulses are actually counted. In other instruments a count-rate meter is used which integrates the pulses and gives a reading in terms of counts per minute (CPM). The count-rate meter operates in this manner. When the gas in the Geiger tube is ionized by the incident radiation, the tube breaks down and discharges. The current pulse produced is used to charge a capacitor. The voltage built up across the capacitor by a succession of pulses, which are all of the same value, will be proportional to the rate at which the pulses are being produced. This voltage is then measured by the output meter which is calibrated in counts per minute. In addition, each current pulse is fed through a power amplifying tube to the neon indicator lamp and the output speaker.

Different types of Geiger counter tubes are used for the detection of different kinds of particles. When the walls of the tube are made comparatively thick, the tube is used for the more penetrating radiations, such as X rays or gamma rays. If the tube is to be used for less penetrating radiations, such as alpha or beta particles, then very thin aluminum windows or glass bubble windows are used to permit the particles to enter the tube. One type of Geiger counter uses a thin-walled stainless steel tube for the detection of beta and gamma rays.

The Geiger counter described in this experiment is the Anton 44 Radioactivity Ratemeter. This instrument is a versatile count-rate meter especially designed to provide accurate measurement of radioactivity for industrial, college, and medical laboratories. It indicates radioactivity in a three-fold manner: first, by means of a loudspeaker, where each click indicates the passage of a single particle; second, by means of vivid neon flashes for the visual observation of the count rate; and finally, by an accurate panel meter for an actual numerical indication of the count rate. This panel meter has two ranges: 0–5000 counts per minute and 0–50,000 counts per minute. The same meter is also used to measure the voltage applied to the Geiger tube. This operation is done by means of a meter-selector switch that can be turned to select H.V. (high voltage), $1 \times$ CPM, or $10 \times$ CPM. The Geiger tube used in this instrument is the Anton 106C thin-walled tube for beta and gamma detection. The recommended operating voltage is 900 volts.

Note: The Geiger counters produced for this purpose by other manufacturers are of the same general type. The main differences are in the recommended operating voltage and the range or ranges of the meter. Except for these two differences, the operating instructions are very similar. The appearance of a Geiger counter of this general type is shown in Figure 62.

The proper operation of the tube as a counter is dependent upon the voltage applied to the tube. If the voltage is too low, the passage of any radiation through the tube will not cause any current pulse. If the voltage is too high, on the other hand, there will be a discharge within the tube even without the passage of any radiation through it. Hence it is very important to determine the characteristic curve of the Geiger tube which is to be used in a set of measurements. This curve shows the effect of the voltage applied to the tube on the operation of the Geiger tube as a counter and clearly shows the voltage needed for the proper results.

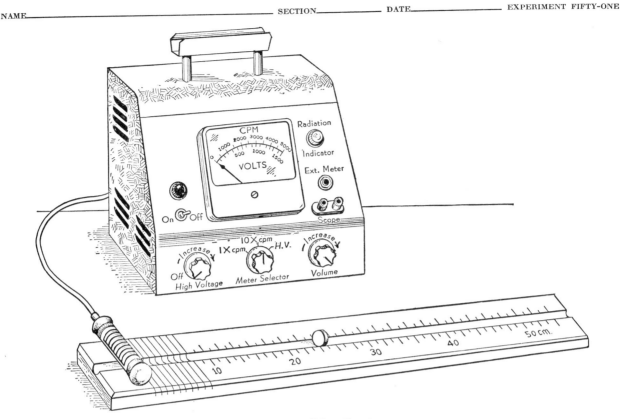

Fig. 62. The Geiger Counter.

Each tube has its own characteristic curve and its own best operating voltage. The curve also provides an understanding of how the Geiger counter operates.

The *characteristic curve* of a Geiger tube is obtained by measuring the counting rate of the tube when placed near a radioactive source of moderate and constant intensity. The distance between the tube and the source is kept fixed. The counting rate is then determined for each of a series of increasing voltages applied to the Geiger tube. At low voltages no counts are produced. As the voltage is increased, a particular voltage is reached at which the tube just begins to produce counts, at a slow rate. This is the *threshold voltage*, or the starting voltage. As the applied voltage is increased, the counting rate also increases, until a region is reached, in the operation of the Geiger tube, where the counting rate is practically constant for an increase of voltage of 100 to 200 volts. This region is known as the *plateau*, or the flat portion of the curve. As the applied voltage is increased still further, the counting rate increases rapidly, because of spurious counts. The *operating voltage* for the Geiger tube is usually taken at approximately the center of the plateau region.

APPARATUS

1. Geiger counter; i.e., a laboratory-student type having a count-rate meter and equipped with a probe.
2. Source of beta-gamma radiation.
3. Calibrated mounting board.

Note: The Geiger counter of the general type used in these experiments and produced for this purpose can be supplied by several manufacturers. Some of these are:

The Anton 44 Radioactivity Ratemeter, supplied by Anton Electronic Laboratories, 1226–1238 Flushing Avenue, Brooklyn 37, New York.

The Atomic Educator, Model AK–2, supplied by Nucleonic Corporation of America, 196 Degraw Street, Brooklyn 31, New York.

The Cenco Radioactivity Demonstrator, supplied by Central Scientific Company, 1700 Irving Park Road, Chicago 13, Illinois.

The Classmaster Radioactivity Demonstrator, supplied by W. M. Welch Scientific Company, 1515 Sedgwick Street, Chicago 10, Illinois.

The Raycounter, supplied by Radioactive Products, Inc., 3201 E. Woodbridge Street, Detroit 7, Michigan.

PROCEDURE

1. Turn the high voltage control of the Geiger counter counter-clockwise until the switch clicks off. Also turn the power switch off. That is, make sure that the instrument is turned off.

2. Place the probe, with the Geiger tube, in the holder on the mounting board. Leave the beta shield open and have the Geiger tube openings face the direction in which the source of radiation is to be placed.

3. Plug the line cord into a 110-volt 60-cycle alternating current outlet.

4. Turn the meter selector switch to the H.V. (high voltage) position so that the meter will indicate the voltage applied to the Geiger tube.

5. Turn the power switch on and allow the instrument to warm up for two minutes.

6. Turn the high voltage control clockwise until it clicks on, to turn on the high voltage.

7. Slowly rotate the high voltage control clockwise, increasing the voltage on the Geiger tube gradually until the normal operating voltage of 900 volts is reached. NOTE: The operating voltage recommended for the Anton Type 106C tube is 900 volts. If some other tube is used, the instructor will recommend the proper voltage to be used.

8. Turn the meter selector switch to the $1 \times$ CPM position to get the radioactivity meter in operating condition. With the switch in this position the meter indicates the rate at which the Geiger tube is counting in counts per minute.

9. Place the source of beta-gamma radiation on the mounting board and about 20 centimeters from the Geiger tube. Hold the beta-gamma source perpendicular to the table and facing the Geiger tube openings. Move the source slowly toward the Geiger tube, while you are watching the meter reading, until the meter reads about one half full scale. Keep the positions of the source and probe fixed for the remainder of the experiment.

10. Turn the meter selector switch to the H.V. position. Turn the high voltage control to the minimum voltage. Then increase the voltage on the Geiger tube slowly until the first indication of counting appears. This is shown by a flashing of the neon bulb and by clicks from the loudspeaker. The value of the voltage at which these pulses first appear is called the Geiger tube threshold voltage. Record this voltage.

11. Increase the voltage by 20 volts and record it. Now turn the meter selector switch to the $1 \times$ CPM position. Observe the meter reading for several seconds and record the reading in counts per minute.

12. Now turn the meter selector switch back to the H.V. position. Increase the voltage by another 20 volts and record it. Turn the meter selector switch to the $1 \times$ CPM position. Observe and record the meter reading corresponding to this voltage.

13. Repeat procedure (12) several times, increasing the voltage by 20 volts each time and recording the meter reading corresponding to each voltage. Notice that after the first big increase in the count rate, the readings remain very nearly the same over a fairly wide range of voltage. This is the plateau region of the Geiger tube. Then, with a further increase of voltage, there may be a considerable increase in the count rate. Do *not* increase the voltage any further; lower it quickly to avoid damaging the tube and stop the taking of readings.

DATA

Type of Geiger counter used...

Operating voltage (recommended)..

Threshold voltage...

Plateau region..

Operating voltage (from the curve)...

NAME_____ SECTION_____ DATE_____ EXPERIMENT FIFTY-ONE

GEIGER TUBE VOLTAGE	COUNTING RATE IN COUNTS PER MINUTE	GEIGER TUBE VOLTAGE	COUNTING RATE IN COUNTS PER MINUTE

CALCULATIONS

1. Plot a graph showing the relation between the counting rate and the voltage applied to the Geiger tube. Plot the voltage along the x axis and the corresponding values of the counting rate along the y axis. Choose the scales on the coordinate axes in such a way that the curve will extend over almost all of a full sheet of graph paper. Indicate the position of each point on the graph by a small pencil dot surrounded by a small circle. Then draw a *smooth* curve through the plotted points.

2. Observe the plateau region of your curve; that is, notice the region where the counting rate remains nearly the same for a wide range of voltage. This is the region where the curve is nearly horizontal. Record the width of this plateau region; that is, record the value of the voltage at the beginning and at the end of the flat portion of the curve.

3. Determine and record the operating voltage of your Geiger tube by selecting a voltage that is about 50 volts above the knee of your curve. This voltage should turn out to be no higher than the midpoint of the plateau region. If it is any higher than this, then choose the midpoint of the plateau region and record it as the operating voltage.

QUESTIONS

1. How does the operating voltage that you obtained from your curve compare with that recommended by the manufacturer?

2. Suppose that the voltage applied to the Geiger tube fluctuated by ± 20 volts about the value of the operating voltage which you determined, what would be the per cent fluctuation in the counting rate which this would produce?

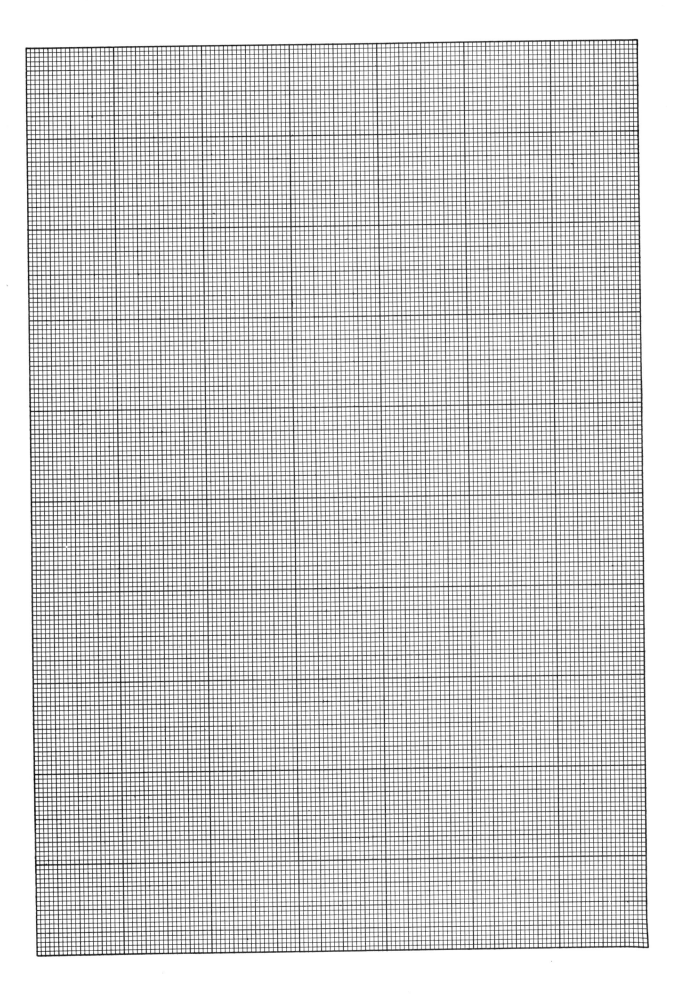

52

RADIOACTIVITY.   THE INVERSE SQUARE LAW OF RADIATION

The discovery of radioactivity has revolutionized our concept of the nature of the physical world and has given us the means by which we can study the innermost structure of an atom, that of the nucleus itself. Radioactive disintegration involves the actual transmutation of elements and the formation of new isotopes. This experiment contains a discussion of the nature of radioactivity and of the radiations from radioactive substances. One of the most important relations used in dealing with radiation is the inverse square law of radiation. It is the purpose of this experiment to show that the intensity of beta and gamma radiation varies inversely with the square of the distance from the source.

THEORY

In 1896 the French physicist Becquerel discovered that minerals containing uranium gave out a radiation which resembled X rays, since it could penetrate an envelope of black paper and affect a photographic paper. These rays could also produce ionization in air and were thus able to discharge electrified bodies. By using a sensitive electroscope they could be easily detected and their intensity measured. This property of uranium was found later to be possessed by a number of the heavy elements, and the name *radioactivity* was applied to it. It was soon found that radioactivity is an atomic phenomenon, for the activity of any given compound of uranium is proportional to the amount of uranium in the substance, and does not depend on the physical or chemical condition of the substance.

Soon more powerful sources of radioactivity were discovered. Madame Marie Curie and her husband, Pierre, began to suspect the existence of other radioactive elements in the uranium ores. After two years of hard labor, during which nearly a ton of uranium ore was worked over chemically, they discovered two new chemical elements, polonium and radium. Both of these elements were found to be thousands of times more radioactive than uranium.

The nature of the radiations from radioactive substances was investigated by Rutherford and his collaborators. It was found that the radiation consisted of three different kinds of rays. These were called α (alpha), β (beta), and γ (gamma) rays. These rays differ in their power of penetrating matter and of producing ionization and also in their behavior under the influence of electric or magnetic fields.

It is easy to show that these rays are different in nature. Suppose a small piece of radioactive material is placed at the bottom of a small hole drilled in a lead block, as shown in Figure 63. A photographic plate is

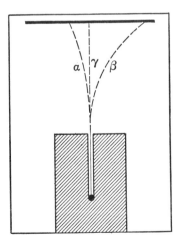

Fig. 63. Separation of Alpha Rays, Beta Rays, and Gamma Rays by a Magnetic Field.

placed at a convenient distance above the lead block, and the whole apparatus is highly evacuated. This arrangement produces a narrow beam of rays emerging from the top of the lead block. A strong magnetic field is then applied at right angles to the plane of the figure. When the photographic plate is developed,

239

three distinct spots are found. One of these was produced by the alpha rays, which were deflected slightly to one side; from the known direction of the magnetic field, we know that the alpha rays consist of positively charged particles. The second spot was produced by the beta rays, which were deflected more strongly in the opposite direction; this shows that they consist of negatively charged particles. The third spot was produced by the gamma rays, which were not deflected at all; this shows that they do not carry any electrical charges.

Actually, it has been proved that *alpha particles* are the same as the nuclei of helium atoms. Each particle has a mass about four times that of a hydrogen atom and each carries a positive charge equivalent to two electron charges. Alpha particles are emitted with a speed of about one twentieth the velocity of light. The *beta particles* have the same mass and the same charge as electrons; they are high-speed electrons emitted from the nuclei of radioactive atoms with speeds that nearly approach the velocity of light. The *gamma rays* consist of electromagnetic waves of extremely short wave length, about 1/100 that of X rays, and are similar to X rays in their properties.

It was found that no physical or chemical process, such as raising the temperature or producing a new chemical compound with some other radioactive substance, could change the radioactivity of a given sample. As a result, it was concluded that radioactivity is a nuclear process and that the emission of a charged particle from the nucleus of an atom results in leaving behind a different atom, occupying a different place in the periodic table. Radioactivity, then, involves the transmutation of elements.

When an alpha particle is given off, the original atom loses four units of mass and two units of charge and thus becomes a new atom of lower atomic weight and lower atomic number. When a beta particle is given off, the new isotope produced will have the same mass number as the parent atom, since the mass of an electron is negligible in comparison with the mass of the nucleus, but the atomic number will be raised by one, since the change produced is equivalent to increasing the net positive charge on the nucleus. In the emission of gamma rays no new elements are produced, since both the atomic number and the atomic weight of the element remain the same. The gamma rays are produced during the transitions from higher to lower nuclear energy states of the same isotope. The emission of alpha particles may be explained by assuming that some of the nuclear protons and neutrons may exist together as alpha particles within the nucleus. To explain the emission of beta particles is not so simple. According to the present belief, electrons do not form part of the nuclear structure. However, when a beta particle is emitted, a neutron within the nucleus becomes a proton and emits an electron.

The occurrence of radioactive disintegration is statistical in nature. For any individual atom of a radioactive substance there is a definite probability that it will disintegrate within a certain time interval. This statement means that when a very large number of atoms are involved, the emission obeys the laws of probability. The rate of disintegration is proportional to the number of atoms present. Accordingly, when the mathematical relation is set up and solved, the radioactive decay is found by using the expression

$$N = N_o e^{-\lambda t}$$

where N is the number of atoms present at any time t, N_o is the number of atoms present at the time $t = 0$, e is the base of natural logarithms, and λ is the decay constant.

A convenient way of representing the rate of radioactive decay is by the *half-life* of a radioactive element, which is defined as the time required for half of a given quantity of the element to disintegrate into a new element. The rate at which a given quantity of a radioactive element decays is found by measuring the intensity of radiation given off by the sample over a period of time and by plotting a graph like the one shown in Figure 64. This figure shows the decay curve for the radioactive element polonium. Thus, for polonium the intensity drops to half of its original value in 140 days; in another 140 days the intensity again drops to half the value it had at the beginning of this time interval, and so on. Since it would take an infinite time for the intensity to drop to zero, the rate of decay is usually specified by the half-life of the atom, and this is one of the important constants to be measured. The same law of decay applies to all the other radioactive elements, except that each one has its own half-life and its own decay constant. The half-life may be extremely short, such as less than one millionth of a second for thorium C′, or it may be quite long, such as 1620 years for radium itself.

The intensity of the rays emitted by a radioactive substance decreases as the distance from the source is increased. Because the rays spread out in all directions, their intensity follows *the inverse square law of radia-*

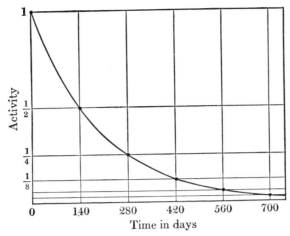

Fig. 64.   Decay Curve for the Radioactive Element Polonium.

tion. This law states that the radiation received on a surface varies directly as the intensity of the source and inversely as the square of its distance from the source. The law applies strictly when the source is a point source of radiation or, in practice, when the distance is very great compared to the size of the source; also the surface must be perpendicular to the rays.

Experimentally, the variation of the intensity of radiation with the distance from the source is obtained in the following manner. The intensity of radiation produced by a beta-gamma source of radiation is measured by means of a Geiger counter placed at a conveniently short, but definite, distance from the source. Then the distance between the source and the Geiger tube is increased in regular steps, and the corresponding intensity of radiation reaching the tube at each distance is recorded.

APPARATUS

1. Geiger counter; i.e., a laboratory-student type having a count-rate meter and equipped with a probe.
2. Source of beta-gamma radiation.
3. Calibrated mounting board.

PROCEDURE

1. Turn the high voltage control of the Geiger counter counter-clockwise until the switch clicks off. Also turn the power switch off. That is, make sure that the instrument is turned off.

2. Place the probe, with the Geiger tube, in the holder on the mounting board. Leave the beta shield open and have the Geiger tube openings face the length of the board.

3. Plug the line cord into a 110-volt 60-cycle alternating current outlet.

4. Turn the meter selector switch to the H.V. (high voltage) position so that the meter will indicate the voltage applied to the Geiger tube.

5. Turn the power switch on and allow the instrument to warm up for two minutes.

6. Place the source of beta-gamma radiation about 10 centimeters from the Geiger tube.

7. Turn the high voltage control clockwise until it just clicks on, to turn on the high voltage.

8. Slowly rotate the high voltage control clockwise, increasing the voltage on the Geiger tube gradually, until the counting of the Geiger tube begins. This is shown by a flashing of the neon bulb and by clicks from the loudspeaker. The value of the voltage at which these pulses first appear is the Geiger tube starting voltage and is normally about 830 volts. Continue increasing the voltage slowly until the normal operating voltage of 900 volts is reached. NOTE: The operating voltage recommended for the Anton Type 106C tube is 900 volts. If some other tube is used, the instructor will recommend the proper voltage to be used.

9. Turn the meter selector switch to the $1 \times$ CPM position to get the radioactivity meter in operating condition. With the switch in this position, the meter indicates the rate at which the Geiger tube is counting

241

in counts per minute. If the meter has two ranges, use whichever range is appropriate for the intensity of radiation being measured.

10. Hold the beta-gamma source perpendicular to the table and facing the Geiger tube openings. Move the source slowly until it is 5 centimeters from the center of the Geiger tube. Do this very carefully, while you are watching the meter reading, making sure that the needle does not go off scale. If the reading gets too close to full-scale deflection, use the shortest suitable distance. Observe the meter reading for this distance for a period of about 30 seconds, taking the average of the maximum and minimum values as the reading. Record this reading, which will be the counting rate of the Geiger tube at this distance.

11. Move the source until it is 6 centimeters from the center of the Geiger tube. Observe the meter reading at this distance for a period of about 30 seconds and record the average of the maximum and minimum values. This value will be the counting rate for this distance.

12. Repeat procedure (11) for distances of 7, 8, 9, 10, 12, 14, 16, 19, 22, and 25 centimeters and record the counting rate for each distance.

13. Measure the background radiation. To do this, remove the radioactive source from the vicinity of the Geiger tube. It should be placed at least 10 feet away so that the intensity of radiation produced by it at the Geiger tube will be negligible. It will be noticed that the tube still continues to count at a slow rate. The number of pulses produced may be counted by listening to the loudspeaker or by watching the neon flasher lamp on the panel. These pulses are produced by the background radiation due mostly to cosmic rays. Count the number of pulses which occur in a one-minute interval and record this value. Do this four separate times.

DATA

Type of Geiger counter used..

Operating voltage..

Cosmic ray background:

    Readings   1.   2.   3.   4.

    Average value..

DISTANCE IN CENTIMETERS	INTENSITY OF RADIATION IN COUNTS PER MINUTE	SQUARE OF THE DISTANCE	RECIPROCAL OF SQUARE OF THE DISTANCE	THEORETICAL VALUE OF INTENSITY
5				
6				
7				
8				
9				
10				
12				
14				
16				
19				
22				
25				

CALCULATIONS

1. Calculate and record the values of the square of the distance for each distance used in the table provided.

2. Calculate and record the values of the reciprocal of the square of the distance; i.e., $1/x^2$, for each distance used. Use three significant figures in these calculations.

3. Using the results of procedures (10–12), plot the values of the distance of the source of radiation along the x axis and the corresponding values of the intensity of radiation along the y axis. Choose the scales on the coordinate axes in such a way that the curve will extend over almost all of a full sheet of graph paper. Indicate the position of each point on the graph by a small pencil dot surrounded by a small circle. Then draw a smooth curve through the plotted points. The curve does not necessarily have to pass through all the points, but it should have on the average as many points on one side of it as on the other.

4. Calculate the intensity of radiation to be expected theoretically in your experiment at each distance used. Use your first reading as the correct value for the intensity of radiation at that distance. Then assume the inverse square law of radiation and calculate the theoretical value of the intensity at each distance used by making the intensity directly proportional to the reciprocal of the square of the distance. Record these values in the table provided.

5. Using the results of calculations (4) plot a second curve on the same graph paper using the same coordinates and the same scale. Plot the values of the distance along the x axis and the corresponding theoretical values of the intensity of radiation along the y axis. Then draw a smooth curve through the plotted points. Label this curve *theoretical* and the previous curve *experimental*.

6. From the data of procedure (13) calculate the number of counts per minute produced by the background radiation, by finding the average of the four readings taken.

QUESTIONS

1. Would you expect your observations to yield very accurate results to prove the inverse square law of radiation? Give your reasons.

2. A source of gamma radiation is of such intensity as to produce 30,000 counts per minute on a Geiger counter placed 5 cm. from the source. At what distance would the source produce 30 counts per minute?

3. An example of radioactive decay is given by the radioactive gas radon, which is a product of radium. Radon loses its activity quite rapidly, its half-life being 3.82 days. A practical use is made of this fact in that thin-walled glass or metal tubes filled with radon are used for therapeutic work. These tubes are inclosed in hollow steel needles which may be inserted into a diseased tissue, which is thus exposed to the radiation given off by the radon. The short life of the radon is a safeguard against overexposure. Calculate the activity of the radon in these tubes after 19.1 days as compared with the initial activity.

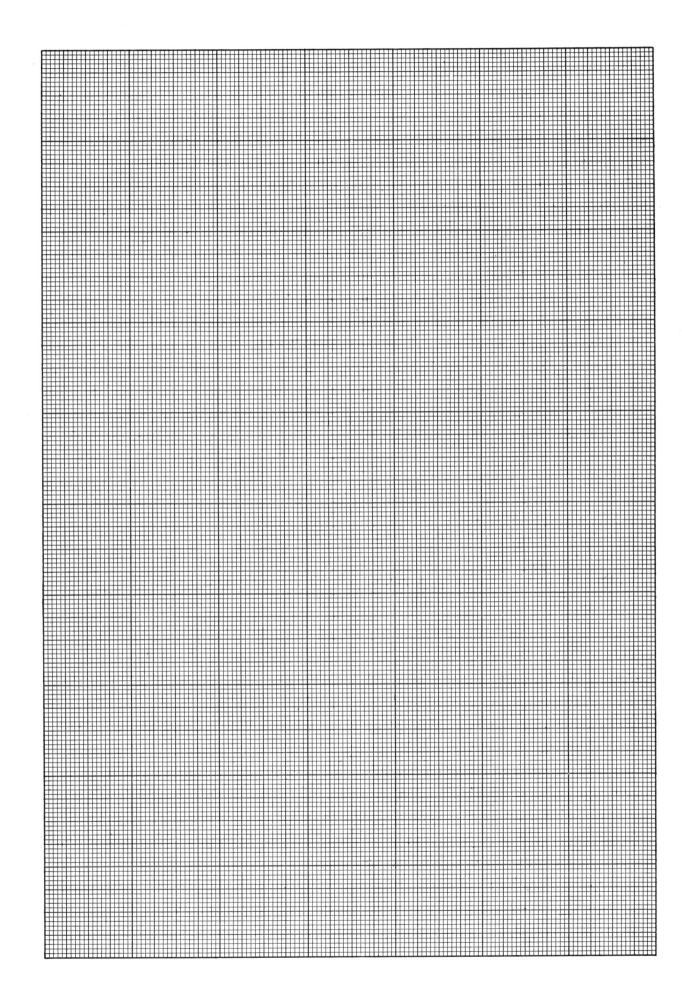

53

THE ABSORPTION OF GAMMA RAYS

Radioactive substances emit one or more radiations known as alpha rays, beta rays, or gamma rays. These rays differ widely in their penetrating power. Thus, a convenient way of distinguishing them is by measuring their intensity after passing through different thicknesses of material; that is, by measuring their absorption in matter. The absorption of beta rays is used in industrial applications for the automatic control of the thickness of metal or plastic films. Absorption measurements of gamma rays are used to determine the energy of the rays. It is the purpose of this experiment to study the absorption of gamma rays by aluminum plates and to determine the linear absorption coefficient and the mass absorption coefficient of aluminum for the gamma rays used.

THEORY

The radiation from radioactive materials, such as uranium, thorium, or radium, is found to contain three different kinds of rays known as alpha rays, beta rays, and gamma rays. These rays can be distinguished from each other by their penetrating power, by their relative ionizing power, and by their deflection in a magnetic or electric field. Under the influence of a transverse electric or magnetic field, the alpha rays are bent slightly in one direction, the beta rays are bent more strongly in the opposite direction, and the gamma rays are not affected at all. The alpha rays are completely absorbed by a few centimeters of air, or by an aluminum foil 0.006 centimeter thick, or by a sheet of ordinary writing paper. The beta rays are about 100 times more penetrating than the alpha rays; they are absorbed by a sheet of aluminum about 3 millimeters thick. The gamma rays are the most penetrating of all; they can be detected after passing through a block of iron 30 centimeters thick. The ionizing power of the three kinds of rays are roughly inversely proportional to their penetrating power.

The *alpha rays* consist of a stream of positively charged particles, each having a mass about four times that of a hydrogen atom and each carrying a positive charge equivalent to two electron charges. In fact, an alpha particle is identical with the nucleus of a helium atom. Alpha particles are emitted with a velocity of about one twentieth the velocity of light. *Beta rays* consist of a stream of negatively charged particles traveling at very high speed. Actually, they are nothing but high-speed electrons emitted by radioactive substances with velocities varying from about 0.2 to 0.9995 the velocity of light. *Gamma rays* are electromagnetic radiations of the same nature as X rays, but of shorter wave length and higher penetrating power. The wave lengths of gamma rays have been measured by crystal diffraction methods and more indirectly from measurements of the velocities of ejected photoelectrons. Their wave length varies from about 0.005 to 1.40 Angstroms. All radioactive elements emit either alpha or beta rays, and either of these rays may be accompanied by gamma radiation.

The measurement of the penetrating power of gamma rays is carried on in the following manner. The intensity of radiation produced by a source of gamma rays is measured by means of a Geiger counter, without any absorber in the path. Then layers of various thicknesses of the absorber are placed between the source and the Geiger tube. The intensity of radiation for each thickness of the absorber is then recorded.

The intensity of a beam of gamma rays after passing through a certain thickness of the absorber is given by the relation

$$I = I_o e^{-\mu d}$$

where I_o is the original intensity, I is the intensity after passing through the absorber, d is the thickness of the absorber in centimeters, e is the base of natural logarithms, and μ is the *linear absorption coefficient*, which is a constant characteristic of the absorbing material and of the wave length of the gamma rays. The law of absorption is illustrated in Figure 65.

From the above equation, by taking the natural logarithms of both sides, we get the relation

$$\ln I = \ln I_o - \mu d$$

This is the equation of a straight line. If the values of the natural logarithm of the intensity, $\ln I$, are plotted along the y axis, and the values of the thickness of the absorber are plotted along the x axis, then the inter-

245

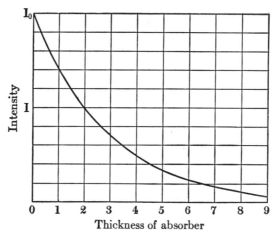

Fig. 65. Absorption of Gamma Rays.

cept on the y axis is the natural logarithm of the original intensity, and the slope of the straight line is the linear absorption coefficient μ. The negative sign for the slope merely shows that the line slopes downward from left to right.

The absorption of gamma rays by a certain element is simply proportional to its density in the absorbing body, irrespective of chemical combination or physical state of the element. It is convenient, then, to introduce another absorption coefficient which is called the *mass absorption coefficient*. This is defined by the relation

$$\mu_m = \frac{\mu}{\rho}$$

where μ_m is the mass absorption coefficient, μ is the linear absorption coefficient, and ρ is the density of the absorber. The use of the mass absorption coefficient is convenient because its value is the same, for a given element, irrespective of physical state or chemical combination of the element. However, it does depend on the wave length of the gamma rays.

A convenient way of representing the penetrating power of a radiation is to use the *half-value thickness*. This is defined as the thickness of the absorber necessary to reduce the intensity of radiation by a factor of two. If the thickness of the absorber is plotted along the x axis and the intensity of radiation along the y axis, the half-value thickness can be read off directly from the curve. It will be the value of the thickness for which the intensity of radiation is one half of the original value.

When a sensitive instrument is used to measure radiation, it is found that it will show a small reading even when no radioactive sources are in the vicinity. This small reading, known as the *background*, is due to cosmic rays coming from outer space and to minute traces of radioactive materials present in the laboratory. To obtain an accurate measurement of the intensity of radiation produced by a sample, a measurement is first made with the sample in position, then with the sample removed. The intensity of radiation due to the sample is obtained by subtracting the second reading, which is the background measurement, from the first.

APPARATUS

1. Geiger counter, i.e., a laboratory-student type having a count-rate meter and equipped with a probe.
2. Source of beta-gamma radiation.
3. Calibrated mounting board.
4. A set of 12 aluminum plates, each about one millimeter thick and about 10 centimeters square.
5. Vernier caliper.

PROCEDURE

1. Measure the thickness of 10 aluminum plates with a vernier caliper and record the value.

2. Turn the high voltage control of the Geiger counter counter-clockwise until the switch clicks off. Also turn the power switch off. That is, make sure that the instrument is turned off.

3. Place the probe, with the Geiger tube, in the holder on the mounting board. Leave the beta shield closed.

4. Plug the line cord into a 100-volt 60-cycle alternating current outlet.

5. Turn the meter selector switch to the H.V. (high voltage) position so that the meter will indicate the voltage applied to the Geiger tube.

6. Turn the power switch on and allow the instrument to warm up for two minutes.

7. Turn the high voltage control clockwise until it clicks on, to turn on the high voltage.

8. Slowly rotate the high voltage control clockwise, increasing the voltage on the Geiger tube gradually until the normal operating voltage of 900 volts is reached. NOTE: The operating voltage recommended for the Anton Type 106C tube is 900 volts. If some other tube is used, the instructor will recommend the proper voltage to be used.

9. Turn the meter selector switch to the $1 \times$ CPM position to get the radioactivity meter in operating condition. With the switch in this position the meter indicates the rate at which the Geiger tube is counting in counts per minute.

10. Place the source of beta-gamma radiation on the mounting board and about 20 centimeters from the Geiger tube. Hold the source perpendicular to the board and facing the Geiger tube. Move the source slowly toward the Geiger tube, while you are watching the meter reading, until the meter reads about two-thirds full scale. Keep the positions of the source and probe fixed for the remainder of the experiment. Observe the meter reading for a period of about 30 seconds, taking the average of the maximum and minimum values as the reading. Record this reading in counts per minute. This value will be the counting rate with zero as the number of plates of the absorber.

11. Place an aluminum plate between the Geiger tube and the beta-gamma source. The plate should be placed perpendicular to the board in such a way as to shield the Geiger tube from the beta-gamma source. Again, observe the meter reading for a period of about 30 seconds and record the average of the maximum and minimum values. This will be the counting rate with one plate as the absorber.

12. Repeat procedure (11) using successive sheets of absorbing material; i.e., increase the number of plates by one each time, until all of the 12 plates are used. Record the counting rate for each set of plates used.

13. Measure the background radiation. To do this, remove the radioactive source and the aluminum plates from the vicinity of the Geiger tube. The source should be placed at least 10 feet away so that the intensity of radiation produced by it at the Geiger tube will be negligible. The tube will still continue to count at a slow rate. The number of pulses produced may be counted by listening to the loudspeaker or by watching the neon flasher lamp on the panel. These pulses are produced by the background radiation due mostly to cosmic rays. Count the number of pulses which occur in a one-minute interval and record this value. Do this four separate times.

DATA

Type of Geiger counter used. . . . .

Operating voltage. . . . .

Cosmic ray background:

Readings	1.	2.	3.	4.

Average value. . . . .

Thickness of 10 aluminum plates . . . .

Thickness of 1 plate. . . . .

Half-value thickness. . . . .

Linear absorption coefficient. . . . .

Mass absorption coefficient. . . . .

Density of absorber. . . . .

NUMBER OF PLATES	INTENSITY OF RADIATION IN COUNTS PER MINUTE		LOGARITHM OF CORRECTED VALUE OF THE INTENSITY
	OBSERVED	CORRECTED	
0			
1			
2			
3			
4			
5			
6			
7			
8			
9			
10			
11			
12			

CALCULATIONS

1. From your readings of the cosmic ray background calculate the average value of the background.

2. From each observed value of the intensity of radiation subtract the average value of the cosmic ray background. These will be the corrected values of the intensity of radiation.

3. Plot an absorption curve for gamma rays. Plot the thickness of the absorber, i.e., the number of absorbers, along the x axis and the corresponding corrected values of the intensity of radiation along the y axis. Choose the scales on the coordinate axes in such a way that the curve will extend over almost all of a full sheet of graph paper. Indicate the position of each point on the graph by a small pencil dot surrounded by a small circle. Then draw a smooth curve through the plotted points.

4. Determine the half-value thickness of aluminum for the gamma rays used. From your absorption curve read off the value of the thickness of aluminum which reduces the original intensity of radiation by 50 per cent. Express the thickness in centimeters of aluminum.

5. Look up the logarithms of the corrected values of the intensity of radiation and record them.

6. Plot a second absorption curve for gamma rays. Plot the thickness of the absorber, i.e., the number of absorbers, along the x axis and the corresponding values of the logarithm of the intensity of radiation along the y axis. Choose the scales on the coordinate axes in such a way that the curve will extend over almost all of a full sheet of graph paper. Indicate the position of each point on the graph by a small pencil dot surrounded by a small circle. Then draw the best fitting straight line through the plotted points. NOTE: If the gamma rays used are made up of different wave lengths, the absorption curve will not be a straight line, because each wave length will have a characteristic value of μ. In that case, the best fitting straight line will give some average value of μ.

7. From your second absorption curve determine the linear absorption coefficient of aluminum for the gamma rays used. The absorption coefficient is the slope of the line obtained when the logarithms of the intensity of radiation are plotted against the thickness of the absorber. Choose two points actually on the straight line and from the coordinates of these points determine the slope. This slope will be given by the expression

$$\mu = \frac{2.303 \,(\log I_1 - \log I_2)}{d_2 - d_1}$$

where μ is the linear absorption coefficient, I_1 is the intensity of the rays after passing through d_1 centimeters of the absorber, I_2 is the intensity of the rays after passing through d_2 centimeters of the absorber, and the factor 2.303 is merely used to change the logarithms with 10 as a base to the natural system of logarithms. The above expression simply gives the value of the slope of the line.

8. From your value of the linear absorption coefficient calculate the mass absorption coefficient of aluminum for the gamma rays used.

QUESTIONS

1. Use the equation

$$\ln I = \ln I_o - \mu d$$

to calculate the half-value thickness of aluminum for the gamma rays used in your experiment. For the value of the linear absorption coefficient use the value obtained in calculations (7). To obtain the natural logarithm of a number you multiply the logarithm to the base 10 by the factor 2.303. How does this half-value thickness compare with the value you obtained in calculations (4)?

2. A beam of gamma rays of energy 1.5 Mev (million electron volts) is passed through an iron plate 10 centimeters thick. If the linear absorption coefficient of iron for these rays is 0.40 per cm., find what fraction of the beam is transmitted by the iron plate. The value of e, the base of natural logarithms, is approximately 2.718.

3. Radium C sends out a group of beta rays whose linear absorption coefficient in aluminum is 13.2 per cm. A beam of these beta rays is passed through an aluminum plate 3.03 millimeters thick. Find what fraction of the beam is absorbed by the aluminum plate. For the absorption of beta rays use the same relation as was used for the absorption of gamma rays.

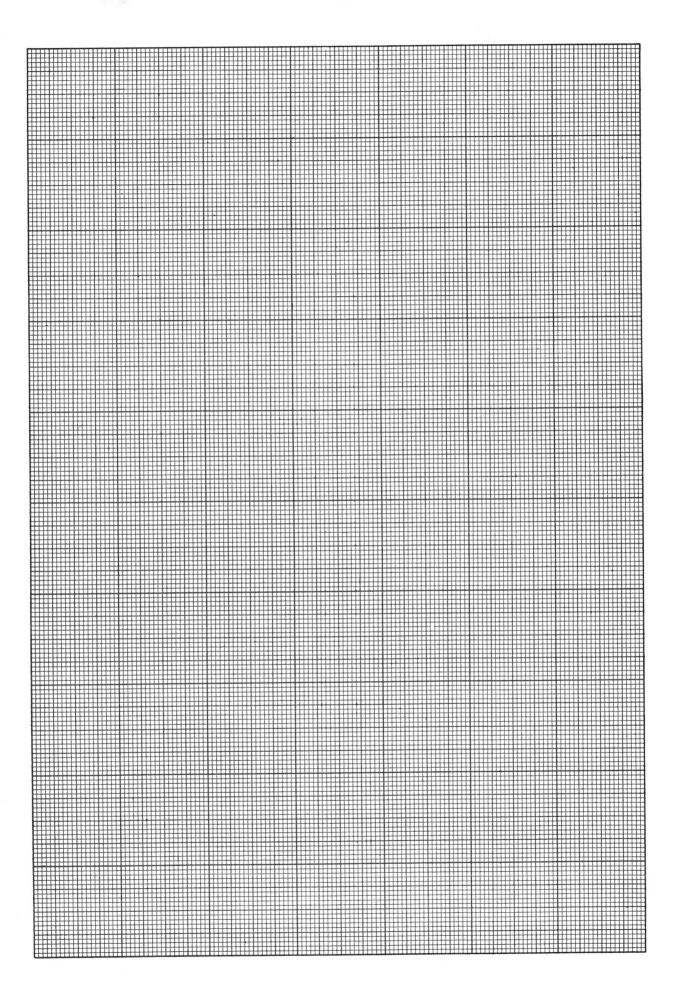

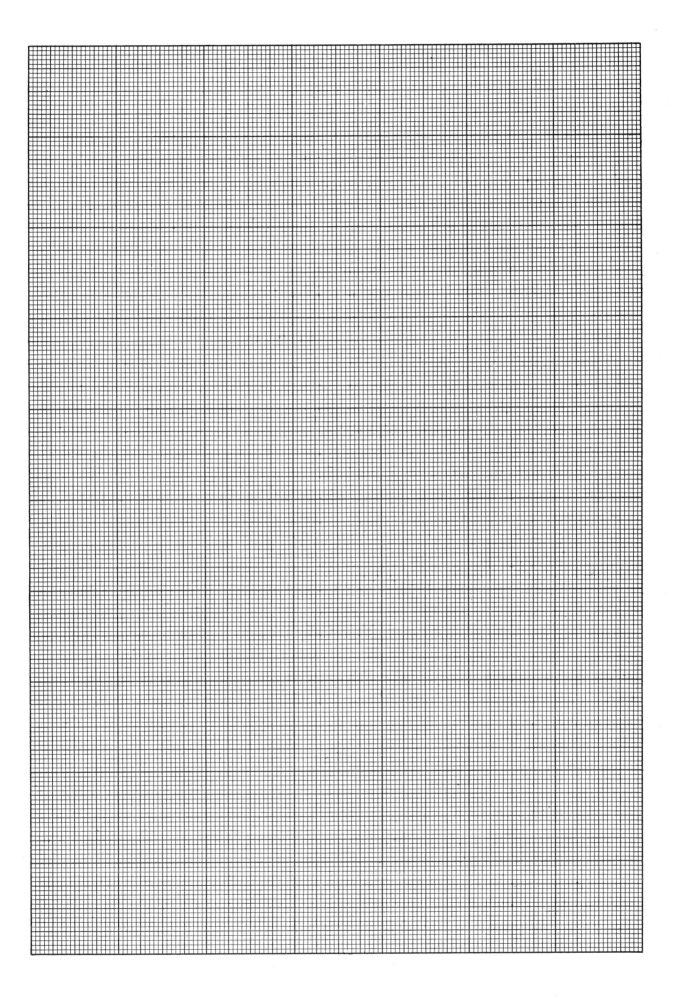

54
HALF–LIFE OF A RADIOACTIVE ISOTOPE

In this modern age, everyone is affected by the utilization of radioactive materials, hence some understanding of the nature of radioisotopes and their potential uses is very essential. Radioactive isotopes are widely used in a variety of practical applications in industry, medicine, agriculture, and in the physical and biological sciences. Some of the techniques that can be employed enable us to perform experiments that seem almost uncanny and permit the detection of amounts of materials far smaller than is possible by ordinary chemical means. One of the most important properties of radioisotopes is their rate of radioactive decay, which is measured in terms of their half-life. It is the object of this experiment to determine the half-life of a radioactive isotope from a series of activity measurements taken over a suitable period of time, and to calculate the decay constant of this radioisotope.

THEORY

The nucleus of an atom is made up of a certain number of protons and neutrons. The number of protons in the nucleus is equal to the atomic number of the element, and all atoms of the same element have the same atomic number. But the atomic weight of an element is equal to the sum of the protons and neutrons in the nucleus of the element. Atoms of the same atomic number but different atomic weights are called *isotopes*. Certain combinations of protons and neutrons produce *stable* isotopes, or isotopes which do not change into other elements. Other combinations of protons and neutrons produce unstable, or *radioactive*, isotopes. The radioactive isotopes reach a stable state by a process of decay which involves the emission of an alpha or a beta particle, usually accompanied by gamma radiation. This spontaneous emission of radiation by the nucleus is called radioactivity. Hence a *radioactive isotope* is an isotope that will spontaneously disintegrate into a new element by the emission of radiation. Some isotopes of the same element are stable, such as carbon-12 and -13, and some are radioactive, such as carbon-11 and -14. Radioactive atoms have the same number of protons as the stable atoms of the same element but a different number of neutrons in the nucleus. They behave chemically and biologically the same as the stable atoms of the same element. This is what makes the tracer technique possible with radioisotopes. Since the mass of a radioactive isotope is slightly different from that of a stable isotope of the same element, their separation involves very special techniques. For example, radioisotopes may be isolated by means of a mass spectrometer, or an ultra high speed centrifuge, or by gaseous diffusion techniques.

Some radioactive isotopes occur in nature, but most of those that are now being used have to be produced artificially. Those which occur in nature are isotopes of the heavy elements which are naturally radioactive, or they are products of the disintegration of these elements. But since the discovery of artificial radioactivity, hundreds of new radioisotopes have been produced. In fact, radioisotopes of all the known elements have been made, including several new elements heavier than uranium and known as the *transuranium elements*. Radioisotopes can be produced artificially in one of two ways. One method is by bombarding stable elements with high energy atomic particles such as electrons, protons, neutrons, deuterons, or alpha particles. The bombardment results in adding one or more particles to the nucleus of the element, or in taking one or more particles away. In either case, the result is a change in the mass number or in the atomic number of the element. Thus a new isotope is formed, either of the same, or of a different element, and it is very likely to be a radioactive isotope. The other method is by breaking elements into pieces in a process known as *nuclear fission*. In the first process, if charged particles are used to bombard the elements, a cyclotron or some other type of high voltage accelerator has to be employed. If neutrons are used, an atomic reactor is employed. Similarly, in producing radioisotopes by nuclear fission, an atomic reactor has to be used. The fission fragments are elements near the middle of the periodic table, and they are likely to have unstable combinations of protons and neutrons; hence they themselves are very likely to be radioactive.

As the number of manufactured radioactive isotopes has increased, very many uses have been found for them. They are used in *industry* to measure radiation intensity, to study diffusion and mixing operations, in thickness gages for paper and plastics, in toxicology studies to check the poisonous effects of many products. Radioisotopes are used in *agriculture* to study metabolism, nutrition, soil fertility, and the action of insecticides. They are used in *clinical research* to study vitamins, hormones, the action of drugs such as antibiotics and anesthetics, and the action of viruses, bacteria, and toxicants. They are used in *medicine* in diagnosis, such as in tumor detection, and in the treatment of thyroid and heart disorders, cancer, and leukemia. In *physics*, radioisotopes are employed in studying the nature of radiations and of radioactivity, and in *physical chemistry* in studying reaction rates, molecular structure, diffusion rates in solids and in solutions. In *biological chemistry* they are useful in research on genetics, metabolic transformations, and the mechanism of enzyme reactions.

In *analytical chemistry* different radioisotopes can be detected from their half-lives and from the different radiations they emit. In quantitative analysis, minute traces of some elements present in compounds or mixtures can be detected by these methods. In some instances quantities smaller than a billionth of a gram can be detected. In *inorganic chemistry* radioisotopes are used as *tracers* to detect impurities. In this way the degree of separation of contaminants from the desired substance can be measured. The *tracer* technique has been one of the most important developments in the studies made with radioisotopes. By means of this technique, the progress of tagged atoms, i.e. radioactive atoms, through a system can be traced. To follow the movements of individual atoms or molecules in a system, one must be able to identify them. If the system is non-homogeneous, the changes in composition can be measured. If the system is homogeneous, the motion of individual atoms or molecules can be followed by using radioactive isotopes and detecting the radiation given off by means of a Geiger counter. For example, by using radioactive sodium it is possible to trace the motion of certain organic and inorganic chemicals passing through the human body, or through plants. The rate at which the blood stream circulates through the body is measured by feeding a person a salt solution containing radioactive sodium. As the solution enters the blood stream, it is distributed to all parts of the body. The presence of the radioactive sodium in the body can be demonstrated by detecting the radiation emitted by the sodium with a Geiger counter. The circulation of the blood through different parts of the body can thus be followed and the rate of circulation measured. A similar technique is used in the study of blood cells, viruses, bacteria, and in many other practical applications which have already been mentioned.

Even though the radioactivity of some materials, such as radium, appears to be quite constant, it has been found that all radioactivity becomes weaker as time goes on. This *radioactive decay*, or loss of activity, is quite apparent in some substances, such as polonium, for example. The rate at which a given quantity of a radioactive element decays is found by measuring the intensity of radiation given off by the sample at regular intervals over a period of time, and plotting a graph like the one shown in Figure 64, page 241. This figure shows the decay curve for the radioactive element polonium. It will be noticed that the intensity of radiation drops to half of its original value in 140 days; in another 140 days the intensity again drops to half the value it had at the beginning of this time interval, and so on. Since it would take an infinite time for the intensity to drop to zero, the rate of decay is specified in terms of the time required for the activity of a given sample to drop to half its original value. This is the half-life of the radioactive isotope and is a very convenient way of representing the rate of radioactive decay of a radioisotope. The same law of decay applies to all the other radioactive isotopes, except that each one has its own characteristic half-life.

The half-life of a radioactive isotope is the time required for the disintegration of half of the atoms in a sample of the isotope. This is also the time required for a given quantity of radioactive material to lose half of its activity. Each isotope has a characteristic half-life that can be determined experimentally. Some isotopes have a very long half-life and some have an extremely short one. For example, the half-life of uranium-238 is 4.50 billion years, that of phosphorus-32 is 14.3 days, while that of thorium C′ is less than one millionth of a second.

The *rate* at which a radioactive material decays is an immutable physical property of each radioisotope and is characteristic of that isotope. The occurrence of radioactive disintegration is statistical in nature. For any individual atom of a given radioisotope, there is a definite probability that it will disintegrate within a certain time interval. This probability does not depend on the past history of the atom nor on the surrounding atoms. Under these conditions, the laws of statistics apply, and when we are dealing with a very large number of atoms, there is a definite probability that a specific proportion of disintegrations will occur in a given time interval. The *rate of disintegration* is then proportional to the number of radioactive atoms present. The rate of radioactive decay can be expressed mathematically as

$$\frac{dN}{dt} = -\lambda N$$

where N is the number of radioactive atoms present; t is the time; λ is the decay constant, which is a constant of proportionality in the above equation, but actually it represents the fraction of radioactive atoms which decay per unit time; and $\dfrac{dN}{dt}$ is the rate of change in the number of radioactive atoms with time, or the number of disintegrations occurring per unit time. The equation merely states that the rate of disintegration is proportional to the number of atoms that have not yet disintegrated. The significance of the negative sign is that the rate decreases with time.

The above equation may be put in the form

$$dN = -\lambda N \, dt$$

or

$$\frac{dN}{N} = -\lambda \, dt$$

The equation may then be solved by integrating both sides. Thus

$$\int_{N_0}^{N} \frac{dN}{N} = -\int_0^t \lambda \, dt$$

This gives

$$\ln N - \ln N_0 = -\lambda t$$

or

$$\ln \frac{N}{N_0} = -\lambda t$$

or

$$\frac{N}{N_0} = e^{-\lambda t}$$

Finally, by multiplying both sides of the equation by N_0, we get the equation mentioned previously (page 240), which is the expression for radioactive decay:

$$N = N_0 e^{-\lambda t}$$

where N is the number of radioactive atoms present at any time t; N_0 is the number of radioactive atoms present at the time $t = 0$; e is the base of natural logarithms; and λ is the decay constant for the particular radioisotope.

The half-life of a radioactive isotope may be obtained from the above equation by finding the value of t for which the ratio $\dfrac{N}{N_0}$ is equal to one half. The half-life will then be given in terms of the decay constant.

The determination of the half-life of a radioactive isotope is very important. In performing experiments with short-lived isotopes, the time that it takes to complete the experiment may be long enough to decrease appreciably the total number of radioactive atoms present, and at the same time, the intensity of radiation produced. This loss of activity has to be taken into account in making accurate measurements. Similarly, in making a chemical analysis of radioisotopes, a determination of the half-life of the radioactive sample will help to identify the isotope present, since each isotope has its own characteristic half-life.

The half-life of a radioactive isotope can also be calculated by measuring the decay constant λ, which is the fraction of radioactive atoms which decay per unit time. For isotopes with very long half-lives, such as thousands of years, it is evident that this procedure must be followed. For isotopes of short half-lives, the usual procedure is to measure the activity of a given sample at regular intervals, over a period of days or weeks, that is, over several half-lives of the given isotope. The activity, in counts per minute, is then plotted as a function of the time, and a smooth curve is drawn through the plotted points. The half-life, or the time for the activity to decrease to half, is read off from the curve directly. Also, the logarithms of the activity may be plotted as a function of the time and the best fitting straight line may be drawn through the plotted points. The half-life can then be calculated from the value of the slope of the line.

In this experiment, the half-life of radioactive iodine, I^{131}, will be determined by taking measurements of the activity of a sample at regular intervals, over a period of several weeks. The net counting rate will be plotted as a function of the time, and the half-life will be obtained directly from the smooth curve drawn through the plotted points. The logarithms of the net counting rate will then be plotted as a function of the time, and from the resulting straight line, both the decay constant and the half-life will be determined.

Radiations from radioactive isotopes may be obtained from two types of sources: a sealed source and an unsealed source. A sealed source contains a definite quantity of a radioactive material usually embedded in a plastic material. This type of source can be easily handled and contains only a few microcuries of the radio-

253

isotope. An unsealed source usually comes in a vial in either powder or liquid form. But the sample to be used in making measurements has to be put in the form of a very thin film of the material. To handle such a source, the cap of the vial should be unscrewed carefully. If the radioisotope is dry, a small quantity of distilled water is added to the vial to dissolve the material. The solution is then poured into a volumetric container and is diluted to the desired volume by adding distilled water. Now it is ready for use. If the sample is already in the liquid form, a definite amount may be obtained by pipetting. Pipets are glass tubes which are used to transfer liquids from one container to another. The liquid is drawn up, usually with a rubber bulb, and then expelled into the other vessel.

Samples of radioisotopes to be used in activity measurements are usually prepared on planchets. Planchets are small, metal, cuplike containers used in counting radioisotope samples. When preparing samples on planchets by evaporation from a solution, it is essential that the deposits be of uniform thickness. To insure even spreading, the planchet must be very clean. The planchet is washed carefully with alcohol, with a thin cotton swab; but a very thin film of alcohol is left on the surface, so that the solution will spread out uniformly. By using a rubber bulb pipet, a one-milliliter sample of the solution is taken into the pipet. The sample in the pipet is then transferred to the planchet. The water in the solution is evaporated by placing the planchet under an infrared lamp, while the solution is kept spread out as evenly as possible. If the solution collects in spots, a few drops of alcohol may be added to make it spread out uniformly over the surface of the planchet. The liquid should then evaporate in a few minutes, leaving a uniform, almost invisible deposit of the radioactive material. The planchet is now ready for use.

APPARATUS

1. Geiger counter, i.e. a laboratory-student type having a count-rate meter and equipped with a probe.
2. Source of beta-gamma radiation; this is a long-lived reference source, such as a radium beta-gamma source, or a cobalt-60 source.
3. Short-lived radioisotope, such as radioactive iodine. This can be a vial of about 10 microcuries of I^{131}, as potassium iodide solution.
4. A holder, such as a calibrated mounting board, or a sample mount.
5. Stop watch or stop clock.

PROCEDURE

1. Turn the high voltage control of the Geiger counter counter-clockwise until the switch clicks off. Also turn the power switch off. That is, make sure that the instrument is turned off.

2. Place the probe, with the Geiger tube, in the holder on the mounting board (see Fig. 62). Leave the beta shield open and have the Geiger tube openings face the length of the board.

3. Plug the line cord into a 110-volt 60-cycle alternating current outlet.

4. Turn the meter selector switch to the H.V. (high voltage) position so that the meter will indicate the voltage applied to the Geiger tube.

5. Turn the power switch on and allow the instrument to warm up for two minutes. Leave the control set at low voltage until the instrument has warmed up.

6. Turn the high voltage control clockwise until it clicks on, to turn on the high voltage.

7. Slowly rotate the high voltage control clockwise, increasing the voltage on the Geiger tube gradually until the normal operating voltage of 900 volts is reached. NOTE: This is the operating voltage recommended for the Anton Type 106C tube. If some other tube is used, the instructor will recommend the proper voltage to be used.

8. Turn the meter selector switch to the $1 \times$ CPM position to get the radioactivity meter in operating condition. With the switch in this position, the meter indicates the rate at which the Geiger tube is counting in counts per minute.

9. Place the source of beta-gamma radiation, the long-lived reference source, on the mounting board about 20 cm. from the Geiger tube. Hold the source perpendicular to the board and facing the Geiger tube. Move the source slowly toward the Geiger tube, while you are watching the meter reading, until the meter reads about one-half full scale. Record the exact position of the source, so that it may be placed in the same spot later. Keep the position of the source fixed while taking the reading. Observe the meter reading for a period

254

of about 30 seconds, taking the average of the maximum and minimum values as the reading. Record this reading in counts per minute. This will be the counting rate for the long-lived reference source.

10. Remove the long-lived radioact've source from the vicinity of the Geiger tube. It should be placed at least 10 feet away so that the intensity of radiation produced by it at the Geiger tube will be negligible. Now place the short-lived source of beta-gamma radiation, the radioactive iodine, on the mounting board about 20 cm. from the Geiger tube. Move the source slowly toward the Geiger tube, while you are watching the meter reading, until the meter reads about one-half full scale. Record the exact position of the source, so that it may be placed in the same spot later, keeping the position of the source fixed while taking the reading. Observe the meter reading for a period of about 30 seconds, taking the average of the maximum and minimum values as the reading. Record this reading in counts per minute. This will be the counting rate for the radioactive iodine. NOTE: If the source is in the form of a vial, it may be used in this form, provided a sufficiently large reading can be obtained on the Geiger counter, and provided the source can be replaced in exactly the same position later. If the source is in a planchet, more accurate results can be obtained. But the planchet should have been already prepared by the instructor. The planchet may be kept in a small beaker, which in turn is kept in a wide-mouth glass container with a metal cap. The planchet may be handled with a pair of forceps. Provision should be made for being able to place the planchet accurately with respect to the Geiger tube, by having a suitable sample mount.

11. Measure the background radiation. Remove the radioactive iodine from the vicinity of the Geiger tube. It should be placed at least 10 feet away so that the intensity of radiation produced by it at the Geiger tube will be negligible. It will be noticed that the tube still continues to count at a slow rate. The number of pulses produced may be counted by listening to the loudspeaker or by watching the neon glow lamp on the panel. These pulses are produced by the background radiation due mostly to cosmic rays. Count the number of pulses which occur in a one-minute interval and record this value. Do this four separate times. Record the day and time of these observations.

12. Repeat procedures (9), (10), and (11) after two or three days. For procedure (9), place the long-lived reference source in exactly the same position as before, while taking the reading. Observe the meter reading for a period of about 30 seconds, taking the average of the maximum and minimum values as the reading. Record this reading in counts per minute. For procedure (10), place the radioactive iodine in exactly the same position as before, while taking the reading. Observe the meter reading for a period of about 30 seconds, taking the average of the maximum and minimum values as the reading. Record this reading in counts per minute. For procedure (11), repeat exactly as before. Record the day and time of these observations.

13. Repeat procedure (12) after one week, counting from the time of the original observations. Record the day and time of the observations.

14. Repeat procedure (12) after two weeks. Record the day and time of the observations.

15. Repeat procedure (12) after three weeks. Record the day and time of the observations.

DATA

Type of Geiger counter used...

Operating voltage...

Position of reference source...

Position of radioactive iodine...

Half-life of radioactive iodine from decay curve...

Decay constant of radioactive iodine...

Half-life of radioactive iodine from decay constant..

Half-life of radioactive iodine, known value...

Per cent error..

TIME OF OBSERVATIONS			INTENSITY OF RADIATION FROM REFERENCE SOURCE IN COUNTS PER MINUTE		
DATE	TIME	ELAPSED TIME IN DAYS	COUNTING RATE	NET RATE	CORRECTION FACTOR

TIME OF OBSERVATIONS			INTENSITY OF RADIATION FROM RADIOACTIVE IODINE IN COUNTS PER MINUTE			
DATE	TIME	ELAPSED TIME IN DAYS	COUNTING RATE	NET RATE	CORRECTED VALUES	LOGARITHMS OF CORRECTED VALUES

TIME OF OBSERVATIONS		BACKGROUND RADIATION				
DATE	TIME	READINGS IN COUNTS PER MINUTE				AVERAGE

CALCULATIONS

1. From your readings of the cosmic ray background calculate the average value of the background radiation for each set of measurements. Use the nearest integral value for the average value.

2. Calculate the net counting rate for the long-lived reference source, at the time of each measurement, by subtracting the average value of the background reading at that time from the corresponding counting rate of the reference source.

3. Calculate the net counting rate for the radioactive iodine, at the time of each measurement, by subtracting the average value of the background reading at that time from the corresponding counting rate of the radioactive iodine.

4. If the net counting rate of the reference source is not the same at the time of all the measurements, then the values of the net counting rate of the radioactive iodine have to be corrected by multiplying each one by the proper correction factor. Calculate the ratio of the net counting rate of the reference source at the time of each set of measurements to the net counting rate of the reference source at the time of the first set of measurements. This will be the correction factor. Correct the net counting rate of the radioactive iodine by multiplying each value of the net counting rate by the value of the correction factor for that time of measurement. This will be the corrected value of the net counting rate for the radioactive iodine.

5. For each set of observations, calculate the time elapsed since the first set was taken. Calculate the time in days, express it in decimals, rounding off the figure to the nearest hundredth of a day, and record the values.

6. Plot a decay curve for radioactive iodine. Plot the time in days along the x axis and the corresponding corrected values of the net counting rate along the y axis. Choose the scales on the coordinate axes in such a way that the curve will extend over almost all of the full sheet of graph paper. Indicate the position of each point on the graph by a small pencil dot surrounded by a small circle. Then draw a smooth curve through the plotted points.

7. Determine the half-life of radioactive iodine. From your decay curve determine the time at which the net counting rate is exactly half what it was at the beginning of the experiment, when the time is zero. This will be the half-life of radioactive iodine as determined from the decay curve.

8. Look up the logarithms of the corrected values of the net counting rate and record them.

9. Plot a second decay curve for radioactive iodine. Plot the time in days along the x axis and the corresponding values of the logarithm of the net counting rate along the y axis. Choose the scales on the coordinate axes in such a way that the curve will extend over almost all of the full sheet of graph paper. Indicate

257

the position of each point on the graph by a small pencil dot surrounded by a small circle. Then draw the best fitting *straight line* through the plotted points.

10. From your second decay curve determine the decay constant for radioactive iodine. The decay constant is the slope of the line obtained when the logarithms of the net counting rate are plotted against the time. Choose two points actually on the straight line and from the coordinates of these points determine the slope. This will be given by the expression

$$\lambda = \frac{2.303 \, (\log N_1 - \log N_2)}{t_2 - t_1}$$

where λ is the decay constant, N_1 is the net counting rate at time t_1, N_2 is the net counting rate at time t_2, and the factor 2.303 is merely used to change the logarithms with 10 as a base to the natural system of logarithms. The above expression simply gives the slope of the line.

11. From your value of the decay constant calculate the half-life of radioactive iodine by using the expression $T = \dfrac{0.693}{\lambda}$, where T is the half-life and λ is the decay constant.

12. Compare the value of the half-life you obtained in calculations (11) with the known value of the half-life of radioactive iodine, which is 8.07 days, by finding the per cent error. How does this calculated value of the half-life compare with the one determined from the decay curve in calculations (7)?

QUESTIONS

1. When working with a short-lived radioisotope, the time that it takes to complete an experiment may be long enough to decrease appreciably the total number of radioactive atoms present, so that the intensity of radiation will be decreased. How long could you work with a given sample of P^{32} before it would have decayed sufficiently to make a 0.5 per cent difference between the initial activity and the activity after a certain time t? The half-life of P^{32} is 14.3 days.

2. A source containing 10 microcuries of radioactive cobalt (Co^{60}) is stored away. What percentage of the cobalt will disintegrate in one year? The half-life of radioactive cobalt is 5.27 years.

3. A solution containing 10 microcuries of radioactive phosphorus (P^{32}) is obtained on the first of the month. What fraction of the radioactive phosphorus remains after 10 days? The half-life of radioactive phosphorus is 14.3 days.

4. Use the equation $N = N_0 e^{-\lambda t}$ to calculate the half-life of radioactive iodine. Since the half-life of a radioactive element is the time required for half of a given quantity of that element to disintegrate, the value of the half-life will be given by the value of t for which the ratio $\dfrac{N}{N_0}$ is equal to one-half. Hence, from the above equation, using this value of $\dfrac{N}{N_0}$, we obtain $\frac{1}{2} = e^{-\lambda T}$ where T now represents the value of the half-life of the given radioisotope. By taking the natural logarithms of both sides of this equation, we obtain

$$\ln 1 - \ln 2 = -\lambda T$$

Use the value of the decay constant (λ) you found in calculations (10) to determine the half-life of radioactive iodine, by employing the above expression.

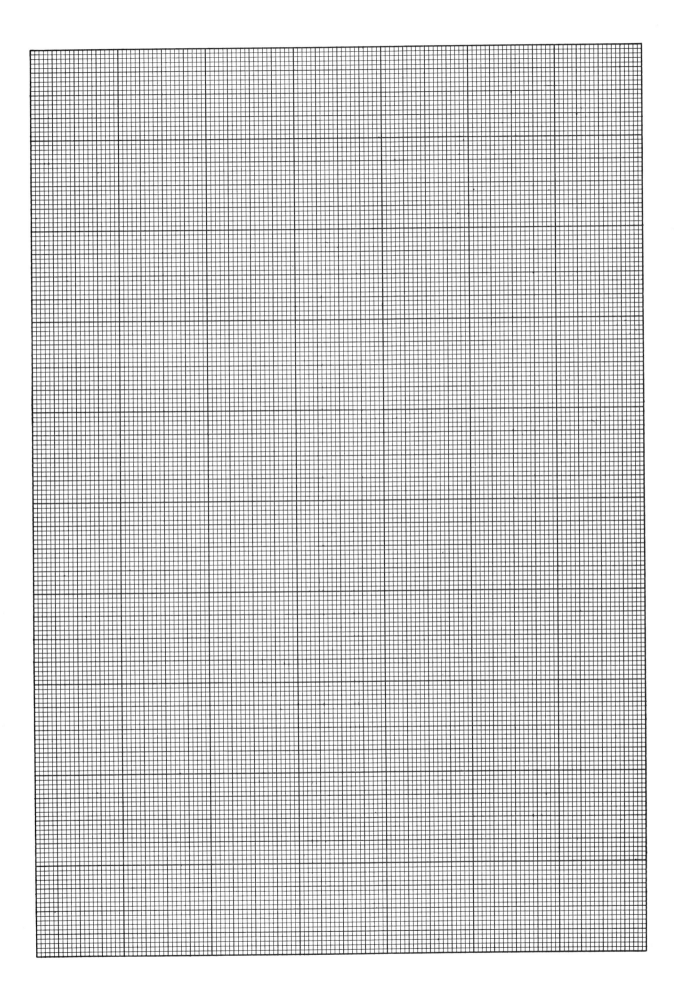

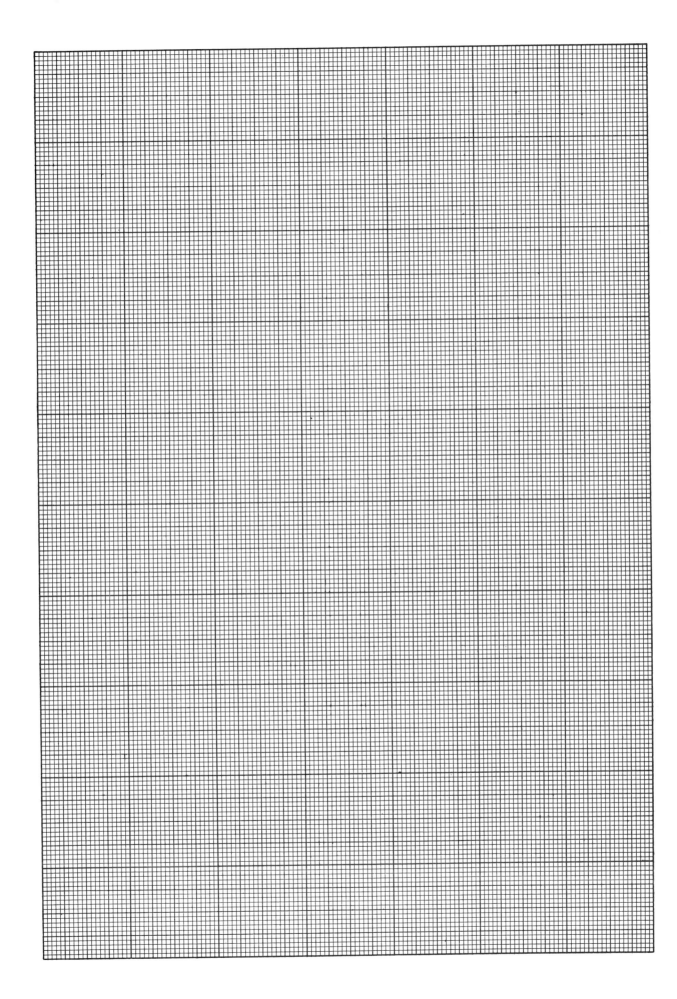

55

STATISTICS OF NUCLEAR COUNTING

Early in the history of radioactivity, it was noticed that there are statistical fluctuations in the number of disintegrations of a radioactive substance occurring in any particular time interval. These fluctuations follow well-known laws of statistics. It is found that while the average number of disintegrations from a steady source is nearly constant when a large number are counted, there are wide fluctuations when small numbers are counted. In expressing the result of a measurement and in determining its accuracy, the laws of statistics have to be applied when dealing with nuclear counting. It is the object of this experiment to study the statistical fluctuations of the disintegration rate of an essentially constant radioactive source, that is, a source whose half-life is very long compared to the time of the experiment.

THEORY

Radioactive material disintegrates in a completely random manner. In any given radioactive substance, there exists a certain probability that any particular atom will disintegrate within a given time interval. This probability is the same for all the atoms of the same substance and is characteristic of the substance. The time at which one atom disintegrates does not affect the disintegration of the other atoms. Although there is no way to predict the time at which an individual atom will disintegrate, it can be shown that when a large number of disintegrations occur, there is a definite average rate of disintegration which is characteristic of a given radioactive substance. However, under these conditions, the observed rate of disintegration fluctuates in a random manner and thus follows the laws of probability. Hence in dealing with data from radioactive measurements, the results of the laws of statistics have to be applied.

In order to be able to apply the laws of statistics to the measurements made in this experiment, a brief survey will be made of the fundamentals of statistics.

Whenever any quantitative measurements are made, or any series of observations involving numerical values are taken, it is desirable to express the results in a simple and compact way. One method is to replace the whole set of observations by a single numerical value which is representative of the whole set. This is some sort of average that can be readily calculated. But this alone does not give a complete picture of the set of observations. It is also important to know how the observations vary among themselves, or how the individual numerical values are scattered around the average value. This is done by calculating certain numerical quantities which give a measure of the dispersion of the individual values.

There are several types of averages which are used in statistical calculations. The most important of these is the *arithmetic mean*, which is used to describe the average of a set of data. Statistical data are obtained by taking observations or measurements on one or more variables. The values of a variable obtained by taking observations are called *variates*. The *arithmetic mean* of a set of variates is defined as the sum of the variates divided by their number. If we use the symbol $\bar{x}$ to represent the arithmetic mean of the N variates x_1, x_2, $x_3, \ldots x_N$, then

$$\bar{x} = \frac{1}{N}(x_1 + x_2 + x_3 + \cdots + x_N).$$

Another type of average that is frequently used is known as the *median*. Suppose that the N variates in a distribution are arranged in the order of their magnitude, or their numerical value. Then, the *median* is defined as the value which is greater than half the variates and less than the other half. That is, the median is the value which lies in the middle of the distribution, when the numbers are arranged in numerical order.

A third type of average is the *mode*, which is that value of the variable which occurs most frequently. This is the kind of average meant by such an expression as the "average man." If the distribution is represented by a frequency curve, the mode is the value of x at which the maximum of the curve occurs.

The aim of statistics is not only to determine average values, but to study variation and the causes of variation. In studying a distribution, then, it is very important to describe how the numerical values are scattered around their average. Two distributions may have the same arithmetic mean and the same total frequency, and yet they may differ in the way the numbers are distributed about the mean. This kind of variation is

261

called *dispersion*. Several quantities are used as a measure of dispersion. Three of these will be described in detail: the *quartile deviation*, the *mean deviation*, and the *standard deviation*.

In analyzing a distribution, it is convenient to divide it into four equal parts. The values of x at which these subdivisions occur are called the quartile values. The first quartile Q_1 is that value of x below which one-fourth of the distribution lies. The second quartile Q_2 is that value of x below which one-half of the distribution lies, and is therefore the median. The third quartile Q_3 is that value of x below which three-fourths of the distribution lies. Half of the distance between Q_3 and Q_1 is known as the *quartile deviation* and is represented by Q. Hence

$$Q = \frac{Q_3 - Q_1}{2}$$

The median does not come at the midpoint of the distance from Q_1 to Q_3 unless the distribution is symmetric.

Another measure of variation about the arithmetic mean is based on the numerical value of the deviations from the mean. A deviation is the difference between an observation and the arithmetic mean. The *mean deviation* is the average of the deviations, or the differences between each observed value and the arithmetic mean, without regard to sign. In adding the deviations their absolute values are used, because regardless of whether the deviations are positive or negative, they represent a variation. Besides, if the algebraic signs are taken into account, the average of the deviations will be zero. Hence, in the calculations, all the deviations are treated as positive. Thus the mean deviation is given by

$$\text{MD} = \frac{1}{N} \left\{ |x_1 - \bar{x}| + |x_2 - \bar{x}| + |x_3 - \bar{x}| + \cdots + |x_N - \bar{x}| \right\}$$

where MD is the mean deviation; N is the total number of observations; $\bar{x}$ is the arithmetic mean; x_1, x_2, etc. are the individual observations; and the vertical bars denote absolute values, that is, the positive values of the expressions. The mean deviation is also known as the *average deviation* from the mean.

The most important measure of dispersion is the *standard deviation*. In order to avoid the difficulty of negative deviations and the use of absolute value signs, the deviations about the mean may be squared and the average of these squares taken; then the square root of the result is calculated. This gives the *standard deviation*, which is the square root of the average of the squares of the deviations taken from the mean of the distribution. Mathematically, this is represented by

$$\sigma = \left[\frac{1}{N} \left\{ (x_1 - \bar{x})^2 + (x_2 - \bar{x})^2 + \cdots + (x_N - \bar{x})^2 \right\} \right]^{\frac{1}{2}}$$

where σ is the standard deviation; N is the total number of observations; $\bar{x}$ is the arithmetic mean; x_1, x_2, etc. are the individual observations. Each expression in parentheses represents a deviation from the mean.

The standard deviation, like the other measures of dispersion, is a measure of how closely the distribution is grouped about the mean. A small standard deviation indicates that the values are closely clustered about the mean; a large standard deviation indicates that the values are spread out widely from the mean. One way of visualizing the significance of the standard deviation is to remember that for a normal distribution, about two-thirds of the distribution is included within the range $\bar{x} \pm \sigma$.

The degree of uncertainty about the accuracy of any measurement can be determined in terms of certain statistical expressions which are related to measures of dispersion. These are called *errors of measurement*. When we speak of errors, we mean deviations from the true value. Since the true value is not known, the errors are expressed in terms of the probability that the true value lies within a certain range of the observed value. Thus different types of errors can be defined. For example, the *probable error* is such a deviation that the probability is 50% that the true value lies within a distance of the probable error from the arithmetic mean of the observations. For a normal distribution, the *probable error* is equal to $0.6745\,\sigma$ where σ is the standard deviation. The *standard error* is equal to σ itself, the standard deviation. In this case, the probability is 68.3% that the true value lies within this distance of the arithmetic mean, i.e. within the range $\bar{x} \pm \sigma$. The *reliable error* is equal to $1.6949\,\sigma$, with a 90% probability that the true value lies within this distance of the arithmetic mean. Of course, the larger the value of the acceptable error, the higher will be the probability that the true value will lie within that range of measurement. However, if the measurements are very accurate, the numerical value of the standard deviation is small, and the errors themselves are small, even with a high degree of probability.

In describing the *accuracy* of any measurement, any desired probability that a new set of measurements will fall within a given range may be selected. This is done by choosing the proper number of standard deviation units. The range of deviation in the observed values for any given probability can then be calculated. The higher the probability selected, the more significant will be the measurement and the greater will be the degree of confidence that if the same measurement were repeated, the new measurement would lie within the given range. Measurements in radioactivity should be expressed in terms of counting rate ± the per cent of deviation at a constant high rate of probability, such as 90% probability, for example.

Whenever any extensive set of data is taken, whether it be in the biological, physical, or social sciences, the methods of statistics must be used to bring out the essential relations from the great mass of detailed information. *Statistics* is the science which deals with the collection, analysis, presentation, and interpretation of numerical data. Because of its mere bulk, sometimes the data is quite incomprehensible. But it may be presented in graphical form, or by means of a few well chosen numerical quantities which give the information necessary to adequately represent the original data.

In making measurements, the observed values can be established only approximately, the error depending upon the precision of the instrument and the care of the observer. The degree of accuracy that can be obtained depends upon the closeness with which the variables can be measured. However, the true value of a measured quantity can never be known exactly. The best that can be done is to make a large number of observations and to calculate from these the value that is most likely to represent the true value. By using statistical methods, it is then possible to calculate the probability that the true value lies within a certain range of the measured value, and thus the *accuracy* of the measurement can be determined.

After the measurements are made, it is necessary to classify them properly, in order to be able to analyze them. The results are arranged in tabular form, being grouped according to a certain range of values. The most important form of tabulation in the analysis of statistics is the frequency distribution. The data are grouped into classes of appropriate size, showing the corresponding frequency of variates in each class, i.e. the number of times that the numbers within a certain range of values occur. When a set of data is arranged in this manner, it is called a *frequency distribution*.

The frequency distribution can be represented graphically by plotting the values of the variates along the x axis and the frequency along the y axis. A series of rectangles are erected at the boundaries of each class interval, with the height of each rectangle proportional to the corresponding frequency, and centered at the middle of the class interval, known as the class mark. The corresponding frequencies are then represented by the areas of the rectangles. This graphical representation of a frequency distribution is known as a *histogram*.

The shape of the distribution represented by the histogram may be shown more clearly by a continuous smooth curve so constructed that the area under the curve between the ordinates at the upper and lower boundaries of each rectangle is equal to the area of the rectangle. If the class intervals are made smaller and smaller and at the same time the number of variates increases, then the shape of the histogram will approach the shape of the curve, and in the limit, when the width of the rectangles approaches zero, the histogram will take on the shape of a smooth curve which is known as a *frequency curve*. The frequency curve represents a mathematical function which gives a relation between the frequency and the value of the variate for a given distribution. Actually, a frequency curve applies only to an ideal distribution which involves an infinite number of variates, but in practice it may be used in describing the properties of any observed distribution, because the results will approach the predicted values as the number of observations is increased.

There are several standard curves to represent different types of distributions. The most important of these is the one known as the *normal curve*. This curve was first discovered by a famous French mathematician, De Moivre, while working on certain problems in games of chance. It was also derived independently by the astronomers Laplace and Gauss, who made statistical use of it, and found that it represents accurately the errors of observations in scientific measurements. The curve is also known as the *normal probability curve*, because of its use in the theory of probability, and as the *normal curve of error*. Here error is used to mean a deviation from the true value. Whenever any measurements are made in which there are random fluctuations, the results predicted by the normal curve are found to be valid. Thus it has been found that this curve describes very well many distributions that arise in the fields of the physical sciences, biology, education, and the social sciences.

The mathematical representation of the normal curve is given by the equation

$$y = \frac{N}{\sigma \sqrt{2\pi}} e^{-\frac{(x - \bar{x})^2}{2\sigma^2}}$$

where y represents the distribution function. This function gives the relation between the variable x and the probability that a given value of x will occur. Actually, the area under the curve is used to represent the probability. In this form of the equation, the total area under the curve corresponds to the total frequency N of all the variates in the distribution. The area under the curve between the values $x = a$ and $x = b$ represents the number of variates with measurements between a and b. The symbol σ represents the standard deviation of the distribution; $\bar{x}$ is the arithmetic mean; e is the base of natural logarithms, which is approximately 2.718.

The curve is bell-shaped and is symmetrical about the line $x = \bar{x}$. It has a maximum for this value of x and falls quite rapidly toward the x axis on both sides. For different normal distributions, the curve has the same general shape, but its steepness, its height, and its location along the x axis will depend on the values of N, $\bar{x}$, and σ. The characteristic properties of the normal curve can be studied very readily by representing it in a new set of variables by means of a mathematical transformation. This is done by considering the total area under the curve as unity, taking the origin at the arithmetic mean, and using the standard deviation as the unit of horizontal measurement. This means that we set $N = 1$, $t = (x - \bar{x})/\sigma$, and represent the function as $\phi(t)$. The normal curve is then represented by the equation

$$\phi(t) = \frac{1}{\sqrt{2\pi}} e^{-\frac{t^2}{2}}$$

This is the *standard form* of the normal curve, where $\phi(t)$ is the distribution function and t is the variable. For this distribution, the average value of t is zero and the standard deviation is equal to one. The advantage of representing the normal curve in the standard form is that the area under the curve between any two values of t may be calculated once and for all. These values are tabulated and can be obtained from tables of probability integrals. Any normal distribution may then be expressed in the standard form and the required calculations of the characteristics of the distribution can easily be made.

It is important to know the *properties of the normal curve* to be able to use it in practical applications. The curve is bell-shaped, and symmetrical about the ordinate at $t = 0$. The ordinates for negative values of t are the same as for the corresponding positive values of t. The curve has a maximum at $t = 0$, falls quite rapidly toward the axis on both sides, and approaches very close to the horizontal axis at both extremities. Theoretically, it extends from $-\infty$ to $+\infty$, but practically it is so close to the axis beyond $t = \pm 3$ that the area under the curve beyond these points is almost negligible.

The mean, the median, and the mode coincide at the origin, where $t = 0$. The distances along the horizontal axis are measured in units of σ, the standard deviation. The total area under the curve is equal to one. Hence the area under any portion of the curve represents the relative frequencies, or essentially the percentage of the total area included in that portion. These values may be obtained from tables and may be changed into actual frequencies by multiplying by N.

The *standard deviation* is approximately 25% greater than the *mean deviation*. The relation is MD $= 0.798\,\sigma$.

The quartiles Q_1 and Q_3 are equidistant from the mean, since the curve is symmetrical. The relation between the *quartile deviation* and the *standard deviation* is $Q = 0.6745\,\sigma$.

The *percentage distribution* of area under the normal curve is given in Figure 66, where σ is the unit of measurement. The significance of the values given in the figure is that if the values of x are normally distributed, the probability that a value chosen at random will fall within the range $\bar{x} \pm \sigma$ is 0.683. The probability that it will lie within the range $\bar{x} \pm 2\,\sigma$ is 0.9545. The probability that it will lie within the range $\bar{x} \pm 3\,\sigma$ is 0.9973. Thus the probability that it will lie outside of this range is only 0.0027 or 0.27%. Hence a deviation of $3\,\sigma$ on both sides of the arithmetic mean includes practically the whole of a normal distribution.

The *standard deviation*, σ, was defined as the square root of the average of the squares of the deviations from the mean. But it can also be shown that whenever a number of independent events occur in a random manner, the standard deviation of the numerical value obtained from a series of observations is equal to the square root of the number of events counted. Thus, when a number N of radioactive pulses are counted, the standard deviation σ is given by $\sigma = \sqrt{N}$. This means that if several observations are made of a certain counting rate which is presumably constant, it will be found that the observed values will be different, and the standard deviation of these values will be given by the square root of the counting rate. In this case, the value of the counting rate is taken to be the arithmetic mean $\bar{x}$ of the observations, and thus the *theoretical value of the standard deviation* will be given by the *square root of the arithmetic mean*. This gives a very simple

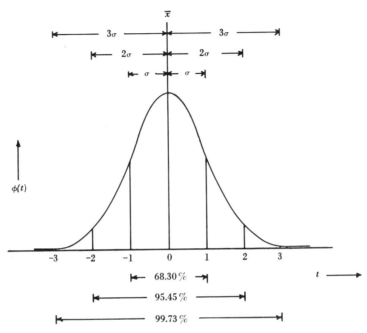

Fig. 66. The Percentage Distribution of Area Under the Normal Curve

way of calculating the standard deviation and also a simple way of calculating the accuracy of the measurement. For example, suppose we wanted to calculate the per cent standard error. As before, error is taken to mean a deviation from the most probable value, which is the arithmetic mean. But the mean is the value N of the observed number of counts. Hence the per cent standard error is

$$\frac{\sigma}{N} \times 100 \quad\text{or}\quad \frac{\sqrt{N}}{N} \times 100 \quad\text{or}$$

$$\%\text{ Standard Error} = \frac{100}{\sqrt{N}}$$

The smaller the % standard error, the higher will be the precision of the counting. It will be seen from the above expression that increasing the number of counts will decrease the per cent error. Hence in any radioactivity measurement, the accuracy may be increased by collecting a larger number of counts in the measurement.

In an actual experiment, there is always some background radiation present. If the intensity of radiation from the sample being measured is very large compared to the background, then the background radiation may be neglected. However, for accurate measurements, and especially if the radioactive sample is weak, the background radiation must be taken into account, since we are interested in the radiation from the sample only. To calculate the average values and the standard deviations involved, we use the following considerations. The difference of two independent distributions, with arithmetic means $\bar{x}_1$ and $\bar{x}_2$ and with standard deviations σ_1 and σ_2, is another distribution with an arithmetic mean $\bar{x}_3$ given by $\bar{x}_3 = \bar{x}_1 - \bar{x}_2$ and a standard deviation σ_3 given by

$$\sigma_3 = \sqrt{\sigma_1^2 + \sigma_2^2}$$

By using these relations and the calculated values for the intensity of radiation from the sample including background, and the values for the background radiation, the intensity of radiation from the sample only can be calculated, as well as the standard deviation of this measurement. In the above expressions, the subscript 1 refers to the radiation from the sample, including background; the subscript 2 refers to the background radiation; and the subscript 3 refers to the radiation from the sample only.

In this experiment on the statistics of nuclear counting, the experiment is performed by measuring the rate of disintegration of a constant radioactive source. A source is chosen whose half-life is very long, of the order of several years, or even several thousand years. A measurement of the rate of disintegration is made over a reasonable interval of time, and the average rate in counts per minute is calculated. Many similar measurements are made, and the average rate is obtained for each measurement and recorded. Even though each value represents a measurement of the same quantity, it will be found that they are all somewhat different. The irregularities are due to statistical fluctuations. A careful study is then made of these fluctuations and the accuracy of the measurement is determined by using the methods of statistics.

If a laboratory-student type counter with a count-rate meter is employed in making the measurements, Procedure A is to be used in the experiment. If a decade scaler is employed in making the measurements, Procedure B is to be used in the experiment.

The decade scaler is a combination of a high voltage source, which activates a Geiger tube, and an electronic adding machine, which counts each ray as it is detected. The scaler is a very useful instrument and is necessary in making accurate quantitative measurements of radioactive disintegrations. The instrument is designed to count and indicate the number of pulses received from an external radiation detector, such as a Geiger counter. The number of pulses counted by the scaler is indicated on two decade strips and a four-digit electromechanical register. Each decade strip contains 10 neon bulbs which light in succession, one at a time, as each pulse from the detector is received. The decade on the right counts in units of one. The decade on the left counts in units of ten. After the ninth pulse has been received and recorded on the right decade, the next pulse causes this decade to go back to 0 and the left decade to advance one digit. Similarly, the register increases one digit each time the decades reach 00. The register indicates the accumulated counts in units of hundreds, thousands, tens of thousands, and hundreds of thousands. To obtain the total number of counts recorded during any interval of time, the register and the decades are merely read from left to right, and the number obtained is the reading.

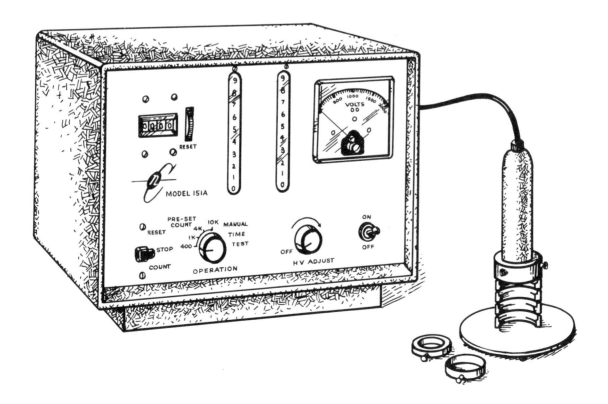

Fig. 67. Decade Scaler with Geiger Tube and Sample Mount

The general appearance of a scaler is shown in Figure 67, which shows Model 151A *Basic Decade Scaler* supplied by Nuclear-Chicago Corporation, as well as the Geiger tube and the sample mount.

The sample mount, as shown at the right in Figure 67, provides support for an end-window Geiger detector. The mount is so designed that radioactive samples may be placed in several positions beneath the detector. Also, absorbers of different materials and thicknesses may be placed between the sample and the detector, for absorption measurements.

In using the scaler, the correct operating voltage for the particular detector being used should be obtained from the instructions received with the detector.

Three different modes of operation are available on the decade scaler: manual, preset count, and preset time mode of operation. The OPERATION selector switch controls the mode of operation. In the *Manual* mode, the starting and stopping of the count are accomplished by manual operation of the STOP/COUNT/RESET switch. In the *Preset Time* mode, the starting and stopping of the count are controlled by the same switch and an externally attached timer. The counting automatically stops after a predetermined time interval. In the *Preset Count* mode, the starting and stopping of the count are controlled by the same switch and the register of the scaler. The counting will stop automatically after a predetermined number of counts has been reached. In this experiment, the manual mode of operation will be used.

APPARATUS

1. Either (A) or (B)
    (A) Geiger counter, i.e. a laboratory-student type having a count-rate meter and equipped with a probe; a holder, such as a calibrated mounting board, or a sample mount.

    (B) Decade scaler, with Geiger tube and sample mount.
2. Source of beta-gamma radiation, of long half-life, such as a radium beta-gamma source, or a cobalt-60 source.
3. Electric timer, or a stop watch.

PROCEDURE A

This procedure is to be used if a laboratory-student type counter with a count-rate meter is employed.

1. Turn the high voltage control of the Geiger counter counter-clockwise until the switch clicks off. Also turn the power switch off. That is, make sure that the instrument is turned off.

2. Place the probe, with the Geiger tube, in the holder on the mounting board. Leave the beta shield open and have the Geiger tube openings face the length of the board.

3. Plug the line cord into a 110-volt 60-cycle alternating current outlet.

4. Turn the meter selector switch to the H.V. (high voltage) position so that the meter will indicate the voltage applied to the Geiger tube.

5. Turn the power switch on and allow the instrument to warm up for two minutes. Leave the control set at low voltage until the instrument has warmed up.

6. Turn the high voltage control clockwise until it clicks on, to turn on the high voltage.

7. Slowly rotate the high voltage control clockwise, increasing the voltage on the Geiger tube gradually until the normal operating voltage of 900 volts is reached. NOTE: This is the operating voltage recommended for the Anton Type 106C tube. If some other tube is used, the instructor will recommend the proper voltage to be used.

8. Turn the meter selector switch to the 1 × CPM position to get the radioactivity meter in operating condition. With the switch in this position, the meter indicates the rate at which the Geiger tube is counting in counts per minute.

9. Place the source of beta-gamma radiation on the mounting board about 20 cm. from the Geiger tube. Hold the source perpendicular to the board and facing the Geiger tube. Move the source slowly toward the Geiger tube, while you are watching the meter reading, until the meter reads about one-half full scale. Keep the positions of the source and the probe fixed while all the readings due to the beta-gamma source are being taken.

10. Observe the reading of the rate meter. You will notice that the reading is not constant, but it fluctuates about some average value, due to the randomness of the nuclear disintegrations. Observe and record a series

of twenty instantaneous readings of the rate meter, in counts per minute, taken at intervals of ten seconds. That is, at the end of every ten-second period, observe the reading of the rate meter and record it. This may be done by keeping an eye on a stop watch and glancing over at the rate meter for an instant at the end of every ten-second interval. Do this twenty times in succession.

11. Measure the background radiation. Remove the radioactive source from the vicinity of the Geiger tube. It should be placed at least 10 feet away so that the intensity of radiation produced by it at the Geiger tube will be negligible. It will be noticed that the tube still continues to count at a slow rate. The number of pulses produced may be counted by listening to the loudspeaker or by watching the neon glow lamp on the panel. These pulses are produced by background radiation due mostly to cosmic rays. Count the number of pulses which occur in a one-minute interval and record this value. Do this ten separate times.

PROCEDURE B

This procedure is to be used if a decade scaler is employed. NOTE: The end-window Geiger-Müller detector will be already mounted in the sample mount and will be connected to the scaler. Do not touch the thin window of the detector in any way, since it can be easily damaged. The timer will also be connected to the scaler and will be ready for operation.

1. Turn the high voltage control counter-clockwise until the switch clicks off. Also turn the power switch off. That is, make sure that the instrument is turned off.

2. Plug the line cord into a 110-volt 60-cycle alternating current outlet. Attach the ground wire to a suitable external ground, such as the metal conduit at the electrical outlet.

3. Turn the power switch on, but do not turn on the H.V. switch. Allow the instrument to warm up for two or three minutes. A number in each decade will light, indicating that power is being applied to the instrument. Leave the control at low voltage until the instrument has warmed up.

4. Turn the H.V. ADJUST control clockwise until a click is heard in the switch. The meter should read below 500 volts. Allow an additional minute for the instrument to warm up, keeping the high voltage at the minimum value.

5. Set the high voltage to the correct operating value for the detector used, by slowly turning the H.V. control clockwise. The correct operating voltage for the detector used should be obtained from the instructions received with the detector.

6. Place the source of beta-gamma radiation on the sample mount, beneath the detector, at some intermediate position.

7. Place the OPERATION switch in the MANUAL position. Starting and stopping the count are accomplished by manual operation of the STOP/COUNT/RESET switch. Momentarily place this switch in the RESET position. This switch has a spring return to the STOP position. The decades should now indicate "00." Manually reset the register to zero by turning the register reset wheel upwards. Also reset the external timer to zero. Before starting any counting run, the decades, the register, and the timer should be reset to zero. Now the counter is ready for operation.

8. The count is begun by placing the STOP/COUNT/RESET switch in the COUNT position and is ended by returning the switch to the STOP position. The external timer will operate as long as the switch is in the COUNT position. If a stop watch is used instead of an external timer, the time interval will be obtained from the stop watch. Begin the count by placing the switch in the COUNT position. At the end of exactly one minute, return the switch to the STOP position. Obtain the total number of counts recorded by reading the register and the decades from left to right.

9. For the purpose of this experiment, the counting rate should be about 2500 counts per minute. The distance between the detector and the radioactive sample should be adjusted until approximately this counting rate is obtained. If the counting rate is higher than this, the radioactive source should be placed farther away from the detector; if it is lower, it should be placed nearer the detector. The counting rate need not be exactly 2500 counts per minute, but should be roughly near that value. To check the counting rate, repeat procedures (7–8) for each position of the radioactive sample, until the proper counting rate is obtained. Record this

position of the source and keep the position fixed while all the readings due to the beta-gamma source are being taken.

10. Take a series of twenty observations of the counting rate, in counts per minute, by observing the total number of counts obtained in a one-minute interval, each separate time. Do this by repeating procedures (7–8) twenty times, and record the total number of counts obtained each time.

11. Measure the background radiation. Remove the radioactive source from the vicinity of the Geiger tube. It should be placed at least 10 feet away so that the intensity of radiation produced by it at the Geiger tube will be negligible. The tube will still count at a very slow rate. These counts are produced by background radiation due mostly to cosmic rays. Take a series of ten observations of the counting rate due to the background radiation, by observing the number of counts obtained in a one-minute interval, ten separate times. Do this by repeating procedures (7–8) ten times, and record the number of counts obtained each time.

DATA

Type of Geiger counter used..

Operating voltage..

Position of radioactive source..

Arithmetic mean..

Mean deviation...

Standard deviation, experimental value..

Standard deviation, theoretical value...

Number of readings within the range $\bar{x} \pm$ MD.......................................

Number of readings within the range $\bar{x} \pm \sigma$...................................

Number of readings within the range $\bar{x} \pm 2\sigma$.................................

Number of readings within the range $\bar{x} \pm 3\sigma$.................................

Background radiation:

Readings, in counts per minute

Average value of background..

INTENSITY OF BETA-GAMMA RADIATION					
READINGS IN COUNTS PER MINUTE	DEVIATIONS $(x - \bar{x})$	SQUARE OF DEVIATIONS $(x - \bar{x})^2$	READINGS IN COUNTS PER MINUTE	DEVIATIONS $(x - \bar{x})$	SQUARE OF DEVIATIONS $(x - \bar{x})^2$

CALCULATIONS

1. Calculate the arithmetic mean, that is, the average value, of the readings you obtained for the intensity of the beta-gamma source. Express the value to the nearest integer.

2. Calculate the deviations of these readings. Subtract the average value from each of the readings obtained, and record the difference. These are the deviations, which may be positive or negative.

3. Calculate the mean deviation. This is found by computing the average of the deviations, disregarding the plus or minus sign, that is, by considering all of the deviations as positive.

4. Calculate the square of the deviations and record them in the table.

5. Calculate the experimental value of the standard deviation. This is found by obtaining the square root of the average of the squares of the deviations.

6. Calculate the theoretical value of the standard deviation. This is found by taking the square root of the arithmetic mean.

7. Count the number of deviations which are numerically less than the mean deviation. This will give the number of readings within the range $\bar{x} \pm \text{MD}$.

8. Count the number of deviations which are numerically less than the experimental value of the standard deviation. This will give the number of readings within the range $\bar{x} \pm \sigma$.

9. Count the number of deviations which are numerically less than twice the standard deviation. This will give the number of readings within the range $\bar{x} \pm 2\,\sigma$.

10. Count the number of deviations which are numerically less than three times the standard deviation. This will give the number of readings within the range $\bar{x} \pm 3\,\sigma$.

11. How do the results of calculations (7–10) compare with those predicted by probability theory? It must be remembered that the results predicted by the theory of probability apply accurately only when we are dealing with an infinite number of observations. For a small number of observations, there is likely to be an appreciable difference between the results obtained and those predicted by the theory of probability.

12. From your readings of the cosmic ray background calculate the average value of the background radiation and record the value. Express the value to the nearest tenth.

QUESTIONS

1. From your readings of the cosmic ray background and the average value of the background radiation, calculate the deviations of these readings. Then compute the experimental value of the standard deviation of the background radiation. How does this compare with the theoretical value of the standard deviation?

2. Express the accuracy of your measurement of the intensity of the beta-gamma source by stating the result, i.e. the arithmetic mean, in terms of the counting rate ± the per cent of deviation at 68.3% probability. This is the probability to be expected that, if new measurements were made, they would lie within the range $\bar{x} \pm \sigma$. Use your experimental value of the standard deviation in making your calculations.

3. In measuring the activity of a radioactive sample it is desired to obtain an accuracy of 1% at 95.45% probability. This is the probability to be expected that, if new measurements were made, they would lie within the range $\bar{x} \pm 2\,\sigma$. What is the number of counts that would have to be taken in a given measurement in order to obtain this degree of accuracy? For σ, assume the theoretical value of the standard deviation, i.e. the square root of the number of counts taken in a given measurement.

4. In making accurate measurements of the activity of a weak radioactive sample, the value of the background radiation has to be taken into account. The intensity of radiation from the sample only is then calculated. In expressing the accuracy of the measurement, the standard deviation of the net measurements is used in the computations.

A certain radioactive sample was measured, and the arithmetic mean of a large number of readings was found to be 74 counts per minute, including background. The arithmetic mean of a large number of readings for the background radiation was found to be 26 counts per minute. Calculate the standard deviation for the intensity of radiation including background, for the background radiation, and for the sample only. Express the accuracy of this measurement of the intensity of radiation from the sample only, in terms of the counting rate ± the per cent of deviation at 68.3% probability.

56

THE HYDROGEN SPECTRUM.   THE RYDBERG CONSTANT

The research work done in the field of spectroscopy, both experimental and theoretical, has contributed a great deal to our knowledge of the physical nature of things, a knowledge not only of the earth, but of the sun, of the stars, and of interstellar space.   This experiment contains a discussion of the Bohr theory of the hydrogen atom, which marked the beginning of a new era in spectroscopy and atomic structure.   The object of this experiment is to measure the wave lengths of the first four lines of the Balmer series of the hydrogen spectrum by means of the diffraction grating spectrometer, and from these measurements to calculate the value of the Rydberg constant.

THEORY

Whenever a narrow beam of light from any ordinary source passes through a glass prism and falls on a screen, a colored band of light is produced.   An array of all the colors of any beam of light is known as the *spectrum* of that light.   The color sensation produced depends on the frequency of the vibrations, and hence on the wave length of the light.   Each chemical element produces its own characteristic spectrum, so that by analyzing the light emitted by a substance, it is possible to identify the elements it contains.   The detailed study of the emission and absorption spectra is called *spectrum analysis*, or *spectroscopy*.

There are three main types of spectra: continuous, bright line, and absorption.   A *continuous spectrum* is produced by light from an incandescent solid or liquid; it contains a continuous gradation of colors, merging with very gradual changes from red to violet, which means that light of all wave lengths in that spectral range is present.   A *bright line spectrum* is produced by exciting an element in the gaseous state by means of an electric discharge or by heating; such a spectrum consists of bright lines, corresponding to light of definite colors, separated by dark spaces.   The number and relative positions of the lines depend on the element used and the method of excitation employed; each line represents light of a definite wave length.   An *absorption spectrum* is produced when light from a source furnishing a continuous spectrum is passed through some cooler absorbing material; the resulting spectrum is crossed by dark spaces or lines which form the absorption spectrum of the material.   Wave lengths of visible light are usually expressed in Angstrom units.   One Angstrom unit is 10^{-8} centimeter.

The frequencies of the light emitted by an excited atom of a gas or vapor at low pressure are characteristic of that particular atom, and the spectrum produced is the bright line spectrum of that element.   When an atom absorbs radiant energy, it absorbs the same frequencies of light it would emit if it were excited.   The sun's spectrum is an absorption spectrum.   The main body of the sun emits a continuous spectrum, but the relatively cooler gases surrounding the sun absorb the energy corresponding to the line spectra of the elements present in the sun's atmosphere.   These absorption lines appear as dark lines or missing lines in the continuous spectrum of the sun.   They were first observed by Fraunhofer and are called *Fraunhofer lines*.

It is found that among the many lines appearing in the spectrum of an element certain ones may be picked out which are clearly related to each other, following a simple law and forming a *series*, and there may be many different series for the same element.   Many attempts were made, over a period of years, to explain the origin of spectral lines and the various relationships found.   It was thought at first that the frequencies of the light emitted by a particular element might be related like the fundamental and the harmonics of a vibrating system.   But this explanation turned out to be unsuccessful.   Finally, in 1885 Balmer found an empirical relation, a simple formula which gave the frequencies of a series of lines emitted by atomic hydrogen.

Since hydrogen is the simplest element, it produces the simplest spectrum, although the spectrum contains many lines.   Under the proper conditions of excitation, atomic hydrogen may be made to emit a sequence of lines, or a *series*, arranged in a definite order, the lines coming closer and closer together as the limit of the series is approached.   Balmer found that the wave lengths of these lines were given very accurately by the formula

$$\frac{1}{\lambda} = R\left(\frac{1}{2^2} - \frac{1}{n^2}\right)$$

where λ is the wave length in centimeters, R is a constant called the Rydberg constant, and n takes on the integral values 3, 4, 5, etc. By letting $n = 3$, the wave length of the first line of the series is obtained. This is the red hydrogen line of the Balmer series. For $n = 4$, the wave length of the second line is obtained, and so on. When n becomes infinite, the limit of the series is obtained. This is the shortest wave length of this series of lines.

Other *series of lines* have since been discovered in the *hydrogen spectrum*. These were named after their discoverers and are known as the Lyman, the Paschen, and the Brackett series. The formula for each of these series is very similar to the one for the Balmer series. The formulas for these series are:

$$\text{Lyman series:} \quad \frac{1}{\lambda} = R\left(\frac{1}{1^2} - \frac{1}{n^2}\right), n = 2, 3, 4, \cdots$$

$$\text{Paschen series:} \quad \frac{1}{\lambda} = R\left(\frac{1}{3^2} - \frac{1}{n^2}\right), n = 4, 5, 6, \cdots$$

$$\text{Brackett series:} \quad \frac{1}{\lambda} = R\left(\frac{1}{4^2} - \frac{1}{n^2}\right), n = 5, 6, 7, \cdots$$

The Lyman series is in the ultraviolet. The Balmer series is in the visible part of the spectrum, and the near ultraviolet. The Paschen and the Brackett series are in the infrared.

The four formulas given above may be combined into a single formula, thus:

$$\frac{1}{\lambda} = R\left(\frac{1}{n_1^2} - \frac{1}{n_2^2}\right)$$

When $n_1 = 1$ and $n_2 = 2, 3, 4$, etc., this formula gives the Lyman series. When $n_1 = 2$ and $n_2 = 3, 4, 5$, etc., the formula gives the Balmer series. The other series are obtained in a similar way. We shall refer to this formula as the *Balmer formula*.

The Balmer formula may also be written in terms of the frequency of the light emitted. The relation between frequency and wave length is

$$c = \lambda\nu, \quad \text{or} \quad \frac{1}{\lambda} = \frac{\nu}{c}$$

where c is the velocity of light in centimeters per second, λ is the wave length in centimeters, and ν is the frequency in vibrations per second. Using this relation in the above expression, the *Balmer formula* becomes

$$\nu = Rc\left(\frac{1}{n_1^2} - \frac{1}{n_2^2}\right)$$

The most successful attempt to explain the origin of spectral lines is *Bohr's theory* of the structure of the atom. On the basis of Rutherford's discovery of the nuclear atom, Bohr introduced his theory of the hydrogen spectrum in 1913, and this proved to be the starting point of a vast development in atomic theory. The hydrogen atom was the object of the first theoretical attack because, since it is the lightest of all the atoms, it must have the simplest structure, and its spectrum is the simplest one. Bohr's aim was to establish a theory from which he could derive the observed hydrogen spectrum as given by the Balmer formula. His theory was essentially an extension of Planck's quantum theory to Rutherford's theory of the nuclear atom, and utilizing Einstein's interpretation of the photoelectric effect, attributing energy quanta to light.

The *Quantum theory* was introduced by Planck in 1900 and was the result of an attempt to derive the law of black-body radiation which would agree with the experimental observations. Planck made some new and radical assumptions about the behavior of radiation. He postulated that any radiation of frequency ν cannot be emitted or absorbed in arbitrary amounts, but is always emitted or absorbed in whole multiples of a discrete quantity, or quantum, of energy. This quantum is given by the relation $E = h\nu$, where E is the energy, ν is the frequency of the emitted or absorbed radiation, and h is a universal constant, now known as Planck's constant.

Making use of the quantum idea, Einstein developed the law of the *photoelectric effect* in 1905. He assumed that light of frequency ν can transfer its entire quantum of energy to a single electron, even though the electron may be far from the source of radiation. This extended the quantum theory to the transfer of radiant energy through space by means of light quanta, or photons.

In 1911 Rutherford proposed the theory of the *nuclear atom* in an attempt to explain the experimental results of the scattering of alpha particles. Rutherford assumed that an atom consists of a positively charged nucleus surrounded by a cluster of electrons. Practically all the mass of the atom is concentrated in the nucleus, which is less than 10^{-12} cm. in diameter. The number of units of charge on the nucleus is equal to the atomic number of the element; each unit of charge is numerically equal to the charge on the electron. Since a normal atom is electrically neutral, it must contain the same number of electrons as the number of charges on the nucleus. These electrons are spread around the nucleus through a region which represents the dimension of an atom, about 10^{-8} cm. To account for the fact that the electrons remain at relatively large distances from the nucleus, in spite of the electrostatic force of attraction of the nucleus, they are assumed to be revolving about the nucleus, the force of attraction providing the centripetal force needed to keep them in their orbits.

The Bohr *model of the hydrogen atom* was based on Rutherford's nuclear atom. Making the assumption that the number of electrons around the nucleus of a neutral atom is equal to the atomic number, Bohr concluded that the hydrogen atom was made up of one electron, with a negative charge, and one proton, with a positive charge equal to the charge of an electron. The *proton* is the nucleus of a hydrogen atom. The electron is assumed to be rotating in a circular orbit with the nucleus as the center. Since the mass of the hydrogen nucleus is 1840 times the mass of the electron, the motion will be approximately the same as the motion of an electron around a fixed central charge of infinite mass. The relative motion of the nucleus will be discussed later.

If an attempt is made to explain the origin of spectral lines on the basis of the electromagnetic theory of radiation, it is found that the theory fails. Assuming the electron to be revolving about the nucleus in a circular path, the theory predicts that the electron must radiate energy; a body moving in a circle is continuously accelerated toward the center of the circle, and the electromagnetic theory predicts that an accelerated electron radiates energy. But the energy is radiated at the expense of the energy stored in the revolving electron. To lose energy, the electron must gradually spiral in toward the nucleus, with an increase in the frequency of revolution. This would mean that the radiation emitted would consist of a continuous spectrum, and that the atom itself would be unstable, since the electron would fall into the nucleus. But this is contrary to the observed facts, since the atom is stable, and the radiation consists of sharp lines.

Thus, in spite of the success of the electromagnetic theory in explaining large-scale phenomena, Bohr was forced to the conclusion that the electromagnetic theory could not be applied to the description of the radiation from atoms. In dealing with processes involving individual atoms, the electromagnetic theory could not be applied, since it led to conclusions contrary to the observed facts. In his *theory of the hydrogen atom*, Bohr introduced some entirely new principles, in fact his theory represents a remarkable combination of principles taken over from classical theory with postulates completely at variance with that theory.

Bohr's *first postulate* was that an electron in an atom can revolve in certain specified orbits without the emission of radiant energy. Permitted circular orbits represented the stationary orbits, or the stationary states of the atom. The electron in any one of these orbits does not radiate, but continues in the same state with the same energy, contrary to the predictions of the electromagnetic theory.

Bohr's *second postulate* specified the conditions under which the non-radiating, or stationary, orbits could exist. In this postulate Bohr introduced the quantum condition that the electron was permitted to rotate about the nucleus only in those orbits for which the angular momentum is some integral multiple of $\dfrac{h}{2\pi}$, where h is Planck's constant. Since the angular momentum of a particle of mass m, moving with velocity v in a circle of radius r, is mvr, the quantum condition may be stated as

$$mvr = n\,\frac{h}{2\pi}$$

where $n = 1, 2, 3$, etc.; n is called the *quantum number*.

Bohr's *third postulate* applied to the atomic theory the quantum ideas developed by Planck, and Einstein's quantum theory of light. In this postulate Bohr assumed that an electron could jump from one allowed orbit to another one of lower energy. When this happened, a quantum of radiation was emitted containing an amount of energy equal to the difference in the energies corresponding to the two orbits, and the atom lost that much energy in the process. The frequency of the light emitted was given by the relation

$$h\nu = W_2 - W_1$$

where ν is the frequency of the radiation, h is Planck's constant, W_2 is the energy of the atom when the electron is in the initial state, and W_1 is the energy when the electron is in the final state. This assumption explains why sharp spectral lines are emitted and indicates that the atom exists only in states of sharply defined energy content. However, it must be remembered that this explanation does not provide any picture of the mechanism by which an atom radiates energy, or of the events during the transition between orbits.

Bohr used these postulates in the mathematical development of his *theory of the hydrogen atom* and succeeded in arriving at a theoretical formula for its spectrum that agrees with observation. The values of the energies allowed in the stationary states for an atom containing a single electron can easily be deduced from the basic assumptions. To make the theory more general, we assume the nuclear charge to be Ze, where Z is the atomic number, and e is the numerical value of the charge on the electron, in electrostatic units. The calculations can then be applied not only to the neutral hydrogen atom, but to a singly ionized atom of helium, a doubly ionized atom of lithium, etc. The electrostatic force of attraction between the electron and the nucleus will be given by

$$F = \frac{Ze^2}{r^2}$$

where F is the force in dynes, and r is the radius of the circular orbit, in centimeters. This force, acting on the electron, is equal to the centripetal force needed for circular motion, which is

$$F = \frac{mv^2}{r}$$

where m is the mass of the electron in grams, r is the radius of the path in cm., and v is the velocity of the electron in cm. per second. Thus, for circular motion we have the condition that

$$\frac{mv^2}{r} = \frac{Ze^2}{r^2}, \quad \text{or} \quad mv^2 = \frac{Ze^2}{r}$$

Since Z, e, and m are constants, the above equation gives a relation between the two variables v and r, which presumably may have any values, over a continuous range.

The *energy* of the electron is partly kinetic and partly potential. The kinetic energy is

$$K.E. = \tfrac{1}{2}mv^2, \quad \text{or} \quad K.E. = \frac{Ze^2}{2r}$$

The potential energy is defined as zero when the electron is infinitely far removed from the nucleus. The potential energy of the electron at a distance r from the nucleus is then given by

$$P.E. = -\frac{Ze^2}{r}$$

The negative sign for the potential energy merely means that work must be done on the electron to move it away from the nucleus, and it is negative as a consequence of the arbitrary definition of the point of zero potential energy. Actually, the potential energy is higher as the value of r increases. The *total energy* of the electron is the sum of the kinetic energy and the potential energy, and is thus given by

$$W = \frac{Ze^2}{2r} - \frac{Ze^2}{r}, \quad \text{or} \quad W = -\frac{Ze^2}{2r}$$

where W is the total energy of the revolving electron, and the other symbols are the same as before.

From the laws of classical physics we obtained the relation between the velocity of the electron and the radius of the orbit, namely

$$mv^2 = \frac{Ze^2}{r}$$

However, from the continuous range of values allowed by this equation, the quantum condition imposed by Bohr's second postulate selects only certain sharply defined *orbits which are allowed*. The condition is

$$mvr = n\frac{h}{2\pi}$$

where $n = 1, 2, 3$, etc. For any quantum number n, the orbit is defined, because now we have two equations with two unknowns, r and v. Solving these two simultaneous equations, we obtain expressions for r and v in terms of n and the constants e, Z, m, and h. The result is

$$r = n^2 \frac{h^2}{4\pi^2 mZe^2} \quad \text{and} \quad v = \frac{1}{n}\frac{2\pi Ze^2}{h}$$

Thus for any given value of n, the values of r and v are sharply defined.

From the allowed values of r, the total energy of the revolving electron can now be calculated in terms of n and the other constants. The total energy of the electron was derived before, and is given by

$$W = -\frac{Ze^2}{2r}$$

Putting the above value of r in this expression, we obtain the relation

$$W = -\frac{1}{n^2}\frac{2\pi^2 me^4 Z^2}{h^2}$$

where W is the total energy of the revolving electron, n is the quantum number, and the other symbols are the same as before. For each value of n, there is a definite value of W, and these different values of W are the *energy levels*, each level representing the *total energy of the electron* in one of the allowed orbits. It should be noticed that the total energy is quantized, since it is given only by integral values of the quantum number n; the other symbols in the expression for the energy are all constant.

The *frequency of the light* emitted is obtained by using Bohr's third postulate, namely that a quantum of radiation is emitted when an electron jumps from one allowed orbit to another orbit of lower energy. The frequency is given by the relation

$$h\nu = W_2 - W_1$$

where ν is the frequency of the radiation, h is Planck's constant, W_2 is the energy state of the atom when the electron is in the upper orbit, and W_1 is the energy state when the electron is in the lower orbit. Thus the frequencies of the spectral lines are given by

$$\nu = \frac{W_2 - W_1}{h}$$

Putting the values of W derived above into this expression for the frequency we obtain

$$\nu = \frac{1}{h}\left[-\frac{1}{n_2^2}\frac{2\pi^2 me^4 Z^2}{h^2} + \frac{1}{n_1^2}\frac{2\pi^2 me^4 Z^2}{h^2}\right]$$

or

$$\nu = \frac{2\pi^2 me^4 Z^2}{h^3}\left[\frac{1}{n_1^2} - \frac{1}{n_2^2}\right]$$

This is *Bohr's formula* for the hydrogen spectrum theoretically derived.

This formula has the same mathematical form as *Balmer's formula*

$$\nu = Rc\left[\frac{1}{n_1^2} - \frac{1}{n_2^2}\right]$$

since the factor in front of the bracket contains only constants. But in addition to this resemblance, Bohr's formula can actually predict the numerical value of the factor Rc which was determined experimentally in the Balmer formula. This is done by merely using the known values of the constants which appear in Bohr's formula. Thus, the numerical value of e is obtained from the oil-drop experiment, the value of m from experiments on cathode rays, and the value of h from the photoelectric effect. When the value of R thus calculated is compared with the value derived from spectroscopic measurements, it is found that they agree exactly, within the limits of experimental error. This was the first outstanding success of the Bohr theory.

In Bohr's formula given above, if we let $Z = 1$, the atomic number for hydrogen, and $R = \frac{2\pi^2 me^4}{ch^3}$, the formula becomes identical with the experimental formula of Balmer for the hydrogen series, even to the calculated value of the Rydberg constant. It is interesting to study some of the characteristics of Bohr's *stationary*

279

states of the atom, such as the radius of the circular orbits, and the velocity of the electron. The expressions for both of these have been obtained before, but it might be well to point out certain results. For example, the radius r of the orbit has the smallest value for $n = 1$. When the electron is in this orbit, the atom is said to be in the *normal state*, or the state in which the energy of the atom is least. An electron can remain indefinitely in this orbit; hence this is the stable condition of the atom. If the atom receives energy from an outside source, such as from collisions with rapidly moving electrons in an electric discharge, or by the absorption of radiation, the electron can be raised to an outer orbit. The atom is then said to be in an *excited state*. This is an unstable state, and after a very short time, the electron falls back to a state of lower energy, emitting a quantum of light in the process.

The radius of the orbit for the normal state of the atom can easily be computed by putting $n = 1$ in the expression for r and using the known values of the other constants. The *radius* of the first Bohr orbit turns out to be 0.53×10^{-8} cm. This is in very good agreement with atomic diameters as estimated by other methods. This was another success of the Bohr theory, for although it was developed to explain the hydrogen spectrum, it successfully predicted the size of the atom. The *velocity* of the electron in any orbit can be calculated by using the expression for v. The velocity in the first orbit turns out to be $1/137$ of the velocity of light. The radius of all the allowed orbits can be calculated by assigning integral values to n in the expression for r. It will be seen that the radius varies as n^2, so that the orbits become progressively larger. Fig. 68 shows a diagram of the Bohr circular orbits of hydrogen and the transitions for the different series of the hydrogen spectrum.

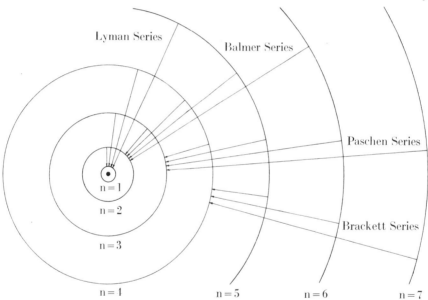

Fig. 68. Bohr Circular Orbits of Hydrogen with Transitions for Different Series of Lines

When the Rydberg constant is calculated from the known values of e, h, c, and m, the frequencies of the lines of the different *series of the hydrogen spectrum* can be calculated from Bohr's formula, expressed simply in the form of Balmer's formula. Thus, when $n_1 = 1$ and $n_2 = 2, 3, 4$, etc., the formula gives the frequencies of the lines of the *Lyman series*. This series is produced by transitions of an electron from any one of the excited states to the first Bohr orbit. The frequencies of the lines of the *Balmer series* are given by the same formula, when $n_1 = 2$ and $n_2 = 3, 4, 5$, etc. This series is produced by transitions of an electron from any one of the excited states to the second Bohr orbit. Thus, the transition from $n = 3$ to $n = 2$ gives the first line of the Balmer series. The transition from $n = 4$ to $n = 2$ gives the second line of the Balmer series, and so forth. The other series of the hydrogen spectrum are produced in a similar manner. These transitions, for the different series of lines, are shown schematically in the diagram of Fig. 68. It should be pointed out that the electron does not have to jump from a high orbit to the lowest orbit in one step; but it may cascade down to the lowest, or normal state in several steps, thus producing several lines belonging to different series.

In trying to represent the stationary states of an atom and the transitions giving rise to the different series of lines, certain difficulties arise. The orbits with large values of n, the higher members of the series, and the series limits cannot be shown in a diagram like that of Fig. 68. In order to include these additional features in the same atomic picture, energy level diagrams are usually drawn. In an *energy level diagram*, each Bohr orbit, or stationary state of the atom, is represented by a horizontal line plotted to an energy scale. The energies of the various quantized orbits are computed and then plotted as shown in Fig. 69. This figure is the energy level diagram of hydrogen. On the right side of the diagram are listed the values of n, which is the *quantum number*. On the left side, for each value of n there is listed the corresponding value of the energy in ergs, as computed from the Balmer formula. Since the energies of the quantized states are negative in value and approach zero as $n \rightarrow \infty$, the zero of energy, for n infinite, is drawn at the top of the figure, and the other states are drawn below. The lowest energy state, or the *normal state* of the atom, is the state for which $n = 1$. The other levels, of higher quantum numbers, represent the energies of the various *excited states*.

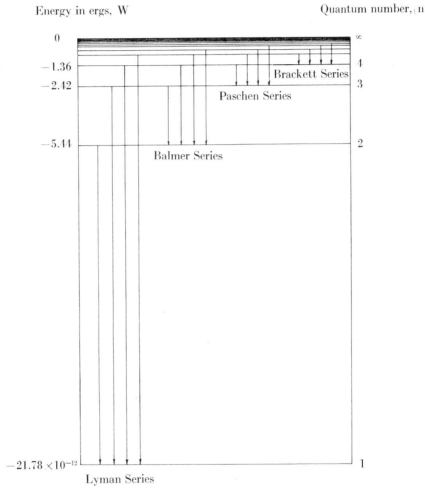

Fig. 69. Energy Level Diagram of Hydrogen

In the absorption of radiation, the electron is lifted from the lowest level to one of the higher levels. In the emission of radiation, the electron spontaneously falls down to a lower level, and in the process light is emitted. A spectral line of a definite frequency is produced when an electron goes from an upper level to a lower energy level, the frequency of the line being proportional to the difference between the two energy levels. The Lyman series, which is characterized by the quantum number of the lower level $n_1 = 1$, is represented by the transitions ending at the normal state of the atom. The Balmer series, which is characterized by $n_1 = 2$, is produced by all the transitions ending at $n_1 = 2$. Similarly, the other series are produced by transitions ending at higher levels, as shown in Fig. 69.

The energy level diagram greatly simplifies the description of the spectrum. It must be remembered that each series is an aggregate of infinitely many lines, and the whole spectrum contains an infinite number of such series. By the use of an energy level diagram, the whole spectrum may be simply represented by only one aggregate of infinitely many levels. From these levels all the lines of all the series can be derived.

281

The energy level diagram clearly represents two important quantities characteristic of the atom, the energies of excitation and ionization. The *energy of excitation* is the energy needed to lift the atom from the normal state $n = 1$ to the lowest excited state $n = 2$. This is the minimum energy required to excite the hydrogen atom, because any change of state can occur only between energy levels. Computed from Bohr's theory as the difference between the two energy levels, the energy of excitation for hydrogen turns out to be 16.34×10^{-12} erg, or 10.20 electron volts (1 electron volt = 1.602×10^{-12} erg). This energy may also be computed from the frequency of the first line of the Lyman series.

The *energy of ionization* is the energy needed to lift the atom from the normal state $n = 1$ to the convergence limit of the energy levels, where $n \to \infty$. When n becomes infinite, the revolving electron is lifted to an infinitely distant orbit, which means that it is separated from the nucleus. This is what is meant by ionization. The energy of ionization for hydrogen, computed from Bohr's theory as the difference between the two energy levels, turns out to be 21.78×10^{-12} erg, or 13.59 electron volts. This energy may also be computed from the convergence limit of the Lyman series.

The original theory of Bohr contained an approximation. In deriving the equations for the stationary states of the atom, the assumption was made that the electron rotates about a fixed nucleus. Actually, according to the laws of mechanics, both the electron and the nucleus rotate about their common center of mass. They revolve with the same angular velocity, but with different radii. Since the mass of the nucleus is very large compared to the mass of the electron, the center of mass very nearly coincides with the center of the nucleus. The assumption that it does coincide amounts to assuming that the nucleus has an infinite mass. But the nucleus has a finite mass. When the mass of the nucleus is taken into account, the *relative motion of the nucleus* has to be considered in calculating the energy of the rotating system. When this is done, the total energy is calculated in terms of the mass of the nucleus, the mass of the electron, their respective distances from the center of mass, and their respective velocities. The mathematical expression obtained can be greatly simplified and put in an elegant form by noticing a peculiar relation. It turns out that this system is equivalent to the rotation of a particle of reduced mass about a fixed force center, where the distance between the force center and the particle is equal to the distance between the electron and the nucleus in the actual atom. It must be remembered that in taking into account the relative motion of the nucleus, the total energy of the system, nucleus and electron, is calculated. But mathematically, the results are the same as would be given by an electron of reduced mass rotating about a fixed nucleus. The *reduced mass* is given by the expression $\dfrac{mM}{m + M}$ where m is the mass of the electron, and M is the mass of the nucleus. When this expression for the reduced mass is used in place of m, the mass of the electron, in Bohr's formula for the spectral lines, it is found that the values obtained agree almost exactly with the experimental values. Also, when the reduced mass is used in the expression for the Rydberg constant, slightly different values of this constant are obtained for the different elements. Some of the values are as follows:

Rydberg constant for hydrogen	R_H	$= 109{,}677.58$ cm.$^{-1}$
Rydberg constant for deuterium	R_D	$= 109{,}707.42$ cm.$^{-1}$
Rydberg constant for ionized helium	R_{He}	$= 109{,}722.27$ cm.$^{-1}$
Rydberg constant for infinite mass	R_∞	$= 109{,}737.31$ cm.$^{-1}$

Thus the *relative motion of the nucleus* results in slightly different values of the Rydberg constant, and this in turn predicts slightly different values for the spectral lines. For example, the difference in the Rydberg constants for hydrogen and deuterium results in a change in the wave lengths of the corresponding Balmer lines of the two isotopes of hydrogen. The accurate measurements of these lines led to the discovery of heavy hydrogen, or deuterium. A knowledge of the nuclear masses of the light elements can be used to calculate the values of the Rydberg constant, and from these to predict accurate values of the wave lengths. Similarly, from a very accurate measurement of the wave lengths, the values of the Rydberg constant can be calculated and from these, the masses of the light nuclei can be determined accurately, as well as the mass of the electron.

Classical physics was developed for large scale phenomena, but it had to be modified by the ideas of quantum physics in dealing with individual atomic phenomena. However, there must be a region in which the two fields overlap, and for this region, the results of quantum physics must agree with those of classical physics. This is essentially the *correspondence principle* of Bohr. Thus classical physics predicts that a revolving electron emits light whose frequency is given by the frequency of revolution of the electron. According to Bohr's theory of the hydrogen atom, the frequency of the radiation emitted is determined by the difference in energy between two orbital states of the atom. In trying to find a correlation between the frequency of revolution in the different electron orbits and the quantum frequency of the emitted energy, Bohr was led to his correspondence principle. This states that for very large quantum numbers n, the quantum theory frequency and the classical orbit frequency become equal.

If we consider transitions between two quantum numbers n_1 and n_2 where $n_2 - n_1 = 1$ and n_1 is very large, we find that the quantum theory frequency and the classical orbit frequency become equal. Actually, the quantum theory frequency lies between the revolution frequencies for n_1 and n_2, and for very large values of n, these two are very nearly the same. If the change in n is greater than 1, such as 2 or 3, it is found that the quantum theory predicts harmonics of the fundamental frequency. Thus, both quantum theory and classical theory make similar predictions.

One of the first outstanding successes of Bohr's theory was its application to the spectrum of ionized helium. Ordinarily helium gas emits a more complicated spectrum than that of hydrogen atoms. But under violent excitation in an electric discharge, an additional spectrum appears with a structure closely resembling the hydrogen spectrum. This spectrum is attributed to ionized helium atoms. The neutral helium atoms have a nuclear charge of $+2$ and two external electrons. A singly ionized helium atom has only one external electron and thus has a structure similar to the hydrogen atom. Hence Bohr's theory can be applied in predicting the spectrum of *singly ionized helium*. Bohr's final equation for the stationary states of the atom contains the factor Z^2, where Z is the atomic number. For $Z = 2$, the constant R in Bohr's formula is replaced by $4R$ and the formula becomes

$$\nu = 4Rc \left[\frac{1}{n_1^2} - \frac{1}{n_2^2} \right]$$

When different values are assigned to n_1 and n_2 this formula is found to represent all of the known series of ionized helium very accurately.

In a similar way Bohr's theory can predict the spectra of other light elements when their atoms are made to have a hydrogen-like structure. It has been found that the third element of the periodic table, lithium, when under violent excitation by a spark discharge at low pressure and high voltage, emits a spectrum which is described by the formula

$$\nu = 9Rc \left[\frac{1}{n_1^2} - \frac{1}{n_2^2} \right]$$

This spectrum is produced by *doubly ionized lithium* atoms, which have a nuclear charge of $+3$ and only one external electron. Here the constant R is replaced by $9R$ and the formula predicts accurately the series for doubly ionized lithium. For the next element, beryllium, which has a nuclear charge of $+4$, it has been found that a spectrum can be produced which is described by the same formula, except that the constant R is replaced by $16R$. This spectrum is produced by *triply ionized beryllium* atoms, or by atoms which have lost three of their four external electrons. Thus Bohr's theory has been successfully used in predicting the spectra of these elements, and at the same time in providing an additional check on the value of the nuclear charge.

The *diffraction grating* provides the simplest and most accurate method for measuring wave lengths of light. It consists of a very large number of fine, equally spaced parallel slits. The lines of a transmission grating are ruled on glass; the unruled portions of the glass act as slits. Gratings usually have about 10,000 to 20,000 lines per inch. The grating used in this experiment is a transmission grating replica.

The theory of the diffraction grating is explained on p. 219. Suppose that a beam of parallel monochromatic light, originally from the same source and having passed through a slit, impinges upon a grating. By Huygens' principle, the light spreads out in every direction from the apertures of the grating, each of which acts as a separate new source of light. The envelope of the secondary wavelets determines the position of the advancing wave. One of the new wave fronts formed is tangent to wavelets which have all advanced the same distance from the slits, and the wave front formed is thus parallel to the original wave front. A converging lens placed in the path of these rays would form the central image. Another wave front is tangent to wavelets whose distances from adjacent slits differ by one wave length. This wave front forms the first order spectrum. The next wave front is tangent to wavelets whose distances from adjacent slits differ by two wave lengths. This wave front forms the second order spectrum. Spectra of higher order may also be formed.

The *wave length* of the light is given by the grating equation

$$n\lambda = d \sin \theta$$

where λ is the wave length of the light in centimeters; n is the order of the spectrum, i.e. the first image, the second image, etc., formed on either side of the central image; d is the distance between the lines on the grating in centimeters; and θ is the angle of deviation from the original direction of the light. If the light is all of one color (monochromatic), a single image of the slit will appear in each order of the spectrum. But if the light is not monochromatic, there will be as many images of the slit in each order as there are different wave lengths in the light from the source, the diffracting angle of each wave length being given by the above equation. The wave length of visible light is usually expressed in Angstrom units. One Angstrom unit is 10^{-8} centimeter.

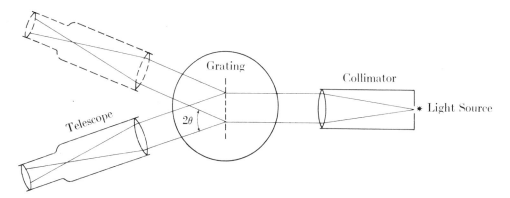

Fig. 70A. The Diffraction Grating Spectrometer

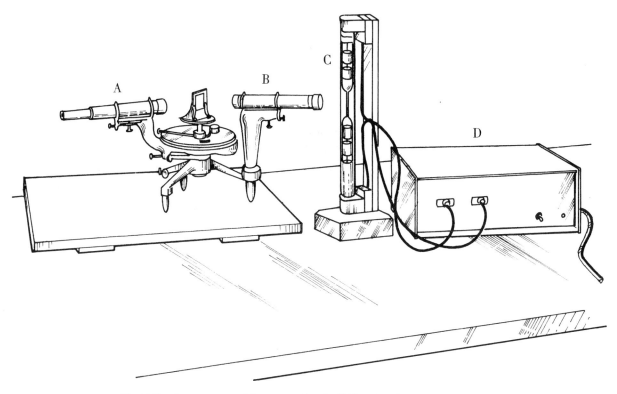

Fig. 70B. Arrangement of Apparatus for the Diffraction Grating Spectrometer:
(A) telescope, (B) collimator, (C) discharge tube, (D) power supply

The arrangement used in this experiment is the *grating spectrometer*, shown in Fig. 70A. By the use of a spectrometer it is possible to measure the diffraction angles very accurately. The grating spectrometer consists of four principal parts: a collimator, a diffraction grating, a telescope, and a divided circle. The collimator is a tube with a converging lens at one end and a fine slit of adjustable width placed in the focal plane of the lens at the other end of the tube. The function of the collimator is to render the rays of light from the slit parallel by means of a lens. The grating diffracts the rays of light and forms spectra of different orders on both sides of the central image. The telescope consists of the objective lens, which brings the parallel rays of light to a focus in its focal plane, and the eyepiece, through which the image of the spectrum is viewed. The position of the image can be read by the setting of the telescope on the divided circle of the spectrometer.

APPARATUS

1. Spectrometer, for prism or grating.
2. Diffraction grating of about 25,000 lines per inch.
3. Grating holder.

4. Atomic hydrogen discharge tube.
5. Discharge tube power supply.
6. Tube holder.

The apparatus listed in this experiment is supplied by Central Scientific Company, 1700 Irving Park Road, Chicago, Illinois. Thus, the hydrogen discharge tube is listed as No. 87206 Balmer Tube (Hydrogen). The high voltage power supply is listed as No. 87207 Power Supply.

PROCEDURE

1. The spectrometer should be already adjusted by the instructor, with the collimator and telescope properly focused and aligned, and the spectrometer table leveled so that its axis of rotation is the same as the axis of the spectrometer. *Caution:* Do not handle the spectrometer at all until the instructor has demonstrated its operation to you, for it is very easy to upset the adjustments. Then, be extremely careful in operating it.

2. Place the diffraction grating in its mounting at the center of the spectrometer table. The unruled side of the grating should face the collimator, and the plane of the grating should be made as nearly perpendicular to the axis of the collimator as can be judged with the eye. The lines on the grating should be parallel to the slit of the collimator, and the center of the grating itself should be as nearly as possible in the center of the spectrometer table.

3. Place the stand containing the hydrogen discharge tube in front of the spectrometer with the discharge tube just outside the slit of the collimator (see Fig. 70B). Connect the terminals of the hydrogen discharge tube to the proper high voltage power supply. Adjust the spectrometer so that the collimator tube is pointing directly at the hydrogen discharge tube. Close the switch of the power supply. *Caution:* Do not touch the discharge tube or high tension wires while the current is on.

4. Observe the central image produced by the diffraction grating. Turn the telescope into line with the collimator and view the central image through the eyepiece of the telescope. This will be an image of the slit of the collimator and will have the same color as that of the hydrogen discharge. The slit should be made as narrow as possible and yet remain visible in the telescope.

5. Move the telescope to the right so as to view the first order hydrogen spectrum. Adjust the position of the telescope until the red hydrogen line falls exactly on the intersection of the cross hairs of the telescope.

6. Directly under the arm supporting the telescope is a clamping device which rotates with the arm and permits the telescope to be clamped by means of a radial screw. A tangent screw on the telescope arm allows a fine adjustment of the setting of the telescope; however, the tangent screw is used only after the telescope has been clamped with the radial screw. Clamp the telescope by means of the radial screw and locate the position of the red hydrogen line by setting the intersection of the cross hairs exactly on the red line by means of the tangent screw. Record the setting of the telescope to the nearest minute of arc, reading the divided circle with the help of the vernier.

7. Repeat procedures (5–6) for the blue-green, the blue, and the violet hydrogen lines. Record the setting of the telescope to the nearest minute of arc, for each of the lines measured.

8. Move the telescope to the left of the central image, so as to view the left-hand first order hydrogen spectrum. Adjust the position of the telescope until the red hydrogen line falls exactly on the intersection of the cross hairs of the telescope. Record the setting of the telescope to the nearest minute of arc.

9. Repeat procedure (8) for the blue-green, the blue, and the violet hydrogen lines. Record the setting of the telescope to the nearest minute of arc, for each of the lines measured.

DATA

Number of lines per inch on the grating. . . . .

Grating constant in centimeters. . . . .

Calculated value of Rydberg constant. . . . .

Accepted value of Rydberg constant. . . . .

Per cent error. . . . .

HYDROGEN LINES		SETTING OF TELESCOPE		CALCULATED VALUES			
WAVE LENGTH ANGSTROM UNITS	COLOR	RIGHT	LEFT	θ	SIN θ	COMPUTED WAVE LENGTH	PER CENT DEVIATION
6562.8	red						
4861.3	blue-green						
4340.5	blue						
4101.7	violet						

CALCULATIONS

1. Compute the grating constant, i.e. the distance between the lines on the grating in centimeters, from the number of lines per inch stated on the grating.

2. Compute the angle of diffraction θ for each of the four lines measured. The angle of diffraction is one half of the angle between the two settings of the telescope, for each line.

3. Compute the value of sin θ for each of the four lines measured.

4. Compute the wave length of each line, using the value of the grating constant previously calculated, and applying the grating equation. The wave length should be expressed in Angstrom units, evaluated to four significant figures.

5. Calculate the per cent deviation of the computed values of the wave lengths from the known values.

6. Calculate the value of the Rydberg constant from the computed wave length of each line.

7. Find the average value of the computed Rydberg constant.

8. Calculate the per cent deviation of the computed value of the Rydberg constant from the known value.

QUESTIONS

1. Calculate the angular separation between the D lines of sodium for a diffraction grating of 15,000 lines per inch in the first order spectrum. Calculate the separation in the second order spectrum. The wave lengths of the lines are 5890 and 5896 Angstroms respectively.

2. Using the Balmer formula, calculate the wave length of the fifth line of the Balmer series of hydrogen lines.

3. Explain the significance of the Fraunhofer lines in the spectrum of the sun.

4. Calculate the wave length of the first line of the Balmer series of deuterium, or heavy hydrogen, lines. Use the Balmer formula which gives the reciprocal wave length, $1/\lambda$, and calculate the wave length in Angstroms to five significant figures. For the Rydberg constant, use the value which is appropriate for deuterium. Also find the wave length difference in Angstroms between this line and the corresponding hydrogen line, by using the known value of the red hydrogen line. It was the accurate measurement of these lines, and the interpretation given by the Bohr theory, that led to the discovery of heavy hydrogen by Urey, Brickwedde, and Murphy in 1932.

57

THE RATIO *e/m* FOR ELECTRONS

The physical nature of cathode rays is revealed by the deflections which they undergo as they pass through electric and magnetic fields. The direction of these deflections shows that these rays consist of particles which have a negative electric charge and a definite mass. The investigations of J. J. Thomson in 1897 led to a measurement of the ratio of charge to mass for these particles, which have been called electrons. The results of these measurements showed that the atom is not indivisible, that the electron is part of an atom, and that it is much smaller than the smallest atom. The object of this experiment is to determine the value of the ratio of charge to mass of an electron. From the known value of the charge on the electron and the value of *e/m* obtained with this experiment, the mass of the electron can be computed.

THEORY

One of the simplest methods of measuring the ratio *e/m*, or the *ratio of charge to mass* of an electron, was devised by Lenard, and consists in measuring the deflection of a beam of electrons in a known magnetic field. The beam of electrons is bent into a circular path. From the known values of the accelerating potential, the strength of the magnetic field, and the radius of curvature of the path, the value of *e/m* can be calculated.

When an electron or any other charged particle moves in a magnetic field in a direction at right angles to the field, it is acted upon by a force which is perpendicular to the direction of the field and the direction of motion of the particle. The *value of the force* on an electron is given by

$$F = Bev$$

where B is the strength of the magnetic field, e is the charge on the electron, and v is the velocity of the electron.

Since the force is always perpendicular to the direction of motion of the electron, it makes the electron move in a circular path; the plane of the circle is perpendicular to the direction of the magnetic field. The *force required* to keep a body moving in a circular path is given by

$$F = m \frac{v^2}{r}$$

where F is the force in dynes, m is the mass of the body in grams, v is the velocity in cm./sec., and r is the radius of the path in centimeters. The required *centripetal force* is provided by the force exerted on the electron by the magnetic field. Therefore we have the relation

$$m \frac{v^2}{r} = Bev$$

When an electron is accelerated by a potential difference V, it gains a kinetic energy equal to the work done on the electron by the electric field, which is Ve. Therefore, the *kinetic energy* of the electron, which is $\frac{1}{2}mv^2$, is given by

$$\tfrac{1}{2} mv^2 = Ve$$

where m is the mass of the electron in grams, v is the velocity in cm./sec., V is the accelerating potential in abvolts, and e is the charge on the electron in abcoulombs. The *velocity* that the electron acquires is therefore given by the relation

$$v = \sqrt{2Ve/m}$$

Substituting this value of v in the expression relating the centripetal force to the force due to the magnetic field, we finally get

$$\frac{e}{m} = \frac{2V}{B^2 r^2}$$

This expression gives the *ratio of charge to mass* of an electron in terms of the accelerating potential, the flux density of the magnetic field, and the radius of the circular path of the beam of electrons. When these quantities are known, the value of *e/m* can be computed. In the electromagnetic system of units, *e* is the charge on the electron in abcoulombs, m is the mass of the electron in grams, V is the accelerating potential in abvolts, B is the magnetic flux density in gauss, and r is the radius of the path in centimeters.

Note on units: To be able to make calculations, one must know the relations between different systems of units.

The electromagnetic unit (emu) of current is the *abampere*. The practical unit of current, the ampere, is $\frac{1}{10}$ of the emu of current.

The electromagnetic unit of charge is the *abcoulomb*. The practical unit of charge, the coulomb, is $\frac{1}{10}$ of the emu of charge.

The electromagnetic unit of potential is the *abvolt*. The practical unit of potential, the volt, is 10^8 abvolts.

Therefore we have the relations

$$\begin{aligned}
1 \text{ abampere} &= 10 \text{ amperes} \\
1 \text{ abcoulomb} &= 10 \text{ coulombs} \\
1 \text{ abvolt} &= 10^{-8} \text{ volt}
\end{aligned}$$

The *equipment* for measuring the ratio of e/m has been designed after the experiment of Bainbridge. The apparatus consists of a large vacuum tube supported at the center of a pair of Helmholtz coils, which provide the uniform magnetic field needed for the operation of the tube. The arrangement of the apparatus is shown in Fig. 71. The beam of electrons is produced by an electron gun composed of a straight filament parallel to the axis of the coils and surrounded by a coaxial anode containing a single slit parallel to the filament. Electrons emitted from the heated filament are accelerated by the potential difference applied between the filament and the anode. Some of the electrons come out as a narrow beam through the slit in the anode. The tube contains a trace of mercury vapor which is used to render the path of the electrons visible. When the electrons collide with the mercury atoms, some of the atoms will be ionized; as these ions recombine with stray electrons, the characteristic mercury light is emitted. Since the recombination and the emission of light occur very near the point where ionization took place, the path of the beam of electrons is visible as a bluish-white streak of light.

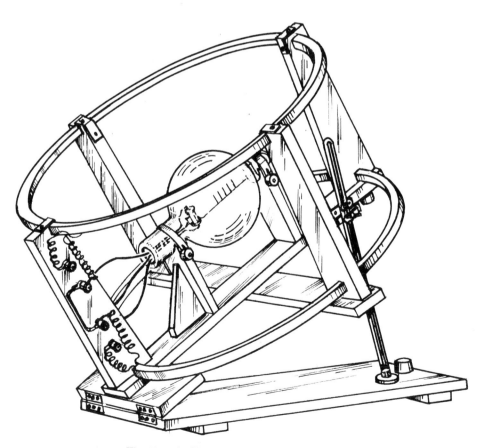

Fig. 71. *e/m* Vacuum Tube and Helmholtz Coils

A pair of *Helmholtz coils* is a particular arrangement of two coaxial, circular coils of radius a with their planes parallel and separated by a distance a equal to the radius of the coils. This arrangement is very useful because it produces an almost uniform magnetic field over a fairly large region near the center of the coils. The magnetic field at the center is parallel to the axis of the coils and its magnitude is given by

$$B = \frac{32\pi NI}{\sqrt{125}\,a}$$

where B is the magnetic flux density in gauss, N is the number of turns of wire on each coil, I is the current through the coils in abamperes, and a is the mean radius of each coil in centimeters. The quantities are expressed here in the electromagnetic system of units.

Each coil of the pair of Helmholtz coils used in this experiment has 72 turns of copper wire with a resistance of approximately one ohm. The mean radius of the coil is 33 centimeters. The coils are supported in a frame which can be adjusted with reference to the angle of dip so that the magnetic field produced by the coils will be parallel to the earth's magnetic field, but in the opposite direction. A graduated scale indicates the angle of tilt.

The *magnetic field* of the Helmholtz coils causes the beam of electrons to move in a circular path whose radius decreases as the magnetic field increases. The magnetic field can be adjusted until the sharp outer edge of the beam coincides with the outer edge of one of the five bars spaced at different distances from the filament. The vacuum tube used in this experiment has been so designed that the radius of the circular path can be conveniently measured. In the manufacture of the *e/m* tube, five cross bars have been attached to the staff wire, and this assembly is attached to the filament assembly in such a way that the distance between each cross bar and the filament is accurately known. The distance in centimeters between the filament and the outer edge of each bar is given below. These distances are the diameters of the circles which the electron beam will be made to describe.

Crossbar Number	Distance to Filament
1	6.48 cm.
2	7.75 cm.
3	9.02 cm.
4	10.30 cm.
5	11.54 cm.

Figure 72 is a sectional view of the tube and filament assembly. A represents the five cross bars attached to the staff wire; B shows a typical path of the beam of electrons; C represents the cylindrical anode, with the slit S; and F represents the filament.

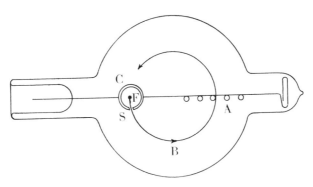

Fig. 72. Sectional View of *e/m* Tube and Filament Assembly

The field circuit for the Helmholtz coils is shown in Fig. 73. The voltage supply E_3 consists of a 12-volt storage battery or a 12-volt battery eliminator capable of supplying 5 amperes of filtered D.C. continuously. Resistance R_2 is the tubular rheostat of about 200 ohms resistance. R_3 is the tubular rheostat of about 10 ohms resistance. A is the D.C. ammeter (0–5 amperes).

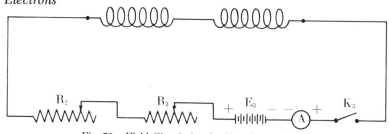

Fig. 73. Field Circuit for the Helmholtz Coils

The circuit for the *e/m* tube is shown in Fig. 74. The voltage supply E_1 consists of a "B" battery with terminals for either 22.5 or 45 volts. The voltage supply E_2 consists of a 6-volt storage battery or a 6-volt battery eliminator capable of supplying 5 amperes of filtered D.C. continuously. Resistance R_1 is the tubular rheostat of about 5 ohms resistance. A is the D.C. ammeter (0–10 amperes).

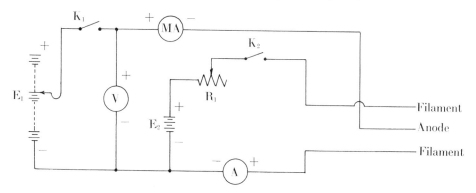

Fig. 74. Circuit for the *e/m* Tube

The action of the *e/m* tube and Helmholtz coils can be used in explaining the principle of the *mass spectrometer*. The expression that was obtained for *e/m* shows that charged particles which have the same ratio of charge to mass will follow the same circular path when they are acted upon by a given magnetic field and are accelerated by the same electric potential. However, if the particles have the same charge, but a different mass, the radius of the circular path which they follow will be different. Thus by measuring the radius of the path, the mass of the particles can be determined very accurately. This is essentially the principle on which the mass spectrometer operates.

The *accepted values* of *e*, *m*, and *e/m* for the electron are the following:

$$e = 1.602 \times 10^{-20} \text{ emu} \qquad \text{charge on the electron}$$
$$m = 9.11 \times 10^{-28} \text{ gram} \qquad \text{mass of the electron}$$
$$e/m = 1.759 \times 10^7 \text{ emu/gram} \qquad \text{ratio of charge to mass for the electron}$$

APPARATUS

1. *e/m* Vacuum Tube.
2. Pair of Helmholtz Coils.
3. 6-volt storage battery or a 6-volt battery eliminator.
4. 12-volt storage battery or a 12-volt battery eliminator.
5. Tubular rheostat of about 200 ohms resistance.
6. Tubular rheostat of about 10 ohms resistance.
7. Tubular rheostat of about 5 ohms resistance.

8. "B" battery ($22\frac{1}{2}$ and 45 volts).
9. D.C. voltmeter (0–50 volts).
10. D.C. ammeter (0–10 amperes).
11. D.C. ammeter (0–5 amperes).
12. D.C. milliammeter (0–10 milliamperes).
13. Three single pole, single throw switches.

The apparatus described in this experiment, the *e/m* Vacuum Tube and the Helmholtz Coils, is supplied by The Welch Scientific Company, 7300 North Linder Avenue, Skokie, Illinois.

PROCEDURE

1. The Helmholtz coils will be already connected in the circuit as shown in Fig. 73. The *e/m* tube will be already connected in the circuit as shown in Fig. 74. These connections should be checked and approved by the instructor. All switches should be open.

2. The Helmholtz coils have been designed to provide the uniform magnetic field required in the operation of the tube. The axis of the coils may be inclined to the dip angle for quantitative measurements in such a way that the magnetic field produced by the coils may be adjusted to cancel the earth's magnetic field. This is done by making the magnetic field produced by the coils parallel to the earth's magnetic field, but oppositely directed. First orient the Helmholtz coils so that the *e/m* tube will have its long axis in a magnetic north-south direction, as determined by a compass. Then measure the magnetic dip at this location by using a good dip needle. Finally tip the coils up until the plane of the coils makes an angle with the horizontal equal to the complement of the angle of dip. The axis of the coils will now be parallel to the earth's magnetic field. For example, in New York State the magnetic dip is about 74° and thus the plane of the coils should make an angle of about 16° with the horizontal. A graduated scale connected to the apparatus indicates the angle of tilt of the plane of the coils. If the dip needle is now placed in a north-south direction on the inclined board supporting the coils, the needle will point along the axis of the coils.

3. Make sure that the axis of the coils has been set so that it points along the earth's magnetic lines of force. Now check to see if the magnetic field produced by each of the coils is in the direction opposing that of the earth's field. To do this, send a small current through the Helmholtz coils. Make sure that there is maximum resistance in the field circuit by checking on the setting of both rheostats R_2 and R_3. Now close switch K_3 and send a small current through the coils. Check the direction of the magnetic field produced by the current in each coil by placing a compass very close to the coil, to see in what direction the needle is deflected when the current is turned on. From this, the direction of the magnetic field produced by the coils can be determined. The direction of the magnetic field produced by each coil should be upward, along the axis of the coils. This will be opposite to the direction of the earth's magnetic field, which is downward along the axis. If one of the coils produces a field in the wrong direction, the current through that coil should be reversed. Now open switch K_3.

4. Apply $22\frac{1}{2}$ volts accelerating potential to the anode of the tube by closing switch K_1.

5. Make sure that there is maximum resistance in the filament circuit by checking on the setting of rheostat R_1. Now close switch K_2 in the filament circuit. Start with a low filament current and increase it very slowly and carefully by gradually decreasing resistance R_1 until the proper electron emission is obtained. This is checked by watching the milliammeter in the plate circuit, which reads the plate current. As soon as the plate current begins to appear, the filament current should be increased extremely slowly and carefully, while the value of the plate current is continually watched. When the plate current reaches a value of 6 milliamperes, do not increase the filament current any further. This will avoid overheating the filament and possibly burning it out. Record the value of the plate current and of the filament current. Record also the value of the plate voltage, which will be kept constant throughout the experiment.

6. The thin path of light produced in the path of the beam of electrons as they pass through the mercury vapor should now be clearly visible. We shall merely call this path the electron beam. If the tube has been properly rotated so that the crossbars extend upward from the staff wire, the electron beam should be horizontal. But the electron beam will be deflected slightly toward the base of the tube by the earth's magnetic field. To balance out the effect of the earth's field, a small current should be sent through the Helmholtz coils. Make sure that there is maximum resistance in the field circuit by checking on the setting of both rheostats R_2 and R_3. Now close switch K_3 and send a small current through the coils. If the magnetic field of the coils tends to straighten the beam, the coils are properly connected. If the field increases the deflection toward the base, the field current is flowing in the wrong direction.

7. Adjust the value of the field current until the electron beam is straight. Slowly increase the value of the current by gradually decreasing resistance R_2. Keep watching the electron beam and slowly increase the current until the beam is perfectly straight, and perpendicular to the long axis of the tube. This adjustment should be made very carefully and accurately. When the electron beam is straight, the magnetic field of the coils is just equal to the earth's magnetic field, so that the resultant field on the electron beam is zero. Record this value of the current as I_1. This current will be constant throughout the experiment, since the accelerating voltage is kept constant.

8. Increase the field current slowly until the electron beam describes a circle. The current is increased by gradually decreasing resistance R_2. Keep on decreasing only resistance R_2 until it is completely out of the

circuit. Then begin decreasing resistance R_3 and from then on, use only resistance R_3 to control the current. This is done to prevent overloading R_2 which cannot carry too big a current. Adjust the value of the current carefully until the bright, sharp outside edge of the beam just clears the outside edge of crossbar number 5, the one that is farthest away from the filament of the tube. Record this value of the current as I_2 in the table.

The outside edge of the beam is used because it contains the electrons with the greatest velocity. The electrons emitted from the negative end of the filament fall through the greatest potential difference between filament and anode, and thus have the greatest velocity. This is the potential difference that the voltmeter measures, and it is the one that we use in our calculations. The electron beam spreads as it goes around the tube, but all of the spreading is toward the inside of the circle. This spreading is produced by electrons which have a smaller velocity, and by electrons which have a component of velocity parallel to the magnetic field.

9. Keep on increasing the field current slowly and adjust its value carefully until the bright, sharp outside edge of the electron beam just clears the outside edge of crossbar number 4. Again record this value of the current as I_2 in the table. Repeat the same procedure for crossbars 3, 2, and 1 and record the value of the current I_2 in each case.

DATA

Number of turns of each coil . . . .

Mean radius of each coil . . . .

Filament current . . . .

Plate current . . . .

e/m calculated value . . . .

e/m accepted value . . . .

Per cent error . . . .

CROSSBAR NUMBER	RADIUS OF CIRCLE	VOLTAGE	I_1	I_2	I	B	e/m
1							
2							
3							
4							
5							

CALCULATIONS

1. Calculate the radius of the circle of the electron beam for each crossbar distance.

2. For each value of the field current I_2 subtract the current I_1 to obtain the value of the current I, which is the current needed to produce the magnetic field which deflects the electrons.

3. For each value of the field current I, calculate the magnetic flux density B of the magnetic field produced within the Helmholtz coils.

4. For each circular path described by the electron beam, compute the value of e/m by using the appropriate value of the accelerating potential, the magnetic flux density, and the radius of the circle.

5. Find the average of the values of e/m obtained in calculation (4) and record this as the calculated value of e/m. Compare your result with the accepted value by finding the per cent error.

QUESTIONS

1. The oil-drop experiment gives a value of 1.60×10^{-20} electromagnetic units of charge on the electron. Using this value and your calculated value for e/m compute the mass of the electron.

2. Name two sources of error in your measurements which are most likely to affect the accuracy of your results.

3. Compute the velocity of an electron which has been accelerated through a difference of potential of 100 volts. Express the result in centimeters per second.

4. Calculate the strength of the magnetic field required to bend electrons which have been accelerated through a potential difference of 100 volts into a circle 10 centimeters in diameter. Express the magnetic flux density in gauss.

5. Show how the action of the *e/m* tube and Helmholtz coils can be used in explaining the principle of a mass spectrometer. In a mass spectrometer, isotopes of the same element can be separated. Charged particles carrying the same charge, but differing in mass, can be produced and studied in this type of tube.

58

THE PHOTOELECTRIC EFFECT. PLANCK'S CONSTANT

The quantum theory has revolutionized our ideas of the nature of radiation, the nature of atoms and molecules, and the interaction between radiation and atomic particles. One of the cornerstones of modern physics, the quantum theory was introduced by Planck in an attempt to derive a law of blackbody radiation that would agree with experimental observations. Planck made some entirely new and radical assumptions about the nature of radiation. He assumed that any radiation of a definite frequency cannot be emitted or absorbed in arbitrary amounts; he postulated that instead it is always emitted or absorbed in whole multiples of a discrete quantity of energy. This quantity of energy, called a quantum, is proportional to the frequency of the radiation. The constant of proportionality is a universal constant, now known as Planck's constant.

Making use of the quantum idea, Einstein developed the law of the photoelectric effect. He assumed that light of a definite frequency can transfer its entire quantum of energy to a single electron, even though the electron may be far from the source of radiation. This assumption extended the quantum theory to the transfer of radiant energy through space by means of light quanta. The purpose of this experiment is to determine experimentally the value of Planck's constant by measuring the photoelectric effect and using Einstein's photoelectric equation.

THEORY

Radiation falling upon bodies is at least partially absorbed by them; some of the radiation may be reflected and some may be transmitted. If the temperature of a body is raised, it will emit radiant energy, or *thermal radiation*. At all temperatures, bodies are emitting and absorbing thermal radiation. If the temperature of a body is constant, the body is absorbing as much radiant energy each second as it is emitting. A body that is a good radiator of energy is also a good absorber of energy. A black rough surface such as that provided by a coating of lampblack is an excellent radiator as well as an excellent absorber of radiant energy. An *ideal black body* is both a perfect radiator and a perfect absorber. Thus, an ideal black body completely absorbs all radiation falling upon it; similarly, all radiation leaving an ideal black body consists entirely of radiation that it emits.

From a theoretical standpoint, *blackbody radiation* is a phenomenon of great interest, since its properties have a universal character, independent of the properties of any particular substance. The temperature of the body is the sole determinant of the amount and quality of the radiation emission. The study of blackbody radiation is very important. It is important to know how the amount of radiation varies with the temperature and what the spectral distribution of the energy is. All this information is of great help in understanding the nature of radiation itself, the nature of atoms and molecules, and the interrelation between atomic processes and the radiation emitted.

Since the quantity and quality of energy emitted by a hot body depend on the temperature of the body, the rate at which an incandescent filament emits radiation increases rapidly with an increase in temperature, and the emitted light becomes whiter. When the heated filament first becomes luminous, it appears dull red. As the temperature rises, the filament grows brighter and yellower; and at a still higher temperature, it becomes very bright and appears white. If the light from the filament is dispersed by a prism or a grating, a continuous spectrum is formed. The relative intensity of the radiation at different wave lengths may be measured, and a curve plotted showing *distribution of energy* among the wave lengths. In the study of blackbody radiation, measurements are made on an ideal radiator, which is a good approximation of an ideal black body. The ideal radiator is approached by way of an enclosed furnace with a small opening through which one may view the interior radiations. The radiation observed through the opening depends only on the temperature of the furnace and not on the material. Hence, the radiation is as close as we can get experimentally to blackbody radiation. Careful measurements have been made of the amounts of energy radiated, under these conditions, at various wave lengths. Fig. 75 shows the experimental results. The curves are obtained by plotting the radiant energy emitted as a function of wave length.   Values for *intensity of radiation,* or energy radiated per unit area per unit frequency interval, have been determined throughout the available frequency range and the results plotted to show distribution of energy.   At very low and very high frequencies the intensity approaches zero, with a maximum value appearing at some intermediate frequency.   The graph shows the distribution of energy to be a function of both wave length and temperature. For each temperature of the black body, there is a definite distribution of energy and a definite wave length at which maximum energy is radiated.   Fig. 75 shows the *intensity distribution curves* for several temperatures.

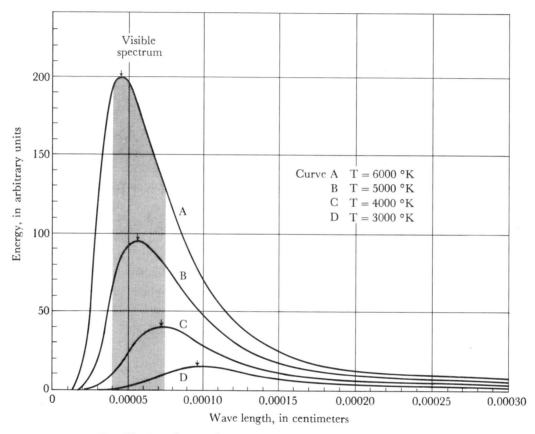

Fig. 75.   Distribution of Energy in the Blackbody Spectrum for Four
Different Temperatures

The radiations from an ideal black body are determined by its temperature alone.   The relation between intensity of radiation and absolute temperature was discovered experimentally by Josef Stefan in 1879. Stefan found that the total energy radiated by a black body is proportional to the fourth power of the absolute temperature.   This relation may be expressed as

$$W = \sigma T^4$$

where W is the total energy radiated per unit area; T is the absolute temperature; and σ is Stefan's constant. Ludwig Boltzmann, using classical thermodynamic theory, later derived the same relationship, which is now known as the Stefan-Boltzmann law.

As the temperature is raised, not only does the total energy emitted by a black body increase, but the quality of the radiation changes.   The *distribution of energy* in the blackbody spectrum is shown in Fig. 75. These curves are obtained by plotting for several temperatures the radiant energy emitted as a function of wave length.   The curves show that an increase of temperature not only causes an increase in the total radiation emitted by a black body but also shifts the peak of the curve toward the shorter wave lengths.   Wilhelm

Wien worked out the shift in wave length, thus giving us Wien's displacement law. The law states that the product of the wave length λ_m, at which the energy density is a maximum, and the absolute temperature of the radiating body is a constant, or

$$\lambda_m T = C$$

where λ_m is the wave length of maximum energy emission; T is the absolute temperature; and C is a constant that has the value 0.289 centimeter degrees when the wave length is expressed in centimeters. Wien's displacement law is a useful relation with important practical applications, since it allows determination of the temperature of inaccessible hot bodies. For example, the maximum energy of the sun is known to be emitted at a wave length of about 0.000045 cm. This corresponds to a temperature of about 6000°C. In a similar way, the temperature of other stars may be determined from the spectral distribution of the light they emit.

Many attempts were made to explain the shape of the observed blackbody emission curves and to derive an analytic expression for the shape of the curves by application of classical electromagnetic theory, but all failed. Reasoning based on thermodynamics, however, reduced the problem of blackbody radiation to one of determining a single unknown function involving λ and T. In 1893, Wien derived a formula for radiation based on special assumptions regarding emission and absorption of radiation. He found an expression for distribution of energy in the blackbody spectrum as a function of both wave length and temperature. *Wien's radiation law* agrees very well with observations for short wave lengths and neighborhoods of maxima of curves, but for long wave lengths it predicts too low a value.

In 1900, Rayleigh applied the principle of equipartition of energy to the problem of blackbody radiation. Collaborating with Jeans, Rayleigh deduced a formula based entirely on classical theory. They assumed that the oscillators in the walls of an enclosure absorbed and emitted radiation constantly, each with its own characteristic frequency. By assigning the average energy prescribed by classical theory to each possible mode of vibration, they arrived at a formula for distribution of energy with wave length. This is the *Rayleigh-Jeans law* for blackbody radiation. For long wave lengths, the formula agrees with observation; but for neighborhoods of maxima of curves and for short wave lengths, the values it predicts are much too large. The law does not predict a maximum at all, and for very short wave lengths the energy density it predicts becomes infinite.

Max Planck in 1900 discovered the first satisfactory formula for blackbody radiation. By introducing certain new and radical assumptions about the behavior of radiation, he derived a formula in complete agreement with experimental results. Hertz's work on electromagnetic waves had confirmed the electromagnetic theory of light, and this convinced Planck that the explanation of the blackbody radiation spectrum would be found in the laws governing absorption and emission of radiation by electric oscillators. In 1900, new and accurate measurements of the blackbody spectrum by Lummer and Pringsheim and by others showed that Wien's formula was not entirely correct. Planck discovered an empirical modification of Wien's formula that fitted the observations. Then he tried to modify the statistical theory of the distribution of energy among a set of oscillators so that the theory would explain his formula. He succeeded only after making a new assumption entirely at variance with classical principles.

Planck assumed that an ideal radiating body contained a large number of oscillators, each having a definite frequency of vibration and each capable of sending out radiation of this frequency. The individual oscillators, he postulated, received the energy from the source that was maintaining the temperature of the radiating body and disposed of this energy in the form of radiation. According to classical theory, the process of absorption and emission of radiation was viewed as continuous. This meant that the energy of a body could change from one value to another through every conceivable intermediate value, no matter how small. To make his theory agree with the experimental radiation curve, Planck abandoned the idea of continuous energy exchange and assumed that each oscillator took on and gave off energy only in intermittent, discontinuous amounts.

Thus, Planck had made some new and radical assumptions about the nature of radiation. He assumed that any radiation of frequency ν cannot be emitted or absorbed in arbitrary amounts, that it must always be emitted or absorbed in whole multiples of a discrete quantity of energy. This quantum he held to be proportional to the frequency of the radiation, its value given by the relation

$$E = h\nu$$

where E is the energy of the quantum in ergs; ν is the frequency of the radiation in vibrations per second; and h is a universal constant, now known as *Planck's constant.*

Planck made another radical assumption, this time with regard to the energy of the oscillators emitting the radiation. He assumed that an oscillator could not have any arbitrary amount of energy, that it could have only energies given by the relation

$$W = nh\nu$$

where W is the energy of the oscillator; ν is the frequency of the oscillator; h is Planck's constant; and n is a number that can take on only integral values. The number n is now called a *quantum number,* where $n = 1, 2, 3, \ldots$ According to this assumption, the energy of an oscillator cannot vary continuously but must take on one of the discrete values 0, $h\nu$, $2h\nu$, $3h\nu$, $\ldots$ This means that the oscillator has a discrete set of possible energy values, or levels; in short, the energy of the oscillator is quantized.

The second assumption that Planck made was that the oscillators did not radiate energy continuously, but only in individual units, or quanta, these quanta of energy being emitted when an oscillator changed from a higher to a lower quantized energy state. Planck held that as long as the oscillator remained in one of its quantized states, it did not emit or absorb energy. If it absorbed energy, it changed from a lower to a higher energy state.

The two new ideas introduced by Planck form part of *modern quantum theory.* Briefly, they are

1. An oscillator has a discrete set of possible energy values, or energy levels; other energy values are not allowed and do not occur.
2. The emission and absorption of radiation are associated with transitions between two of these levels; the energy lost by the oscillator is emitted as a quantum of radiation, and similarly, the energy gained by the oscillator is absorbed as a quantum of radiation. The magnitude of the quantum in either case is $h\nu$, where ν is the frequency of the radiation and h is Planck's constant.

On the basis of his two assumptions, Planck was able to derive his radiation law entirely from theory. He derived it by considering the interaction between the radiation inside an isothermal enclosure and electric oscillators that he imagined as existing in the walls of the enclosure. *Planck's radiation law* is

$$U_\lambda = \frac{8\pi ch}{\lambda^5} \frac{1}{e^{ch/\lambda kT} - 1}$$

U_λ is the energy density for waves with wave length λ; c is the velocity of light; h is Planck's constant; k is Boltzmann's constant; and T is the absolute temperature. The formula shows the variation of energy with wave length and temperature. This is *Planck's formula for blackbody radiation.* Planck's formula reduces to Wien's formula near one end of the spectrum and to the Rayleigh-Jeans formula near the other end. It agrees very well with the experimental observations at both ends of the spectrum. Both the Stefan-Boltzmann law and the Wien displacement law can be derived mathematically from the Planck radiation law.

The quantum theory introduces the idea of an individual unit of energy, a quantum of energy. This is similar to the idea of the atomic structure of matter, or of the atomicity of electricity, in which the electron represents the smallest unit of electricity. However, there is a difference between the latter and the quantum idea. Quanta of energy are not all of the same size; they vary in size with the frequency of the radiation. The thing that does not change is the value of h, or Planck's constant, which is a universal constant. This constant is the new element introduced by the quantum theory. The constant h plays a very important part in a variety of atomic phenomena. Planck's hypothesis of the quantum structure of energy represented the very birth of quantum ideas. It proved to be the beginning of quantum theory, which has revolutionized our concepts of the nature of the processes taking place in emission and absorption of radiation.

One of the earliest applications of the quantum theory was in the explanation of the photoelectric effect. The *photoelectric effect* was discovered by Heinrich Hertz in 1887, when he observed that an electric spark started more readily when the electrodes of a spark gap were exposed to ultraviolet light. The effect was investigated one year later by Hallwachs, who found that a freshly polished zinc plate that was insulated and charged negatively would lose its charge when exposed to ultraviolet light; he also noted that there was no effect if the charge on the plate was positive. Ten years later, both J. J. Thomson and P. Lenard showed that the action of the light caused emission of free negative charges from the metal surface. These charges were found to be the same as other electrons, but they were called *photoelectrons*. Usually, electrons are liberated from substances only by ultraviolet light. This is true for nearly all of the known metals. However, a few elements, namely the alkali metals lithium, sodium, potassium, rubidium, and cesium, are exceptions, for they will eject photoelectrons even when visible light falls on them.

The photoelectric effect is the emission of electrons from a metallic surface by the incidence of a beam of light. The number of electrons emitted per second is directly proportional to the intensity of the light. The energy of the electrons emitted depends only on the frequency of the light and the kind of metal used. It does not depend on the intensity of the light. Early in the study of photoelectricity, certain characteristics of the photoelectric effect were clearly established:

1. The photoelectric current is directly proportional to the intensity of the light falling on the emitting surface.
2. The maximum kinetic energy of the ejected photoelectrons does not depend on intensity of light, but it does depend on frequency; for a monochromatic beam of light, the maximum kinetic energy of the electrons increases with the frequency of the light.
3. For a particular metal, there is a definite cutoff frequency ν_0, below which no photoelectric effect occurs.
4. There is no detectable time lag between the impinging of light on the surface of the metal and emission of the photoelectrons.

For physicists of the nineteenth century, the phenomena of interference and diffraction had firmly established the wave theory of light. Similarly, the discovery of electromagnetic waves by Heinrich Hertz in 1886, and his experimental work with these waves, further confirmed Maxwell's electromagnetic (wave) theory of light. But physicists found that the photoelectric effect could not be explained on the basis of this theory. According to the wave theory, the kinetic energy of the photoelectrons should have increased as the intensity of the light increased. However, the kinetic energy of the photoelectrons was independent of the intensity of the light, depending only on the frequency. According to this theory also, the photoelectric effect should have occurred for any frequency of light, provided that the light had sufficient intensity. However, for each metal there was a characteristic cutoff frequency below which the photoelectric effect did not occur, no matter how intense the illumination. According to the wave theory, the energy of light waves was distributed equally over the wave front. Hence, if an electron obtained its energy by the ordinary process of absorption, there should have been a considerable time lag between the beginning of illumination and the start of the photoelectric current. But there was no such detectable time lag. Thus, it could only be concluded that the electromagnetic theory of light failed to explain the photoelectric effect.

To explain the photoelectric effect, Einstein introduced a fundamental change in the concept of the nature of light. Making use of Planck's quantum idea, Einstein introduced the idea that radiation is not a smooth, continuous flow of energy, as it would be according to the wave theory. He viewed it instead as a series of discontinuous, concentrated packages of energy, called *photons*. Thus a photon was a single quantum of electromagnetic radiation. The energy of a single photon was determined as

$$E = h\nu$$

where E is the energy of the quantum in ergs; ν is the frequency of the radiation; and h is Planck's constant. Einstein further assumed that the energy in each photon was so concentrated that the photon could transfer its whole energy content to a single electron. These ideas of Einstein concerning the nature of light extended the quantum theory to the transfer of radiant energy through space by means of light quanta.

By using the extension of the quantum theory just described, Einstein arrived in 1905 at a satisfactory explanation of the photoelectric effect. He assumed that in the photoelectric process a whole quantum of radiant energy was absorbed by a single electron. He assumed further that a certain amount of energy was required to liberate the electron from the metal, and that any additional energy the electron absorbed was used to give it its kinetic energy. Applying the principle of conservation of energy, Einstein arrived at the expression

$$h\nu = \phi + \tfrac{1}{2}mv^2$$

This is the *Einstein photoelectric equation* and represents energy transfer between photon and electron. The first term, $h\nu$, is the total energy content of a single quantum of light, the incoming photon, where h is Planck's constant and ν is the frequency of the light. The term ϕ is the energy needed to get the electron free from the atoms and away from the metal surface; it is called the *work function* of the metal. The last term, $\tfrac{1}{2}mv^2$, is the kinetic energy of the ejected electron, where m is the mass of the electron and v the maximum velocity of the electron.

Einstein's application of the quantum theory to the photoelectric effect explains in a simple way all the characteristics of the photoelectric effect that could not be explained by the wave theory of light. According to Einstein's quantum theory of light, the high intensity of light is due to a large number of quanta passing a point per second in a ray of light. Thus, the photoelectric current is directly proportional to the intensity of the light, because the number of photoelectrons emitted (current) is proportional to the number of photons reaching the surface. The maximum kinetic energy of the electrons ejected from a surface by a monochromatic beam of light increases with the frequency of the light. This is explained simply by the original assumption of the quantum theory—that the energy in a quantum of radiation is directly proportional to the frequency—and by Einstein's assumption that a whole quantum of energy is absorbed by a single electron. The theory accounts for the existence of a low frequency limit for the photoelectric effect, because the quantity of energy ϕ, the *work function*, is the least amount of energy that an electron can receive and still escape from the surface of the metal. The energy that an electron receives is proportional to the frequency of the light; if the frequency is less than a certain lower limit, the energy the electron receives is less than the amount needed for the electron to escape. Thus the theory predicts what is observed—that the work function ϕ is a constant characteristic of the metal, while Planck's constant h is a universal constant that depends on the nature of light. Finally, there is no measurable time lag between the arrival of the first photons and the emission of the photoelectrons. This confirms the assumption of the *photon theory*, that the energy in each photon is so concentrated that the photon can transfer its whole energy content to a single electron. Thus Einstein's application of the quantum theory to the photoelectric effect not only explains the effect completely but gives additional insight into the nature of light.

Experimental investigations of the photoelectric effect were carried out in 1912 by A. L. Hughes, and by O. W. Richardson and K. T. Compton. Their experiments showed that the energy of the photoelectrons increased proportionately with the frequency of the light, and that the constant of proportionality was approximately equal to Planck's constant h. This was the first experimental confirmation of Einstein's photoelectric equation. In 1916, R. A. Millikan carried out many experiments that established the photoelectric equation completely and led to a very accurate determination of the value of Planck's constant. Millikan carefully planned and carefully executed an extensive series of experiments. He systematically studied the photoelectric effect by varying separately the intensity of the light, the wave length, and the metal illuminated. In the first set of experiments, Millikan varied the intensity of the light, while keeping the wave length of the light and the metal unchanged.

When monochromatic light falls on a metal plate, it will liberate photoelectrons, which can be detected as a current if a potential difference V is applied between the metal plate, which is the cathode, and a collecting wire, which is the anode. When the potential on the anode is positive with respect to the plate, the current will flow; if the value of V is increased on the anode, the photoelectric current reaches a certain limiting value, at which all the photoelectrons ejected from the plate are collected by the anode. Photoelectric current thus produced was found by Millikan to be directly proportional to the intensity of the light over an extremely wide range of values. If V is made negative with respect to the plate, the photoelectric current flows in the same direction as before, and it decreases but does not drop to zero immediately. The current decreases as the negative value of V is increased, until a value of V is reached at which the photoelectric current drops to zero. This value of V is called the *stopping potential*, and it is a measure of the kinetic energy of the fastest-ejected photoelectrons. When V is negative with respect to the plate, the electric field opposes the motion of the electrons; for small values of V, however, some of the electrons still reach the anode, which shows that the electrons are emitted from the plate with a finite velocity. But as V is made more and more negative, only the faster-moving electrons reach the anode, until a point is reached at which no electrons reach the anode. This point is the stopping potential. From measurements of the stopping potential, Millikan found that the maximum kinetic energy of the ejected photoelectrons is independent of the intensity of the light for light of equal wave length.

If monochromatic light of different wave lengths is used, the stopping potential is found to have a definite value for each wave length. If the stopping potential is plotted as a function of the frequency of the light, in the case of an individual metal, a linear relation is found to exist between these variables. Millikan discovered that for an individual metal, such as sodium, a straight line of definite slope and definite intercept is obtained. These results can be simply explained in terms of the photoelectric equation

$$h\nu = \phi + \tfrac{1}{2}mv^2$$

which may also be written in the form

$$\tfrac{1}{2}mv^2 = h\nu - \phi$$

From this form it may be seen that there is a definite value of ϕ for which the kinetic energy term, $\tfrac{1}{2}mv^2$, becomes zero. Since ϕ is an energy term that is the work function of the metal, it may be represented as the energy of a photon by $\phi = h\nu_0$. In this expression, the term ν_0 is the *photoelectric threshold frequency*, which is the frequency of light that, as light falls on a surface, is just able to liberate electrons without giving them any additional kinetic energy. The photoelectric equation can therefore be written as

$$\tfrac{1}{2}mv^2 = h\nu - h\nu_0$$

When an electron is accelerated by a potential difference V, it gains in kinetic energy an amount equal to the work done on the electron by the electric field, which is Ve, where e is the charge on the electron. Therefore, the *kinetic energy* of the electron, which is $\tfrac{1}{2}mv^2$, is given by $\tfrac{1}{2}mv^2 = Ve$. For negative values of potential difference, the electron's motion is retarded, and thus it loses kinetic energy. If a negative potential is large enough to stop the flow of the fastest-moving electrons to the anode, it is a stopping potential. Thus, a measurement of the stopping potential enables us to calculate the kinetic energy of the fastest-moving electrons and the velocity of these electrons. The photoelectric equation can then be written in the form $Ve = h\nu - h\nu_0$. Finally, the equation can be put in the form

$$V = \frac{h}{e}\nu - \frac{h}{e}\nu_0$$

In this equation, V is the stopping potential; ν is the frequency of the light; ν_0 is the photoelectric threshold frequency, or the frequency below which no photoelectric effect occurs; e is the charge on the electron; and h is Planck's constant. If the stopping potential is plotted as a function of the frequency of the light, the plot is a straight line. Thus, the equation for the stopping potential is the equation of a straight line,

$$y = mx + b$$

where y is the value of V; x is the value of ν; the slope m is the value of h/e; and the intercept b is the value of $-(h/e)\nu_0$. The value ν_0 is the value of ν when V is equal to zero. Thus, from the slope of the straight line obtained from the experimental observations, the value of *Planck's constant h* may be calculated. And from the intercept, the value of the *photoelectric threshold frequency* ν_0 may be calculated, as well as the value of the *work function* $h\nu_0$.

In his final set of experiments, Millikan varied the metal exposed to the light. He found that if the stopping potential were plotted as a function of the frequency of the light, a straight line plot could be obtained for each metal; each line was noted to have the same slope as the one obtained for sodium, but there was a different intercept for each metal. Such results meant that h was a constant and the same for all metals, or a *universal constant*, while the work function ϕ, or $h\nu_0$, was a constant characteristic of the metal. The value of the photoelectric threshold frequency ν_0 usually lay in the ultraviolet for most metals, but for the alkali metals and for barium and strontium it lay in the visible region; for potassium it lay in the red; and for cesium, in the infrared. From the results of his systematic series of experiments, Millikan was able to verify Einstein's photoelectric equation completely, in every detail.

This experiment involves an investigation of some characteristics of the photoelectric effect. A monochromatic beam of light of constant intensity is sent into a vacuum photoelectric cell and made to strike the cathode of the cell. Photoelectrons are emitted from the surface of the cathode and collected by the anode, or the collecting wire, of the cell. This flow of electrons constitutes the photoelectric current. We shall study the variation of the photoelectric current as the voltage between the cathode and the anode is varied. When the potential of the anode is positive with respect to the cathode, the photoelectric current flows. Even when the potential is zero, some current flows, because the photoelectrons are emitted with enough kinetic energy to be able to reach the anode. When the potential is made negative with respect to the cathode, the current decreases until a large enough value of negative potential is reached, at which the photoelectric current drops to zero. This is the stopping potential, a measure of the kinetic energy of the fastest-ejected photoelectrons. This experiment involves a measurement of the stopping potential for different wave lengths of light.

The best light source for our purpose is a high-intensity mercury arc lamp. This source will produce very intense mercury lines that are apart far enough to be separated and used as an intense monochromatic beam of light. To accomplish this, two types of light filters are used. One type transmits only light of a desired wave length. The other type of filter, known as a cutoff filter, transmits light of wave lengths down to a certain limit but no light from below this limit. Both types of filters are used in this experiment. The filters on our list that have been given first choice are those that transmit only a desired wave length. If a filter transmits more than one line, the intense line of shortest wave length is the one to be used, as the shortest wave length controls the stopping potential. This is the way the filters are labeled. In measuring the stopping potential for different wave lengths of light, we use the appropriate filter for each wave length.

For each filter used and for light of a definite wave length, a curve is plotted to show the relation between anode voltage and photoelectric current. The general appearance of these curves is shown in Fig. 76, in which are the curves obtained for four different wave lengths, plotted from data obtained under actual laboratory conditions. From curves such as these, the value of the stopping potential corresponding to each wave length can be read off. Another curve is then plotted showing the relation between the frequency of the light and the stopping potential. This curve turns out to be a straight line. Such a curve is shown in Fig. 77, which was plotted from the data obtained from Fig. 76. Such a straight line can easily be shown to correspond to one plotted from the final form of Einstein's photoelectric equation (given above). Therefore, from the slope of this straight line, the value of Planck's constant h can be determined. How this is done can best be explained by the following example, which uses the straight line of Fig. 77.

The slope m of the straight line is given by

$$m = \frac{V_1 - V_0}{\nu_1 - \nu_0}; \qquad m = \frac{2.00 - 0.00}{(8.45 - 3.60) \times 10^{14}}; \qquad m = 0.4124 \times 10^{-14}$$

The value of Planck's constant h is given by

$$h = m \times 1.602 \times 10^{-12}; \qquad h = 0.4124 \times 10^{-14} \times 1.602 \times 10^{-12};$$

$$h = 6.60 \times 10^{-27} \text{ erg sec}$$

This is the calculated value of Planck's constant, which in this case comes to within less than 1% of the accepted value.

The circuit and components used in this experiment are shown in the schematic diagram of Fig. 78. The voltage supply consists of two good dry cells of 1.5 volts each, connected in series. Resistance R_1 is the tubular rheostat of about 1400 ohms resistance. Resistance R_2 is the resistance box, three-dial type, used as a shunt for the galvanometer. V is the D.C. voltmeter, 0–3 volts. P is the vacuum phototube. G is the galvanometer.

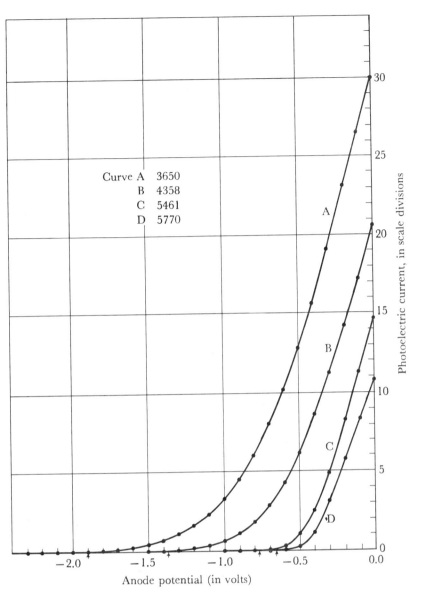

Curve A 3650
B 4358
C 5461
D 5770

Photoelectric current, in scale divisions

Anode potential (in volts)

Fig. 76. Variation of Photo-electric Current with Anode Potential for Light of Different Wave Lengths

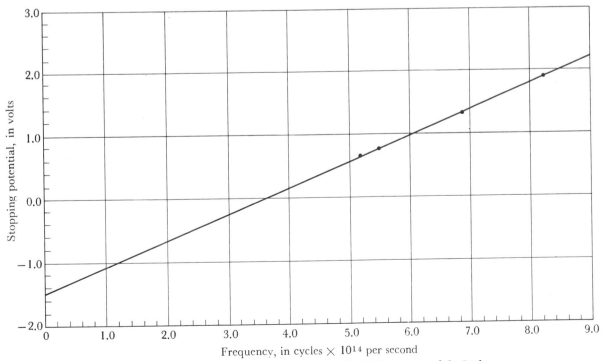

Stopping potential, in volts

Frequency, in cycles × 10¹⁴ per second

Fig. 77. Variation of Stopping Potential with Frequency of the Light

305

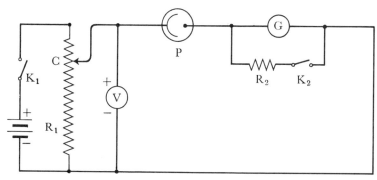

Fig. 78.   Circuit Diagram for Planck's Constant Experiment

The optical arrangement used in this experiment is shown in Fig. 79.   The light source is the high-intensity mercury arc lamp, which is enclosed in a metal housing provided with an adjustable projection lens.   The lamp is mounted on an adjustable support stand.   The lens should be adjusted to produce a beam of light.

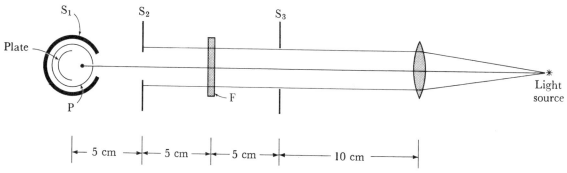

Fig. 79.   Optical Arrangement for Measurements on Photoelectric Effect

The remainder of the apparatus is mounted on the auxiliary optical bench, about 50 cm long, which provides an easy and convenient means of lining up the optical parts.   P is the vacuum phototube in a tube socket.   The socket is mounted on a wooden block $6 \times 6 \times 1.5$ cm, supported on a metal rod 14 cm long and 10 mm in diameter.   This mounted tube socket is held in place by a carriage on the optical bench. S_1 is a light shield that covers the phototube.   It may be easily made by using a cardboard tube about 12 cm long and 4 cm in diameter, big enough to slide over the phototube and rest on the tube socket.   At a point directly in front of the plate of the phototube, when the cardboard tube is in place, an aperture 1.5 cm wide and 2.5 cm high is cut in the cardboard tube.   This serves as the wide slit through which the light enters the phototube. S_2 is the mounted iris diaphragm, held in place by a carriage on the optical bench.   The iris diaphragm is used to regulate the amount of light entering the phototube and also to prevent any light that has not passed through the filter from entering the phototube.   F is the light filter, mounted, and held by a lens holder. S_3 is a screen with an aperture 2.0 cm wide and 3.0 cm high, used to regulate the amount of light passing through the light filter.   The screen may be made from a square piece of cardboard, 7.5×7.5 cm, with the aperture cut in the center.   The screen is then mounted on a clear glass plate (7.5×7.5 cm) for rigid support, and held by a lens holder.   A metal screen, with adjustable slit, suitable for this purpose, is also available commercially (Welch, Cat. No. 3640).

The pieces of apparatus on the optical bench should all be lined up accurately so that the center of the light beam entering the phototube passes through the center of all the apertures.   Similarly, the height of the mercury arc lamp should be properly adjusted so that the beam of light is accurately centered with the rest of the optical system.

When the optical arrangement described above is used, the experiment does not have to be performed in a dark room.   It can be performed in a dimly lighted room with very good results, since not enough stray light can enter the phototube to spoil the accuracy of the measurements.

The type of photoelectric cell best suited for the purpose of the experiment is the vacuum phototube listed under Apparatus as No. P38307 Vacuum Phototube. It has an octal radio tube base and is a highly sensitive emissive phototube. It has maximum sensitivity for light of 4000 Angstroms, and the sensitivity decreases to zero for light above 7000 Angstroms. Under the conditions described in our experiment, the photoelectric current produced is appreciable and well suited to the purpose, since good experimental results can be readily obtained. The vacuum phototube is an RCA Type 929 Phototube.

Connecting the photoelectric cell in the circuit calls for care to be taken that the connections are made to the proper terminals in the octal tube socket. In the preliminary adjustments, the opening in the iris diaphragm should be small so that not too much light enters the phototube. The size of the diaphragm opening should be carefully regulated according to the need.

The type of galvanometer found to be best suited for this experiment is listed under Apparatus as No. 82162 Mirror Type Galvanometer. This same type of galvanometer is supplied also by the Welch Scientific Company, listed by them as Reflecting Galvanometer, Cat. No. 2702. This galvanometer has a sensitivity of 0.06 microampere per mm scale division; the coil resistance is 100 ohms. The inclined 80-division scale has one set of numerals with zero at the left, and one set with zero at the center. The zero adjustment knob has sufficient range to set the zero on either scale. In our experiment, the zero is set at the center of the scale. The galvanometer contains a taut-suspension D'Arsonval movement with attached mirror and has an enclosed 6-volt lamp with built-in transformer. A sharp index line is projected onto the scale in a small, bright field.

The galvanometer should be properly connected in the circuit as shown in Fig. 78. Resistance R_2 is the resistance box, a three-dial type, used as shunt for the galvanometer. In any preliminary adjustments, the key K_2 should always be kept closed, so that the galvanometer is being used at reduced sensitivity. In a check of the sensitivity of the galvanometer when the shunt is being used, the value of R_2 should be set at 12 ohms. With key K_2 closed, key K_1 should now be closed and the value of the anode voltage set at zero. The aperture of the iris diaphragm should be very small. Now the cord connected to the galvanometer should be plugged into the 115-volt A.C. line to light up the galvanometer lamp, which projects an index line onto the scale. With no light entering the photoelectric cell, the adjustment should be carefully made so that the index line is on zero at the center of the scale when the galvanometer current is zero. Now the high-intensity mercury arc lamp cord should be plugged into the 115-volt A.C. line. The lamp reaches high intensity in about 3 minutes. The beam of bluish white light will be limited by the screen S_3 and also by S_2, which is the iris diaphragm. The aperture of the iris diaphragm should still be very small. Under these conditions, and with key K_2 closed, the galvanometer reading should be less than 3 mm scale divisions. If it is less than 3 divisions, the setting of the iris diaphragm should be slowly and carefully adjusted until the galvanometer reading is exactly 3 scale divisions. Now key K_2 should be opened momentarily to test whether galvanometer sensitivity during these adjustments has been reduced by a factor of 10. If so, the galvanometer reading at full sensitivity should be 30 scale divisions. The exact value of the reading is not important so long as it is near 30 divisions. The shunt is merely to protect the galvanometer in making preliminary adjustments; it is not used during actual measurements. If the reading is too different from 30 scale divisions, a slightly different value of R_2 may be chosen. But this must be done very carefully. Once chosen, the value of R_2 must not be changed during the course of the experiment. Now key K_2 should be closed, and should be kept closed, unless actual readings are being taken.

The light filters listed under Apparatus are the ones that have been found to be best suited for the purpose of the experiment. However, other filters may be used with satisfactory results. For example, for the 5770 mercury line, the Wratten gelatin filter No. 21 can be used; this filter is listed by Cenco as No. 87310-11 Light Filter. Similarly, for the 4358 mercury line, the light filter listed by Cenco as No. 29874 can be used; this filter is called Optical Filter, Series B, Coleman B-3. Both of these filters give very good results.

Another set of filters that can be used in this experiment is supplied by the Welch Scientific Company in their Planck's Constant Apparatus, Cat. No. 2120. This is a set of three sharp cutoff filters mounted on a card 5.4 × 8.9 cm; the aperture in front of each filter is 2.5 × 1.3 cm. The filters are labeled with the wave length of the highest frequency spectral line of mercury they will transmit, namely the wave lengths 5770 A, 5461 A, and 4358 A. Each filter transmits waves of lengths longer than the specified cutoff wave length, but this condition is acceptable for the purpose of this experiment. The card on which the filters are mounted may be held by a screen holder, of the type supplied by Central Scientific Company, Cat. No. 86020. This type of holder is suitable for holding screens or filters mounted on a card, because the holder can be held in place by a carriage on the optical bench. Each screen or filter may be accurately aligned horizontally by moving the card on the holder and clamping it, and aligned vertically by moving the holder itself and clamping it on the carriage.

In work with the filters listed under Apparatus, the gelatin filters must first be properly mounted. The Wratten gelatin filters can be fitted on the cardboard mounts made for 35-mm slide projectors. The cardboard mounts have apertures 35 × 23 mm and are supplied by the Eastman Kodak Company. The gelatin filters are in 3-inch-square pieces. A filter should be handled by the edges or at the extreme corners only. The gelatin filter, when being cut, should be between two pieces of clean, fairly stiff paper, with sharp scissors used. The cutting line can be marked on the paper. The filter is then carefully placed in the cardboard mount, which is then folded over, with edge sealed, according to the instructions given. The filter and mount can be held in place on the optical bench by the screen holder No. 86020.

The ultraviolet filters UV-1 and UV-2 are supplied already mounted on a glass plate 2.7 × 4.9 cm. This type of filter, mounted in this manner, can be conveniently held in place on the optical bench by the lens holder No. 72288. The optical bench already provides the horizontal alignment, and the adjustment for the vertical alignment is made by moving the lens holder itself and clamping it on the carriage.

APPARATUS

1. Photoelectric cell, a vacuum phototube.
2. Mercury arc lamp, high-intensity.
3. Light filters for the mercury lines: Yellow, 5770; Green, 5461; Blue, 4358; Ultraviolet, 3650.
4. Galvanometer, reflecting, with enclosed lamp and scale.
5. Auxiliary optical bench, about 50 cm long.
6. Iris diaphragm, mounted.
7. Two lens holders. Two screen holders.
8. Four hinged carriages, for optical bench.
9. Socket, 8-pin, for mounting phototube.
10. Four clear, square glass plates, 7.5 × 7.5 cm.
11. Tubular rheostat (about 1400 ohms).
12. Resistance box, three-dial type (1 to 999 ohms).
13. D.C. voltmeter (0–3 volts).
14. Two good dry cells of 1.5 volts each.
15. Two single-pole, single-throw switches.

Most of the apparatus listed for this experiment is available in the average physics laboratory. But in order that the type best suited for the experiment may be obtained, some items are listed more in detail. For example, apparatus of this type supplied by Central Scientific Company, 1700 Irving Park Road, Chicago, Illinois, is listed in their catalog as follows:

No. P38307   Vacuum Phototube.
No. 80912-2 Socket, 8-pin.
No. 87268   High Pressure Mercury Arc, Light Source.
No. 82162   Mirror Type Galvanometer, No. 3.   Sensitivity 0.06 μA/mm div.
No. 85810   Auxiliary Optical Bench.
No. 86105   Iris Diaphragm, Mounted.
No. 72288   Lens Holder.
No. 85802   Hinged Carriage.
No. 82519-2 D.C. Voltmeter 1.5/3.0/30, Weston 281.
No. 29842-1 Filter, Ultraviolet, Primary, Coleman UV-1.
No. 29842-2 Filter, Ultraviolet, Primary, Coleman UV-2.

The two items listed below are supplied by Special Sensitized Products Sales, Eastman Kodak Company, Rochester, New York.

No. 22   Wratten Gelatin Filter, 3 inches square.
No. 74   Wratten Gelatin Filter, 3 inches square.

Filter No. 22 transmits the 5770 mercury line; filter No. 74 transmits the 5461 mercury line; the Coleman filters UV-1 and UV-2 transmit the 3650 and 4358 mercury line, respectively.

PROCEDURE

1. Record the type of photoelectric cell supplied to you, the type of light filter to be used for each of the four mercury lines, and the current sensitivity of the galvanometer in microamperes per millimeter scale division. If the galvanometer sensitivity is to be checked, review this procedure in the theory section of this experiment.

2. Begin the experiment by putting filter 5770 in place on the optical bench. The apparatus to be used in measuring should already have been arranged on the optical bench, as shown in Fig. 79, and lined up so that the center of the light beam entering the phototube passes through the center of all the apertures. The lens of the mercury arc lamp should now be adjusted to produce a beam of light. For the preliminary measurements, close the key on the galvanometer and keep it closed. This puts the shunt resistance R_2 (see Fig. 78) across the galvanometer and reduces the galvanometer sensitivity by a factor of 10, thus protecting the galvanometer. Plug the cord connected to the galvanometer into the 115-volt A.C. line. Light from the galvanometer lamp causes a sharp index line to be projected onto the scale. The adjustment should already have been made for the index line to be on zero, at the center of the scale, when the galvanometer current is zero.

3. Close switch in the phototube circuit (K_1 in Fig. 78). The circuit connections are such that a negative voltage is applied to the anode of the phototube. The cathode is connected to the positive terminal. Thus the voltmeter reads the positive voltage on the cathode, which is also the value of the negative voltage on the anode. Adjust the rheostat until the voltage on the anode of the phototube is zero, as read on the voltmeter.

4. Plug the cord connected to the mercury arc lamp into the 115-volt A.C. line. Allow about 3 minutes for the lamp to reach high intensity. The beam of bluish white light will be limited by the screen, so that a rectangular beam of light reaches light filter 5770. This is a cutoff light filter that does not allow any wave lengths below 5770 Angstroms to pass through it. The light passing through the filter and reaching the second screen and finally the phototube will be yellow in color. Check the iris diaphragm of the second screen, making sure that the aperture is wide open. The entire system should be well centered so that the maximum amount of light reaches the cathode of the phototube. The room should be dimly lighted, so that there will not be enough stray light entering the phototube to spoil the accuracy of the results.

With the anode voltage set at zero, and the galvanometer key (hereafter designated as key K_2) closed, observe the reading of the galvanometer. The galvanometer is now reading at one-tenth sensitivity. The reading should now be no higher than it would be at the maximum scale reading at full sensitivity. Thus, since the maximum scale reading is 40 divisions, the reading should now be no higher than 4 divisions. If it is higher, slowly close the aperture of the iris diaphragm until the reading is about 3 scale divisions. Now open key K_2 to allow the galvanometer to read at full sensitivity. This key should be kept open while the actual measurements are being taken. The galvanometer should now read ten times as high as before, or about 30 scale divisions. For the measurements with filter 5770, adjust the setting of the iris diaphragm very slowly and carefully until the galvanometer reading is about 20 scale divisions when the anode voltage is zero. Record this reading of the galvanometer to the nearest tenth of a millimeter scale division, estimating a tenth of a division carefully.

5. Do not disturb the setting of the iris diaphragm or move any of the apparatus while making the remainder of the measurements with filter 5770. Set the anode voltage exactly at 0.10 volt by adjusting the rheostat. The galvanometer reading should now be lower than before if the connections to the phototube have been properly made. Record this reading of the galvanometer to the nearest tenth of a scale division.

6. Set the anode voltage exactly at 0.20 volt and record the new reading of the galvanometer. Now increase the anode voltage by 0.10 volt each time, until a reading of 1.50 volts is reached. Record the reading of the galvanometer to the nearest tenth of a scale division for each setting of the anode voltage. It will be found that as the anode voltage is increased, the photoelectric current decreases, until it becomes zero for some definite value of the anode voltage. Make sure to take the readings near the zero value of the current carefully and accurately to the nearest tenth of a scale division.

7. Now close key K_2 to protect the instrument from any surge of current. Remove filter 5770 from the optical bench and replace it by filter 5461. This is a filter that lets through only the green mercury line 5461, or else it does not allow any wave lengths below 5461 Angstroms to pass through it. Make sure that the filter is properly lined up so that the center of the beam of light passes through the center of the filter. With the anode voltage still at 1.50 volts, and key K_2 closed, the reading of the galvanometer should be close to zero. Slowly reduce the anode voltage to zero while observing the reading of the galvanometer. With the anode voltage set at zero, the reading of the galvanometer should be no higher than 4 divisions. If it is higher, slowly close the aperture of the iris diaphragm until the reading is about 3 scale divisions. Now open key K_2 to allow the galvanometer to read at full sensitivity. Keep this key open while the actual measurements are being taken. The galvanometer should now read about 30 scale divisions. For the measurements with filter 5461, adjust the setting of the iris diaphragm very slowly and carefully until the galvanometer reading is about 20 scale divisions when the anode voltage is zero. Record this reading of the galvanometer to the nearest tenth of a scale division.

8. Do not disturb the setting of the iris diaphragm or move any of the apparatus while making the remainder of the measurements with filter 5461. Set the anode voltage exactly at 0.10 volt and record the new reading of the galvanometer to the nearest tenth of a scale division. Increasing the anode voltage by 0.10 volt each time until a maximum reading of 1.50 volts has been reached. Record the reading of the galvanometer to the nearest tenth of a scale division for each setting of the anode voltage. Make sure to take the readings near the zero value of the current very carefully and accurately to the nearest tenth of a scale division.

9. Close key K_2 to protect the galvanometer. Remove filter 5461 from the optical bench and replace it by filter 4358. This is a filter that lets through only the blue mercury line 4358, or else it does not allow any wave lengths below 4358 Angstroms to pass through it. Again make sure that the filter is properly lined up. With the anode voltage still at 1.50 volts and key K_2 closed, the reading of the galvanometer should be close to zero. Slowly reduce the anode voltage to zero while observing the reading of the galvanometer. With the anode voltage set at zero, the reading of the galvanometer should be no higher than 4 divisions. If it is higher, slowly close the aperture of the iris diaphragm until the reading is about 3 scale divisions. Now open key K_2 so the galvanometer may read at full sensitivity. This key should be kept open while the actual measurements are being taken. The galvanometer will now read about 30 scale divisions. For the measurements with filter 4358, adjust the setting of the iris diaphragm very slowly and carefully until the galvanometer reading is just about 30 scale divisions when the anode voltage is zero. Record this reading of the galvanometer to the nearest tenth of a scale division.

10. Do not disturb the setting of the iris diaphragm or move any of the apparatus while making the remainder of the measurements with filter 4358. Set the anode voltage exactly at 0.10 volt and record the new reading of the galvanometer to the nearest tenth of a scale division. Keep increasing the anode voltage by 0.10 volt each time until a maximum voltage of 2.00 volts has been reached. Record the reading of the galvanometer to the nearest tenth of a scale division for each setting of the anode voltage. Be sure to take the readings near the zero value of the current very carefully and accurately to the nearest tenth of a scale division.

11. Close key K_2 to protect the galvanometer. Remove filter 4358 from the optical bench and replace it by filter 3650. This is the ultraviolet filter UV-1 that transmits the 3650 mercury line. Make sure that the filter is properly lined up so that the center of the beam of light passes through the center of the filter. With the anode voltage still at 2.00 volts and with key K_2 closed, the reading of the galvanometer should be close to zero. Slowly reduce the anode voltage to zero while observing the reading of the galvanometer. With the anode voltage set at zero, the reading of the galvanometer should be no higher than 4 divisions. If it is higher, it can be made lower by slowly closing down the aperture of the iris diaphragm until the reading is about 3 scale divisions. Now open key K_2 to make the galvanometer read at full sensitivity. This key should be kept open while the actual measurements are being taken. The galvanometer will now read about 30 scale divisions. For the measurements with filter 3650, adjust the setting of the iris diaphragm very slowly and carefully until the galvanometer reading is just about 30 scale divisions when the anode voltage is zero. Record this reading of the galvanometer to the nearest tenth of a scale division.

12. Do not disturb the setting of the iris diaphragm or move any of the apparatus while making the remainder of the measurements with filter 3650. Set the anode voltage exactly at 0.10 volt and record the new reading of the galvanometer to the nearest tenth of a scale division. Keep on increasing the anode voltage by 0.10 volt each time until a maximum voltage of 2.50 volts has been reached. Record the reading of the galvanometer to the nearest tenth of a scale division for each setting of the anode voltage. Make sure to take the readings near the zero value of the current very carefully and accurately to the nearest tenth of a scale division. Now close key K₂ and keep it closed. Pull out the plug to disconnect the mercury arc lamp. Pull out the plug to disconnect the galvanometer lamp. Open the key in the circuit (K₁ in Fig. 78) to disconnect the battery. Leave the switch open.

13. Plot a curve to show the relation between the anode voltage and the photoelectric current for light of a definite wave length. Using the data for the ultraviolet mercury line 3650, plot the anode voltage along the x axis and the corresponding values of the photoelectric current along the y axis. Use a volt for the unit of voltage, and a galvanometer scale division for the unit of current. Choose the scale on the graph paper in such a way that the curve will cover practically the whole page. (See Fig. 76.) Keep in mind that the anode voltages are negative. Each plotted point should be a small dot surrounded by a small circle, so that the point will be clearly visible on the graph. A smooth curve should be drawn through the plotted points in such a way as to fit the points as closely as possible. Plot a second curve on the same piece of graph paper, with the same coordinates scale as before, using the data for the green mercury line 5461. Again plot the anode voltage along the x axis and the corresponding values of the photoelectric current along the y axis. Draw a smooth curve through the plotted points. The two curves will be distinct, so that it will be easy to notice the effect of a change of wave length on the stopping potential.

14. Plot a third curve on a separate piece of graph paper with the same coordinates and the same scale as before. For this plot, the data for the blue mercury line 4358 are to be used. As before, plot the anode voltage along the x axis and the corresponding values of the photoelectric current along the y axis. Draw a smooth curve through the plotted points. Plot a fourth curve, using the same piece of graph paper, the same coordinates, and the same scale as for the third curve. Using the data for the yellow mercury line 5770, plot the anode voltage along the x axis and the corresponding values of the photoelectric current along the y axis. Draw a smooth curve through the plotted points. Again, the two curves will be distinct, and the effect of a change of wave length on the stopping potential will be easily seen.

15. From each of the four curves obtained in procedures (13) and (14), read off and record the value of the stopping potential corresponding to each wave length. The cutoff voltage, or the stopping potential, is the voltage at which the photoelectric current becomes zero, for light of a given wave length. It is the voltage needed to prevent the fastest-moving electrons produced by light of a given frequency from reaching the anode. This voltage can be read from any curve that shows the relation between the anode voltage and the photoelectric current. NOTE: When determining the stopping potential, the student may find that the photoelectric current does not approach zero as a limit, but some other value close to zero. This is usually owing to some spurious photoelectric current produced by emission from the anode. In this case, the stopping potential is taken as the point at which the curve is tangent to the direction of the x axis for each individual curve. This point should be read as carefully as possible to the nearest hundredth of a volt.

16. Plot another curve to show the relation between the frequency of the light and the stopping potential. For each wave length used, plot the value of the frequency of the light corresponding to that wave length along the x axis, and the corresponding value of the stopping potential along the y axis. Choose the scale on the coordinates in such a way that the value of the frequency can be plotted from 0 to 9.0×10^{14} cycles per second, and the stopping potential from -2.0 to $+3.0$ volts. Notice that in this curve the stopping potential is plotted as a positive voltage, which is the voltage actually read by the voltmeter. This voltage is a measure of the kinetic energy of the fastest-moving photoelectrons ejected by light of a given frequency. Draw a smooth curve through the four plotted points, extending it to both the x and y intercepts. (See the curve shown in Fig. 77.)

DATA

Type of photoelectric cell used ....

Type of light filters used for the mercury lines: ....

    Yellow, 5770 ....

    Green, 5461 ....

    Blue, 4358 ....

    Ultraviolet, 3650 ....

Current sensitivity of the galvanometer ....

Calculated value of Planck's constant ....

Accepted value of Planck's constant ....

Per cent error ....

MERCURY LINES		FREQUENCY	STOPPING POTENTIAL
WAVE LENGTH ANGSTROM UNITS	COLOR	CYCLES PER SECOND	VOLTS
5770	YELLOW	5.20×10^{14}	
5461	GREEN	5.50×10^{14}	
4358	BLUE	6.88×10^{14}	
3650	ULTRAVIOLET	8.22×10^{14}	

ANODE VOLTAGE	PHOTOELECTRIC CURRENT GALVANOMETER READINGS			
	FILTER 5770	FILTER 5461	FILTER 4358	FILTER 3650
0.00				
−0.10				
−0.20				
−0.30				
−0.40				
−0.50				
−0.60				
−0.70				
−0.80				
−0.90				
−1.00				
−1.10				
−1.20				
−1.30				
−1.40				
−1.50				
−1.60				
−1.70				
−1.80				
−1.90				
−2.00				
−2.10				
−2.20				
−2.30				
−2.40				
−2.50				

CALCULATIONS

1. From the curve obtained in procedure (16), read and record the value at the point of intercept of the straight line with the frequency axis. This value is the photoelectric threshold frequency, or the frequency when the stopping potential is zero. Calculate the wave length of light that corresponds to the value of the threshold frequency. In the calculations, use the relation $c = \lambda \nu$, where c is the velocity of light in centimeters per second; ν is the frequency; and λ is the wave length in centimeters. Represent the wave length in Angstroms.

2. Calculate the value of Planck's constant h. This is determined from the slope of the straight line obtained in procedure (16), which shows the relation between the frequency of the light and the stopping potential. The photoelectric equation may be written

$$\tfrac{1}{2}mv^2 = h\nu - h\nu_0 \qquad \text{or} \qquad Ve = h\nu - h\nu_0$$

where the term Ve represents the kinetic energy of the fastest-moving photoelectrons; V is the stopping potential in volts, and e is the charge on the electron. If the last equation is put in the form

$$V = \frac{h}{e}\nu - \frac{h}{e}\nu_0$$

and the stopping potential V is plotted as a function of the frequency of the light ν, then the final form of the equation is the equation of a straight line, with a slope m given by $m = h/e$. With determination of the value of the slope m of this straight line, the value of Planck's constant h may be calculated.

The slope of the straight line may be determined if two points on the line are known. The slope m is given by

$$m = \frac{V_1 - V_0}{\nu_1 - \nu_0}$$

One point that may be chosen is the point on the line where the stopping potential is zero. This makes $V_0 = 0$. Then ν_0 will be the value of the photoelectric threshold frequency. The other point on the line may be chosen at some other suitable value, such as at $V_1 = 2.00$. The value of ν_1 will then be the value of the frequency, taken from the curve, that corresponds to this value of the voltage. From these four values, the slope m may be calculated.

The numerical value of the slope of a line depends on the units used. The value of m obtained by the method just described is the slope when V is expressed in volts and e is set equal to one, so that the kinetic energy of the electron is expressed in electron volts. But in the original photoelectric equation, the term Ve represents the kinetic energy of the ejected photoelectron expressed in ergs. Then the constant h is the value of the slope of the straight line obtained when the kinetic energy of the electron expressed in ergs is plotted as a function of the frequency of the light. The term Ve can be expressed in ergs by expressing the voltage V in esu of voltage and the charge e on the electron in esu of charge. But the conversion can be made more simply by changing the numerical value of the kinetic energy expressed in electron volts to the same energy expressed in ergs, using the relation 1 electron volt $= 1.602 \times 10^{-12}$ erg. When this is done, the slope of the straight line obtained by plotting the kinetic energy in ergs as a function of the frequency will be the value of h. Then, the relation between the value of m just obtained and the value of h is simply

$$h = m \times 1.602 \times 10^{-12}$$

Calculate the slope of the straight line obtained in procedure (16), using the method just explained. From your value of the slope m, determine the value of Planck's constant h by using the above relation. Use at least three significant figures in your calculations.

3. The accepted value of Planck's constant is $h = 6.625 \times 10^{-27}$ erg sec. Compare your calculated value of Planck's constant with the accepted value by finding the per cent error.

QUESTIONS

1. What do you think is the biggest source of error in determining the stopping potential for photoelectrons produced by light of a given wave length? Explain.

2. Using the value of the photoelectric threshold frequency obtained in this experiment, calculate the work function for the metal of the photoelectric cell used. In the calculations, use the accepted value of Planck's constant, and express the result both in ergs and in electron volts. Compare the value of the work function, expressed in electron volts, with the value of the y intercept of the straight line obtained in procedure (16).

3. The work function for a metal used in the cathode of a photoelectric cell is 2.40×10^{-12} erg. Calculate the value of the longest wave length for light that has just sufficient energy to cause the emission of photoelectrons from the surface of this metal. What is the color of this light?

4. Calculate the amount of energy contained in a photon, or a quantum of visible light, of wave length 5900 Angstroms. Express the energy in ergs. Suppose that a lamp, a source of yellow light, is sending out radiation of a single wave length, 5900 A, at the rate of one watt, or one joule per second. How many quanta of radiation are emitted each second?

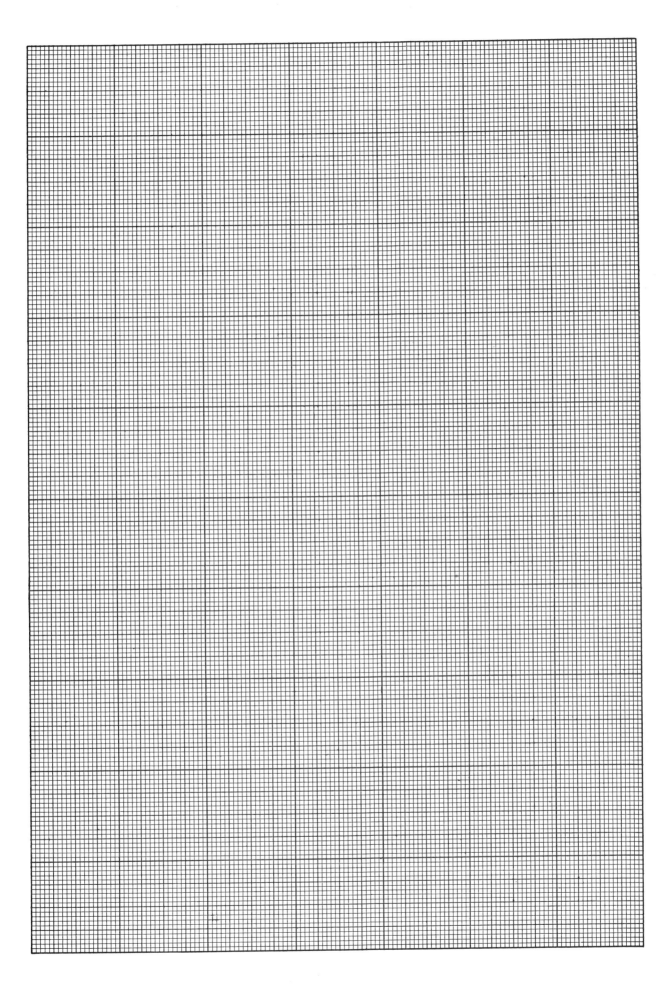

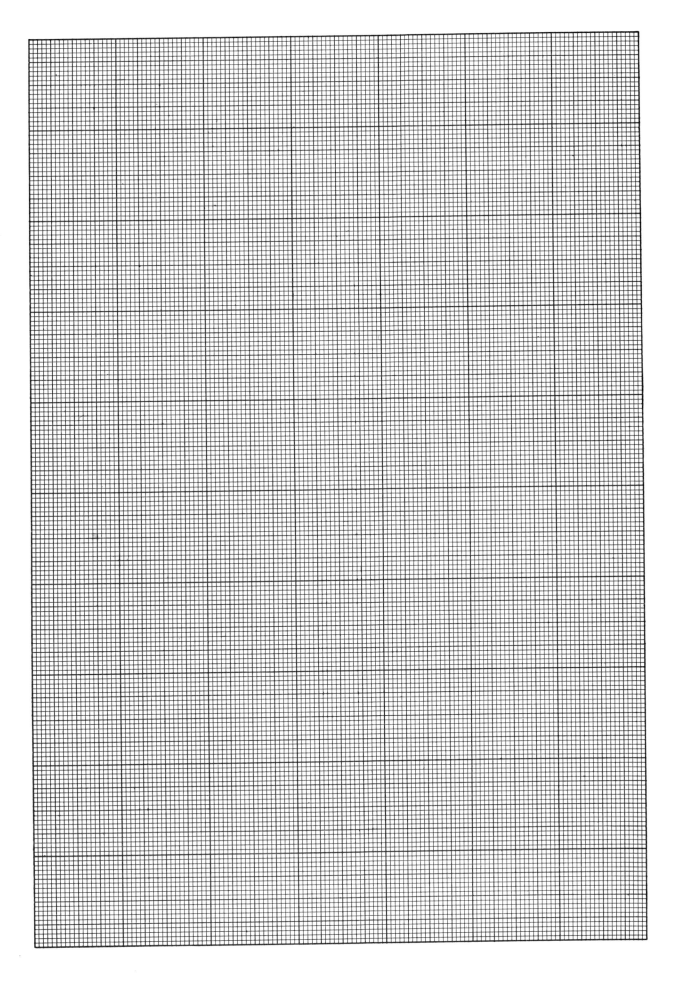

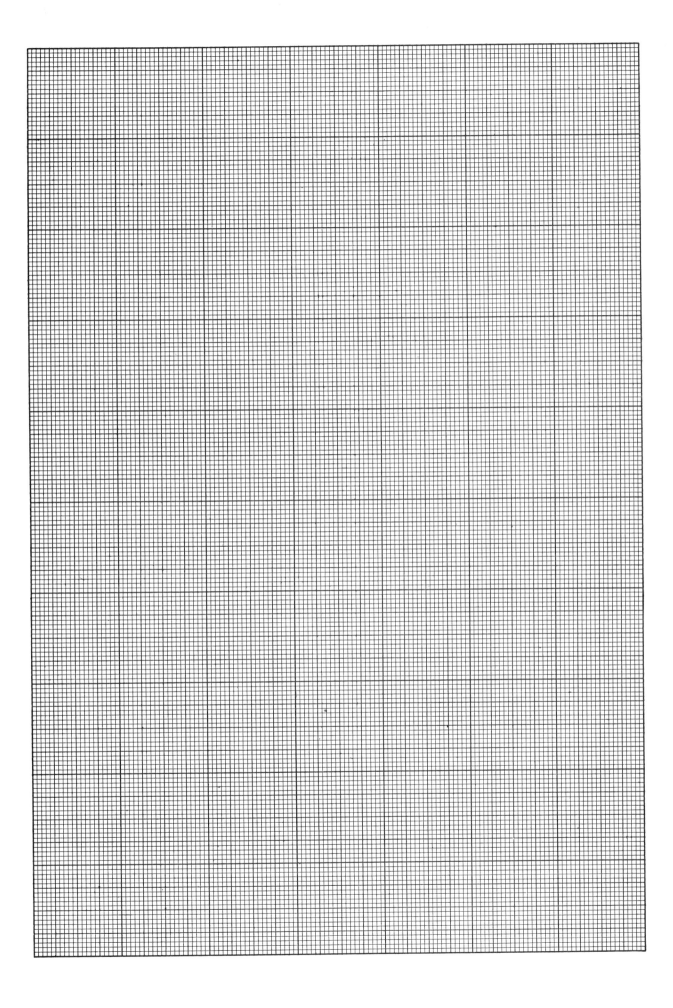

59

THE CHARGE OF THE ELECTRON. MILLIKAN'S OIL DROP EXPERIMENT

The charge of the electron is one of the most important and fundamental physical constants. R. A. Millikan's determination of the value of the charge of the electron in his oil drop experiment proved to be the simplest and most direct method of finding the value of this constant. The experiment showed that electric charges are not infinitely divisible, it provided the evidence for the existence of an elementary electric charge, and it gave us the means of determining the value of this charge very accurately. It is the object of this experiment to determine the charge of the electron using Millikan's oil drop experiment.

THEORY

The charge of the electron is a constant that is fundamental in modern physics. Some early attempts to measure the charge of the electron were made during the study of the charge on gaseous ions such as are produced in a gas by X rays. To measure these charges, Townsend in 1897 used the clouds that form about the ions in saturated air. By observing the rate of fall of a cloud, which is made up of small droplets of water, and applying Stokes's law for the free fall of spheres through a viscous medium, he could determine the size of the droplets. From a measurement of the total amount of water in the cloud, he could calculate the number of droplets it contained. By assuming that each droplet contained one ion, and measuring the total charge in the cloud, he could then calculate the charge on a single ion. For this charge he obtained a value of 3.4×10^{-10} electrostatic unit. In 1903, H. A. Wilson used the same method, with the exception of the addition of an electric field. His method was thus somewhat similar to Millikan's oil drop method, except that Wilson used water drops and made his measurements on the entire cloud instead of on a single drop. For the charge on a single ion, Wilson obtained the value of 3.1×10^{-10} electrostatic unit. The values of both Townsend and Wilson are of the right order of magnitude for the charge of the electron, but because of the errors involved in the measurements, neither is very accurate. One of the errors introduced was the assumption that each droplet contained one electron. Another error resulted from the loss of water droplets in evaporation during the course of the experiment.

The most accurate method yet devised for measuring the charge of the electron was developed by Millikan during the years 1909 to 1913. He used oil droplets to make the first accurate measurement of the value of this constant and to show that the charge of the electron has a single, discrete value. Hundreds of times he determined the electrical charge on individual drops of oil located singly between two horizontal parallel plates of an electrical condenser. By measuring the velocity of fall of the drop under gravity and the velocity of rise when the plates were at a high electrical potential difference, he obtained data from which the charge on a drop could be calculated. He found that the charge was always an integral multiple of a certain small amount of charge, which he presumed to be the charge of a single electron.

In our experiment, fine watch oil is used; there will then be no loss of weight of the droplet by evaporation. The oil droplets are charged as they are sprayed from an atomizer, and then allowed to fall through a small hole in the center of the top plate of the condenser. Air currents are avoided by enclosing the chamber with two glass plates, which also permit the viewing of the droplets. In the measuring process, a single oil drop is observed with a measuring microscope, and the velocity of fall determined by means of a scale contained in the eyepiece of the microscope. This method is extremely sensitive and very accurate, since the effect of a single electron on the motion of the oil drop can be detected and measured.

During the experiment, the oil drop is subject to three different types of forces: gravitational force, viscous resistance of the air, and electrical force. For very accurate measurements even the buoyant force of the air has to be taken into account, but we can neglect the effect of this force. By analyzing the effect of the other forces on the motion of the oil drop, we can derive an expression that allows us to calculate the charge on the oil drop and eventually to determine the charge on the electron.

317

When there is no electric field present, the oil drop will fall slowly, acted upon by the downward pull of the force of gravity and the retarding frictional force that contact with air molecules provides. Whenever a body is moving through the air or any other viscous material, the motion of the body is opposed by a frictional force owing to the viscous resistance of the medium. This resisting force is known experimentally to be proportional to the velocity of the moving body. Thus, when the oil drop falls through the air, the frictional force of the air quickly increases as the velocity of the drop increases, and the frictional force soon becomes equal to the force of gravity on the oil drop. The net force acting on the oil drop is then zero, and the oil drop no longer accelerates but moves with a constant velocity. This constant, or terminal, velocity is quickly reached by a very small droplet, and its value depends on the radius of the droplet.

The resistance of a viscous fluid, such as air, to the steady motion of a moving sphere can be obtained from Stokes's law, from which the retarding frictional force acting on the sphere is given by

$$f = 6\pi r \eta v$$

where r is the radius of the sphere; η is the coefficient of viscosity of the fluid; and v is the velocity of the sphere.

For an oil drop that has reached a constant, or terminal, velocity, the upward retarding force is equal to the downward gravitational force,

$$f_1 = mg = 6\pi r \eta v_1$$

where f_1 is the frictional force; m is the mass of the oil drop; g is the value of the acceleration of gravity; mg represents the gravitational force; r is the radius of the oil drop; η is the coefficient of viscosity of the air; and v_1 is the terminal velocity of the oil drop for free fall under gravity.

If an electric field exists between the plates of a condenser on both sides of an oil droplet, the field can be applied in such a direction and be of such magnitude as to make the oil drop move upward with a new terminal velocity. The frictional force again opposes the motion, but in this case the frictional force is directed downward. The electric force upward now balances the frictional force and the gravitational force, which are both downward. Taking the direction of these forces into account, we see that the retarding frictional force is given by

$$f_2 = Eq - mg = 6\pi r \eta v_2$$

where v_2 is the upward terminal velocity of the oil drop under the influence of the electric field E. In all three expressions for the retarding frictional force, this force is equal to some constant times the velocity of the oil drop, and the constant in all cases is the one given by Stokes's law. In the last expression, f_2 is the frictional force; E is the value of the electric field; q is the charge on the oil drop; and Eq represents the electric force on the oil drop, since the force on a charge q placed in an electric field E equals Eq. Putting the value of mg from the expression for f_1 into the expression for f_2, we obtain

$$Eq - 6\pi r \eta v_1 = 6\pi r \eta v_2$$

Simplifying, and solving for q, we obtain

$$q = \frac{6\pi r \eta}{E}(v_2 + v_1)$$

This expression gives the value of the charge q in terms of the electric field E, the radius of the oil drop r, the coefficient of viscosity η, the velocity v_1 of the oil drop for free fall under gravity, and the upward velocity v_2 of the oil drop under the influence of the electric field E.

The value of the electric field can be easily computed. The intensity of the electric field between two parallel plates is given by

$$E = \frac{V}{d}$$

where E is the electric field; V is the voltage, or the potential difference, between the plates; and d is the distance between the plates.

The radius of the oil drop can be obtained by using Stokes's law, which gives the relation between the radius of a small sphere falling through a viscous gas such as air, and the velocity of the sphere. Stokes's law states that when a small sphere falls freely through a viscous medium, for instance, a drop of oil falling through air, it acquires a constant, or terminal, velocity, given by the equation

$$v = \frac{2gr^2(\rho - \rho_1)}{9\eta}$$

where v is velocity of fall under gravity; g is the acceleration of gravity; r is the radius of the oil drop; ρ is the density of the oil; ρ_1 is the density of the air; and η is the coefficient of viscosity of the air. Since the density of the air is very much smaller than the density of the oil, the term ρ_1 may be neglected in the above equation. When the equation is thus solved for r, it gives the radius of the oil drop as

$$r = \sqrt{\frac{9\eta v}{2g\rho}}$$

where the radius is expressed in terms of velocity of fall of the droplet and of the other constants.

Now the charge on the oil drop can be calculated from the equation given above. Remember that all the data used for calculating the charge on an oil drop must be for the same oil drop. The velocity of fall under gravity will be the same for the same oil drop. But the upward velocity under the influence of the electric field will be different if the electric charge on the oil drop has changed during the course of the experiment. Each different upward velocity will correspond to a different value of the charge on the oil drop.

When many values for charge on the oil drops have been determined, all of these charges will be integral multiples of a certain small amount of charge, which is the smallest charge that can be found. Assuming that this smallest charge is the charge of the electron, each charge found may be represented by the expression

$$q = ne$$

where q is the charge, n is a small integer, and e is the charge of the electron. After the different values of the charge have been determined, the value of the charge e can be found by dividing each value of q by the appropriate n, which is an integer between 1 and about 20. These values of e will be the calculated values, obtained from the experiment, of the charge on the electron.

When Millikan determined the value of the charge on the electron, he found the value to depend somewhat on the size of the oil drop used. But experimental evidence had shown that the value of the charge on the electron was a constant, since an oil drop gains or loses charges of a definite amount regardless of the size of the drop. Millikan suspected that the discrepancy was due to Stokes's law, which he found did not hold accurately for very small drops. The motion of very small droplets is actually affected by the bombardment of air molecules, and this affects the predicted value of the velocity. Thus, he had to make a correction to Stokes's law in expressing the velocity of the oil drop, a correction that depended on the air pressure and on the size of the oil drop. The correction involved replacing the velocity v, given by Stokes's law, with the expression

$$\frac{v}{(1 + (b/pa))}$$

Since the expression for the charge on the oil drop, as well as the expression derived for the unit charge, contains the velocity to the three-halves power, the correction for the charge on the electron can be put simply in the form

$$e = \frac{e'}{(1 + (b/pa))^{3/2}}$$

where e is the corrected value of the charge on the electron; e' is the value of the charge on the electron obtained from the experiment; b is a constant of numerical value 0.000617; p is the barometric pressure in centimeters of mercury; and a is the radius of the oil drop.

319

The apparatus used in this experiment is an adaptation of that used by Robert A. Millikan.   The design of the apparatus was developed by the Welch Scientific Company, based upon the recommendations of J. B. Hoag, and thus the apparatus is called the Hoag-Millikan Oil Drop Apparatus.

The essential components of the apparatus are a specially designed condenser, a measuring microscope, a light source, and a toggle-switch assembly, all mounted on a common support.   The general appearance of the apparatus is shown in Fig. 80.

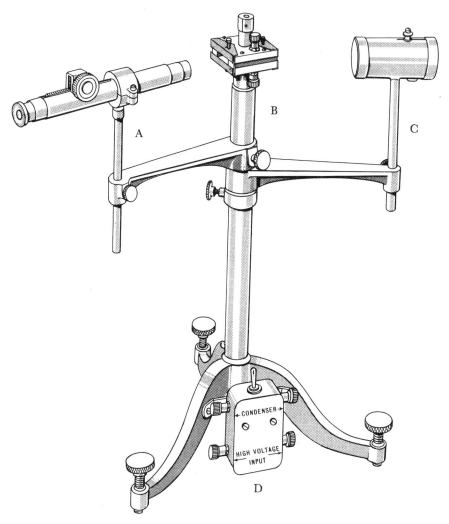

Fig. 80.   Hoag-Millikan Oil Drop Apparatus: (A) measuring microscope, (B) condenser unit, (C) light source, (D) switching assembly

The condenser unit consists of two horizontal metal plates, 5 cm square, separated by bakelite strips of equal and uniform thickness.   The plates are about 4.5 mm apart, and mounted on the central support shaft, completely insulated from the shaft and from each other.   A single small hole in the center of the upper plate allows the oil droplets to fall from the spray chamber above the plate into the observation chamber.   The spray chamber in the more recent models is about 6 cm high and slips over the viewing chamber.   Oil from the atomizer is sprayed into a small hole near the top of the spray chamber.   The oil droplets fall freely in the spray chamber, and many of them pass through the small hole into the viewing chamber.   Two glass windows, one at the front and one at the rear of the chamber, permit the illuminating and viewing of the oil droplets, while eliminating air currents within the chamber.   The glass windows are removable to allow measurements of the plate separation to be made with calipers.   A binding post is provided on each plate for high voltage connection.

The light source is an incandescent lamp, which should be operated on 6.3 volts A.C. but may also be operated from a 6-volt battery.   The light can be focused to a narrow beam to illuminate the center of the

The Charge of the Electron. Millikan's Oil Drop Experiment

NAME————————————————— SECTION————— DATE————————— EXPERIMENT FIFTY-NINE

viewing chamber. This is done by varying slightly the position of the bulb in its housing and by carefully adjusting the orientation and the elevation of the light source.

The measuring microscope has a magnification of approximately 22 ×. Measurements are made by means of a graduated scale contained in the microscope, which first has to be calibrated with the calibration scale supplied. The depth of focus is sufficiently short that the calibration remains unchanged so long as the object is in sharp focus. The microscope is provided with a rack-and-pinion fine-focusing arrangement. Focusing involves inserting a small pin through the small hole in the center of the upper plate of the viewing chamber; the sharp point of the pin is then put into focus. In the focusing process, both elevation and orientation of the microscope should be carefully adjusted.

The switching assembly is mounted at the base of the apparatus. It contains four binding posts—two to be connected to the high voltage supply, and two to the condenser plates. It also has a toggle switch that reverses the polarity of the plates; when placed in the vertical position, this switch disconnects the power source and short-circuits the plates, thus allowing free fall of the oil droplets.

As part of the apparatus, several additional items are supplied: calibration scale, atomizer, and bottle of high quality watch oil. The calibration scale is 10 mm long, divided to 0.1 mm, on a glass disk cemented into a metal frame. In calibration of the microscope, the scale is supported in vertical position on the condenser at the center of the upper plate. The atomizer is a specially designed nonflooding oil aspirator. Usually Nye's watch oil, which has a density of 0.890 gm/cm^3, is supplied.

The remainder of the apparatus needed to perform the experiment is listed and explained under Apparatus. For example, the condenser plates require a voltage supply adjustable from about 0 to 300 volts D.C., drawing negligible current. A D.C. voltmeter (0–300 volts) is needed, preferably one having a sensitivity of 10,000 ohms per volt. A stop watch is also required.

The oil drop apparatus described and illustrated in this experiment is listed as Cat. No. 0620. Its advantages include ease of setting up and of operation, and a relatively low potential requirement, about 200 volts. All the component parts are in clear view, making it easy to understand the principles on which the apparatus operates.

A later model of the apparatus, which has been developed by the Welch Scientific Company, is listed as Cat. No. 0620B. In this model, the latest improved design, the spray chamber is about 6 cm high and slips over the viewing chamber. The oil droplets can be produced, seen, and controlled with great ease. One can produce and see oil droplets of widely different sizes, and then control any selected one in the field of view for a long time. The charge on a droplet can be changed to other values by means of a built-in ionizing source. The operation of the apparatus is the same as that described for the older model.

The oil drop apparatus should be assembled as shown in Fig. 80. The toggle switch at the base of the apparatus is initially placed in the vertical position, to disconnect the power source and short-circuit the plates. The condenser plates are then connected to the two binding posts on the switching assembly marked "condenser." Next, the high voltage supply is connected to the two binding posts on the switching assembly marked "high voltage input." The voltmeter is also connected to the latter binding posts, so that it will not be reversed when the polarity of the plates is reversed.

If the power supply unit does not include a 6.3-volt A.C. outlet, a separate voltage supply must be used for the light source. This may be either a 6-volt storage battery or a 6-volt dry cell battery, such as Cat. No. 2239 supplied by the Welch Scientific Company. A single-pole, single-throw switch is also included in the circuit.

The light source and the microscope are arranged on the stand as shown in Fig. 80. The condenser is oriented so that the small glass window is facing the light source and the larger one is facing the microscope. The entire apparatus should be leveled so that the condenser plates are horizontal.

For a determination of the distance separating the condenser plates, one of the glass plates on the condenser should be removed and the distance between the inner faces of the plates measured, using a suitable metric caliper. If the glass plates appear foggy or misty in any way, they should be removed, cleaned, and then replaced.

The proper illumination of the oil drop is very important. The initial adjustments of the light source are as follows.   First, the lamp housing is raised slightly so that the beam of light passes just over the top of the condenser plates.   Then the nut on top of the light source is loosened and the lamp moved to focus the beam of light at a point exactly above the center of the condenser.   This is done by holding a small piece of white cardboard, perpendicular to the light, at the center on top of the upper plate and focusing the light on the cardboard.   The spray chamber must first be removed from the top of the condenser.   The lamp housing is now lowered to a position where the beam of light passes through the small window and illuminates the edges of the upper and lower plates equally.   This face of the condenser should be oriented perpendicular to the light beam.   Now the bright beam of light is directed at the center of the viewing chamber.

The initial focusing of the microscope may be done as follows.   The arm supporting the microscope should be oriented at an angle of about 30° from the direction of the beam of light from the light source (see Fig. 80).   The height of the microscope is adjusted and the microscope oriented so that it is pointing directly at the center of the viewing chamber.   First of all, make sure to short-circuit the condenser plates by setting the toggle switch vertical; the power supply should also be disconnected.   All of this is done to ensure that high voltage is not accidentally applied to the plates.   Now with the bulb lighted, a small pin is inserted vertically through the hole in the center of the upper plate of the condenser and the microscope focused on the point of the pin and, if possible, on the bright streak of light reflected from the pin.   The focusing is done by turning the knob of the focusing device.   When the point of the pin and the bright streak of light from the side of the pin are both in sharp focus, the microscope is focused for viewing the region where the oil drops will appear.   The eyepiece of the microscope contains at its focus a graduated scale by which measurements are made.   The eyepiece should be rotated about its optical axis until the scale is vertical, with the highest number on top.   The microscope being already pointed toward the dark corner of the chamber, roughly at the orientation suggested above, its angular position is now varied slightly until the background of light just permits the scale to be clearly distinguished.   The focus of the microscope and of the eyepiece should then be carefully adjusted so that there is no parallax between the image of the pin and the scale.   The focusing of the microscope should not be disturbed for the remainder of the experiment.

The next step is to calibrate the microscope scale so that correct measurements may be made.   In calibration, the scale, divided to 0.1 mm, is supported in a vertical position on the condenser, at the center of the upper plate.   With no moving of the arm that supports the microscope, and no disturbing of the focus, the microscope is raised enough to point just over the top of the condenser and in the direction of the center of the condenser plates, where the small pin is still inserted.   An additional light source is used to illuminate the scale in the microscope.   A lamp with a 40-watt incandescent bulb, placed directly in front of the microscope and about one foot away, is a satisfactory source.   The microscope is next pointed at the small pin and adjusted so that the image of the pin appears exactly on top of the microscope scale.   The small pin should now be removed.   The calibration scale is now placed on top of the condenser, with the side of the glass on which the scale is etched facing the microscope, and with the part of the frame marked "down" touching the top of the condenser.   The scale is thus in a vertical position, with the face perpendicular to the optical axis of the microscope, and as near to the center of the top plate as possible.   The exact location of the calibration scale is checked by making sure that the scale itself is sharply in focus in the microscope and superimposed on the scale in the microscope.   Only the moving of the calibration scale slowly and carefully, a very minute amount, along the direction of the microscope for focusing and perpendicularly for lateral adjustment, will do this.   When both scales are sharply in focus and superimposed, the calibration can be carried out.

Select two points on one of the scales, such as 6.00 and 10.00, and read off the corresponding values on the other scale to three significant figures.   From these measurements, the scale in the microscope can be calibrated in centimeters.   Thus, the measurement of the distance that an oil drop falls will be in centimeters.   Now the calibration scale should be removed.   The small pin is again inserted through the small hole in the center of the upper plate of the condenser, and the microscope lowered to its original position without moving the arm which supports the microscope and without disturbing the focusing in any way.   The height of the microscope is adjusted, and the microscope oriented so that it is pointing directly at the pin, with the image of the point of the pin exactly on the scale in the microscope.   The small pin should again be removed and put away where it is usually kept.   With this orientation, the scale will be at the point where the image of

The Charge of the Electron. Millikan's Oil Drop Experiment

NAME——————————————————— SECTION——————— DATE——————— EXPERIMENT FIFTY-NINE

the oil drops will appear, the oil drops will be sharply in focus, and the background of light will just permit the scale to be clearly distinguished.

The accepted values for e, m, and e/m for the electron are the following:

$$e = 4.803 \times 10^{-10} \text{ esu} \qquad \text{(charge on the electron)}$$
$$m = 9.11 \times 10^{-28} \text{ gram} \qquad \text{(mass of the electron)}$$
$$e/m = 5.273 \times 10^{17} \text{ esu/gram} \qquad \text{(ratio of charge to mass for the electron)}$$

APPARATUS

1. Oil drop apparatus, Hoag-Millikan.
2. Power supply unit, 0 to 300 volts D.C.
3. D.C. voltmeter (0–300 volts).
4. Watch oil, ¼-oz bottle.
5. 6-volt storage battery or 6-volt battery eliminator.
6. Stop watch or stop clock.
7. One single-pole, single-throw switch.

Some of the apparatus listed for this experiment may be available in the average physics laboratory, but for clear specification of the type best suited for the experiment, some of the items will be listed in more detail.   For example, the oil drop apparatus described is the one supplied by the Welch Scientific Company, 7300 North Linder Avenue, Skokie, Illinois.   The other items listed here are also supplied by the same company.   They are as follows:

No. 0620   Oil Drop Apparatus, Hoag-Millikan.
No. 0620L   Power Supply, 0 to 300 volts D.C. (includes 6.3-volt A.C. outlet).
No. 3035E   Voltmeter, Cadet, 15/150/300 volts D.C.
No. 0620J   Watch oil, ¼-oz bottle.
No. 0823   Stop watch, single-action, ⅕-second.

PROCEDURE

1. Record the reading of the barometer in centimeters of mercury.

2. Record the spacing of the condenser plates in centimeters.   Spacing should already have been determined by the instructor.

3. Record the calibration of the scale in the eyepiece of the microscope in centimeters per scale division. This should also have been determined previously by the instructor.

4. The microscope and also the light source should have already been focused by the instructor, according to the instructions given.   The microscope should have been accurately focused on the region through which the oil drops will come.   With all the adjustments properly made, the oil drops will appear as bright stars in a dark background, they will be sharply in focus, and the background of light will just permit the scale to be clearly visible.   The oil drops will appear to fall right along the scale.   Do not disturb the focusing of the microscope, or the adjustments of either the microscope or the light source.

5. Make certain that the pin has been removed from the small hole in the upper plate of the condenser and that the toggle switch is in the vertical position.   Replace the spray chamber on top of the upper plate.   Plug the line cord of the high voltage supply unit into a 115-volt, 60-cycle A.C. outlet.   Turn the power switch on.   Adjust the voltage to 200 volts.   Close the switch to light the lamp of the light source.   CAUTION: Do not touch the condenser plates or the high-tension wires while the current is on.

6. Now the apparatus is ready for operation.   Gently spray some oil into the spray chamber by placing the nozzle of the atomizer close to the small hole near the top and directing the spray toward the top of the chamber.   Do not spray toward the small hole in the upper plate of the condenser.   Being small, the hole could easily be clogged with oil.   The oil spray should be fine and uniform within the chamber, a condition that indicates that the droplets are of the proper size.   The oil drops will become charged in the atomizing process.

7. As soon as the oil has been sprayed, look through the microscope. At first, a diffused light will be seen. This will thin out, and small individual bright spots will appear, which are reflections of light from the oil drops and appear like stars of different magnitudes. The oil drops are all falling under the force of gravity, but note that they are moving at diverse speeds. The large ones fall fastest and quickly disappear from the field of view; they are too large to use. The one suitable for our purpose is moving slowly and is the one on which measurements are to be made. It can be kept in the field of view for a long time by properly manipulating the toggle switch. When the switch is in the vertical position, the oil drop falls freely under gravity, since no voltage is being applied to the plates. When the switch is placed to the right, one plate is made positive and the other negative. When the switch is placed to the left, the polarity of the plates is reversed. Determine the position of the switch that makes the upper plate positive by noticing when the oil drop moves upward. This will be the position of the switch during the procedure, to make the oil drop move upward. When the switch is placed in the opposite position, the oil drop moves downward, in the same direction as when it is under gravity, although much faster. The switch is not used in this position to make any measurements because of the danger that the oil drop will quickly disappear from view and be lost. It is better to rely only on gravity for the downward pull. It is important to remember that the downward motion of the oil drop is seen as upward motion in the microscope, and the upward motion is seen as downward motion—the image in the microscope is inverted.

8. Begin by observing the motion of a slow-moving droplet falling freely under gravity; the toggle switch is in the vertical position. By manipulating the switch, practice making the oil drop move up and down. Be sure not to let the oil drop fall out of the field of view in either direction. Rely on gravity for the downward motion and apply the electric field only for the upward motion. Remember that directions are reversed in the microscope.

Choose two points on the scale, such as 2.00 and 8.00, and record their value. With a stop watch, measure time of transit for the oil drop between these two points, for both upward and downward motions. Select an oil drop that requires about 20 seconds for the downward motion and about 30 seconds for the upward motion. Keep the oil drop under observation as long as possible—for 30 minutes or longer. Determine and record time of transit alternately for the downward motion, or free fall, and for the upward motion, under the influence of the electric field. Do this until you have made five observations of the downward motion and five of the upward motion. Thereafter, record only time of transit for the upward motion, for the same oil drop, and observe as long as possible. The values of time of transit for the downward motion will be very nearly equal. Those for the upward motion will differ but are likely to fall into groups, in which intra-group values will differ by only a fraction of a second, and intergroup values by several seconds. For the downward motion, the time of transit will remain the same for the same oil drop, since velocity depends only on the size of the drop and the force of gravity, which remain the same. For the upward motion, the time of transit will be different if the charge on the oil drop changes by one or two electrons, since the velocity of the oil drop depends on the electric force, which in turn depends on the electrical charge on the drop. Thus, in measuring the time of transit for the upward motion, one is likely to observe a sudden change in the velocity of the oil drop, when it gains or loses an electron. It is better not to record that particular reading of time of transit, but to wait for the next one, when the velocity has settled down to a new value.

NOTE: It is advisable to have two observers make the measurements. One observer manipulates the toggle switch, watches the oil drop continuously, and handles the stop watch. The other observer reads the stop watch and records all the readings. Make a total of at least 30 readings of time of transit for the upward motion, whether for a single oil drop or for several. For the downward motion, a total of 5 readings for each oil drop used is sufficient.

9. The table (see Data) for recording downward motion of the oil drop has three oil drops listed. This is done to provide space for recording data if it becomes necessary to make measurements on three different oil drops. It is quite possible, however, to make all the measurements needed for the experiment on a single oil drop. The only condition is that there should be several different groupings of the velocities for upward motion of the oil drop, representing different values of the electric charge on the same oil drop. This condition will be met if the oil drop gains or loses an electron under the influence of radiation or through collisions. If this is the case, all of the data can be taken on a single oil drop.

The reason for listing three oil drops is that sometimes an oil drop may be accidentally lost after a series of measurements have been made, but not enough measurements to be very conclusive. Then another oil drop must be used and a new set of measurements made. But in calculations for determining the value of the electric charge on an oil drop, all the data used must be for the same oil drop.

When sufficient observations have been made, the power supply should be turned off. Open the switch to shut off the lamp of the light source. Turn the power switch off. Pull out the plug of the high voltage supply unit. Leave the toggle switch in vertical position to short-circuit the condenser plates.

DATA

Barometer reading ....
Separation of the condenser plates ....
Calibration of the scale in the eyepiece ....
Density of the watch oil ....
Distance traversed by oil drop, in scale readings, from _____ to _____. ....
Distance traversed by oil drop, in centimeters ....
Voltage applied to the plates of the condenser ....
Electric field between the plates of the condenser ....
Calculated value of the charge on the electron ....
Accepted value of the charge on the electron ....
Per cent error ....

DOWNWARD MOTION OF OIL DROP FREE FALL UNDER GRAVITY		
OIL DROP NO. 1 TIME OF TRANSIT	OIL DROP NO. 2 TIME OF TRANSIT	OIL DROP NO. 3 TIME OF TRANSIT
1.	1.	1.
2.	2.	2.
3.	3.	3.
4.	4.	4.
5.	5.	5.
AVERAGE TIME _____	AVERAGE TIME _____	AVERAGE TIME _____
VELOCITY OF OIL DROP _____	VELOCITY OF OIL DROP _____	VELOCITY OF OIL DROP _____
RADIUS OF OIL DROP _____	RADIUS OF OIL DROP _____	RADIUS OF OIL DROP _____

UPWARD MOTION OF OIL DROP UNDER INFLUENCE OF ELECTRIC FIELD		
OIL DROP NO. 1 TIME OF TRANSIT	OIL DROP NO. 2 TIME OF TRANSIT	OIL DROP NO. 3 TIME OF TRANSIT

(Continued)

The Charge of the Electron. Millikan's Oil Drop Experiment

UPWARD MOTION OF OIL DROP UNDER INFLUENCE OF ELECTRIC FIELD		
OIL DROP NO. 1 TIME OF TRANSIT	OIL DROP NO. 2 TIME OF TRANSIT	OIL DROP NO. 3 TIME OF TRANSIT

UPWARD MOTION OF OIL DROP UNDER INFLUENCE OF ELECTRIC FIELD		
OIL DROP NO. 1 AVERAGE TIME	OIL DROP NO. 2 AVERAGE TIME	OIL DROP NO. 3 AVERAGE TIME
GROUP I _____	GROUP I _____	GROUP I _____
GROUP II _____	GROUP II _____	GROUP II _____
GROUP III _____	GROUP III _____	GROUP III _____
VELOCITY OF OIL DROP	VELOCITY OF OIL DROP	VELOCITY OF OIL DROP
GROUP I _____	GROUP I _____	GROUP I _____
GROUP II _____	GROUP II _____	GROUP II _____
GROUP III _____	GROUP III _____	GROUP III _____

CALCULATED VALUES OF ELECTRICAL CHARGE ON OIL DROP	ASSUMED VALUES OF SMALL INTEGER n TO OBTAIN $q = ne$	CALCULATED VALUES OF CHARGE ON THE ELECTRON

The Charge of the Electron. Millikan's Oil Drop Experiment

NAME————————————————————— SECTION———————— DATE———————— EXPERIMENT FIFTY-NINE

CALCULATIONS

1. Calculate the distance traversed by the oil drop from the value of the distance expressed in scale readings and the calibration of the scale in the eyepiece.   Express the distance in centimeters.

2. Calculate the average time of transit for free fall under gravity for oil drop No. 1.   If measurements have been made on oil drops No. 2 and No. 3, calculate the average time of transit for these drops also.

3. Calculate the velocity of free fall for oil drop No. 1, using the value of the distance traversed and the value of average time of transit for free fall.   Express the velocity in centimeters per second.   If measurements have been made on oil drops No. 2 and No. 3, calculate the velocity of free fall for these drops also.

4. Calculate average time of transit for upward motion of oil drop No. 1, which is under the influence of the electric field.   Notice that observed values of time of transit listed in the table are likely to fall into groups, where the values belonging in any one group do not differ by more than a fraction of a second.   The values belonging to a different group differ by several seconds from those of the first group.   From the values of time of transit for oil drop No. 1 make a list of those belonging to the same group and call it Group I. Calculate the average time of transit for Group I and record it in the table.   Make a separate list of the values of time of transit for oil drop No. 1 belonging to a different group and call it Group II.   Calculate the average time of transit for Group II and record it in the table.   If there is another group present, make another list of the values of time of transit for oil drop No. 1 belonging to this group and call it Group III.   Calculate the average time of transit for Group III and record it in the table.   If more than one oil drop has been used in making measurements of time of transit for upward motion under influence of the electric field, calculate

average time of transit for each of these by the method just described. Do this even if there is only one group present for an individual oil drop.

5. Calculate the velocity of the upward motion of oil drop No. 1, under the influence of the electric field, by using value of distance traversed and value of average time of transit for each group listed. Express the velocity in centimeters per second and record in the table. If measurements have been made on oil drops No. 2 and No. 3, calculate velocity of upward motion for these oil drops also, for each of the groups listed. Record data in the table.

6. By using Stokes's law and your value of the velocity of oil drop No. 1 for free fall under gravity, calculate the radius of the oil drop. Stokes's law states that when a small sphere falls freely through a viscous medium, such as a drop of oil falling through air, it acquires a constant velocity, given by the equation

$$v = \frac{2gr^2(\rho - \rho_1)}{9\eta}$$

where v is the velocity of fall under gravity; g is the acceleration of gravity; r is the radius of the oil drop; ρ is the density of the oil; ρ_1 is the density of the air; and η is the viscosity of the air. Since the density of the air is very much smaller than the density of the oil, the term ρ_1 may be neglected in the above equation, in solving for the radius of the oil drop. When the equation is thus solved for r, it gives the radius of the oil drop as

$$r = \sqrt{\frac{9\eta v}{2g\rho}}$$

where the radius is expressed in terms of velocity of fall of the droplet and of the other constants.

In making the calculations, use 980 cm/sec² for the acceleration of gravity; 0.890 gram per cubic centimeter for the density of Nye's watch oil; and 0.000182 poise, or dyne-sec/cm², for the viscosity of air. The radius of the oil drop will be expressed in centimeters. If measurements have been made on oil drops No. 2 and No. 3, calculate the radius of these oil drops also. Record the values of the radius of the oil drops in the table of the downward motion of the oil drop.

The Charge of the Electron. Millikan's Oil Drop Experiment

NAME————————————————————— SECTION——————— DATE————————— EXPERIMENT FIFTY-NINE

7. Compute the value of the electric field used in your measurements. The intensity of the electric field between two parallel plates is given by

$$E = \frac{V}{d}$$

where E is the electric field; V is the voltage, or the potential difference, between the plates; and d is the distance between the plates. In our calculations, the electrostatic system of units will be used. Thus E is the electric field in dynes per esu of charge; V is in esu of voltage; and all mechanical quantities are expressed in the cgs system of units. Computing the value of the electric field requires dividing the value of the voltage V by 300 to change it into esu of voltage, since 300 volts = 1 esu of voltage. The distance d between the plates is expressed in centimeters. The value of the electric field E will be in dynes per esu of charge.

8. Calculate the value of the electrical charge on oil drop No. 1 from the expression that gives the value of the charge in terms of certain known quantities, and of other quantities determined in the course of the experiment. The expression for the charge on the oil drop is

$$q = \frac{6\pi r \eta}{E} (v_2 + v_1)$$

where q is the value of the charge on the oil drop; E is the intensity of the electric field; r is the radius of the oil drop; η is the coefficient of viscosity of air; v_1 is the velocity of the oil drop for free fall under gravity; and v_2 is the upward velocity of the oil drop under the influence of the electric field. In these calculations the electrostatic system of units will be used. Thus the value of the charge will come out in esu of charge, and all mechanical quantities will be expressed in the cgs system of units.

Calculate the value of the electrical charge on oil drop No. 1 from the value of the upward velocity of the oil drop, found for Group 1, as listed in the table. This is the term v_2 appearing in the above equation. The term v_1 is the velocity of oil drop No. 1 for free fall under gravity, as given in the table for the downward motion. The term r is the value of the radius of oil drop No. 1 as found in calculation (6). The term E is the value of the intensity of the electric field as found in calculation (7). The term η is the coefficient of viscosity of air, which may be taken as 0.000182 poise, or dyne-sec/cm². The value of π may be taken as 3.14 in these calculations. The value of the charge will be in esu of charge.

Similarly, calculate the value of the electrical charge on oil drop No. 1 from the value of the upward velocity of the oil drop, under the influence of the electric field, found for Group II, and also for Group III, as listed in the table.

9. If measurements have been made on oil drops No. 2 and No. 3, calculate the electrical charge on each of these oil drops, as described in calculation (8). Do this even if there is only one group of velocities present for an individual oil drop.

10. List all the values of the electrical charge found on all of the oil drops measured, for the different groups represented. Assume that each charge found may be represented by the expression $q = ne$, where q is the charge; n is a small integer; and e is roughly equal to the known value of the charge on the electron. Next to each charge, list the small integer n, between 1 and about 20, that best fulfills the condition of the above equation. Assuming the relation to hold, calculate the value of e that will be obtained for each value of the charge listed, and record the value of e thus found. These values of e represent the calculated values of the charge on the electron, obtained from the experiment.

The Charge of the Electron. Millikan's Oil Drop Experiment

NAME———————————————— SECTION——————— DATE——————— EXPERIMENT FIFTY-NINE

11. Find the average of the calculated values of the charge on the electron, obtained in calculation (10), and record this in the data as the calculated value of the charge on the electron. Compare your result with the accepted value by finding the per cent error.

QUESTIONS

1. Name at least three possible sources of error in this experiment that are likely to affect the accuracy of the results.

2. By using your calculated value for the radius of oil drop No. 1, as found in calculation (6), compute the volume of this oil drop. The volume of a sphere is given by $V = \dfrac{4}{3}\pi r^3$, where r is the radius of the sphere; the value of π may be taken as 3.14 in the calculations. Express the volume in cubic centimeters.

Compute the mass of the oil drop, if the density of the oil is 0.890 gram per cubic centimeter.

3. Assume that oil drop No. 1 used in the experiment was suspended in the electric field of the condenser plates, held stationary under the influence of the electric field and the force of gravity. Calculate the value of the voltage that would have to be applied to the plates of the condenser to accomplish this, assuming that the charge on the oil drop was equal to that produced by five electrons. For the mass of the oil drop, use the value obtained in question (2).

Under these conditions when the oil drop is suspended, the gravitational force is equal to the electric force acting on the oil drop. The relation between the two forces is $mg = Eq$, where mg is the force of gravity; m is the mass of the oil drop in grams, and g is the value of the acceleration of gravity in cm/sec². The term Eq represents the electric force on the oil drop, since the force on a charge q placed in an electric field E is equal to Eq. As before, we are using the electrostatic system of units. Then, the value of the charge q has to be expressed in esu of charge. The value of the electric field E will be in dynes per esu of charge. The electric field between two parallel plates is given by $E = V/d$, where E is the electric field in dynes per esu of charge; V is the voltage between the plates in esu of voltage; and d is the distance between the plates in centimeters. To change the value of the voltage to volts, it must be remembered that 1 esu of voltage = 300 volts.

4. In determining the charge on the electron, Millikan found that a small error was introduced if the oil drop used was too small. This is due to a failure of Stokes's law to predict accurately the velocity of very small droplets. If a correction to Stokes's law is introduced, the velocity can be predicted much more accurately. When this is done, and an expression for the charge on the electron is derived, the charge can be determined more accurately. The correction for the charge on the electron is expressed as follows:

$$e = \frac{e'}{(1 + (b/pa))^{3/2}}$$

where e is the corrected value of the charge on the electron; e' is the value of the charge on the electron obtained from the experiment; b is a constant equal to 0.000617; p is the barometric pressure in centimeters of mercury; and a is the radius of the oil drop.

By using the above expression, calculate the corrected value of the charge on the electron. For e', use your calculated value of the charge on the electron, as recorded in the data. For the radius of the oil drop, use the one that corresponds to oil drop No. 1. Compare the corrected value of the charge on the electron with the accepted value by finding the per cent error.

5. The accepted value for the ratio of charge to mass for the electron is $e/m = 5.273 \times 10^{17}$ electrostatic units of charge per gram. Using this value of e/m and your calculated value for the charge on the electron, compute the mass of the electron.

APPENDIX

Table I. Physical Constants

Velocity of light in vacuum	$\begin{cases} = 3.00 \times 10^{10} \text{ centimeters per second} \\ = 186{,}000 \text{ miles per second} \end{cases}$
Velocity of sound in air at 0° C.	$\begin{cases} = 331.4 \text{ meters per second} \\ = 1087 \text{ feet per second} \end{cases}$
Acceleration of gravity	$\begin{cases} = 980 \text{ centimeters per second per second} \\ = 32.2 \text{ feet per second per second} \end{cases}$
1 standard atmosphere	$\begin{cases} = 76 \text{ centimeters of mercury} \\ = 14.7 \text{ pounds per square inch} \end{cases}$
1 horsepower	$\begin{cases} = 550 \text{ foot-pounds per second} \\ = 746 \text{ watts} \end{cases}$
1 faraday	= 96,500 coulombs
Avogadro's number	$= 6.023 \times 10^{23}$ molecules per mole
Mechanical equivalent of heat	= 4.186 joules per calorie
Absolute zero	= − 273.18° C.

Table II. Metric and English Equivalents

1 inch	= 2.540 centimeters		1 centimeter	= 0.3937 inch
1 foot	= 30.48 centimeters		1 meter	= 39.37 inches
1 mile	= 1.609 kilometers		1 kilometer	= 0.6214 mile
1 ounce	= 28.35 grams		1 gram	= 0.03526 ounce
1 pound	= 453.6 grams		1 kilogram	= 2.205 pounds
1 quart	= 0.9463 liter		1 liter	= 1.057 quarts

Table III. Densities

(in grams per cubic centimeter)

SOLIDS				LIQUIDS		GASES *(at 0° C., 760 mm. pressure)*	
Aluminum	2.7	Glass, crown	2.5 –2.7	Alcohol, ethyl	0.79	Air	0.001293
Brass	8.4	Glass, flint	3.0 –3.6	Alcohol, methyl	0.81	Carbon dioxide	0.001977
Copper	8.90	Granite	2.7	Carbon tetrachloride	1.60	Helium	0.0001785
Gold	19.3	Marble	2.6 –2.8	Ether	0.74	Hydrogen	0.00008988
Iron	7.85	Wood		Gasoline	0.68	Nitrogen	0.001251
Lead	11.3	Balsa	0.11–0.13	Mercury	13.6	Oxygen	0.001429
Nickel	8.75	Cork	0.22–0.26	Olive oil	0.92		
Platinum	21.5	Ebony	1.11–1.33	Turpentine	0.87		
Silver	10.5	Maple	0.62–0.75	Water, pure	1.000		
Steel	7.8	Oak	0.60–0.90	Water, sea	1.025		
Zinc	7.1	Pine	0.35–0.50				

Table IV. Young's Modulus

(in dynes per square centimeter)

Aluminum	7.0×10^{11}
Brass	9.2×10^{11}
Copper	12×10^{11}
Phosphor bronze	12×10^{11}
Steel	19.2×10^{11}

Table V. Coefficient of Linear Expansion

(per degree Centigrade)

Aluminum	0.000024	Lead	0.000029
Brass	0.000018	Nickel	0.000014
Copper	0.000017	Platinum	0.000009
German silver	0.000018	Silver	0.000019
Glass	0.000009	Steel	0.000011
Gold	0.000014	Tin	0.000027
Iron	0.000012	Zinc	0.000026

TABLE VI. Specific Heat

Aluminum	0.22	Mercury	0.033
Brass	0.092	Nickel	0.11
Copper	0.093	Steel	0.12
Glass	0.16	Tin	0.054
Iron	0.11	Water	1.00
Lead	0.031	Zinc	0.093

TABLE VII. Resistivity of Metals

(in ohm-cm.)

Aluminum	2.6×10^{-6}	German silver	33.0×10^{-6}
Brass	$6.4\text{–}8.4 \times 10^{-6}$	Iron	10×10^{-6}
Constantan	44.1×10^{-6}	Manganin	44.0×10^{-6}
Copper	1.72×10^{-6}	Nichrome	100×10^{-6}
		Silver	1.63×10^{-6}

TABLE VIII. Electrochemical Data

ELEMENT	ATOMIC MASS	VALENCE	ELECTROCHEMICAL EQUIVALENT, GRAMS PER COULOMB
Aluminum	27.1	3	0.0000936
Copper	63.6	2	0.0003294
Copper	63.6	1	0.0006588
Gold	197.2	3	0.0006812
Hydrogen	1.008	1	0.00001046
Iron	55.8	3	0.0001929
Iron	55.8	2	0.0002894
Lead	207.2	2	0.0010736
Nickel	58.7	2	0.0003040
Oxygen	16.0	2	0.00008291
Silver	107.9	1	0.0011180

TRIGONOMETRIC FUNCTIONS

ANGLE	SINE	COSINE	TANGENT	COTANGENT	ANGLE
0	0.0000	1.0000	0.0000	∞	90
1	0.0175	0.9998	0.0175	57.2900	89
2	0.0349	0.9994	0.0349	28.6363	88
3	0.0523	0.9986	0.0524	19.0811	87
4	0.0698	0.9976	0.0699	14.3007	86
5	0.0872	0.9962	0.0875	11.4301	85
6	0.1045	0.9945	0.1051	9.5144	84
7	0.1219	0.9925	0.1228	8.1443	83
8	0.1392	0.9903	0.1405	7.1154	82
9	0.1564	0.9877	0.1584	6.3138	81
10	0.1736	0.9848	0.1763	5.6713	80
11	0.1908	0.9816	0.1944	5.1446	79
12	0.2079	0.9781	0.2126	4.7046	78
13	0.2250	0.9744	0.2309	4.3315	77
14	0.2419	0.9703	0.2493	4.0108	76
15	0.2588	0.9659	0.2679	3.7321	75
16	0.2756	0.9613	0.2867	3.4874	74
17	0.2924	0.9563	0.3057	3.2709	73
18	0.3090	0.9511	0.3249	3.0777	72
19	0.3256	0.9455	0.3443	2.9042	71
20	0.3420	0.9397	0.3640	2.7475	70
21	0.3584	0.9336	0.3839	2.6051	69
22	0.3746	0.9272	0.4040	2.4751	68
23	0.3907	0.9205	0.4245	2.3559	67
24	0.4067	0.9135	0.4452	2.2460	66
25	0.4226	0.9063	0.4663	2.1445	65
26	0.4384	0.8988	0.4877	2.0503	64
27	0.4540	0.8910	0.5095	1.9626	63
28	0.4695	0.8829	0.5317	1.8807	62
29	0.4848	0.8746	0.5543	1.8040	61
30	0.5000	0.8660	0.5774	1.7321	60
31	0.5150	0.8572	0.6009	1.6643	59
32	0.5299	0.8480	0.6249	1.6003	58
33	0.5446	0.8387	0.6494	1.5399	57
34	0.5592	0.8290	0.6745	1.4826	56
35	0.5736	0.8192	0.7002	1.4281	55
36	0.5878	0.8090	0.7265	1.3764	54
37	0.6018	0.7986	0.7536	1.3270	53
38	0.6157	0.7880	0.7813	1.2799	52
39	0.6293	0.7771	0.8098	1.2349	51
40	0.6428	0.7660	0.8391	1.1918	50
41	0.6561	0.7547	0.8693	1.1504	49
42	0.6691	0.7431	0.9004	1.1106	48
43	0.6820	0.7314	0.9325	1.0724	47
44	0.6947	0.7193	0.9657	1.0355	46
45	0.7071	0.7071	1.0000	1.0000	45
ANGLE	COSINE	SINE	COTANGENT	TANGENT	ANGLE

N	0	1	2	3	4	5	6	7	8	9
10	0000	0043	0086	0128	0170	0212	0253	0294	0334	0374
11	0414	0453	0492	0531	0569	0607	0645	0682	0719	0755
12	0792	0828	0864	0899	0934	0969	1004	1038	1072	1106
13	1139	1173	1206	1239	1271	1303	1335	1367	1399	1430
14	1461	1492	1523	1553	1584	1614	1644	1673	1703	1732
15	1761	1790	1818	1847	1875	1903	1931	1959	1987	2014
16	2041	2068	2095	2122	2148	2175	2201	2227	2253	2279
17	2304	2330	2355	2380	2405	2430	2455	2480	2504	2529
18	2553	2577	2601	2625	2648	2672	2695	2718	2742	2765
19	2788	2810	2833	2856	2878	2900	2923	2945	2967	2989
20	3010	3032	3054	3075	3096	3118	3139	3160	3181	3201
21	3222	3243	3263	3284	3304	3324	3345	3365	3385	3404
22	3424	3444	3464	3483	3502	3522	3541	3560	3579	3598
23	3617	3636	3655	3674	3692	3711	3729	3747	3766	3784
24	3802	3820	3838	3856	3874	3892	3909	3927	3945	3962
25	3979	3997	4014	4031	4048	4065	4082	4099	4116	4133
26	4150	4166	4183	4200	4216	4232	4249	4265	4281	4298
27	4314	4330	4346	4362	4378	4393	4409	4425	4440	4456
28	4472	4487	4502	4518	4533	4548	4564	4579	4594	4609
29	4624	4639	4654	4669	4683	4698	4713	4728	4742	4757
30	4771	4786	4800	4814	4829	4843	4857	4871	4886	4900
31	4914	4928	4942	4955	4969	4983	4997	5011	5024	5038
32	5051	5065	5079	5092	5105	5119	5132	5145	5159	5172
33	5185	5198	5211	5224	5237	5250	5263	5276	5289	5302
34	5315	5328	5340	5353	5366	5378	5391	5403	5416	5428
35	5441	5453	5465	5478	5490	5502	5514	5527	5539	5551
36	5563	5575	5587	5599	5611	5623	5635	5647	5658	5670
37	5682	5694	5705	5717	5729	5740	5752	5763	5775	5786
38	5798	5809	5821	5832	5843	5855	5866	5877	5888	5899
39	5911	5922	5933	5944	5955	5966	5977	5988	5999	6010
40	6021	6031	6042	6053	6064	6075	6085	6096	6107	6117
41	6128	6138	6149	6160	6170	6180	6191	6201	6212	6222
42	6232	6243	6253	6263	6274	6284	6294	6304	6314	6325
43	6335	6345	6355	6365	6375	6385	6395	6405	6415	6425
44	6435	6444	6454	6464	6474	6484	6493	6503	6513	6522
45	6532	6542	6551	6561	6571	6580	6590	6599	6609	6618
46	6628	6637	6646	6656	6665	6675	6684	6693	6702	6712
47	6721	6730	6739	6749	6758	6767	6776	6785	6794	6803
48	6812	6821	6830	6839	6848	6857	6866	6875	6884	6893
49	6902	6911	6920	6928	6937	6946	6955	6964	6972	6981
50	6990	6998	7007	7016	7024	7033	7042	7050	7059	7067
51	7076	7084	7093	7101	7110	7118	7126	7135	7143	7152
52	7160	7168	7177	7185	7193	7202	7210	7218	7226	7235
53	7243	7251	7259	7267	7275	7284	7292	7300	7308	7316
54	7324	7332	7340	7348	7356	7364	7372	7380	7388	7396

N	0	1	2	3	4	5	6	7	8	9
55	7404	7412	7419	7427	7435	7443	7451	7459	7466	7474
56	7482	7490	7497	7505	7513	7520	7528	7536	7543	7551
57	7559	7566	7574	7582	7589	7597	7604	7612	7619	7627
58	7634	7642	7649	7657	7664	7672	7679	7686	7694	7701
59	7709	7716	7723	7731	7738	7745	7752	7760	7767	7774
60	7782	7789	7796	7803	7810	7818	7825	7832	7839	7846
61	7853	7860	7868	7875	7882	7889	7896	7903	7910	7917
62	7924	7931	7938	7945	7952	7959	7966	7973	7980	7987
63	7993	8000	8007	8014	8021	8028	8035	8041	8048	8055
64	8062	8069	8075	8082	8089	8096	8102	8109	8116	8122
65	8129	8136	8142	8149	8156	8162	8169	8176	8182	8189
66	8195	8202	8209	8215	8222	8228	8235	8241	8248	8254
67	8261	8267	8274	8280	8287	8293	8299	8306	8312	8319
68	8325	8331	8338	8344	8351	8357	8363	8370	8376	8382
69	8388	8395	8401	8407	8414	8420	8426	8432	8439	8445
70	8451	8457	8463	8470	8476	8482	8488	8494	8500	8506
71	8513	8519	8525	8531	8537	8543	8549	8555	8561	8567
72	8573	8579	8585	8591	8597	8603	8609	8615	8621	8627
73	8633	8639	8645	8651	8657	8663	8669	8675	8681	8686
74	8692	8698	8704	8710	8716	8722	8727	8733	8739	8745
75	8751	8756	8762	8768	8774	8779	8785	8791	8797	8802
76	8808	8814	8820	8825	8831	8837	8842	8848	8854	8859
77	8865	8871	8876	8882	8887	8893	8899	8904	8910	8915
78	8921	8927	8932	8938	8943	8949	8954	8960	8965	8971
79	8976	8982	8987	8993	8998	9004	9009	9015	9020	9025
80	9031	9036	9042	9047	9053	9058	9063	9069	9074	9079
81	9085	9090	9096	9101	9106	9112	9117	9122	9128	9133
82	9138	9143	9149	9154	9159	9165	9170	9175	9180	9186
83	9191	9196	9201	9206	9212	9217	9222	9227	9232	9238
84	9243	9248	9253	9258	9263	9269	9274	9279	9284	9289
85	9294	9299	9304	9309	9315	9320	9325	9330	9335	9340
86	9345	9350	9355	9360	9365	9370	9375	9380	9385	9390
87	9395	9400	9405	9410	9415	9420	9425	9430	9435	9440
88	9445	9450	9455	9460	9465	9469	9474	9479	9484	9489
89	9494	9499	9504	9509	9513	9518	9523	9528	9533	9538
90	9542	9547	9552	9557	9562	9566	9571	9576	9581	9586
91	9590	9595	9600	9605	9609	9614	9619	9624	9628	9633
92	9638	9643	9647	9652	9657	9661	9666	9671	9675	9680
93	9685	9689	9694	9699	9703	9708	9713	9717	9722	9727
94	9731	9736	9741	9745	9750	9754	9759	9763	9768	9773
95	9777	9782	9786	9791	9795	9800	9805	9809	9814	9818
96	9823	9827	9832	9836	9841	9845	9850	9854	9859	9863
97	9868	9872	9877	9881	9886	9890	9894	9899	9903	9908
98	9912	9917	9921	9926	9930	9934	9939	9943	9948	9952
99	9956	9961	9965	9969	9974	9978	9983	9987	9991	9996

1 2 3 4 5 6 7 8 9 10